Cover illustration by JANE EVANS

A montage of the Sun (God, or universal center), Man, reaching
for his god-hood, the tree, symbolizing the beauty and mystery
of all life. God-Sun is above the Earth, but immersed in it.

MAN, GOD AND THE UNIVERSE

Is man, as some insist, an accidental intruder into a basically hostile world? Is he doomed to self-destruction through his own unbridled passions and violence? Or is his destiny to bring to fruition the seeds of ultimate Reality which lie hidden in the secret places of his own being and which he himself must discover and nourish? In this profound and inspiring book, a scientist-philosopher and specialist in yoga takes the last view.

The deepest concern of thinking man must surely be with the nature of, and the relationship between, the three great factors mentioned in the title: with man, his origins, his purpose, and his destiny; with God, not as an anthropomorphic deity but as the source of all life and being; and with the universe, the environment in which the stupendous drama of evolution—involving both divine and human—is enacted. Despite the majestic sweep of the concepts offered, they are made easily comprehensible by the clarity with which they are presented and the many diagrams and charts with which they are illustrated. And the enlightening synthesis of Eastern and Western approaches should make the book rewarding to thoughtful readers the world over.

Dr. I. K. Taimni, now retired, was for many years a chemistry professor at Allahabad University in India, specializing in guided research; technical journals in several countries have published his many research papers. In addition to his professional work, Dr. Taimni is the author of a number of books, outstanding among which are *The Science of Yoga* and *Glimpses into the Psychology of Yoga*.

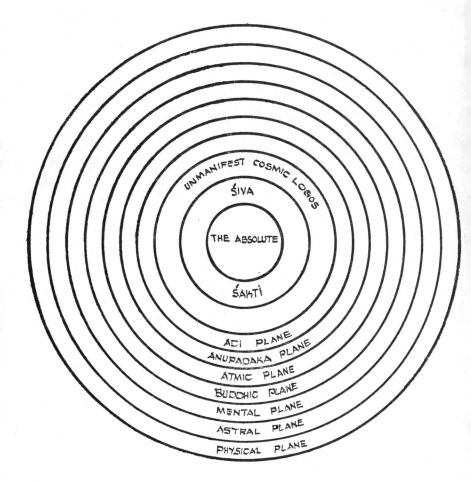

THE DIFFERENT LEVELS OF REALITY

MAN, GOD
AND THE
UNIVERSE

by

I. K. TAIMNI

A QUEST BOOK

Published under a grant from the Kern Foundation

THE THEOSOPHICAL PUBLISHING HOUSE
Wheaton, Ill., U.S.A.
Madras, India / London, England

© The Theosophical Publishing House, Adyar, 1969

First Quest Edition published by the
Theosophical Publishing House, Wheaton, Illinois,
a department of The Theosophical Society in America, 1974

ISBN: 0-8356-0447-0
Library of Congress Catalog Number 74-4167

PRINTED IN THE UNITED STATES OF AMERICA

PREFACE

1. *Man from the materialistic and spiritual standpoints*

Any intelligent person who is capable of serious thought and even vaguely aware of the realities of his life cannot but feel that there is a great mystery hidden behind the universe and his own life and until this mystery is unravelled his life can have no real meaning and he cannot be at peace. He may ignore this mystery or try to forget it by plunging into work or other distracting pursuits but it will continue to haunt him and sub-consciously poison whatever happiness he is able to snatch from his experiences in the outer world.

The vast majority of people are not even vaguely aware of this mystery and are so completely assimilated with their environment and the current of life in which they find themselves that the deeper problems of life do not trouble them at all. There is, of course, a definite reason for this strange incapacity to see what is quite obvious. They have still to go through more experiences and through these experiences, both pleasant and painful, to develop that discriminative faculty which is called *viveka* in Sanskrit. It is *viveka* which is the hall-mark of a soul which is spiritually mature and thus qualified to undertake the task of tackling the deeper problems of life.

Any one who is spiritually awake and inclined to understand and if possible to unravel the great mystery of life can look for knowledge on this subject in three directions. He can try to find out what religion, philosophy and science have to say about it and how they try in their own respective ways to unravel it. It will be shown later how the Occult method of approach to this fundamental problem, based as it is on its systematic and direct investigation through the combined methods of religion, philosophy and science, can alone provide a satisfactory theoretical explanation as well as an effective technique for the solution of the problem. But before we can appreciate the value of the Occult method for unravelling the mystery of man and the universe it is necessary to give some thought to the vital question: what is the significance of man and his life according to the fundamentally different materialistic and spiritual points of view.

We are so engrossed in our ordinary pursuits and passions aroused by passing events that we are not even vaguely aware of the hard facts of our existence which stare us in the face and which would make us pause and tremble if we could only see their real significance. Materialistic philosophy based as it is on the intellect alone cannot in its spiritual blindness see the significance of these facts and the implications of its own conclusions regarding the nature and destiny of man and the meaning and purpose of human life. We shall take only one of these obvious facts of existence from the field of science to illustrate how blind scientific materialism is to the implications of scientific discoveries.

The researches of astronomers have shown that our earth is a mere speck of dust as compared with the vast and limitless universe containing billions of solar systems separated by unimaginable distances which are measured in terms of light-years. Its life which to us appears so long is no more than a flash in the long stretches of time during which the universe is supposed to exist. On this insignificant and evanescent planet the present humanity has been in existence only for a few thousand years. Its past is shrouded in the uncertain evidence of geological strata and fossils of animals, and its future is anybody's guess as far as materialistic philosophy can see.

Surely, with these hard scientific facts before us we cannot refuse to consider the conclusions to which they point inevitably and obviously. One of these conclusions which is awful in its import, if only we had eyes to see it, is that man in his physical aspect has practically no significance and is of no consequence to Nature. A bevy of ants occupying a log of wood floating in the Pacific Ocean has far greater significance than our humanity occupying this planet which is floating in the limitless universe and will inevitably be swallowed up in empty space and oblivion leaving no trace behind it. And, of course, when we consider an individual human being as a unit of this continuing but ever-changing humanity the significance of our physical life is reduced to practically nothing. We have only to recall how mighty civilizations which once flourished have been swallowed up completely by the advancing tide of time and change to realize what kind of fate awaits every one of us as physical entities, the high and mighty as well as the poor and the meek.

If this is the basic reality of our existence as *merely* physical entities, should we not pause and consider carefully our aims and ideals, this feverish pursuit of purely materialistic aims however realistic or spectacular they might appear outwardly. Should we not try to go deeper into the question of human life and its problems instead of ignoring these problems and pursuing our pet aims thoughtlessly. It requires only a little commonsense and intelligent detachment from our engrossing interests and preoccupations to see how utterly meaningless and dreamlike the whole drama which is being played on the world stage would be if there were nothing more to it, hidden behind the shadow play which we are witnessing.

As a matter of fact there is something more, and it is what is hidden behind this otherwise meaningless passing show which gives meaning and importance to the march of events and things which we witness in time and space. It is what is present in the background, in the invisible but tremendously more real mental and spiritual realms of Nature which gives significance to crowds of self-important politicians strutting about on the world stage, to scientists making frantic efforts to probe into the secrets of Nature, to common people acquiring fragmentary knowledge and skills of various kinds, to philosophers spinning endless theories about human life and the universe, to religious people striving to reach an ideal of goodness and perfection which is obviously beyond their present capacities.

If we ignore this reality which is hidden in the background we reduce man to the status of a mere animal who has evolved through the agency of blind evolutionary forces and who is destined to remain a mere animal essentially though acquiring more and more knowledge and intelligence through the slow processes of evolution. But this accumulation of knowledge and growth of intelligence is only for that elusive and ever-changing collection of human beings which is referred to as the human race. The individual human being cannot be anything but an utterly insignificant creature of apparently accidental circumstances who is doomed to die and disappear into the nothingness of oblivion after spending a few years in feverish excitements and meaningless pursuits of various kinds. The artificial and self-deceptive means of satisfaction which he creates for himself endlessly are of no avail in this resistless march of time and the destruction of everything which he holds dear.

This is the status and prospect which materialistic philosophy has given to man and which a large number of even intellectual people have thoughtlessly accepted because they are unable to see the real significance of things around them. If the tendency to take things of our life for granted were not so common and we were not hypnotized by the glamour of scientific achievements we would see that the pragmatic

attitude upon which materialistic philosophy is based is
nothing but a means of escape from the hard and frightening
realities of the physical world. It provides the scientific
world with an ostensible justification for the thoughtless
pursuit of aims which cannot be justified in the face of
these realities. We want to bury our heads in the immediate
and limited problems because we dare not face the larger
and very real problems which are always present in the
background.

The pragmatic attitude is considered to be justified and
the scientific position is thought to be invincible because the
scientist claims to base all his work and conclusions on facts
which can be proved as facts. He can always turn round
and tell the occultist in effect: " Prove your case. Show me
that there is anything else in existence besides the physical
world which can be cognized by the sense-organs or physical
instruments that are really extensions of the sense-organs.
Show me that subtler and invisible worlds exist within the
physical world and all these worlds are derived from one
Ultimate Reality which is eternal, all-pervading and an integrated Whole." Now, the occultist cannot meet this
challenge by means of an ordinary physical experiment and
demonstrate before the sceptic what he is asserting and
trying to communicate. The things which he is asked to
demonstrate cannot be handled in this manner simply because
they are not material. They belong to the realms of mind
and consciousness and it is absurd to demand that mental
and spiritual facts of existence be demonstrated by physical
means. Each investigator has to explore and discover these
inner realms by methods which are applicable to those realms.
Any fool can see that mental and spiritual realms can be
explored only by mental methods, by diving into the deeper
recesses of our own mind and Spirit. Others can only point
to their existence and show the way to this deeper knowledge.
The subtler worlds of Reality cannot be brought to the

sceptic. He has to go into the deeper realms of his mind to find those worlds.

As regards the question of proof a careful study of scientific theories and facts on which they are based will show that the position of the orthodox scientist is not as invulnerable as it is considered to be by the layman. The scientist considers himself competent to pronounce high-sounding views on any subject, even such a profound subject as the nature and the origin of the vast, limitless and complex universe. If we examine the basis of his views on these questions we find that he bases them almost entirely on the flimsy evidence of extremely limited phenomena observed with purely physical instruments such as the telescope, the microscope and the photographic camera. He ignores the limitations of these instruments and on the basis of data collected with the help of these instruments he builds up elaborate theories even with regard to those things which are beyond the scope of his investigation.

While he considers himself justified in holding and propounding very definite views about the most profound problems of life on the basis of such flimsy and insufficient evidence he regards the clear and overwhelming testimony of innumerable occultists, sages, saints and mystics about the existence of subtler worlds as unreliable and not even worth considering. Some of these great souls like the Buddha, the Christ, Śaṃkarācārya and Patañjali stand out like Colossuses in their intellectual and spiritual stature whom a vast number of people all over the world have held in reverence and have been following for thousands of years. Other *Mahātmās* equally great and living in the present who prefer to remain unknown also bear their personal testimony to the existence of these subtler and far more real worlds. Surely, no sensible person can brush aside all this overwhelming and reliable evidence based on the direct experiences of these great souls unless his mind is completely closed by prejudice or preconceived ideas.

It is not a question, as is sometimes supposed, of one view being based on facts of the objective world and the other on the subjective perceptions in the realm of the mind. Both are based on the mind. Both are objective in one sense, subjective in another. For, is not knowledge derived through the sense-organs based upon the perception of mental images present in our own mind and so subjective in its essential nature? People do not realize that sense-organs are merely out-posts of the mind and knowledge of the so-called objective world is essentially subjective in character. So, both views of the world around us—the materialistic and the spiritual—are based on the mind and human experience. It is therefore merely a question of giving credence to one because it suits us and we like to remain involved in the seductive experiences of the lower life and rejecting the other because we do not want to face the real problems of life and undertake the task of getting rid of the illusions and limitations in which we are involved.

In considering the relative reliability of the materialistic and spiritual standpoints let us not bring into the picture the doctrines of Occultism which are meant to give us some idea with regard to the subtler and more real universe which is hidden within the visible physical universe. Let us not complicate the issue by going into these details at the initial stage. Let us consider merely the simple basic question: Is the physical world which we can cognize with our five sense-organs and with the help of the physical instruments the only reality in existence or is it merely an outermost shell of the far greater and more real universe which exists hidden within it? Let us not complicate this question and its consideration with details concerning the nature of the invisible part of the universe. For, if it is true that there is an invisible subtler universe of many degrees of subtlety hidden within the physical universe or that the apparently material universe which we know is essentially mental in nature, then the whole edifice of scientific materialism crashes to the ground and all its conclusions and pompous pronouncements with regard to the nature of man and the universe and the materialistic aims and objects of human life become worthless and meaningless. It is only then that the way becomes clear for giving serious thought to the nature of this real though invisible universe and its relation to the visible universe which we can cognize with our five sense-organs.

Let us now leave the question of the nature of the universe and come to man. Here again we find a marked and refreshing contrast between the standpoints of scientific materialism and Occultism. Let us consider first what man is according to scientific materialism. He is referred to as 'man the unknown' by which it is implied that we do not know and cannot know what man is except what we can cognize through our sense-organs and physical instruments. In other words, man is nothing but his physical body and whatever mental expressions that may take place through it as by-products of its functioning. He is thus essentially an animal who has mysteriously developed some mental faculties and intelligence as a further step in the evolutionary process and will continue to develop in that direction if he does not in the future involve the world in a holocaust of atomic war and revert to the simian stage.

This view of the nature of man may appear shocking when put in this manner but it is implicit in the theories of science which are current these days and which are accepted without question by the modern intellectuals and their followers. They have not only accepted this view but are very proud of their rational and scientific outlook upon which this view is supposed to be based. The view that man is divine in his origin, divine in his nature and has unlimited divine potentialities hidden within him is considered obsolete and based upon wishful thinking.

If man is considered to be a highly evolved animal who has developed a mind as a by-product in the natural course of evolution then it is natural for those who consider themselves responsible for his welfare to treat him basically as an animal. They try to prolong his life and make it as comfortable as possible. They try to provide him with amusements for his emotional needs and art, literature, etc. for his intellectual needs. They give him a decent burial when he disappears behind the curtain of death and his life as an individual is supposed to be extinguished for ever. What more can a mere animal want?

From this conception of man as a glorified animal also follows the utter disregard for his individuality and the right to use him in any way the community thinks is desirable or necessary. He has no right to hold even any individual opinions, to live his life as he thinks best, when these are contrary to or interfere with the plans of the majority or those in power. It is considered quite justifiable to destroy individuals or people en masse when those who consider themselves responsible for his welfare think this is desirable or necessary. It will be seen how strikingly similar is this attitude to our behaviour towards animals. We feed them properly, make them as comfortable as possible but when we need meat we slaughter them mercilessly.

It is refreshing to turn from this degrading concept of human origin, nature and destiny which materialistic philosophy has created for us to the spiritual concept of Occultism. This spiritual concept is not the product of arbitrary thinking of an individual or group of individuals who, without knowing or even caring to enquire into the realities of life formulate elaborate theories of human nature and ideals and methods of realizing them, basing their theories solely on the observation and study of superficial and passing phenomena of life. It is based on the wisdom and direct experience of great Adepts who have been able to penetrate into the deepest mysteries of life and found that Reality which lies at the basis of and contains the whole universe within itself in a mysterious but very real manner. It is only such liberated Beings who have transcended the limitations and illusions of the lower worlds and are permanently established in that Reality who are in a position to give sound and reliable opinion on all these vital questions concerning man and the universe. Those who base their conclusion with regard to these things on what they can see through microscopes and telescopes and are still involved in the grossest illusions of the lower worlds are obviously incompetent to do so, simply because their knowledge is so incomplete, uncertain and divorced from wisdom. If any proof is needed for this it is amply provided by the chaotic, conflicting and extremely dangerous conditions which have resulted in the world by following the philosophy of materialism. After all, a philosophy has to be judged by its fruit.

Besides this, any one who compares the different methods of ensuring and promoting human welfare with an unprejudiced mind will have to concede that the humane methods advocated by the spiritual philosophy of life are far more in conformity with our ideas of civilized behaviour than the barbarous methods followed by the votaries of the materialistic philosophy. One recommends conflict and struggle, the other cooperation and brotherhood. One depends upon hatred and violence for solving international problems, the other on reason, understanding and justice. One is callous in its attitude towards the common man and without the slightest hesitation inflicts unnecessary suffering on large masses of people, the other is very sensitive and careful with regard to the manner in which policies and decisions affect the life of the people. One respects and cherishes the individuality of man and tries to bring about a happy and harmonious adjustment between the needs and interests of individuals and society. The other considers the individual as of no account and does not mind crushing him ruthlessly in achieving its aims.

Surely, any one who looks at the above two pictures of the ideals and methods of the two philosophies will see at once that these differences arise from and are the inevitable consequences of regarding man as an evolved animal on the one hand and a spiritual being rooted in divinity on the other. If, therefore, we find that the materialistic philosophy has created intolerable and dangerous conditions the obvious remedy lies in adopting the other philosophy at least as an experimental measure. History has shown again and again that the mere fact of large masses of people subscribing to a particular ideology or mode of life does not mean necessarily that they are right. The mass mind is very amenable to suggestion and regimentation and can be influenced easily by appeals to the lower instincts, narrow prejudices and baser passions of mankind. The time has come to do some rethinking with regard to the vital problems which face us and see whether we should not now give the spiritual philosophy of life a fair trial. Let us honestly and earnestly substitute cooperation for conflict, love for hatred, reason for violence, wisdom for naked power, intelligent facing of life's problems for mechanical pursuit of arbitrary idealogies, a sense of individual responsibility for blind following of a leader or party. In short, let us admit the failure of the materialistic philosophy and try to give the spiritual philosophy a fair trial.

We need not enter here into the question of the nature and contents of this philosophy of Occultism for this is a very comprehensive subject and the whole of this book is meant to provide glimpses of it under the tremendous limitations which thought and especially language necessarily impose on the presentation of such truths. But it is necessary at least to point out here very briefly and in a general way what is the conception of man according to this philosophy so that we may be able to compare it with the conception of man according to the materialistic philosophy.

Occultism *knows* man to be a mental being working through the physical body which serves as his instrument for gaining experience on the physical plane. He is not only a mental entity but has a spiritual core of unlimited potentialities in which he can realize himself as one with the Reality which underlies the universe and is generally and vaguely referred to as God. It is through this spiritual or rather divine Centre hidden within the many layers of the mind that he can contact the whole universe in all degrees of subtlety and solve within the innermost depths of his own consciousness the total, eternal mystery of his own nature, of the universe and of that Reality from which both are derived. It is because he holds the ultimate mystery of his existence hidden within the innermost depths of his mind that he can become aware of it by transcending systematically the different layers of the mind.

The philosophy of Occultism is based upon the systematic unravelling of this mystery in this manner by a large number of adepts of Occultism, some of whom have appeared in the world as sages, saints and mystics from time to time. It is this body of men who have gathered this Eternal Wisdom, verified it again and again in their own experience and preserved it throughout the ages in trust for humanity as a whole. They are the real guardians of humanity who work constantly behind the scenes and guide humanity along the destined path of evolution with their unerring wisdom and unfaltering will.

It should be clear from what has been said above that there can be really no comparison between this philosophy and that of materialism. The latter is based on the sensuous perceptions of people who are still involved in the limitations of the lower mind and who with incomplete and uncertain data try to evolve tentative and constantly changing theories about man and the universe. The former is based on the direct experience of Self-realized and liberated beings who have not only systematically investigated the subtler worlds but found the ultimate Truth of existence and tried to mirror it in the realms of thought for the benefit of those who are still imprisoned in their minds.

A great deal is being made these days of the achievements of Science, of how man is discovering the secrets of the atom, probing into greater and greater depths of space, hunting for microbes and controlling diseases etc., and many naive people think that Science will ultimately solve all human problems and bring a Godless heaven upon earth in course of time. It would be absurd to belittle the achievements of Science. They are really wonderful but let us not exaggerate their importance or efficacy in the solution of the deeper problems which face humanity. Already Science has created very serious and urgent problems because it has ignored the realities of life and the development of our moral and spiritual nature has not kept pace with the development of the intellect. At no time perhaps was there greater unrest, fear, conflict, uncertainty, greater accumulation of means of mass destruction, concentration of power in individuals, many of whom, by a mere accident or error of judgment, can destroy whole populations, inflicting enormous suffering on innocent and helpless people. Even the innumerable amenities and means of entertainment which Science is providing in increasing number are not an unmixed blessing, for they are making man more and more outward-turned, superficial and cut off from the only source of real strength, peace and wisdom which exists within him. The almost universal and increasing dissatisfaction of youth which seeks relief in constant change, excitements of various kinds and even in drugs are all symptoms of the basic malady which afflicts our civilization—the disintegration of psyche which sets in when man disowns his spiritual nature and is cut adrift from his Divine Centre. All this is due, of course, not to Science itself but to the materialistic philosophy which has been developed and adopted by those who are working for the advancement of Science or exploiting it for their short-sighted political and social purposes.

Let us also not in considering the philosophy of Occultism confuse it with the philosophies which are generally associated with the doctrines of orthodox religions. It is true that the great religions of the world have been given by spiritual teachers who were in touch with the inner realities, and so the fundamental doctrines of these religions reflect more or less the doctrines which form part of Occultism. But no religion can remain in its pristine purity, free from the accretions which gradually accumulate with the passage of time, unaffected by the prejudices and weaknesses of those who transmit it from one generation to another after losing touch with the inner realities. It is inevitable that every religion should therefore become more and more debased, ineffective and formal. That is why discrimination is necessary in the study and practice of every religion and the serious seeker for Truth should try to separate carefully what is true and fundamental from what is false and non-essential, the result of accretions which have taken place in the course of time.

The same kind of caution is needed in the study of various philosophies which have been put forward by academic philosophers in different countries from time to time. They should be studied with discrimination and an effort should be made to separate what is based on pure speculation from what is based on knowledge. The ultimate test in the case of every doctrine whether it is of a religious or philosophical nature is whether it is based upon direct experience and can be verified experimentally by any one who possesses the necessary qualifications. This test may not be easy to carry out but every religion and philosophy has to submit to it in order to justify and prove its validity.

2. *Necessity of an integrated approach*

It has been pointed out already that an enquirer can look for light on the great mystery which surrounds his life in three directions—religion, philosophy and science. But if he is earnest and genuinely interested in unravelling this mystery he will fail to find real satisfaction in any of these quarters. If he goes to the academic philosophers they give him all kinds of hypotheses, each dealing with a few limited aspects of the mystery and discussing the great problem in a very superficial manner. He finds that these hypotheses differ from one another and frequently contradict each other. For this reason, and the fact that they are admittedly mere guesses by intellectual people without any foundation of experience or experiment, he gets no help in unravelling the mystery or even ordinary intellectual satisfaction. In fact, the more he studies these academic philosophies the more confused he becomes by their contradictions and inability to answer the vital questions concerning human life directly and satisfactorily.

Those who are in touch with the development of philosophical thought in modern times and study it with discrimination will agree that the above is not an exaggerated and unfair statement. Philosophy is drifting away more and more from its real purpose and getting bogged down in futile discussions of artificial questions which are not of vital interest to anybody and which do not throw any light on the fundamental problems of life. The mill for producing philosophical thought has to be kept running and grist has to be found for this mill. Anything which can enable academic philosophers to keep themselves engaged in outwardly philosophical discussions and fill the pages of philosophical journals is good enough for this mill. The very nature of the human mind is such that it can serve as an inexhaustible source of ideas on any subject.

If the enquirer turns to religion for understanding the mystery of life he finds religious people and their leaders divided into different groups or folds each group subscribing to a particular creed or set of religious ideas derived from a spiritual teacher or teachers in the near or distant past. If we examine the fundamental doctrines of these different religions carefully we find a remarkable general resemblance between them. This points to a common source and their essential unity. But this essential body of pure and true teaching is so debased by admixture with all kinds of dogmas, traditions and religious practices that different religions seem to have hardly anything in common or to have any basis in fact. Instead of bringing people together in a common bond of brotherhood based upon the fatherhood of God they divide people more and more in water-tight compartments and serve frequently as instruments of hatred and violence instead of love and understanding. There is perhaps nothing more tragic and ironical in human life than religious fanaticism which nullifies the very purpose of religion and reason for its existence by promoting hatred and conflict in man and shutting off completely all his higher potentialities. It is inevitable that under these conditions religion should tend to become more and more formal, a matter of following routines and elaborating outer paraphernalia of religious life. Blind belief is substituted for experience, learning is taken for spirituality and charitable work is considered as the same thing as love.

The above conditions prevailing in the sphere of religious life may be adequate for the spiritual needs of the man who takes his life for granted and in whose life religion plays a very minor part. But they can not satisfy the aspirant who has begun to question life and wants not the outer forms of religious life but its inner realities. It is because a much larger number of people in the world are becoming spiritually awake that they have begun to question the prevailing religious values and forms of religious life. It is because they can see through its inadequacies and perversions that so many of them now do not want to have anything to do with religion. In the case of others the reaction is not so violent, but still they are internally dissatisfied and fail to find in religion the knowledge and certainty which can help them to transcend their present limitations. They do not want the superficial satisfactions and escapes of formal religion but the enlightenment, peace and strength of real spiritual life.

If the seeker after Truth turns to science for any light on the problems which are troubling him he finds an entirely new situation facing him. Here, all is experiment, experience, proved facts, certainty, but a complete absence of interest and information concerning the deeper problems of life which are present in the background of human life and questions about which should arise naturally in the minds of all intelligent people including the scientists. The scientists have deliberately adopted a pragmatic approach to life and arbitrarily decided to confine their attention to the investigation of physical phenomena through physical means. They refuse to have anything to do with the larger and deeper problems of life, many of which have been created by the discoveries of science itself.

But these deeper problems of life do not cease to exist because they are ignored. They appear in the form of other problems, generally more serious and sometimes deadly. If you ignore the needs of your spiritual nature and consider morality as unnecessary for progress you may be able to put God in cold storage and do freely and without any inhibition what you like, but then the problem will appear in the form of a hydrogen bomb and the dreadful possibility of an atomic war which may exterminate humanity itself. So a scientific philosophy based merely on experiments carried on in a very limited field of investigation and divorced from the consideration of problems which are supposed to belong to the province of religion and philosophy is not only inadequate but extremely dangerous and may lead ultimately to the destruction of the very people who profess it and thoughtlessly propagate it. The seeker after Truth will therefore not be able to find in the realm of science the knowledge and satisfaction which he seeks and the mystery which he wants to unravel will remain as impenetrable as ever.

What then is wrong with these different methods of approach which are adopted in unravelling the mystery of life and finding the Truth underlying the phonomenal world in which we find ourselves involved? Why can not they help the earnest enquirer who wants light on the deeper problems of life and is not prepared to pursue blindly the limited aims which religion, philosophy and science have set for themselves in their respective fields of work.

If we consider the matter carefully and with an open mind we shall find that the ultimate aim of all the three is the same or should be the same and they represent different ways of looking at and finding the ultimate truth about man, God and the universe. If this fact is recognized then we shall be able to see why they are not able to fulfil effectively their respective purposes in their own fields as well as their common and ultimate purpose. The reason obviously lies in the lack of integrated approach and the wrong tradition and practice of working in water-tight compartments. Let us see how this lack of integrated approach works to the detriment of all the three and prevents them from reaching the consummation of their effort in their respective fields of endeavour.

The isolation of religion from philosophy deprives it of the philosophical thought without which there can be no sound and definite basis of true religious endeavour. If the ultimate aim of religion is not merely to follow an external code of conduct but to find and live in communion with God, we must first have some idea with regard to the nature of the human soul and God and the relation existing between the two. We must know the nature of the mind and its illusions and limitations and how these illusions and limitations can be transcended. All these questions and many more fall within the province of philosophy and the aspirant must have thought about and clarified his ideas about them. It is only with such a philosophical mental back-ground that he can know with some clarity what his aim is and how that aim can be achieved. Otherwise, he will continue to drift in a vague world of religious aspiration and ideas at the mercy of others who may try to invite him into their own little folds and exploit him for their own purposes.

Many people think that there is some inherent antagonism between science and religion. This is a misconception resulting from our having very narrow and preconceived ideas about the real purposes of religion and science. It is true that in the recent history of scientific development the orthodoxies of religion and science have come into frequent conflict but this was because of their limited vision and misconceptions with regard to their true purposes. The most important feature of scientific development is the experimental altitude towards all problems and the devising of definite and effective techniques for the solution of those problems. Both these are necessary for the aspirant who wants to realize in his own experience the realities of the religious life. The divorce of religion and science therefore means that the real aim of religion remains unfulfilled and so religious life remains barren.

The isolation of philosophy from religion and science leads to similar detrimental consequences for philosophy. The real purpose of philosophy is to enquire into and obtain a clear and true understanding with regard to the nature of man and the universe. Since both are ultimately derived from that Reality which we refer to as God, a divorce of philosophy from religion means that this enquiry cannot be pursued to its final end and the mystery of life being deprived of its central clue remains unresolved. It is for this reason that purely academic philosophy without association with deep religious thought and spirit remains futile, a matter of interesting speculative thought evolved for the amusement of philosophers, with no vital purpose behind it.

But it is not enough to associate philosophy with religious thought. If the conclusions of philosophy are to have any real value they must become matters of realization. Realization can come only when the aspirant treads that path of experience and direct knowledge with which the science of Yoga deals. So we should not only have a marriage of philosophy and religion but this marriage should also be consummated by the fructifying technique of science.

What happens when science is isolated from religion and philosophy has already been indicated to some extent in the earlier part of the Preface. Science means knowledge of the facts of existence and laws of Nature. Such knowledge brings power. Power without wisdom is a dangerous thing and can lead to very undesirable consequences. Wisdom can come only from true religion and philosophy.

Also, without the wider vision which can come only from association with religion and philosophy, science must remain very narrow in its outlook and purpose and be confined to the extremely limited knowledge of the phenomena of the physical world. With a truly philosophical and religious background science can see the phenomena of Nature from a deeper and wider point of view and also in a better perspective. It can have a better sense of values and organize the search for Truth from a higher standpoint and with a more profound purpose. It need not then be obliged to serve merely the physical and intellectual needs of man and to become a tool of unscrupulous politicians and governments.

As there is only One Reality at the basis of the universe, seen and unseen, there must be only one ultimate Truth which is the object of pursuit along the three different lines of religion, philosophy and science. It is the knowledge of

this Truth, ' knowing which everything is known ' which is
the goal of all occultists. Adepts of Occultism have attained
to this transcendent knowledge which has not only liberated
them from the illusions and limitations of the lower worlds
but enables them to guide humanity with unerring wisdom
and certainty.

We can also see from what has been said above why
the three kinds of knowledge obtained along the three different
lines in the earlier stages, as well as the methods of obtaining
them, begin to merge into one another as we penetrate inwards
into the deeper levels of consciousness. So the development
of the integrated approach is inherent in the very nature of
things and as religion, philosophy and science succeed in
understanding their real object they must draw nearer to
each other.

When we understand the true and wider purposes of
religion, philosophy and science we begin to see the absurdity
of workers in these different fields working in water-tight
compartments and frequently regarding the workers in other
fields with feelings bordering on hostility or contempt. The
reason as pointed out above is the narrowness of outlook
which has resulted in confining their respective scope of
work within very narrow and unjustifiable limits. But the
pressure of evolutionary forces is bound to bring about a
progressive expansion of outlook in mankind and break down
the artificial barriers of every kind, including those existing
at present between religion, philosophy and science. We
shall then all work together, collaborate in different ways
and make common cause against the ignorance, illusion and
misery in which all of us are equally involved, although
many of us are not conscious of these limitations. We shall
take advantage of all that is useful and essential in the points
of view and techniques of workers in other fields and thus
be able to work more effectively and usefully in our own
sphere.

This collaboration is not only desirable but absolutely necessary for effective work because the roles of religion, philosophy and science in the discovery of Truth are really complementary. Religion provides us with the urge or motivating power to find this truth and gives us the benefit of the experience and advice of those religious teachers, saints and sages who have trodden this path and found that truth within their own heart by their own efforts. Without the indomitable faith in the existence of this Truth (which is generally referred to as God) and the tremendous attraction and love for it which religion alone can arouse it is impossible to tread that difficult path which leads to Self-realization.

Philosophy prepares the ground for this divine adventure by encouraging the spirit of enquiry, by bringing about a proper appreciation of the deeper problems of life, by giving us some idea of our own nature and the nature of the universe in which we are involved, and by giving us some indication of the direction in which our efforts should be directed. But a philosophy can be really helpful only when it is not speculative but based upon experience, upon facts discovered by those who have tried and succeeded in solving these problems and can therefore speak with authority and confidence. It is only such a philosophy which can be accepted with confidence, though tentatively, until we are in a position to verify the facts of the inner life in our own experience.

It is science which provides us with the experimental attitude and techniques by the application of which the truths of the inner life can be made real to us. Without such realization we cannot rise above the illusions and limitations of the lower worlds. So, the understanding given by philosophy, the attraction aroused by religion and the means provided by science are all needed by the seeker after Truth if he is to succeed in his difficult task.

It is to be expected that fanatics and orthodox people in these different spheres of enquiry and endeavour will

insist on remaining confined within their narrow outlooks
and limited spheres of work and will not be able to see the
necessity, the effectiveness and the grandeur of this alliance
of religion, philosophy and science in the discovery of Truth.
But there is no reason why really intelligent people who are
genuinely interested in the deeper problems of life should find
it difficult to accept this principle and adopt it whole-heartedly
in their work. And so rational and full of commonsense is
this attitude that it is bound to wear down gradually the
orthodoxies and narrow outlooks of workers in these separate
fields and bring them together, sooner or later, in a common
brotherhood of seekers after Truth. And when this brotherhood becomes a reality we shall not only find it possible to
organize the search for truth more purposefully and effectively
but many of the problems which are hindering the progress
of humanity and producing chaos and conflict everywhere
will begin to dissolve naturally and rapidly.

Syntheses and integrations of various kinds are taking
place in different spheres of life everywhere but the synthesis
of religion, philosophy and science which must come sooner
or later is the grandest synthesis which one can think of and
is fraught with the most beneficent possibilities. It will end
not only the conflicts of religions with one another, of philosophies with one another but will enable us to see life and its
problems from a deeper and broader point of view and to
co-operate whole-heartedly and effectively in every sphere of
human activity.

That such a synthesis is possible will be evident from
what has been said above already. Hinduism recognized
the impossibility of separating religion and philosophy and
so these two branches of knowledge are interwoven in the
development of Hindu culture and thought. One cannot
say where one ends and the other begins. Hindu religious
teachers, called *Ṛṣis* were philosophers and the great philosophers were generally Yogis devoted to the task of unravelling

the mystery underlying the human soul and the universe by direct experience. Even where the philosophy they propounded was based on reason and presented in terms of the intellect it was associated intimately with the problems of religion and frequently derived from their direct realizations of the realities of the inner life. They first realized the truths in their own lives by diving into their own minds and then presented them in the form of a reasoned and rational philosophy.

The synthesis of religion and philosophy is not the final synthesis in the realm of thought dealing with the deeper problems of life. As pointed out above we need to include in this synthesis another important branch of knowledge—science—to make it richer if not final. As a matter of fact the elements of science were included in the synthesis of religion and philosophy attempted by Hinduism, because Yoga is an experimental science and Yogic philosophy and technique are an integral part of Hinduism. All genuine occult knowledge which is part of Hindu religion and philosophy is based ultimately on the direct experiences and systematic experiments of Yogis, most of whom preferred to remain unknown to the world and are not therefore historical figures. They communicated their experiences to their advanced disciples or embodied them in treatises in a somewhat veiled form. But as physical science was not developed to a considerable extent as in modern times, the element of science was not properly and explicitly represented in the synthesis of knowledge which was accomplished. Now that science has developed tremendously in the recent past it is possible to attempt this greater and fuller synthesis more satisfactorily. This can be done in several ways, some of which are given below:

(1) By interpreting the truths of religion and philosophy in terms of modern scientific thought as far as possible, thus making them more easily understandable and acceptable.

(2) By inculcating the scientific spirit in the pursuit of religious or philosophical aims, which means laying greater emphasis on the experimental attitude and the experimental method and the need and importance of testing and experimenting with the truths of religion and philosophy.

(3) By encouraging students and aspirants to push into the unknown and deeper realms of the mind in which the realities of life are hidden. This is not easy, but a cautious beginning can be made by encouraging the study of higher Yoga and the practice of its elementary techniques. This will prepare the ground for and make the practice of higher Yoga and the realization of the truths of spiritual life possible.

It is necessary to point out here that in the present state of the world and the mood and temper of scientists, academic philosophers and religious leaders in general, it is not possible to bring about immediately the kind of co-operation and collaboration which is desirable and possible. The chief stumbling block in the achievement of this highly desirable purpose is orthodoxy. Orthodoxy is not a vice from which only religious people suffer, although this is the common impression. The orthodoxies of philosophers and scientists are in a way more deep-rooted and rigid and more difficult to overcome for they are based on the knowledge of the intellect alone with not much light of intuition. It is intuition which gives understanding and makes the softening and liberalization of attitudes possible. As far as science is concerned this attempt to promote greater understanding and co-operation has, therefore, for the time being to be confined to opening up of channels of communication, using the discoveries and theories of science for a clearer understanding of the Occult doctrines and providing clues to scientists which may help them to get out of the contradictions and difficulties in which they have become involved.

This work requires a great deal of caution and discrimination and enthusiastic but unwise attempts of people who want to promote this understanding and collaboration can do more harm than good. It is easier to spread these ideas among the general public whose minds have not been conditioned so much, and then let the pressure of public opinion thus built up, slowly influence scientific thought. It is the general public which is the ultimate court of appeal in the battle of ideas in the case of people who represent different points of view in any sphere of life—politicians, scientists, religious people etc. And all changes of a vital nature have necessarily to be brought about gradually through the changes in the minds of people in general. The individual problem is the world problem.

One hopeful feature of the difficult situation referred to above is that the discoveries which have been made in the rapid and unexpected development of science have produced a chastening effect on the scientific mind. For a long time, in the first flush of advancement, scientists as a class were cocksure, triumphant and contemptuous of views different from their own. They thought and made it appear as if they would soon be able to unravel the ultimate mystery of the universe and bring a heaven upon earth. But the unexpected and frequently confusing facts which they have come across and the serious and apparently insoluble problems which they have created as a result of their discoveries and inventions and ignoring of moral and spiritual values has made the more open-minded among them question their idealogies and general aims.

Matter which formed the basis of scientific materialism has disappeared into energy and radiation and so really scientific materialism has had the very ground cut away from under its feet. The perfect design found everywhere in Nature, the intelligent co-ordination of different natural forces in the achievement of all natural objectives, the mathematical precision with which all natural laws work, has exploded the theory that ' the universe is a fortuitous concourse of atoms' and made some thoughtful scientists to talk of a possible Architect of the universe who 'must be a mathematician'. The tremendous amounts of energy which are needed and the potentials to which these must be raised in starting a universe has suggested to their mind the possibility of there being a Creator, for insentient energy cannot raise its own potential. The very recent discovery of quasars has thrown astronomers 'into a state of exciting confusion' and is making many of them doubt their theories about the universe and the premises upon which they were based. All this is to the good, for it is bound to soften the attitude of the orthodox scientists and make them realize that there are forces and realities to be reckoned with which they had so far ignored and which cannot be ignored. When Nature wants to break a rigid mould which we have created for ourselves by our prejudices and orthodoxies it generally throws us into a state of confusion and puts us in impossible situations from which we can get out only by unlocking the doors of our mind and crying out for the light.

We find similarly in the case of religion and philosophy that situations are arising which are gradually leading to the softening of attitudes and making people slowly realize the necessity of co-operation in these three different fields. It cannot be said that the old prejudices and habits of thought have disappeared and people are yet ready to adopt a synthetic and co-operative approach, but anyway, the desirability and inevitability of such an approach is recognized among the more thoughtful people. Movements of this nature and fundamental changes in the attitudes of people in general take time to materialize and gain roots in their mind. We should not, therefore, expect a rapid and spectacular transformation in this respect. But those who believe in this synthetic approach should emphasize it everywhere, and what is more important, should by practical applications show its obvious superiority over the narrow and extremely limited points of view which imprison the life and mind of man. They should remember the Sanskrit maxim: *satyameva jayete nānritam*—It is truth which prevails ultimately, not falsehood.

3. *Plan and Purpose of the book*

It has been pointed out above that an integrated approach in the work of unravelling the mystery of life is not only desirable but necessary for tackling this difficult problem. The best proof of this is the fact that the profound knowledge regarding the inner realities of life which we refer to as Occultism has been acquired by adopting this integrated approach. This knowledge is based on the direct experiences of those who have been able to penetrate into the very heart of the Great Mystery and obtained that transcendent vision in which man, God and the universe are seen in their true and essential nature, as different aspects of one Reality. This transcendent vision of the underlying Reality of the three in which the Great Mystery is unravelled and the Truth of truths is revealed cannot be formulated in terms of the intellect nor can it be communicated to others. It must be obtained by each individual by his own efforts within the deepest recesses of his own consciousness. But it is possible to communicate the essential aspects of this knowledge in very general terms to the public at large, enough to give to the aspirant some idea of the realities of the inner life and to enable him to take those preliminary steps which will prepare him for treading the path of practical Occultism. Every human being has the inherent right to free himself from the illusions and limitations of the lower life and must be given a chance to make a beginning whenever he feels inclined to do so. He can always make a beginning by taking up earnest enquiry and learning to lead a righteous life which opens the door of the inner life. But few are yet ready to tread the difficult occult path which leads ultimately to

Enlightenment. This is all that even the greatest spiritual teachers can do for the common man.

It is this knowledge, communicable and understandable, which we find in its fragmentary form in the literature of revealed religions and in the schools of gnostics and mystics. It is called Occultism, or *Gupta-vidyā*—' the Secret knowledge' —because its deeper aspects are truly esoteric in nature, i.e. can be communicated only through direct and definite experience to those who are initiated or otherwise properly qualified. It is not necessary to say here what Occultism is. The whole of this book is meant to provide the student glimpses of this transcendent knowledge as far as this can be done on the plane of the intellect.

Occultism has both its theoretical and practical aspects. The former is concerned with the philosophical background of the wisdom while the latter deals with the techniques which enable the aspirant to tread the path of inner unfoldment and verify in his own experience the truths with which the philosophy is concerned. For the mere student a study of theoretical Occultism is enough. This will give him a clear understanding of the meaning of human life, his place in the universe, the nature and destiny of the human soul and its evolution through experiences gained in a series of lives according to the laws of Nature, including the law of Karma. But then he must remain content with second-hand intellectual knowledge and all the inadequacies which characterize such knowledge. He should not hope for the certainty and enlightenment which can come only by treading the path of practical Occultism.

Although this theoretical knowledge of Occultism is of limited usefulness, still, even in this form it provides the human mind with some of the profoundest and most reliable philosophical and religious conceptions regarding the nature of man, God and the universe and enables him to grasp mentally the realities of the inner life in the best possible manner. The earnest enquirer will find it not only of fascinating interest from the philosophical point of view but will acquire through its mastery a deep understanding of the problems of human life which perhaps cannot be obtained in any other way.

A subject which deals with the vast universe, both in its visible and invisible aspects, with man, the known and unknown, and with that Reality which underlies and is the source of both, must by its very nature be of limitless scope and unfathomable depths and must be able to satisfy the needs of people of all stages of mental and spiritual development. This is very true of Occultism which according to the words of a Christian devotee ' contains shallows in which a child could wade and depths in which a giant must swim '. Some of the lower aspects of Occultism can be studied and understood by almost any enquirer who brings to the subject on open mind and sincere desire to know the truths of the inner life. But its higher aspects which are related to the transcendental realities of existence and are meant to throw some light on the ultimate questions in the field of philosophy and psychology require for their study a trained intellect and sustained interest. An enquirer who wants to understand really the deeper problems of life and make his study fruitful must therefore be prepared to give some time and study the subject systematically. This is necessary because we cannot understand fully the real significance of any part of a whole unless we have some idea of the essentials of the whole and can see the part in its correct perspective. This is particularly true of Occultism which deals especially with the Whole, with the fundamental realities of existence, with the totality of life in all its aspects. To know such a subject only superficially or in parts is really not to know it at all.

It is necessary to point out that the Truth with which Occultism deals is so vast, transcendent and infinite in its nature that it is impossible to formulate it in any system, however comprehensive and profound this might be. Every system of philosophy, religion or science can at best represent only a glimpse of this transcendent Truth from a particular point of view. That is why all systems of philosophy in Hinduism are called *Darśanas*, *Darśana* broadly meaning a glimpse of Truth. Every great teacher of the Eternal Wisdom comes to present such a view of this Truth and so every presentation of this nature must be limited more or less by its very nature. The whole Truth in its perfection and transcendent beauty can be realized only within the innermost depth of one's consciousness when all the limitations and illusions of the mind have fallen away. We are then not looking at this Truth from a *particular* point of view. We have then become the Truth itself.

If this patent fact regarding the nature of Truth were more widely recognized and accepted it would prevent the formation of personality cults, the fanatical adherence to religious creeds, the antagonisms between different systems of philosophy, the isolation of the mind and its confinement in the prison of a particular teaching. People will begin to see that the claim of finality or completeness on behalf of any teaching or system of thought is as absurd as the claim that the reflection of the sun in a cup of water is the sun itself.

So, while Occultism claims to deal with this transcendent Truth underlying all forms of existence and tries to make its presentation as true and effective as possible, it does not claim that any particular presentation of occult truths on the plane of the intellect represents the whole Truth or the Real Truth. At best such a presentation can be an attempt to provide faint and blurred glimpses of this Truth in order that people may intuitively feel its beauty and grandeur within their heart, and begin to seek it there earnestly and purposefully. For the same reason no Teacher of the true Wisdom ever tries to put forward the claim that his teaching is new or exclusive. Even the Buddha said ' I have seen the ancient way, the old road that was taken by the former awakened beings and that is the path I follow.'

All this book therefore attempts to do is to draw the attention of the enquirer to a few fundamental problems of philosophy and to present as clearly as possible the Occult point of view with regard to these problems. Occultism has no creed and no doctrines which are meant to define different aspects of truth rigidly and formulate them in a final form. As it deals with realities which have innumerable aspects and unfathomable depths and not with limited objects or forces, it gives freedom to the enquirer to study these truths in his own way and come to his own conclusions and understanding, knowing that this understanding is bound to remain partial and imperfect on the purely intellectual plane any way, and when direct perception is obtained in the advanced stages there is no question of error, or doubt or disagreement between those who obtain the vision of the Truth.

This freedom of thought should not, however, be interpreted as license. Even when we are dealing with realities and not products of imagination or speculation we are free to believe what we like and understand them in our own way. But we entertain wrong beliefs and understand things in the wrong way to our own disadvantage and maybe at our own peril. The freedom of thought we have in regard to Occultism is similar to the freedom of thought in the field of science. A man is free to believe that the law of gravitation does not exist and to jump from a roof, but if he exercises his freedom in this foolish manner and does jump he will break his neck and learn the hard way that gravitation is a reality. When we are dealing with these things pertaining to the inner realities of existence, let us be very careful and not misuse our freedom of thought to interpret things as we like, and in our foolishness and egoism tread the path of error.

This freedom of thought also makes it necessary for us to exercise discrimination constantly. As everybody is free to believe what he likes and interpret things in any way he likes a vast literature has grown on the subject. Only a small part of it is genuine, essential and reliable and this is embedded in a vast mass of spurious or non-essential thought. Discrimination is needed to sort out all these ideas and separate the essential and the true from the non-essential and false. Our time and energy being limited, it would be foolish to waste them by becoming engrossed in the non-essential literature or entering paths of pseudo-occultism which lead nowhere or lead into the dangerous realms of the lower occult arts. It would, however, be equally foolish to reject Occultism as a whole because it is mixed up with ideas which are spurious and in many cases false. If we are too lazy to separate the grain from the chaff we must be prepared to remain hungry and spiritually starved.

No authority is claimed for the views expressed in the book except that it tries to represent broadly the knowledge and points of view of those who throughout the ages have seen the Truth and borne testimony to it in an unequivocal manner. An enquirer is free to accept or reject any view but it is expected that he would give serious consideration to it with an open mind before rejecting it. It is better in studying such things not to reject anything outright but to keep it aside for the time being. It is possible that with greater knowledge and deeper insight gained with more intensive study he may be able to see and appreciate the truth behind an idea which repelled him at first sight. A student will find probably that if he goes through the whole book several times and acquires a clear idea of the subjects it deals with, many points which had remained obscure before become illuminated in the light of what he has learnt later.

The study of such a book which deals with the most fundamental things in existence and problems which are of vital importance to us should not be expected to be easy. Patience and perseverance are needed. But once we catch an intuitive glimpse of the inner realities which it deals with, we shall feel that the labour spent has been worth while. It has given us not only an insight into the realities of our inner life but also a definite capacity to live and move and be at ease in the realms of higher thought. This is where the real life of man begins. He shares with animals all other attributes and capacites—desires, emotions, concrete thoughts and physical needs and propensities—but only he is capable of developing and living in his higher mind.

It may also be pointed out that in dealing with different topics only glimpses of the realities with which they are concerned have been given. Vast and limitless regions of thought and realization still remain to be explored. The purpose of the book is not to prove anything but to provide such partial glimpses of the philosophy of Occultism, in order that the student may see intuitively for himself that here is a source of knowledge which can throw some light on the deeper problems of life and enable him to gain direct and certain knowledge concerning the realities of the inner life of the soul. As the book deals particularly with the deeper and more fundamental aspects of Occultism, the simpler aspects had to be left out in this treatment. For these the student can consult simpler and more elementary treatises.

The reader may find in the book one or two references to Part II. This discrepancy is due to the fact that the book was originally planned to be in two parts, Part II dealing with some problems which could be considered more of a psychological nature. After a considerable portion of the book had been printed it was decided to leave out most of the chapters in Part II and incorporate them in another book dealing with the psychology of Yoga.

The arrangement of the subjects in the order in which they have been dealt with in the book does not follow any rigid order dictated by logic. When we are viewing a big beautiful diamond with many and different kinds of facets, we can start with any facet and view them in any order. For, they are all related and together constitute the whole diamond. It is more important that we get a view of all the facets, one by one, and be able to visualize the whole diamond simultaneously. It is not so important in which order we begin and carry out our observation.

Still, as the universe is an expression of a Central and Ultimate Reality which manifests at different levels, one derived from the other, there is a certain sequential relationship existing between its different aspects, and it is perhaps helpful if we consider these aspects in a certain order determined by the above consideration. An attempt has been made to follow this order as far as possible, but a different order of treatment may be equally helpful. This order as pointed out above is not of great importance, for the serious student will have to read the book several times and refer to different points backwards and forwards in order to gain a clear and satisfying comprehension of the philosophical side of Occultism as a whole.

With this rather lengthy but necessary preface the reader is invited to take a plunge into the intellectual aspect of the great mystery which surrounds our life and see what Occultism has to say about it. Later on, if he is convinced that Occultism points out correctly the direction in which we have to seek for the Light he can take a different kind of plunge into the depths of his own mind to enable him to unravel the mystery, step by step, by direct realization.

21-3-1968   I. K. Taimni

CONTENTS

LIST OF DIAGRAMS

CHAPTER I

THE CONCEPT OF THE ABSOLUTE—I

Void or Plenum?

The nature of the Absolute is the most enigmatic though fascinating problem of philosophy and religion and although the problem is bound to remain always unsolved by philosophy, it will continue to engage the attention of philosophers for all time to come. Because the Ultimate Reality which is denoted by the word 'Absolute' or 'Parabrahman' is the very core of our being as well as the cause and basis of the universe of which we are a part, we can no more get away from it than our solar system can get away from the sun round which it revolves and from which it receives everything which keeps it alive and moving.

Although the Absolute is sometimes referred to by such epithets as the Void, Ever-Darkness, etc. and is beyond intellectual comprehension, still, from the intellectual point of view it is the most profound concept in the whole realm of philosophy. The fact that it is called 'Unknowable' does not mean that it is beyond the range of philosophical or religious thought and something on which thinking is impossible or undesirable. The very fact that it is the heart and the basis of the universe should make it the most intriguing object of enquiry within the realms of the intellect.

Although the Vedas and the Upaniṣads emphasize again and again that this highest and subtlest Principle in existence is beyond speech and thought, still, their main purpose seems to be to give to those who read these revealed books a certainty that such an Ultimate Reality does exist at the heart of the manifested universe and to realize it in increasing measure is the highest object of human endeavour. They are full of indirect hints, beautiful descriptions and symbolic representations of this unknown and intellectually unknowable Principle and the means which may be adopted for gaining more and more vivid realizations of its nature within the unfathomable depths of our own consciousness.

So, it is obvious that thinking and making enquiries about the Absolute or Parabrahman is not discouraged, but is, on the other hand, considered as the highest object of pursuit and enquiry for the intellect. What the student of the Divine Wisdom or the *Sādhaka* has to guard against is not thinking about this Ultimate Reality but to consider his thoughts as knowledge of that Reality. It is unknowable and yet the highest object of realization, unthinkable and yet the most profound object of philosophical enquiry. But this enquiry must be a joint effort of earnest thought and deep devotion and not mere speculation or exercise of sterile logic if it is to be of any practical use.

In dealing with such a profound and inexhaustible concept all that is possible is to place before the reader, one by one, certain ideas which throw some light on its different aspects. These ideas are like the pieces of a jig-saw puzzle. Each piece when taken by itself may not mean much or anything. But when they are put together properly, one after another, a stage comes when the whole picture flashes suddenly in our mind and we see not only the significance of the pieces which have been fitted already but also catch a faint glimpse of those pieces which are still missing. The intellect can deal only with disjointed aspects of any concept. It is the function of the Higher Mind, and especially of Buddhi or intuition in the case of spiritual realities, to fuse

together these separate aspects and to grasp to some extent
that reality of which they are the broken images.

Herein comes the value of intellectual effort in the pursuit
of the Divine Wisdom. The intellect cannot give us perception of the truths we are seeking. This comes only from
the light of Buddhi. But it can prepare the ground for
acquiring that perception by gathering essential intellectual
material and working upon it with great concentration and
earnestness and with the set purpose of finding those truths
which are hidden behind the ideas. In thus straining perseveringly to go beyond the ideas, consciousness becomes
more and more free from the obscuring influence of the
intellect and acquires in an increasing measure the direct
perception of those truths.

Before we begin to clarify our ideas about the Absolute
we must remind ourselves of the tremendous limitations under
which we are undertaking this difficult but fascinating task.
We are trying to understand through the instrumentality of
the intellect a Reality which is not only beyond the range
of the intellect but beyond the range of Buddhi and Ātmā
and even beyond the range of the experiences of those high
Adepts who can dive even deeper into the recesses of their
own consciousness. We are trying to peer into a mystery
which is called the Ever-Darkness and the Unknowable and
can only hope that a faint glimmer of light from the deeper
recesses of our being will be able to filter down into our
minds, at least partially satisfy our hunger for this knowledge,
and perhaps draw us a little nearer to that Reality which is
shrouded in impenetrable mystery.

If we are conscious of our tremendous limitations and
regard our efforts merely as trying to get information about
a country with the help of a map, and not to know it in any
sense of the term, we may be able to maintain the right
attitude of reverence and humility. This is the only way
of avoiding the error into which the ordinary scholar or

divine falls when he mistakes his intellectual knowledge for real knowledge and on the basis of this begins to consider himself superior to those who do not have even this knowledge. Consciousness of our ignorance is the beginning of wisdom and the first step toward acquiring true knowledge. There is no greater enemy of real knowledge than complacency which completely stops our progress by making us live in a world of false and illusory security and satisfactions.

Although for the sake of convenience in dealing with the subject we have separated the concept of the Absolute from the other two concepts, namely those of the dual Father-Mother Principle and the triple Unmanifest Cosmic Logos, we should remember that the three together are the Ever-Unmanifest and really constitute one indivisible, impenetrable Mystery which lies at the basis of the manifested universe. Therefore, after we have considered the three aspects of the Unmanifest separately, we should take them together and by bringing out their relationships integrate them into one concept which is self-contained and a harmonious whole.

In considering the nature of the Absolute, as far as this is possible within the realm of the intellect, it would be of great help if we first consider a few facts and natural phenomena which by their analogous relationships can give us some insight into this Mystery of Mysteries. By a strange irony of circumstances these facts have been provided by Science which owing to its hostility to the doctrines of religion and philosophy was generally considered an enemy by orthodox adherents of religion and philosophy. These, and other instances of this nature, show how the discoveries of Science, instead of being prejudicial to the Occult Doctrine are really of great help in enabling us to understand and appreciate that doctrine. This is so because the phenomena in the lower worlds are shadows of realities in the higher and by examining and understanding the shadows below we can sometimes gain a clue or glimpse into the nature of the realities above. It is this fact which made one of the Adepts say, 'Science is our greatest ally'. Truth has nothing to fear from any quarter, least of all from Science which is also devoted to the discovery of Truth, although at a much lower level and in a very limited field. If some things are proved wrong in some of the minor occult doctrines or in the investigations made by occultists it is good that they are proved wrong in the interest of the greater Truth, for the occultist also, like the scientist, wants the Truth, and nothing but the Truth.

The first of the natural phenomena which we shall briefly consider is the dispersion of white light by a prism as shown in Fig. 1. Those who have knowledge of even elementary science are familiar with the experiment in which a beam of white light is passed through a prism and the emergent beam

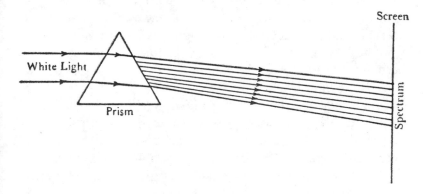

FIG. 1. Dispersion of White Light.

allowed to fall on a white screen. The image which is produced is not that of the original beam but we get a band of colours which is called a spectrum. If the original beam of white light was derived from the sun then there is also an invisible spectrum on either side of the visible spectrum which is called infra-red and ultra-violet. What has happened is that the beam of white light has been dispersed or differentiated by the prism and all the vibrations, visible and invisible, have been separated from each other, according to their wave lengths, forming a continuous spectrum. By putting another inverted prism in the path of the emergent rays it is possible to recombine or integrate them again into the original beam of white light. So the whole process is reversible.

Let us now note a few facts about this simple experiment which will throw some light on the problem we are considering. The first point we note is that it is possible to integrate a graded series of things in a perfectly balanced state in which none of the individual things is present as such but it is possible to get all the constituent things by differentiation. Considering the phenomenon further we see that the conditions prevailing on the two sides of the prism are entirely different. On the side on which the light enters the prism we have only the integrated white light and no colour, as such, and on the side on which it leaves the prism there are only colours and no white light. If there is an entity who has lived only on the side of colours and has never been to the other side he cannot have the slightest idea of what white light is like from his experience of different colours although they are all derived from white light. He will have to pass through the prism and emerge on the other side to realize what white light is like. And also, if he has always been in the realm of white light he can have no experience and not even an idea of colours as long as he does not pass into the realm of colours. The two experiences seem to be mutually exclusive. Another fact we should note is that the wholeness of the incident white light is not destroyed when in its progress it passes through the prism and is broken up into colours on the other side. The white light on the side of incidence is not affected by what happens to it on the side of emergence because it is not a static but a dynamic phenomenon ever renewing itself.

The significance of this light phenomenon in its various aspects in enabling us to understand to some extent the nature of the Absolute in a very general way is quite obvious and we need not go into it beyond pointing out the analogies which are self-evident. We can see at once how the Absolute itself can be without any attributes although it is the source of all those principles, *tattvas*, forces which invest all things in the realm of the manifest with attributes. To a world which knows only colours the absence of colours can only be interpreted as darkness and not as white light which is fundamentally different from darkness, for darkness means the complete absence of colours while white light means the presence of all colours but in an integrated form. So it is easy to see how the Absolute is said to be without any attributes whatsoever, the Ever-Darkness, or the Nirguna-brahman.

Again, we see how it is impossible to know a principle or reality from which a series of derivatives have been obtained by differentiation until we can transcend the realm of these derivatives and emerge into the realm of the parent principle. We must transcend the realm of particulars if we are to know and not merely conceive the archetype from which they are derived. We must leave the world of shadows if we are to know the realities which cast these shadows. We must leave the world of the mind if we are to know Consciousness in its purity and, lastly, we must leave the world of relativity if we are to know the Absolute, if this is at all possible.

The reverse of this proposition is perhaps also true in another sense and may provide a clue to the question why the Monad has to descend into the lower worlds to gain the necessary experience for his mysterious unfoldment. Living as he has always done in the bosom of the Father in the bright radiance of only white light he must come down into the world of manifestation where alone he can find the colours which are obtained by the differentiation of that white light. And since this can be done only through the instrumentality of a proper mechanism on the lower planes he must get involved in the building up and use of that mechanism. It is this, we may take it, that necessitates his evolution on the lower planes.

Let us try to look at this problem from another point of view. We have seen already that to people living in a world of only colours, white light will be conceived as darkness although it is fundamentally different from darkness. It may be said in general that when we cannot respond to a series of vibrations we always get the impression of an absence of vibration, for consciousness is related to anything through vibration and if our vehicle is unable to respond to a set of vibrations, the object which produces those vibrations must remain non-existent as far as we are concerned. We know as a matter of scientific fact that on both sides of the visible spectrum there is the infra-red and ultra-violet spectrum, but we cannot see it because our eyes cannot respond to vibrations of those wave lengths. Those realms of light are darkness to us although they can affect us in other ways. Similarly with sound. Our ears can respond only to a limited number of vibrations of sound and vibrations of greater or smaller wave length mean only silence to us although they can be detected and utilized by Science in various ways. The same holds true in the case of our mind. What is beyond the range of our mental comprehension appears meaningless and untrue to us. When we grow mentally we not only begin to understand those things but continue to see deeper meaning and significance in them. So, we must be on our guard when we encounter these words like silence and darkness in dealing with the realities of the inner realms and should not associate these words with the absence of any kind of reality but only with the absence of response on our part. As a matter of fact darkness and silence contain even on the physical plane far more than visible light and audible sound. This fact is brought home to us if we remember that on becoming blind and deaf the visible spectrum also passes into the realm of darkness and the audible spectrum into the realm of silence.

The word 'Ever-Darkness' used for the Absolute in occult literature therefore means only that the Ultimate Reality which it denotes is beyond the range of not only our senses and mind but even beyond the range of experience of the still higher principles like the Ātmā which are within the experience of the highest Adepts on our globe. From the many references we see in Hindu religion and occult literature it appears that it is only the Logos of a solar system who can have some kind of access into that impenetrable mystery but nothing definite on this point has been said.

We have so far been considering the whole question from what we may call the qualitative point of view. Let us now dwell for a while on its quantitative aspect. And in dealing with the quantitative aspect of the problem we cannot do better than consider very briefly the nature of the zero. The zero, as all those who have some knowledge of mathematics know, is the most intriguing, baffling and unpredictable entity in the whole field of mathematics with the exception of its counterpart, infinity. It is not possible to go here in detail into the extraordinary properties of zero and infinity but we may consider a few facts which are relevant to our problem and which may throw some light on the concept of the Absolute.

Zero and infinity appear to be polar opposites. If we go on increasing the quantity of anything we approach the limit of infinity but never seem to reach it. If we go on decreasing the quantity we approach the limit of zero but again never seem to reach it. Between these extreme and unattainable limits are contained all possible magnitudes of the thing we can imagine. The zero and infinity will thus be seen to be analogues of the point and space in geometry.

Now, a wonderful thing about the ideal point and boundless space is that they appear to be the same ultimately and indistinguishable. If we imagine a point expanding *ad infinitum* it will merge ultimately into infinite, boundless space and then appear mysteriously again out of nowhere at its original position and in its infinitesimal form. One can see why this should be so. The point and boundless space are the two polar vestures of the Absolute, and Cosmic Rhythm, as we shall see later, is an eternal oscillation of consciousness between them. The properties of the zero and infinity are analogous to those of the point and space.

An extraordinary property of zero is that it can contain within itself a quantity of any magnitude provided that quantity is balanced by another quantity which is equal and opposite in sign. You can write on a blackboard a figure of a hundred digits indicating a huge amount of anything and then if you write against it the same figure with an opposite sign the two disappear together in a zero. Not only large figures, but you can write a complex fraction large enough to cover the wall and then if you write another complex fraction which is equal and opposite in sign, the two together disappear into the unlimited potentiality of a zero. The interesting point to note is not only that you can reduce anything to zero by introducing its equal and opposite but also that the zero can contain both the +ve and −ve quantities in any number and of any magnitude without being affected in any manner. In short we may say, therefore, that the zero has the potentiality of containing within itself an infinite number of magnitudes from the smallest to the largest, all perfectly balanced, by each quantity being neutralized by an equal and opposite.

The significance of these extraordinary properties of zero can throw some light on the concept of the Absolute. They show mathematically how the existence of an Ultimate Reality, with the possibility of containing an infinite number of potential systems in any number and of any magnitude, is possible provided they are such that each separate item is balanced by its equal and opposite. We should note that there is no limit to the number, size or quality of the different items provided each is balanced by its equal and opposite. And we see also that this Reality in spite of the presence of these multifarious contents can be a void, containing everything and yet nothing.

The consideration of these two simple facts, one quantitative, the other qualitative, derived from the field of Science shows us that the two principles of balanced integration and balanced summation give us a significant clue to the attributeless and contentless nature of the Absolute which has potentially all attributes and yet is without any attributes, which has everything in itself which finds expression in an infinite series of manifestations and is yet without content. It is needless now to ask the question whether the Absolute is a Plenum or a Void. The question has answered itself.

The presence in an integrated form in the Unmanifest of all equal and opposite principles in a potential state naturally finds expression in the manifested universe in opposites called *dvandvās* or pairs of opposites, although it may not always be possible, on account of the limitations and illusions in which we live to correlate these opposites in every case. But they are seen everywhere and sometimes in a very striking form if we look at life intelligently and enquiringly. The active and passive functions of volition and cognition, involution and evolution, spirit and matter, subject and object, descent and ascent, +ve and —ve electricity, are a few of these well known pairs of opposites which may be traced backward to their source in the Unmanifest, where they remain perfectly balanced and potential and from which they spring forth into active functioning when manifestation takes place. The presence of these opposite aspects of the Unmanifest has been hinted at in a very beautiful verse of the *Iśāvāsyopaniṣad* (5) like this:

> " It moves, It does not move, It is further than the furthest,
> It is nearer than the nearest, It is within all this universe and It is also out of this All."

These pairs of opposite forces, processes and properties are well known and it is not necessary to go into the question of their nature here. I would rather deal very briefly with a few pairs of opposites which are generally not recognized as such but are implicit in the perfect balance, harmony and wholeness of the Absolute in which the whole universe, manifest and unmanifest is rooted. The recognition of these opposites is important not only from the academic standpoint but also from the practical point of view because it can affect our attitudes in life and be of help in the work of discovering that Reality within ourselves.

Let us first take a question of great personal interest to many people and on which there appears to be some confusion of thought amongst us. I mean the question of Saguna- and Nirguna-brahman or in other words Personal and Impersonal God. There is an impression prevalent among some people that Occultism considers God as a purely impersonal Principle who is unapproachable in a personal capacity and it is therefore not possible to establish any kind of personal relations with Him in our inner life. Any attempt to regard Him also as a personal God is frowned upon by these people and generally considered the result of anthropomorphic tendencies in man. Personal God does not necessarily mean a God sitting on a throne high up in the heavens. He is a God who is approachable and with whom personal relationships can be established although He remains invisible, intangible. This impression has to

some extent been created by those who under the strong
influence of Buddhistic teachings have taken into account
only one point of view and practically ignored its opposite.

It is true that in the very core of the Unmanifest, the
Absolute, the two aspects called Saguna- and Nirguna-brahman must be present in a balanced state and it is therefore
impossible to establish any kind of individual relationship
with that impenetrable Ultimate Principle. But when we
descend to the next lower level, the result of the primary
differentiation into two +ve and —ve Principles, called *Śiva-
Śakti* in Hindu philosophy and Father-Mother in *The Secret
Doctrine*, this impersonality and inaccessibility should disappear and it should not only be possible to establish personal
relationship with any aspect of that Reality at any level but
this should be of tremendous help to us in the work of Self-
discovery. We shall deal in a subsequent chapter with this
Father-Mother Principle and Its relation to the Monads
and try to show that we should trace our birth as Monads
and spiritual origin to that ultimate dual Principle which
is called Father-Mother not without reason, and we should
not talk thoughtlessly, and if I may say so unscientifically,
of having come out of the bosom of the Father, ignoring
completely our spiritual Mother who must have in those
mysterious and unimaginable realms a more important role
to play both in giving us birth and bringing us up as Monads,
as Her shadow in the physical world down here has.

We are, however, not concerned here with the question of
our origin but with that of our relationship with that Father-
Mother Principle or other lower manifestations of that Principle in any form. It may be asked in all seriousness whether
it is possible that the Father-Mother Principle which is the
prototype of all fathers and mothers in the physical world
and thus the ultimate source of all parental love, tenderness
and care, can itself be devoid of all these attributes. Is it not
more reasonable to suppose that It is the very fountain-head

of that love which even in its feeblest expression on the lower planes provides the most exquisite and blissful experience to human beings, nay even to animals? If our spiritual Parents are so impersonal and indifferent to us, their children, as individuals, as is sought to be made out, then why are they referred to as the Father-Mother?

I think that this view about the impersonality of God is the result of taking into consideration only one point of view and ignoring the opposite. The Reality which lies at the basis of this universe of such vast magnitude and complexity must be impersonal in one of its aspects. But this very fact of its utter impersonality must be balanced by its exact opposite, i.e. the fact that there must exist the most intimate and exquisite personal relationship between the Divine Parents and each individual soul. If He is utterly impersonal in one of His aspects He must be utterly personal in its opposite aspect. If His love holds in His vast embrace the whole universe in an impersonal manner, then He must also hold each individual soul within His bosom as the most loved and cared for child as no human mother can do. We must ponder carefully this idea that personality and impersonality are two opposite principles and utter impersonality in its Universal aspect must be balanced by utter personality in the individual aspect. It is upon this fundamental principle, derived from our concept of the Absolute, that the idea of a Saguna-brahman and the possibility of establishing the most intimate relationship of lover and beloved between the individual soul and the Universal Soul is based. And it is through the development of this relationship that the *Bhaktimārga* or the path of love is trodden.

From a question which is of personal interest and in which many must be interested I now come to a rather impersonal question of philosophical significance which is really what we call an *atiprasna* or ultimate question—beyond the comprehension of the intellect. I mean the question of the 'why' of the universe. Why was the universe created and even if there is no creation and merely alternation of *Sṛṣṭi*, creation, and *Pralaya*, dissolution, why this alternation? I think we can turn again to the concept of the Absolute for a partial answer to this question. It is obvious that the Manifest and the Unmanifest are two opposite states of Being. Forthgoing and returning are two opposite processes connected with these two states of Being and one cannot be without the other, its opposite, in a balanced whole. If there is the Unmanifest there must also be the Manifest and if there is the going forth from the Unmanifest there must also be the return to that state. So both the Manifest and the Unmanifest and their alternation at various levels must be inherent in the very nature of Reality and there is no question of any motive or exertion of will by any being in bringing about this alternation. There can be no Ultimate Reality without these two opposite aspects being inherent in It and producing the alternation of *Sṛṣṭi* and *Pralaya*.

We have taken here for the sake of illustration only these two implications of the concept of the Absolute. We could take many other implications of this wonderful concept of integration and balance in the Absolute and find that these throw some light on many problems in the field of philosophy which seem to baffle us.

A state in which all possible principles, forces, etc. exist in perfect balance and equilibrium would not only be a void as shown above but would also be a state of perfect stability. According to modern conceptions of Science if such a state of equilibrium is disturbed in any way the disturbance will be followed by such changes and adjustments as tend to neutralize the disturbance and tend to restore the original stable equilibrium.

Are there any indications in the phenomena of Nature to show that there exists an Ultimate Reality at the core of the universe which is in perfect equilibrium and which tends to restore the equilibrium whenever and wherever it is disturbed in any way? There are many natural laws and phenomena which point to the existence of perfect stability and equilibrium at the heart of the universe and the neutralisation of any kind of disturbance by corresponding changes and adjustments. Let us consider briefly a few of such laws and phenomena.

The first of such generally observed laws which may be considered is the law of compensation. Every advantage in the life of an individual is balanced by a disadvantage. Every pleasure is compensated by actual or potential pain. If we feel elated we must feel depressed correspondingly. If we want to accomplish anything in a shorter time we must spend energy at a faster rate. If we want things of the higher life we must give up things of the lower life. It is because we can get only a very limited view of one life that we are not able to see clearly the law of compensation at work, but it is of universal application.

It is not only in ordinary life that we can vaguely see the working of this law. In the field of Science also we see it working under different forms with mathematical exactitude. For example, there is the well-known Le Chatelier's principle in chemistry according to which " if a system in equilibrium is subjected to any change the system reacts in such a manner as to annul the effect of the change ". In simple language this means that if a system in chemical equilibrium is disturbed in any way it reacts in such a manner as to undo the effect of the disturbance. In the field of biology the development of immunity may be cited as an expression of this law.

So we see that there can exist simultaneously a state of perfect balance and dynamic change provided the change introduced is compensated by another change of an equivalent nature. But because there is generally a time lag and it is not possible to see all the resultant changes which have taken place in a complex system in equilibrium the law of compensation cannot be seen at work always.

It will be seen from what has been said above that when any kind of impulse is given to any part of the universe the whole of the universe reacts to it theoretically, though the reaction may be too feeble to be detected. The reaction is of such a nature that it tends to neutralize quantitatively the disturbance which has been created. This fact which is recognized by Science shows the underlying unity of the whole universe, the manifest and unmanifest, and its being alive or conscious at every point. It is the development of this reaction to every impulse of whatever nature which may be considered as the Law of Cause and Effect in its widest sense. The original action or impulse is the cause and the reaction is the effect.

The Law of Karma is nothing but the Law of Cause and Effect operating in the realm of human life and bringing about adjustments between an individual and other individuals whom he has affected by his thoughts, emotions and actions. The adjustments which restore the equilibrium in Nature are of two kinds. They are either immediate or delayed or follow a period of accumulation. Natural reactions in the realm of insentient matter are generally immediate while those in the case of human beings who are conscious are more or less delayed. It is these accumulated reactions involving a large number of souls which pile up in the invisible realms and produce cataclysmic results like wars, pestilences and revolutions. It is this keeping in abeyance of destructive reactions which is symbolized by the drinking of poison by Śiva during the churning of the ocean in the well-known Purāṇic story. ' Poison ' of undesirable reactions once generated cannot be destroyed but it can be held back and released in such a regulated manner and at such an appropriate time that it does the least harm and does not paralyse or unduly hamper the evolution of individuals or humanity.

Most thoughtful people are vaguely aware that there is a law of compensation underlying the phenomena of life.

But very few people realize that this law of compensation is not a law which governs only limited spheres of life or natural phenomena but is universal in its application. And it is universal and inviolable because it is the expression of the fact that a perfectly balanced Ultimate Reality which we refer to as the Absolute lies at the core of manifestation. It is because the universe is rooted in the Absolute and is an expression of the Absolute that compensation rules every sphere of life and Nature. Like a gyroscope which has been tilted to one side it immediately tends to come back to the position of equilibrium automatically. In fact the whole phenomenon of manifestation is the result of this tendency to regain equilibrium. The clock of the universe is wound up to a higher potential of existence by the Divine Will and then the machinery of the manifested universe begins to run in order to regain the perfect harmony and equilibrium of the Absolute which has been disturbed by this manifestation.

CHAPTER II

THE CONCEPT OF THE ABSOLUTE—II

Cosmic Rhythm

In dealing with the concept of the Absolute it was pointed out that such an Ultimate Principle must be a perfectly harmonious synthesis of all possible opposites and must contain in an integrated form all principles, qualities, etc. which find expression in and are the basis of a manifested universe. Let us examine more fully these two ideas, namely the perfect neutralization of opposites and harmonious integration of principles and states. We shall take a few more important cases of the neutralization of opposites which produces a neutral state devoid of positive and negative characters and consider some inferences of fundamental importance which may be drawn from the conception of such a neutral state.

One such inference is that there must exist eternally an ideal Point in the unmanifest state of Reality from which all kinds of manifestation start. The presence of such an eternal ideal point follows from several considerations. The primary differentiation of the One Reality into a dual and polar *Śiva-Śakti Tattva* assumes the existence of another subtler *tattva* functioning through a point or centre just as the existence of an ellipsoid assumes the existence of a sphere from the centre of which the two focii of the ellipsoid separate when the sphere degenerates into an ellipsoid as shown below:

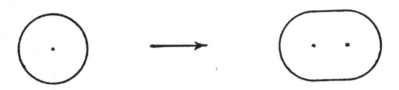

The same assumption becomes necessary from the consideration of the mathematical series of natural numbers given below:

0, 1, 2, 3, 4, 5, 6, 7, 8, 9, 10 ....

These numbers, as has been shown in another chapter, are the mathematical representatives of the fundamental realities in existence and each of them corresponds to a particular level of reality which is related to both, the one above and the other below it. In this series of numbers 0 obviously represents the perfectly undifferentiated Absolute and 2 the *Śiva-Śakti Tattva*. There is 1 between 0 and 2 and this must represent some aspect of Reality coming between the two aspects mentioned above. The undifferentiated Ultimate Reality or the Absolute which is a Void and is called *Nirviśeṣa* cannot have any centre or particular point in It as this will mean distortion and lack of uniformity. Yet without such an eternal centre there can be no manifestation as has been shown in another chapter. If such a centre exists it can exist only if it is balanced by its exact opposite. Now, what is the exact opposite of a point which can neutralize or perfectly balance the Point and thus serve to maintain the perfectly undifferentiated state of the Ultimate Reality? Obviously, boundless, infinite, empty Space. So the Space to which reference is made in *The Secret Doctrine* is that aspect of Reality which balances the Point and thus maintains the perfectly undifferentiated condition required in that highest state. Both eternal Ultimate Space and eternal Ultimate

Point are recognized in Occultism and Hinduism. The eternal Ultimate Space which is referred to as the 'container' or 'vesture' of the Ultimate Reality is called *Mahākāśa* in Hindu philosophy to distinguish it from *Cidākāśa* or mental space which comes into existence on manifestation and serves as the medium of Divine Ideation. The eternal Point which serves as a centre round which manifestation takes place is called a *Mahābindu*. It is this Point which by its primary differentiation into polar opposites produces the focii of the dual *Śiva-Śakti Tattva* and contains within its unfathomable depths the mental centres of all Solar Logoi and Monads.

If we analyze the conceptions of mathematical point and mathematical space we shall find that they are two opposite and limiting aspects of the same reality which underlies the idea of magnitude and which may be referred to as 'extension'. If we begin to contract a sphere of any size it must ultimately be reduced to a point, which is a dimensionless ideal mathematical entity without magnitude—no length, breadth or thickness. Similarly, if we go to the other extreme and begin to progressively enlarge the sphere *ad infinitum* it must ultimately assume the form or formlessness which we generally associate with boundless, infinite space, i.e. space extending in all directions without any limiting boundary and so attenuated that it is a perfect void.

We have to assume that boundless infinite space must be the ultimate form of an *expanding sphere* because it is only a sphere which on contraction to the utmost limit will give a point. Any other figure like a cube or a tetrahedron of any size on contraction to the utmost limit will not give a point as can be seen quite easily without any proof. The corners of such a figure will prevent it from contracting perfectly into a point. So the ideal point and ideal space are the two ideal limits of our conception of 'extension', the point being the limit in the direction of the infinitesimally small and space being the limit in the direction of infinitely large.

This idea is of the utmost importance in our concept of the Absolute because it shows that the Ultimate Point and the Ultimate Space must be the two opposite eternal forms or vestures of the Ultimate Reality. That is to say, on the one hand the Absolute must have the form of space and on the other that of point both being opposite to each other and therefore perfectly balancing or neutralizing each other and maintaining the voidness of that Ultimate State. It is not a question of the Absolute resting in space in its unmanifest state and appearing through a point in its manifest state but existing through both simultaneously. This means that the unmanifest and manifest states of the Absolute related to this Space and Point are not two alternative but co-existing states which exist simultaneously and eternally. They may be considered as polar states indissolubly bound together. In the Absolute, the eternal Point or the *laya* Centre round which the manifested universe crystallizes on the lower planes, as it were, is eternally there. It is not that the ideal Point *appears* when manifestation is to take place. It exists eternally and simultaneously with the Ultimate Space and is the vehicle of the Nirguna-brahman, the Reality which comes between the Absolute and the *Śiva-Śakti Tattva* and which corresponds to number 1 in the series of numbers referred to above.

The conception of the Absolute as a super-integrated state in which all principles, etc. are present in a perfectly harmonized condition is a necessary part of the philosophical concept of the Ultimate Reality. But on deeper thought it will be seen to be only one aspect of that transcendental state. For such a state must be purely static in nature a state of frozen immobility and it is difficult to imagine how this dynamic universe with movement everywhere and all the time could have its source in such a static Reality. In order to clear up this doubt we have therefore to turn to the other side of the coin and dwell for a while on the dynamic aspect of this Reality which is the exact opposite of the static aspect and must necessarily exist as a complement of that aspect. This can best be referred to as Cosmic Rhythm and we shall now consider this matter briefly.

We find generally that a natural phenomenon of whatever nature, after it has started, goes on gaining momentum but a time comes when it reaches its zenith and the reverse process of decay or decline begins to set in. This also gains momentum until the movement dies and either disappears from the realm of manifestation or reappears with a fresh impulse. This phenomenon takes place at all levels, from the level of the atoms which vibrate in simple harmonic motion to the level of the manifested systems which are born, grow, reach their zenith, decline and then disappear when *Pralaya* takes place.

The action of this almost universal law in the phenomena of Nature taking place in the manifest points to the presence of a periodic movement or rhythm in the Unmanifest which is like harmonic motion, i.e. going in opposite directions about a neutral point. Taking the phenomenon of manifestation itself at the highest level we find that there is alternate movement towards manifestation and dissolution in the eternal succession of *Śṛṣṭi* and *Pralaya*. This should correspond in the realm of the Unmanifest to an outward and inward movement about a neutral or *laya* centre. By outward and inward movement is meant a movement in which there is alternate expansion and contraction about a central point, corresponding to centrifugal and centripetal movements in mechanics.

We have to remember that in these cosmic phenomena there is not only a recurrent periodical movement from *Śṛṣṭi* to *Pralaya* but also a movement from *Pralaya* to *Śṛṣṭi*, or in other words, a manifested system not only passes into the state of *Pralaya* after a period of active functioning but it also emerges from the state of *Pralaya* after a certain period and enters the phase of active functioning which is called

Sṛṣṭi. Now, since *Pralaya* is a state of quiescence corresponding to the zero level there must be not only a force which pulls back the manifested system into the state of *Pralaya* but also a corresponding opposite force which comes from the other side of the zero level and after passing the zero level pushes the system, as it were, into manifestation. The manifested system continues to develop and grow until the outward wave is exhausted, the reverse process of decay and decline sets in, the system is pulled back below the zero level into the state of *Pralaya* and the whole cycle is repeated over and over again.

The zero potential of the *laya* centre cannot by itself produce a positive thrust outward towards manifestation just as an organism which is dead cannot by itself revive and become alive again. A battery which is discharged cannot become charged by itself. A sun which has cooled off or is dead cannot become active again unless an external agency acts upon it, puts energy into it and sets it going again.

Since the Ultimate Reality is by Its very nature an independent, self-sufficient (*nirālamba*) Reality and there can be no other Reality above It or outside It to produce such changes, it follows logically that we must look for such forces and the changes which they bring about within the Ultimate Reality Itself. In other words, there must be an eternal periodic movement in the Ultimate Reality Itself which accounts for and *automatically* brings about these periodic changes of *Sṛṣṭi* and *Pralaya* and all other periodic changes in the realm of manifestation.

If the above view is correct then the period of *Pralaya* for any system is not a period of sleep, a state of inactivity almost amounting to a moribund condition which it appears to the illusion-bound intellect. It is a period in which the whole gamut of changes or rather movements hinted at above takes place behind the screen which separates the Manifest

from the Unmanifest. We can ' see ' intellectually only
what happens when the wave of manifestation emerges from
behind the screen. This is the birth of the universe (or a
smaller system), its growth, zenith, decline and disappearance
into the state of *Pralaya*. What next? What happens when
the reverse wave recedes into the darkness of *Pralaya*? Does
the whole thing become dead, frozen into immobility until
the time of *Sṛṣṭi* or creation comes again and a manifested
system starts functioning? This cannot be, as life cannot come
from death, energy from inertia. What happens behind the
screen in the darkness of *Pralaya*—it is darkness only to us
who are on this side of the screen—is the completion of the
rhythmic movement of which only one half is intellectually
visible on this side. This movement may be represented
diagrammatically as shown below:

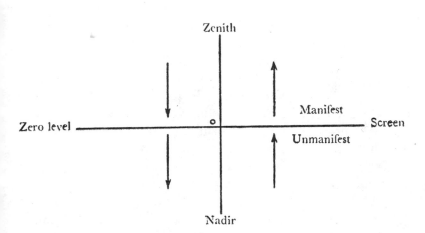

The receding wave at the time of *Pralaya* descends into
the Unmanifest, reaches the nadir and then again returns to
the zero level with a certain momentum which accounts
for the new urge for *Sṛṣṭi* after a period of *Pralaya*. The

movement will be seen to be analogous to the movement
of a pendulum in a clock as shown below:

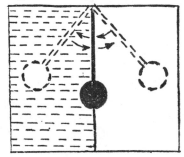

FIG. 2.   Oscillation of a pendulum

If we cover half the lower
portion of the clock we
shall see only half the total
movement of the pendulum.
The movement behind the
covered portion on the left
will remain invisible to us.
The phenomenon of mani-
festation is analogous to the
visible movement of the
pendulum on the right side.   One interesting point to be
noted in the movement of such a pendulum is that it can
continue to oscillate indefinitely by itself in a non-resistant
medium like a vacuum if the resistance at the point from
which it hangs can somehow be eliminated.

It will be seen from what has been said above that we
can replace the ordinary conception regarding *Sṛṣṭi* and
Pralaya by another conception which is breath-taking in its
beauty, harmony and philosophical grandeur. We replace
the partial and unsatisfactory picture of the cosmic process
in which a universe appears out of nowhere and disappears
into nowhere, without any cause, with another picture in
which we get a glimpse of the whole process which is simple,
harmonious, self-contained, eternal and in harmony with the
scientific laws with which we are familiar.

The student should note that this kind of eternal rhythm
in the Unmanifest can account very satisfactorily for a number
of universal phenomena in the realm of the manifest such as
the following:

(1) Periodicity which seems to pervade the phenomena of
     Nature.   The whole universe appears like a gigantic
     clock in which wheels of all kinds and sizes are

revolving continuously and steadily in spite of the fact that energy is being spent and the machinery will ultimately stop.

(2) Phases, which are accompanied by waxing and waning, ebb and flow, in different spheres in the universe.

(3) Raising and lowering of energy level in manifested systems and smaller organisms.

These phenomena are symbolized by the crescent moon and *Damru* in the symbology of Maheśa.

As the idea of an eternal rhythm pervading the cosmos is extremely interesting both from the philosophical and scientific points of view and serves to throw light on many doctrines of Occultism and natural phenomena we shall go into it a little more in detail. Let us first see what it means and whether we can visualize it to some extent with the help of mathematical symbols and scientific analogies.

The visualization of the Ultimate Reality as existing only in unlimited, unbounded Space or *Mahākāśa* or alternatively in a Point called *Mahābindu* is philosophically unsatisfactory. If it exists solely in unlimited, unbounded Space how are we to account for Its manifestation through a Point, for, the Point seems to be the very basis of all phenomena of manifestation from the lowest to the highest planes. If, on the other hand, that Reality is to be conceived as existing in a Point how can we account for its existence in *Mahākāśa*. These two mathematical conceptions, the dimensionless Point and the unbounded Sphere of infinite diameter are, as shown above, two ultimate opposite conceptions in which this Reality can be conceived to exist but actually it can exist neither in one nor the other exclusively. This is really a trick of the intellect which conceives every reality or idea as a pair of opposites or *dvandva*. Both these are really static and materialistic conceptions while Reality by its very nature must be of the nature of consciousness and dynamic. The simple idea of

Cosmic Rhythm reconciles and fuses together conceptions of the dimensionless Point and unbounded Space into an intelligible concept which is in accord with modern scientific ideas. In this the Ultimate Reality is conceived as an oscillation of consciousness in which it alternately expands to an unbounded sphere of infinite radius and then contracts to an ideal point, thus sweeping through all the intermediate stages represented by concentric spheres of different radii as shown below:

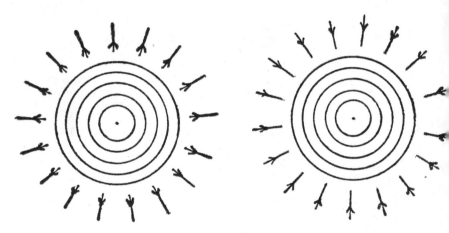

Fig. 3.   Alternate expansion and contraction

This alternate contraction to a point and expansion to infinity brings out on the one hand the dynamic nature of Reality and on the other shows how the ideal Point and unbounded infinite Space both serve alternately as vestures of that Reality.   Those who are familiar with modern scientific ideas will see in this alternate assumption of two extreme and opposite states an analogy with the state of resonance which is assumed in a natural phenomenon when it shows the characteristics of two opposite states simultaneously.   The thing showing such opposite characteristics is considered to assume the two extreme states corresponding to these characteristics alternately and with extreme rapidity.   Under these circumstances the thing is neither one nor the other but a dynamic equilibrium between the two.

It should also be noted that this oscillation between the two ultimate limits means that all the intermediate states between the two extreme states are also passed through with inconceivable rapidity and are therefore contained in the over-all state. So all possible states of existence are fused together, as it were, in one State. This concept, therefore, affords us a new glimpse into the nature of Reality and brings out the dynamic nature of the superintegrated state.

The idea given above gives us a satisfying picture of the cosmic process but it does not give a complete picture, for it deals only with the contraction and expansion in the positive realm of manifestation corresponding to the process above the zero level in the figure given above. Without the corresponding contraction and expansion in the negative realm below the zero level there can be no balance and automatic movement and it is difficult to account for the reversal of the impulse which results in bringing a universe into manifestation after a period of *Pralaya*. A pendulum, if it is to swing continuously must swing on both sides of the mean position. We cannot imagine it swinging only on one side of the mean position.

What makes the manifested universe to start contracting after the impulse to expansion has exhausted itself? What makes it come out into manifestation after a period of *Pralaya*? The clue to all these questions lies in combining the idea of expansion and contraction in the positive realm above the zero level with the idea of expansion and contraction in the negative realm below the zero level, thus making the whole cycle of the cosmic process complete, automatic and analogous to similar cycles in the field of natural phenomena.

It is observed in the case of physical phenomena that a moving body continues to move unless stopped by the application of a force in the form of resistance of some kind. A pendulum must continue to oscillate indefinitely unless it is stopped by some kind of resistance however small this might be. This is due to *tamas* or inertia. This tendency which is inherent in Nature has been formulated in the form of a definite law of dynamics and is at the basis of all natural movements which continue indefinitely like the movements of electrons in atoms or movements of planets in a solar system. It is really the expression of one of the three fundamental *guṇas* which in their harmonized condition are referred to as *Prakṛti* in Sāṃkhyan philosophy.

Let us look at the whole cosmic process a little more closely to understand the significance of the completed cycle. When the wave of contraction reaches the limit of the ideal Point it does not reverse its direction and start expanding again. It goes through the Point and emerges on the negative side as a wave of expansion. In thus going through the Point it not only changes its direction and from a contracting wave is transformed into an expanding wave but it also goes through a change in its nature which may be likened to that of turning a glove inside out. Let us follow the movements of the wave front by means of a diagram. The contraction and expansion at the point where this repeated reversal in direction takes place may be represented diagrammatically as shown in Figure 4.

We see in the figure how the wave changes its direction at the point 0, an expanding wave becoming a contracting wave or vice versa. In the illustration the reversal at the point 0 has been shown within the limited range of a sector but the student by using his imagination can easily visualize the whole process in terms of a contracting and expanding sphere centred in the point 0.

We can visualize in this illustration the reversal of the movement at the point 0 but not its reversal in the realm of infinity when after expanding to infinity the wave front starts to contract again both in the realm of the Manifest

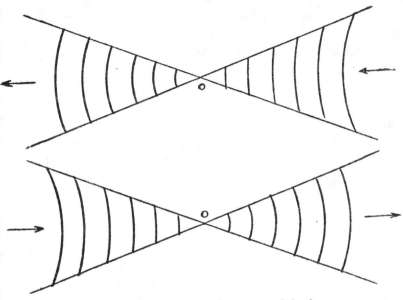

FIG. 4. Reversal of wave-front at the Point 0

and Unmanifest. But that such reversal does take place will be obvious if Cosmic Rhythm is a fact and the cosmic process with its periodical alternation of *Ṣṛṣṭi* and *Pralaya* is an automatic and eternal activity in the Absolute requiring no initiatory impulse for creation or dissolution either from within or without.

We cannot hope to understand or visualize these ultimate mysteries of existence except in a very vague and fragmentary manner but we can sense intuitively their tremendous nature and awful grandeur. Mathematics can sometimes help us in these things by enabling us to symbolize these transcendental realities through mathematical diagrams. But these diagrams are mere symbols and cannot give us any comprehension of the *modus operandi* of the processes except in a very vague and general manner. In the present case, for instance, according to mathematics, if a wave starting from a centre begins to expand outwards it must again after expanding to infinity ultimately appear at the same centre *from within.* This means that in the realm of infinity existing within the Unmanifest it has somehow been reversed in direction, though how, we cannot visualize or conceive in any manner.

If Cosmic Rhythm as envisaged above lies at the basis of all periodic movements and changes in the cosmos, then the whole of the manifested state in the positive sense as we know it must have its negative counterpart and we should have a negative manifested state which balances the positive manifested state and thus maintains the void state of the Absolute. Corresponding to the basic realities which we find in the positive manifested universe there should be their counterparts in this negative world. There should be negative time, negative space, negative matter, etc. though it is difficult to conceive what these constituents of the negative world mean. Scientists have already begun to talk of antimatter and those who travel in fast jet planes have some kind of idea of what negative time—time running backward —may mean. So the idea of there being negative time, space, matter, etc. though it sounds fantastic, is not as absurd as it may appear on the surface. Veiled references to these negative worlds, negative time, space, etc. are found in occult literature but for some reason the truth about this negative state of manifestation which exists behind the screen, as it were, has been withheld from the general public for the present. Let us, therefore, not try to peer into these things for the time being.

That the concept of Cosmic Rhythm is not a product of pure fancy and is within the realm of possibility even according to modern scientific knowledge will be clear from the following simple diagram which illustrates the repeated reflection of light waves coming out of a point light situated at the centre of a glass sphere. The outer surface of the sphere is silvered and so the inner surface serves as a spherical mirror and reflects the light waves which strike it along the radii of the sphere. The light rays advance along the radii of the sphere and each ray when it strikes the surface of the sphere is reflected back along the same radius. All reflected rays pass through the centre and the contracting wave front is thus converted into an expanding wave front again. The whole process, as has been pointed out in another context, is repeated *ad infinitum* with the speed of light if the sphere is perfect in shape and the silvering is also perfect, or in other words, under ideal conditions:

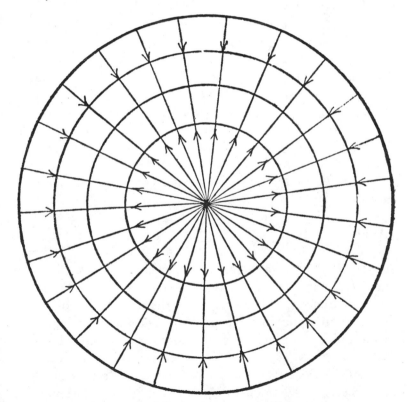

FIG. 5. Repeated reflection of light within a spherical mirror

It will be seen that in this simple scientific experiment we have almost a perfect illustration of the idea of Cosmic

Rhythm which we are considering. The wave-front emerges again and again from the centre, after being reflected back from the sphere wall and disappearing into the centre, these two processes corresponding to *Śṛṣṭi* and *Pralaya* or creation and dissolution. The only difference is that in this case the reversal, other than the one at the centre, takes place at the inner surface of the sphere and can be seen while in the case of Cosmic Rhythm the reversal takes place in the dark realm of the Unmanifest and cannot be seen or comprehended.

It should, however, be remembered that it is only the Ultimate Space or *Mahākāśa*, the vehicle of the Ultimate Reality which is not only infinite but also boundless. A manifested universe according to the Occult doctrine is a relatively limited phenomenon although it appears stupendous and infinite to us. It is called *Brahmāṇḍa* or ' the Egg of the Creator ' and it is probable that the impulses of Cosmic Rhythm are reflected from the inner surface of this *Brahmāṇḍa* in a manner analogous to the reflection of light from the inner surface of a sphere as illustrated above. On account of the very close relation of light and consciousness it may be that the analogous physical phenomenon is merely a case of a reflection of a reality according to the occult maxim ' As above, so below '.

The conception of Cosmic Rhythm in the Ultimate Reality or what may be called an eternal alternate expansion and contraction of consciousness between the Point and Ultimate Space is in harmony with the phenomena of Nature in the visible and invisible realms. The rhythms observed in the universe in larger and smaller cycles, the contractions and expansions which alternate in different spheres and at different levels, the inflow and outflow of energy, the advances and recessions, all point to the existence of a mysterious all-embracing Cosmic Rhythm at the very heart of the manifested universe, and as the manifested universe is derived from and based upon the Unmanifest, they point to the source of these movements ·or alternation of states in the Ultimate Reality itself.

To sum up what we have been discussing in the previous pages we may say that the concept of the Absolute as an Ultimate Reality which is perfectly neutral, balanced, perfect, whole, outside which nothing can exist requires that this Reality in its totality must be self-adjusting, requiring no external agency or cause to start any process like that of creation or dissolution. Being eternal it should have no beginning or end and all movements in it should be like movements in a circle. The ideas and illustrations given above will perhaps serve to throw some light on how such a State, such a self-contained and self-adjusting Reality, including both the Manifest and the Unmanifest, can exist and function, dispensing with the necessity of supposing that the Absolute has to initiate certain movements or changes periodically, an idea which is philosophically untenable.

It is this dynamic aspect of the Ultimate Reality or Cosmic Rhythm which is referred to as the dance of Śiva and is represented symbolically in the well-known form of Natarāja. It lies at the basis of all rhythmic, harmonious movements which we find everywhere in Nature. The rhythmic movements in the infinitesimal atom as well as the expansions and contractions of the universe are merely its reflections and expressions at the lowest level. The art of dancing is a futile effort to express the mystery of Cosmic Rhythm in the movements of the physical body. Still, dancing at its highest, when it is truly creative and takes the dancer and those who witness it out of themselves in an ecstasy, is in some mysterious manner a reflection and faint expression of that rhythm which underlies the universe. Such a dancing by its very nature cannot be repetitive based only upon technique and memory, but must depend upon a temporary and partial rapport of the dancer with the rhythmic movements which are taking place eternally within the heart of the universe and therefore within the heart of every human being. So it cannot be the product of mere technique or even ordinary creativeness, though these are necessary. An inner attunement of the lower with the higher, in whatever manner this is attained, is a necessary condition.

It may also be pointed out that this Cosmic Rhythm has been expressed as an alternate inward and outward movement of consciousness from the great Centre embracing in its vast sweep the whose cosmos. But this is so because we cannot conceive any movement in more than three dimensions as long as our consciousness is confined to this physical world of three dimensions. As a matter of fact, Cosmic Rhythm by its very nature must be a movement above the dimensions of space but having the potentiality of producing any kind of rhythmic movement in the worlds of any number of dimensions. It is thus that fundamental integrated form of rhythmic movement which can serve as an inexhaustible source of an infinite variety of such movements.

CHAPTER III

COSMIC CONSCIOUSNESS AND POWER

(The Śiva-Śakti Tattva)

THE Unmanifest is the core of the Manifest, as it were, and the Absolute is the core of the Unmanifest. We have already considered this Ultimate Reality in the previous two chapters and tried to deal with a few ideas which might enable us to have some slight comprehension of this incomprehensible Principle which is hidden within the universe and also within each individual Monad. We shall now proceed to deal with the next lower Principle, namely the dual Principle which is known in Hindu philosophy as the *Śiva-Śakti Tattva*. I may repeat what I have already pointed out in the first chapter that the three Principles in the Unmanifest really constitute one indivisible Reality and to separate them in this manner for convenience in dealing with the subject makes it necessary to refer to them back and forth and makes inevitable a certain amount of overlapping of our ideas. But we shall try to avoid this as far as possible and also the metaphysical jargon in which these transcendental truths are generally enwrapped by academic philosophers.

It follows logically that if the Ultimate Reality which we denote by the word 'Absolute' is to differentiate, this primary differentiation must be into two, and not only into two, but into two polar opposites, for the differentiation of the One Reality which is neutral, void and a balanced whole cannot be in any form except that of two polar opposites. We have numerous instances of this kind in the field of Science. Take, for instance, an electrolyte like sodium chloride or ordinary table salt whose molecules are neutral as a whole in the solid form but dissociate into positively charged sodium ions and negatively charged chloride ions when dissolved in water; or frictional electricity, which is always produced in equal amounts of opposite charge on rubbing non-conductors of electricity.

The relation between the two components of this primary duality which we are now dealing with is one of the most interesting questions of philosophy and its extraordinary nature follows from the polarity which characterizes it. Before proceeding further I would like to point out a few general characteristics of a polar relationship for the sake of those who do not possess the necessary knowledge of Science. A polar relationship is characterized by the following facts:

1. The two components are derived from a unity and given favourable conditions can again disappear into that unity.

2. The two poles are in a way attached to each other and are interdependent.

3. They are related to each other as equal and opposite.

4. They can draw together more and more and can also draw apart more and more with the alteration of tensions between them. These tensions can have the elements of both attraction and repulsion.

5. The two poles appear and disappear together and we cannot have one without the other.

With such an elementary knowledge regarding a polar relationship we can attempt to understand this primary polarity which underlies the universe and which in a manner divides both the Manifest and the Unmanifest into two equal and opposite counterparts facing each other, repelling each other and also attracting each other. For, all reactions between all kinds of polar opposites in the manifested universe are rooted in the two poles of the primary differentiation. If these were to fuse together, nothing would be left but the Absolute, for every element on one side is matched and balanced by its counterpart on the other side, although we may not be able to trace the counterparts in every case.

After these preliminary considerations let us now come to the essential nature of the two elements of this polarity which are called Śiva and Śakti or the Father and Mother Principles. Broadly, these two elements may be referred to as Consciousness and Power although we should carefully understand what these terms mean in their transcendent state and not confuse them with the usual meanings and connotations associated with them. Considering the transcendent nature of these two Principles, the phrases ' Root of Consciousness ' and ' Root of Power ' will be more appropriate but provided we keep the above important fact in view we may continue to use the simpler names in the treatment of the subject.

Before we deal separately and in detail with the nature of the two elements of the *Śiva-Śakti Tattva* or the Positive-Negative Principle and their mutual relationship let us dwell for a while on the relation of will and power which play a very important part in our life and with the expression of which most people are familiar. Will and power are very closely related to Śiva and Śakti respectively, are in fact faint reflections or degraded expressions of these two polar Principles, and by studying and properly understanding the lower reflections or expressions we may be able to gain a glimpse into the nature of the realities which they imperfectly reflect and partially express.

What do these two words denote in psychology? How are they related. The first thing we have to note is that will and power are two aspects of the same principle and the difference between these aspects is very subtle and rather difficult to grasp. What is the essential characteristic of will? We may say in a general way that it is that faculty or quality of human nature which enables an individual to decide on a course of action to gain a definite end and to pursue that course until the end is achieved. The will merely fixes its aim and adopts that attitude of *saṃkalpa* or fixed determination which makes the accomplishment of that aim almost a certainty. When a person of really strong will decides to do something you know that the thing will be done while this certainty is absent in the case of a weak-willed person. Where lies the difference between the intentions and accomplishments of the two persons? In the unalterable nature of the determination and the relentless pursuit of the aim until it is accomplished. It is a quality which is very difficult to define or understand and you can merely get glimpses of it in the life of men who have brought about great revolutions or changes in the face of tremendous odds either in the outside world or within themselves. One can almost see in their life the working of a mysterious force which is able to break down all resistance, overcome all difficulties and ultimately accomplish the desired aim.

It is a very peculiar fact that in the will itself there is no indication or presence of an idea of *how* the thing will be accomplished or achieved. It is a pure determination or purpose without any reference to ways and means and can exist in the absence of any predetermined means of achieving the determined aim. This peculiar characteristic of pure will, i.e. the absence of any predetermined and fixed method of achieving the objective, should be kept in mind, for it is this flexibility upon which depends its efficacy and the certainty of finally gaining the end. It is this freedom to adopt one means or another or adjusting means to ends, giving up a particular course of action when necessary so that the accomplishment of the end is ensured, it is this relentless flexibility which ensures that the end will be accomplished sooner or later, by one means or another. The will concentrates its effort and attention on the *end* and leaves the question of *means* open. It is thus merely a state of consciousness capable of bringing to bear a tremendous concentration of purpose on any aim which has been deliberately chosen and pursuing that aim until it is accomplished.

Now, this kind of expression on the lower planes which we refer to as will is a very weak reflection of that aspect of Divine Consciousness which we refer to as *Sat* and it has its source in the Unmanifest, in the Principle which we refer to as *Śiva Tattva*. It is His Will which in its repeated reflections produces the extraordinary and sometimes awe-inspiring expressions of human will that are capable of bringing about vast changes in the world against tremendous odds. And it is His Will which is at the back of the Divine Plan for every manifested system and brings it to its appointed, destined end without any chance of failure.

In the case of aims pursued by human beings there can be failure because the will may not be sufficiently strong, or where the will is adequately strong the aim may be against the Divine Will. But Śiva represents and is the embodiment of that infinite Cosmic Will which is at the back of manifestation and which pushes it irresistably and yet wisely towards its appointed end. Because it is infinite it is equal to any finite end. Because its potential is unlimited it can break down ultimately any resistance or hindrance which develops during the course of evolution. For, such resistances and hindrances are bound to develop in a system which is governed by law and which has to provide for the unfoldment of innumerable unevolved Monads. These Monads are fragments of the Divine Life, children of the Most High, and have to develop in freedom so that they learn to cooperate with the Divine Will not from outer compulsion but inner choice, born of experience and enlightenment.

The Divine Plan according to the Occult Doctrine is
not implemented in a mechanical way and an inexorable
destiny does not rule our life. There is plenty of room for
us to blunder and go along wrong paths and learn our lessons
through suffering. The Divine Plan is sufficiently flexible
and alternative paths will be taken by powers that direct
evolution to meet any deficiencies or derelictions on our part,
but the appointed end shall be reached as hinted at in the
Yoga-sūtras of Patañjali (IV-12). The Divine Will and the
Divine Wisdom are equal to any situation which may develop
during the course of evolution. It is this knowledge, direct
or intuitional, which enables people who are in touch with
the realities of the inner life to remain calm in the face of the
gravest dangers and the most undesirable developments which
sometimes take place in the world.

Having considered Śiva in His aspect of Cosmic Will let
us now turn for a while to its correlate, Cosmic Power,
represented by Śakti. Here again, it will help us to understand the Divine Principle if we first examine the nature of
its reflection in human life.

We have seen that in our life will merely determines
and concentrates on the attainment of the end. It is power
which provides the necessary means for the attainment of
the end. As will is concerned with the end so power is
concerned with the means for attaining that end. In this
fact will be seen the inevitable and intimate relation of
will and power. Will, without power which provides the
means, is helpless. Power, without will which provides the
end and continued concentration on that end, is purposeless. If you have an object in view and also will to
achieve it but with no power or means to achieve it you are
helpless. On the other hand, if you have all kinds of
means available but no object or purpose in view, all those
means mean nothing and remain unutilized. This fact
concerning the relation of will and power is not generally

realized but if we think deeply over it we shall find that it is essentially true.

The role of will and power in our life pointed out above shows not only the intimate relation between the two but also gives us another glimpse into the nature of the *Śiva-Śakti Tattva* as well as the concept of Cosmic Will and Cosmic Power which they represent. At the level of the *Śiva-Śakti Tattva* in the Unmanifest, although both Principles are infinite they must be potential because there is at that level no manifested system in existence for the exertion of the Cosmic Will and for providing an infinite variety of energies in various forms for working a Divine Plan. It is only when Mind comes into existence and a manifested system is created (universe, galaxy or solar system) that conditions are produced for the exertion of the Divine Will of Śiva and the application of the Divine Power of Śakti. Then only can there be a definite end represented by a Divine Plan behind which the Divine Will can exercise a constant pressure. Then only can there be all kinds of means available owing to the emergence of *Prakṛti* from its *sāmyāvasthā* or harmonized condition. So, although the *Śiva-Śakti Tattva* is eternal and in its highest form an aspect of the Ever-Unmanifest, it comes into play only on the appearance of a manifested system created by a Logos. Otherwise, it remains potential in the darkness of the Ever-Unmanifest as the intellect sees it. What is present in that supreme Consciousness which is eternal and ever remains the same, whether the shadow of a manifested system is or is not present, who can tell?

It will also be seen that the polarity and mutual dependence of the ultimate Positive and Negative Principles is also reflected in its lower expressions in the form of will and power. As we have seen above, will without power is helpless and power without will is purposeless. This mutual relationship of the two is unconsciously recognized and indicated by using the compound word 'will-power' foɪ the essentially dual principle.

Having dealt with the general nature of the ultimate Positive and Negative Principles let us now consider a few other aspects of these two components, the Positive Principle of Consciousness referred to as Śiva and the Negative Principle of Power referred to as Śakti. Considering the transcendental nature of these Principles and the fact that they lie at the very basis of the Manifest and the Unmanifest, we should regard our efforts to understand them in the proper perspective and approach the problem with the necessary humility born of a sense of our tremendous limitations.

Since the word 'power' conveys the idea of a non-sentient Principle the first question we have to ask and answer is: What is the nature of this Power? There is a great deal of confusion in Hindu philosophical thought about the nature of this Power. Some writers confuse it with *Prakṛti*, others raise it to the status of the Ultimate Reality, depending on the school of thought to which they belong. At the level of the primary differentiation of the One Reality which is above the realm of manifestation it is obvious that Śakti or Power cannot be joined with a mechanism of any kind and cannot therefore be associated with any kind of activity even of a mental and spiritual nature. It must be potential and must have the potentiality of initiating any kind of activity needed in the manifestation of the lower worlds which are mental or in the Divine worlds on which the Logoi with their triple aspects function. For the appearance of a Logos from the latent Consciousness of the Cosmic Logos or Maheśvara also requires the exercise of Power and so this Power must be above the realm of the innumerable Logoi in the cosmos. It is in this potential state, above the realms in which Brahmā, Viṣṇu and Maheśa function that it is really called Ādi-Śakti, the consort of Ādi-Śiva.

If Śakti is not associated with any mechanism even of a spiritual nature and is inactive or potential at this level the question arises whether it is conscious or not. The answer to this question is found in the very nature of the polar relationship which exists between Śiva and Śakti and their mutual dependence and inseparability. There can be no power without consciousness and no consciousness without power in that duality which we are considering. Or, we may say that it is potential Power associated with integrated Consciousness. If you look at the head of a coin you know that the tail is at the back and vice versa. We really need a specific word for this polar combination of consciousness and power corresponding to the Sanskrit word *Śiva-Śakti Tattva* to denote the simultaneous presence of both aspects in the One Reality which they really are.

We now come to the question why Śakti is called the Root of Power. Science tells us that the whole universe with the smaller units of the solar systems is declining in the level of energy and when it reaches a dead level the universe will die out. It is like a clock which has been wound up and allowed to run. Slowly it uses up energy which has been put into it and when the energy is exhausted the clock of the universe or a solar system comes to a stop. Of course, this end is too far off to bother about, but that it is inevitable is the considered opinion of all orthodox physicists. But the question arises who put this energy into the universe or raised it to the needed energy level in the beginning from which it is steadily declining. Science has no answer to this question, though there are some less orthodox physicists who have now begun to talk of the possibility of there being a Creator or Architect who may have, in the act of creation, endowed the universe with the needed energy. This is regarded merely in the light of an interesting speculation. But the Occult Doctrine has a clear answer to this question. The energy required for running the machinery of the universe, visible and invisible, comes from the transcendent *Śiva-Śakti Tattva.* How?

The Ultimate Reality, as has been pointed out, is a state of perfect equilibrium and balance. We know that when we want to disturb such a state we have to use force and the more stable the equilibrium the greater the force required for the purpose. But once this state has been disturbed, energy becomes available for work in the scientific sense of the term until the equilibrium is restored. But in manifestation it requires an outside agent to disturb such an equilibrium and put in energy. Since the Unmanifest is a self-sufficient and self-directed Principle from which everything else comes, this disturbance must be self-created and the separation of the two foci from the one Centre must be a self-initiated act of the Divine Will. Only Consciousness can initiate such a move within itself and not anything which is insentient like *Prakṛti.* So we see that the power needed for the universe must come from a self-initiated action of Cosmic Consciousness which by drawing apart the two poles from the one static Centre by the force of Divine Will creates the unlimited amount of power needed for the purpose. The potential power thus available can then be transformed and stepped down to lower levels through different kinds of spiritual, mental and material mechanisms. Just as electrical energy generated at very high voltages in hydro-electric systems is transformed into currents of lower voltages by transformers for ordinary use, so the potential Power in the *Śiva-Śakti Tattva* which is universal, is transformed by the presiding Logos of a particular system for His work in that system. Every Īśvara or Logos in His negative aspect may therefore be considered as a sort of sub-station which steps down and makes available at a suitable voltage this universal and unlimited power for running His system. After the energy has been appropriated and specialized in this manner it runs off into different channels at different voltages doing different kinds of work in a network, as it were, and the powers which control and direct this energy into different channels are the *devis* or goddesses of Hinduism. It will be seen, therefore, why there should be a hierarchy of *devis* and why each *devī* should be wedded to her consort—a *devatā* who represents a particular Divine function in manifestation.

The fact that the *Śiva-Śakti Tattva* is an unlimited universal storehouse of power is not the only aspect which we have to consider in dealing with this Principle. There are others which are equally important and which throw a flood of light on many problems and phenomena of life. Before we take up some of these, let us recall a simple experiment which everybody has seen, namely the stretching of a piece of indiarubber by pulling apart its two extreme ends. This illustrates in a simple and easily understandable manner the drawing apart of the two foci from a single stable centre in the Ultimate Reality and enables us to have some idea of the types of forces which are developed in this manner and the phenomena which are associated with them.

One of these, namely the development of potential energy which can be made to do any kind of work we have already considered. Let us take a few other aspects of the simple experiment and see how they throw light on the nature of the *Śiva-Śakti Tattva*.

The first thing which will strike anybody is the tendency developed in the two sides to draw together again. It appears as if all the particles in the piece of indiarubber have developed a tendency to resume their original condition of equilibrium. In fact, this tendency is so strong that only a steady force applied to the two ends prevents them from flying to their original position. Not only this, but also one half of the particles on one side tend to move in one direction and the other half in the opposite direction. In other words a tremendous attraction between the particles develops and the attraction works through the agency of a polar relationship.

Now, let us see the significance of this phenomenon in relation to the fragments of Divine Life which have been scattered far and wide as a result of being thrown into the realm of manifestation. We see that all these fragments seem to be actuated consciously or unconsciously by an over-powering tendency to regain their lost state of oneness with that Whole from which they have been separated. We see also that the search throughout the period of their evolution is characterized by association of the fragments in pairs. The positively and negatively charged atoms tend to combine with each other and derive from the union a temporary though unconscious satisfaction. The animals and human beings pair off either as male and female, father and son, mother and daughter, or in any other of a number of relationships which always has a kind of polarity hidden behind it. For polarity is not confined to the male and female bodies only. The attitudes of the two components in any such pair are opposite to a great extent and therefore polar in nature. It seems, therefore, that all life has become polarized and is functioning through attractions and repulsions which characterize a polar relationship.

It is only when love has been sufficiently developed by means of these different kinds of temporary relationships between different fragments of the Divine Life that the love of a fragment for the Whole is born within it. Then, instead of seeking satisfaction of love in this piecemeal manner the fragment seeks it in the Whole, and through the Whole in the other fragments. It is in this way that the desire to become one with the Whole is developed and ultimately consummated.

Not only is there this universal all-pervading tendency for different fragments of Divine Life to come together but also the satisfaction of this tendency, in whatever measure it may be achieved, is the only source of happiness, bliss or *ānanda* there is in the world. In whatever little measure we succeed in any situation in life in satisfying this tendency to come together and become one in spirit, to that extent we feel happy and at peace. Because, if we are all one in essence, going towards that supreme source of bliss, and to become one again is our ultimate destiny it is inevitable that in every little effort in which we succeed in achieving this unity there must be present a quantum of a corresponding amount of happiness or bliss according to the level and degree to which this unity is attained. The awareness of our unity is the basis of love and the satisfaction of love is the basis of real happiness. Where the drawing together involves association of matter or mind owing to our identification with our body or mind we have simple pleasure or happiness based on possession, passion or sensation. Where, owing to non-association with mind and body there is pure awareness of unity without the complications which attend association with mind and matter we have real peace and *ānanda* of the spiritual and still higher planes. But we should not forget that the ultimate source of every kind of bliss from the lowest to the highest is that Reality whom we refer to as Śiva in His *Ānanda* aspect.

Then we come to another aspect of the *Śiva-Śakti Tattva* which is fundamentally different from the aspect we have been considering so far. In this primary differentiation so far considered we have the drawing apart of the one Centre into two poles, one positive, the other negative. The second kind of differentiation we shall now consider is the basis of manifestation. It may be considered as an outward thrust of Consciousness which in its *Cit* aspect projects a manifested system outside itself and establishes a relation of Self and Not-Self within the *Śiva-Śakti Tattva*. It is this thrust outside its fundamental innermost nature—*Sat*—and yet within the realm of Its own Consciousness, which is the basis of Cosmic Ideation and lays the spiritual foundation of the universes which come into existence one after another in the eternal

alternation of *Sṛṣṭi* and *Pralaya*.   This second kind of differentiation, also in the realm of the Unmanifest, will be seen to
be the basis of the subjective-objective relationship and the
root of the mind which functions through such a subjective-
objective relationship.   But we must remember that we are
still dealing with a change—if a change it may be called—
within the realm of the Unmanifest.   There is no mental
activity as yet, but this Cosmic Mind in the innermost realms
of Reality is the mysterious and ultimate foundation upon
which are erected edifices of the manifested universes in time
and space both on the spiritual and mental planes.   This
subtlest Cosmic Ideation is even subtler than the Divine
Ideation of the manifest Logoi who derive from this primary
source the material or plan for ideating their respective
worlds.   This primary subjective-objective relationship and
the Cosmic Ideation which is its product remains potential
like its counterpart, the Power which resides in the *Siva-Sakti
Tattva*.   It becomes active only when a Triple Logos comes
into being and utilizes it for His work in a manifested
system.   But as this subtlest kind of Ideation belongs to the
function of the Unmanifest Cosmic Logos, we need not go
into this question here.   We shall consider it in the next
chapter.

We shall close the study of the *Siva-Sakti Tattva* with the
consideration of one of its important functions.   According to
Hindu philosophy the Consciousness of Śiva serves as a
receptacle in which the universe rests during the period of
Pralaya.   After every period of manifestation the cosmos or
a solar system passes into His Consciousness until the time
comes for it to emerge again into manifestation according to
the eternal alternation of *Sṛṣṭi* and *Pralaya* which is inherent
in the Absolute.   This state has been described very beautifully and graphically in the first stanza of Cosmogenesis in
The Secret Doctrine though the poetic description given there
is liable to give quite a wrong impression if we do not grasp

the real significance of the words and phrases and are carried away by the superficial meanings. But we need not go into that question here. The point we have to note is that the Consciousness of Śiva serves as a receptacle for the universe in the state of *Pralaya*. As a matter of fact, the universe remains in His Consciousness all the time and the changes incidental to *Sṛṣṭi* and *Pralaya* may be considered to affect only the periphery of His Consciousness. His Consciousness may be regarded as receiving within its deeper levels all the minor systems as they pass into *Pralaya*, and during a *Mahā-pralaya*, the great dissolution, the whole universe as explained in another chapter.

The question arises: how is the constant disturbance which must be produced by these changes to be reconciled with the state of utter peace or *śānti* which is maintained in His Consciousness, for He is called *Śivam, Śāntam, Sundaram*? *Śivam* means " in Whom all things lie " or " the Auspicious One ". *Śāntam* means " the Peaceful ". *Sundaram* means " the Beautiful ".

To understand how a state of utter peace or *Śānti* can coexist with the disturbances incidental to manifestation, we have only to imagine the different layers of water in an ocean. Even when the surface of an ocean is disturbed by the most violent storms the lower layers of the water remain absolutely tranquil without even a trace of any kind of disturbance. The stresses and strains created by the disturbances at the surface are progressively absorbed by the successive layers of water and as we go deeper we find less and less disturbance, until at a certain level below the surface it ceases altogether. So the lower levels of an ocean always remain perfectly calm and we can understand from this fact how the essential inner Consciousness of Śiva can remain *Śānta* in spite of the disturbances in the periphery.

The same experience is reflected, at a much lower level, in the consciousness of a human being. Those who can dive into the deeper levels of their consciousness can always experience the utter peace which always exists in those layers. The deeper they dive the more subtle and perfect the peace which is found in those layers. And it is this peace which is present within all of us, which every one can enter if he knows the technique of diving within himself. When the passage between the inner Self and the outer personality becomes partially open this inner tranquillity can filter down, to some extent, into the realm of the mind and suffuse it with an indescribable peace which passeth understanding. And the ultimate source of this peace is that *Sānti* which abides eternally in the Consciousness of Śiva.

CHAPTER IV

THE UNMANIFEST COSMIC LOGOS

(COSMIC MIND)

THE nature of the Cosmic Logos is one of the most fascinating concepts of the Occult philosophy because of its many interesting aspects constituting some of the most profound mysteries underlying the universe. Some of these important aspects are sought to be represented in the well-known symbolical form of Maheśa with which every Hindu is familiar. Every thing associated with this Divine form hints at some function or attribute of the Cosmic Logos and a careful and deep study of this form in the light of the Occult doctrines can enable us to enrich very greatly our concept of this Reality which forms as it were the base of the manifested universe. The symbology of Maheśa which means ' the Great Lord ' has been dealt with very briefly in *An Introduction to Hindu Symbolism* but even a brief study like this will show not only the extraordinary richness of this conception of Godhood but also how the profound ideas associated with Divinity can be ingeniously represented in a symbolical form. This form thus enables not only the devotee to develop his devotion but also the philosopher to see many of his philosophical concepts embodied very effectively in an integrated form.

There is no doubt that the concepts of Maheśa and Śiva have been somewhat mixed up in Hindu religious and philosophical thought but the student who has studied the subject carefully and critically and grasped the essential ideas in the two concepts can easily separate them mentally and get a clear comprehension of the two concepts which are quite distinct from each other. The distinction is however so subtle and the concepts are so much beyond the realm of the intellect that there is nothing to be surprised at in this mixing up of the two concepts which had to be presented to the human mind frequently in a popular form. The student of the Divine Wisdom who wants to go deeper into these things and study them from the philosophical and scientific point of view would however do well to clarify his ideas on the subject and separate the two concepts from the mytho-logical lore in which they are embedded. We shall deal in this chapter with a few deeper aspects of the function which the Cosmic Logos exercises as the Presiding Deity of the cosmos and His essential nature.

The first point we have to note in dealing with this difficult subject is that the Cosmic Logos has a dual nature. On the one hand, He is part of the Ever-Unmanifest and on the other, His consciousness is the ultimate basis of the Mani-fest. As part of the Ever-Unmanifest He is *Mahesvara-Mahesvari Tattva*, the Logoic Principle which is the seat of Cosmic Ideation and the source of the infinite number of universes which follow one another in the eternal succession of *Srsti* and *Pralaya*. As the ultimate basis of a manifest universe He is Visvesvara, the Presiding Deity of the whole manifested universe containing countless galaxies and solar systems and existing in all possible grades of subtlety. As the former His consciousness may be considered to be inward-turned. As the latter it may be considered to be outward-turned. It is this mystery of His dual nature, this alternation of consciousness between the Manifest and the Unmanifest which is sought to be represented by the *Damru* in the symbology of Mahesa.

The student will see in this dual nature correspondence with the bifurcation of the Ātmic and mental planes. Just as these alternate planes are the meeting grounds of two principles, so the Ādi plane may be considered to be the meeting ground of the Ever-Unmanifest and the Manifest.

This correspondence shows how the Ever-Unmanifest is the source and prototype of everything we find in the Manifest and how the Manifest is merely a repeated projection and reflection of the Unmanifest at different levels. The Ever-Unmanifest is projected and reflected in the Divine, the Divine is projected and reflected in the spiritual and the spiritual is projected and reflected in the temporal. And it is because there is the projection and reflection of the same Reality at different levels we find similarities and correspondences everywhere when we are dealing with different levels of manifestations both in the macrocosm and the microcosm.

It is necessary to note this interesting correspondence between the Ever-Unmanifest on the one hand and the different levels of the Manifest on the other. We recognize somehow the correspondences between the Divine, spiritual and temporal worlds but the Ever-Unmanifest is generally considered as apart from this process of projection and reflection. The above considerations will show that the Ever-Unmanifest is also mysteriously a part of this process and is in fact the source and prototype of the three different levels of Reality referred to above. This conception which is breathtaking in its grandeur and all-embracing synthesis will be seen to integrate into One Whole the Ever-Unmanifest and the Manifest and abolish the arbitrary distinction which we make between these two aspects of the One Reality.

Although our universe functions as a cosmos, governed by the same laws and pervaded by an underlying Intelligence, Science has not been able to discover any central sun round which the life of the universe revolves, just as the life of our solar system revolves round the sun. This is in harmony with the Occult Doctrine according to which the Cosmic

Logos is represented on the lower planes only by the Solar Logoi functioning through their respective solar systems. This means that there is no central source on the physical plane through which His life flows into the universe just as the life of a Solar Logos flows into the solar system through its physical sun. But all the same He is the Presiding Deity of the cosmos and His Consciousness pervades and controls the cosmos from within through the cosmic planes.

The fact that the Cosmic Logos has no separate centre of expression in the cosmos and we have no evidence of the existence of the cosmic planes is to be expected from the Occult Doctrine regarding the relation of the cosmic and solar planes. The solar planes are built upon the cosmic planes and so contact with the cosmic planes can be established only through the consciousness of those Beings who can function consciously on the cosmic planes. As far as we know it is only the Solar Logoi who can function in this manner on the cosmic planes and it is therefore only through the consciousness of the Logos of his system that a Monad can contact the cosmic planes, if at all. This will also be clear from the figure in the chapter on ' The Manifest Logos ' which shows that the Monads evolving in a solar system are linked directly only with their Solar Logos and only indirectly with the Cosmic Logos. This means that their consciousness must function within the limits set by the consciousness of their Solar Logos and cannot go beyond it. It is this fact which is probably hinted at in aphorism I-25 of the *Yoga-sūtras*: ' In Him [Īśvara] is the highest limit of Omniscience '.

This does not mean that we are completely deprived of the contact and knowledge of the higher Principles which all undoubtedly exist within the deeper levels of our own consciousness right up to the Absolute. The Solar Logos is a micrososm which reflects or rather expresses the consciousness of the Cosmic Logos and because it is a highly developed microcosm it contains all aspects of Divinity in almost a fully developed state. So it is a mirror and focus of the life of the Cosmic Logos, and for all practical purposes is the Cosmic Logos to the still undeveloped Monad. In trying to reach the deeper levels of Divine Consciousness of our Solar Logos we therefore qualitatively come in contact with the Consciousness of the Cosmic Logos, as well as the still higher Principles hidden within Him. We should not, however, forget that our spiritual nature is still so little developed that our contact with these innermost Realities and Principles, at its best, can be extremely superficial. Differences in the Consciousness of the Solar Logos and the Cosmic Logos, tremendous though they must be, do not therefore have any real significance for us. A student of the sixth year in a university differs greatly in knowledge from one still studying in the first year. But to a child still trying to master the three 'R's these differences do not matter much. He can learn all that the sixth year student can teach him equally well from the first year student. And he cannot appreciate the differences existing between the knowledge of the two university students, considerable though these must be. Let us therefore try to see these things in the correct perspective and not forget our limitations and lose our sense of proportion when we are trying to comprehend them as far as possible through the instrumentality of the intellect.

After having dealt with the philosophical concept of the Cosmic Logos in its general and dual aspect let us now consider a few interesting questions relating to His unmanifest nature. He is part of the Ever-Unmanifest as well as the Manifest Logos of the whole cosmos and in these two aspects exercises different functions. Let us now consider these two aspects separately keeping in mind the fact that it is the same Reality we are dealing with.

The essential point to note about the Unmanifest Cosmic Logos or *Mahesvara-Mahesvari Tattva* as He is called in Hindu philosophy is that He is the source of Cosmic Ideation as the *Śiva-Śakti Tattva* is the source of Cosmic Power. But, as in the case of the *Śiva-Śakti Tattva*, the Cosmic Ideation is potential and not active. Now ideation, whether it is potential or active, means projection from the whole or the integrated state of consciousness something inside itself, as an artist projects a picture in his mind or a dramatist projects a play in his imagination. This kind of projection is the beginning of the subject-object relationship, though this subject-object relationship is potential. It is potential in the sense that it is confined within the consciousness of the projector, and there is nothing outside consciousness to which attention is directed, as it were. Active subject-object relationship, on the other hand, is a relationship between a subject and an object outside himself. To take the simile of the artist and his picture, as long as the picture is only in the mind of the artist, it can be considered to be in the realm of potential subject-object relationship or potential ideation. When the picture is being actually drawn, it goes out from the realm of the mind into the realm of objects, and the relation then established between the artist and the picture is an active subject-object relationship. So we may say in a general way that Cosmic Ideation of the Cosmic Logos belongs to the realm of potential subject-object relationship in contrast with the active subject-object relationship which comes into play when a manifest universe comes into existence and actual objects, whether on the subtle or gross planes, are present to enable an active subject-object relationship to be established. This is the realm of the Manifest Cosmic Logos working through the innumerable Solar Logoi in different conditions of time and space.

So, here we have a dim picture of the two most fundamental Principles hidden in the realm of the Unmanifest— the *Śiva-Śakti Tattva* and the *Maheśvara-Maheśvarī Tattva*. The first is considered to be concerned with the generation of power, and the second with the production of the blueprint of the cosmos, which finds expression in an unending series of manifestations after every *Mahāpralaya*. The two may be considered to be correlated, for power without a plan to embody and guide it can never become active and a plan without power to execute it will always remain on paper. Both are necessary for running the machinery of the universe when it is manifested. It is probable that not only are the two related, but closely interlinked so that the power generated depends upon the requirements of the plan to be worked out.

A discovery has been made very recently in the field of Science which may throw some light on this correlation of power and plan in the realm of the Unmanifest. Research had been going on for a long time for devising a mechanism which can enable us to harness the energy of the sun falling upon the earth. A tremendous amount of energy coming from the sun falls upon our earth, and if a proper mechanism could be invented, our power problem would be solved for ever. It has been calculated that enough energy pours down on a hundred square miles of desert in one day to operate all the industries of any highly developed country, round the clock. Research workers have at last been able to perfect a mechanism which is called a silicon cell and which converts sunlight into electricity. Light rays striking the surface of a wafer of silicon dislodge electrons which are drawn off as electrical current. When a number of silicon cells are connected to form a solar battery substantial voltage is generated.

Now, the important point to note in this device is the co-ordination of light and electricity. Light can form visible patterns on the surface of the silicon wafer, and these are accompanied by the generation of electricity according to the pattern and intensity of light. We can see in this relation of the two phenomena—light phenomenon corresponding to production of plan, and electrical phenomenon corresponding to production of power—a faint analogy to the relation of

Cosmic Plan and Power required to implement that Cosmic Plan. In view of the perfect and harmonious adjustment of everything in the realm of the Divine, may it not be that there is perfect co-ordination and correspondence between the Divine Plan and the Divine Power?

These two different types of differentiation represented by *Śiva-Śakti Tattva* and *Maheśvara-Maheśvarī Tattva* lie at the basis of the symbol of the cross which has been considered so sacred from times immemorial. The primary differentiation into the positive and negative principles is represented by a horizontal line between the two poles, as follows, because the negative pole is on a par with the positive pole:

$$+ \underline{\hspace{3cm}} -$$

Consciousness (Śiva)   Power (Śakti)

(PRIMARY DIFFERENTIATION)

The secondary differentiation into Self and Not-Self which is the basis of Cosmic Ideation is represented by a vertical line because it denotes a vertical thrust down into manifestation, though that thrust is still confined to the potential realm of the Unmanifest.

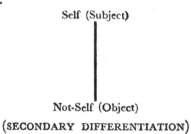

Self (Subject)

Not-Self (Object)

(SECONDARY DIFFERENTIATION)

The combination of the two is represented by the Cross, as shown below:

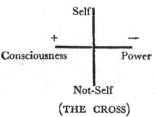

Self

+   —
Consciousness   Power

Not-Self

(THE CROSS)

This combination of the two in the form of a cross, both potential, both within the realm of the Unmanifest, lies at the basis of the manifest universe. From this is derived the profound significance and sacredness of the cross as a universal symbol. Let us note a few points in this connection:

1. That the Consciousness-Power differentiation precedes and lies at the basis of the Self-Not-Self differentiation. This is so because both Consciousness and Power are needed for the secondary differentiation. The Self-Not-Self relationship grows out of Consciousness, for it is really a further differentiation of integrated Consciousness into a dual subject-object relationship which makes Divine Ideation possible. It also needs Power, for the downward thrust towards manifestation means disturbing the equilibrium of the integrated and balanced Consciousness in the *Śiva Tattva*. This Power can come only from Śakti. We see, therefore, that the *Śiva-Śakti Tattva* is the parent of Maheśvara, for both contribute to the differentiation of Consciousness into the duality of the Self and Not-Self. The Unmanifest Cosmic Logos or the Logoic Principle is therefore called the Son for this reason. The Father and Mother Principles precede and are the cause of the Son ' born ' to Them.

2. That both Power and Divine Ideation are potential and not active in the two Unmanifest *Tattvas* considered above and do not function actively as long as a manifested system has not come into being as a result of a further thrust into actual manifestation. This is brought about by the appearance of the Manifest Cosmic Logos with His three well-known aspects and innumerable Solar Logoi, each ruling over His own solar system independently yet under the overlordship of the Manifest Cosmic Logos. The Ādi plane is the plane of the manifestation of the Manifest Cosmic Logos, and it is from this plane that His Will to manifest operates and further differentiation into the three aspects takes place before the fivefold manifested universe comes into being.

3. It should also be noted that the manifest Cosmic Logos on the cosmic Ādi plane, and his innumerable expressions in the form of the Solar Logoi on the solar Ādi planes still remain in the background and are partly within the realm of manifestation and partly outside it. They are within the realm of manifestation because Their Will has begun to work on their respective fields of manifestation. They are outside the realm of manifestation in the sense that they are still hidden behind the scenes though they are the Inner Rulers of the manifested systems over which they preside. It is the Second Logos who is the active ruler and like a prime minister carries out the will of the king in his kingdom. It is thus Viṣṇu or the Second Logos who is the actual manifest Logos. The relation between the First and Second Logos will be seen to be reflected in the two highest principles in man, his Ātmā and his Buddhi. The Ātmā is the inner ruler, and Buddhi is his agent through which his will finds expression on the spiritual planes.

During all the stages referred to above, which are really stages of the downward thrust towards manifestation, the cross formed by the two differentiations remains stationary until the Third Logos appears on the scene and starts His activity by first creating the next five planes. These planes are pervaded by all the three Logoi, the Third Logos being the basis of the material aspect, the Second Logos of the life aspect, and the First Logos of the consciousness aspect of the manifested solar system. It is with the creation of the five planes—Ātmic, Buddhic, mental, astral and physical— that manifestation really begins and the mechanism of the universe begins to function. This active functioning, or the turning of the wheels of the machinery of the universe is symbolized by the revolving *Svastikā* which is nothing but a cross revolving round its axis like a whirling wheel in fire-works. It is this principle which has been utilized in the modern jet-engine for propulsion of vehicles at incredible speeds even in empty space where there is no air to offer resistance and make propulsion of an ordinary aeroplane possible. These different stages in the progress towards manifestation which have been outlined above may be represented diagrammatically, as follows:

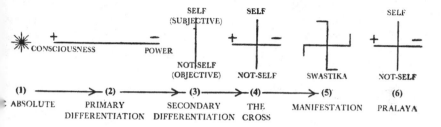

1. Represents the undifferentiated Ultimate Reality or the Absolute.

2. Represents the primary differentiation into Consciousness and Power.

3. Represents the secondary differentiation into Self and Not-Self.

4. Represents the combination in the form of the cross.

5. Represents the turning of the wheels of the machinery of the manifested universe.

6. Represents the cessation of the turning when the plan has been completed and the power apportioned to it has been exhausted.

(Then the revolving *Svastikā* again becomes the stationary Cross.)

This completes our brief and imperfect study of the functions and nature of the Cosmic Logos and His relation to the principles above and below Him.

We shall now turn to another matter, the origin of the Monads. It appears that the origin of the Monads has not been properly understood and the interpretations generally given with regard to this are not quite satisfactory. Let us see why. According to the teachings of the Occult Doctrine the unfoldment of the Monads is at least one if not the only reason why the manifested universe comes into existence. The Monads are eternal and each has the potentiality of becoming a Logos as a result of this unfoldment. This means that the Monads are microcosms which have the same nature, powers, and potentialities as the macrocosm or the Cosmic Logos. That is why they continue to unfold continuously and seemingly endlessly in the same way as water which is derived from the reservoir of a high dam continues to rise higher and higher trying to reach the level of the water in the reservoir.

If these Monads have the same nature and potentiality as the Cosmic Logos and differ from Him only in the degree of unfoldment, just as a sapling differs from the tree in the degree of growth, then they must have the same origin and same status as the Cosmic Logos, in the same way as the younger children in a family have the same status as the eldest son. In *The Secret Doctrine* we find that while the Cosmic Logos is called the Son of the hidden Father, the Monads are also called sons, showing conclusively that they have the same status and nature as the Son. He is the First Born from the Eternal Parents and provides for the younger sons a field of evolution in the same way as the eldest son of a family may provide the wherewithal for the upbringing of all the younger sons who follow him and take advantage of the facilities he provides.

One can be excused for putting these highest and most profound mysteries of existence in these rather anthropomorphic forms, for, we are trying to understand these mysteries and must use the best means at our disposal for this purpose. We know well that the ordinary phenomena of life are the shadows of the realities above and they provide the best clues for understanding those realities. I do not think we

are guilty of sacrilege or impropriety of any sort in treating
these things in this manner provided that we know what we
are doing and maintain the proper attitude of reverence and
humility in this obviously imperfect intellectual treatment of
these profound and unimaginable mysteries.

This mystery of the origin of the Monads, as I have
pointed out already, has not been clarified or at least not
clearly stated and all kinds of nebulous and indefinite ideas
have been put forward in this connection. Some writers
place the origin in the Ādi solar plane, some on the
Anupādaka plane thus implicitly assigning a somewhat indefinite and lower status to these Monads than that of the
Cosmic Logos, although the word ' son ' has been used for both.
Not only is the origin not clearly placed where it belongs,
but even the Mother is not allowed to come into the picture
at all. The Monads are supposed to come out of nowhere
and are found for the first time in the bosom of the
Father on the Anupādaka plane. Where is the Mother—
She who has given them spiritual birth and who will be
responsible for their bringing up throughout the unending cycle of unfoldment in which they rise from one stage
to another in an apparently unending process which has
no limit?

We have seen already that the Father-Mother Principle
is the spiritual origin of the Monads as that of the Cosmic
Logos, and if the Mother Principle has a mysterious part to
play in the birth of the Monads it should also have an equal
if not more important part to play in the unfoldment of the
Monads at every level of evolution, right down to the level
of the personality. This means that the Divine Mother
Principle should be definitely and clearly recognized, and
given its proper place in the life of human beings. If people
have the right to call upon the Inner Source of their being
and address Him as a Father, they have an equal right to
call upon that Source as Mother. For, from their very nature

and on account of the polar relationship between the two aspects of Divinity, they are inseparable.

This is the basis of the Śakti worship in some Hindu schools of occultism. These people also sometimes make the same mistake of excluding or ignoring the other aspect, or giving a predominant place to the Śakti aspect, but it is generally recognized that in order to make worship successful both aspects have to be invoked.

Of course, this tendency to lay emphasis on one or the other aspect is a question of point of view. If we look at an ellipsoid which is used as a symbol of the *Śiva-Śakti Tattva* from a side, along its axis, only one focus is visible, the other remaining hidden from view behind the first, and the ellipsoid is seen as a sphere. The real relationship is seen on looking from the side when both foci are visible and seen to be in polar relationship, as illustrated in Fig. 6.

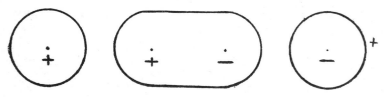

Fig. 6. An ellipsoid as seen along the axis and from the side

CHAPTER V

THE NATURE OF THE EVER-UNMANIFEST

In dealing with the nature of the Ever-Unmanifest Reality
in the previous chapters we have divided it into three aspects
for the sake of convenience in grasping intellectually this
profound concept. These three aspects have been called
(1) The Absolute (2) *Śiva-Śakti Tattva* and (3) The Unmanifest Cosmic Logos and we have tried to understand, as far
as this is possible, how these three aspects of the same Reality
differ from one another. In considering these aspects separately it is but natural that the underlying unity of the Ever-
Unmanifest is lost sight of to a great extent and we become
inclined to take the three aspects as three different Realities,
just as in considering the three aspects of the Manifest Logos
—Brahmā, Viṣṇu and Maheśa—we begin to regard them
as three different Persons instead of three functions of the
same Īśvara. It is, therefore, desirable that we now consider the three aspects of the Ever-Unmanifest together with
a view to make clear in our mind its underlying essential
unity. But before we deal with the nature of the Ever-
Unmanifest as a whole let us briefly recapitulate the essential
facts we have learnt in studying the three aspects separately.

(1) The Absolute is the Ultimate Reality or Parabrahman
of Hindu philosophy in which not only what finds expression
in the manifested universe but also what is present in the
Unmanifest potentially, exists in a perfectly harmonized,
balanced and integrated state so that this state appears as a

void and plenum at the same time. Not only all the principles, forces, functions, powers, etc. which form the basic
realities of the manifested universe are perfectly blended and
integrated into a void state in the Absolute but even the
products of primary and secondary differentiation which
constitute the other two components of the Ever-Unmanifest
are harmonized and integrated so perfectly and completely
that nothing can be distinguished in that Ultimate Reality.
That is why it is called *Nirviśeṣa*, i.e. without any distinction
or special property.

The nature of the Absolute as a perfect void does not
mean that it is unrelated to all the other levels or aspects of
Reality or even the lowest states of manifestation. In spite
of its voidness and apparently impenetrable nature it is in
some mysterious manner the ultimate and causeless cause of
not only the Unmanifest but also the manifested universe.

The concept of the Absolute as a Self-sufficient, Self-
determined Ultimate Reality in which all processes of manifestation, dissolution, etc. take place automatically as a result
of an underlying Cosmic Rhythm, requires the existence of a
Point through which this eternal Cosmic Rhythm takes place,
and a manifested universe is projected periodically in the
eternal alternation of *Sṛṣṭi* and *Pralaya*. This Point corresponds
to the number ' 1 ' coming between ' 0 ' representing the
void state of the Absolute and ' 2 ' representing the primary
duality of the *Śiva-Śakti Tattva*. So the Point should be
properly considered as a vehicle of the Absolute, as the
opposite of boundless infinite Space which is considered in
the Occult Doctrine to ' contain ' the Ultimate Reality. It is
the door between the Absolute as a void and the rest of the
Unmanifest and Manifest states.

(2) The second aspect or component of the Ever-Unmanifest is the *Śiva-Śakti Tattva*, sometimes referred to as Positive-
Negative or Father-Mother Principle. This is the product of
the primary differentiation of the Ultimate Reality and the

primary duality which results divides, as it were, the whole manifest and unmanifest Reality into two opposite counterparts which by their action and reaction and baiancing of opposites weave the fabric of the universe. The nature of this dual and polar Principle has already been dealt with at some length in a previous chapter. Very briefly stated, this dual Principle may be considered to be the very essence and foundation of the universe.

Śiva-Śaktyātmakam viśvam.

'Śiva and Śakti are the innermost Essence of the universe.'

In this dual Principle are to be traced the mysteries and relationships of consciousness and power, of will and action, of attraction and repulsion, of love and bliss. It is these fundamental realities of existence which are rooted in the *Śiva-Śakti Tattva* that descend gradually, step by step, to lower and lower realms of manifestation and produce by their interactions the multifarious and universal phenomena of life, mind and consciousness at all levels.

(3) The third aspect or component of the Ever-Unmanifest is the *Maheśvara-Maheśvarī Tattva*, the Mind-Principle with its essential characteristic of subject-object relationship. This Mind-Principle which is the root of mental phenomena at all levels finds expression in Cosmic Ideation of the Unmanifest Cosmic Logos at the highest level and is then reflected in mental phenomena of all degrees of subtlety in the different realms of manifestation. Wherever there is any mental phenomenon there is a subject or the ' seer ' and there is the object of perception which comes out of the ' seer ' and is bound up with it in a kind of polar relationship. Although the *Maheśvara-Maheśvarī Tattva* is also dual and polar, this duality and polarity is of a different kind and results in phenomena of a different nature. A comparison with the *Śiva-Śakt Tattva* will show that while the duality and polarity of the *Śiva-Śakti Tattva* is connected in one way or another with the

manifestation of power and forces, that of *Maheśvara-Maheśvarī Tattva* is connected with manifestations of a mental nature.

Just as the integrated Consciousness of Śiva is the root of mind functioning through the subject-object relationship, so the integrated Power of Śakti is the root of all manifestations of energy taking place through *Prakṛti* in its triple aspect. The two polar components of the primary differentiation must be necessarily affected equally in the secondary differentiation though the products at the two poles will be different. Consciousness differentiates into *Sat-Cit-Ānanda*, the root of Mind and the Power into *Tamas-Rajas-Sattva*, the root of Matter or *Mūlaprakṛti*.

Without grasping this fundamental idea we cannot understand the relation existing between Śakti and *Prakṛti* and cannot remove the confusion which surrounds this relationship in Hindu philosophy. Everywhere Śakti is confused with *Prakṛti* and the failure to distinguish between them and to clarify our ideas with regard to their nature and functions has led to all kinds of philosophical inconsistencies. What has been said above will show that the word *Prakṛti* stands or should stand for a reality at a lower level than that of Śakti. It is the correlate of the Mind-principle while Śakti is the polar opposite and correlate of the principle of Consciousness. *Prakṛti*, according to Hindu philosophy, is the *sāmyāvasthā* or the balanced state of the *guṇas* while Śakti is the conscious Power which is the polar opposite of the pure Consciousness in which Power is potential. When the pure integrated Consciousness descends into manifestation it appears as mental phenomena. When pure integrated Power descends into manifestation it appears as *Prakṛti* with its play of the *guṇas*. When mind or *Citta* merges into integrated consciousness of the *Puruṣa* on the attainment of *Kaivalya* the play of the *guṇas* is over and *Prakṛti* merges into potential power as pointed in the last aphorism of the *Yoga-sūtras* of Patañjali (IV-34).

Although the essential unity of the Ever-Unmanifest must be kept in mind, still, we have to remember that the three aspects or states referred to above are inherent in that oneness in an integrated state and when the Unmanifest becomes manifest they become more and more prominent with each further descent into manifestation. We are apt to overlook the fact that the triplicity of the manifested Reality as it descends lower and lower in manifestation in the form

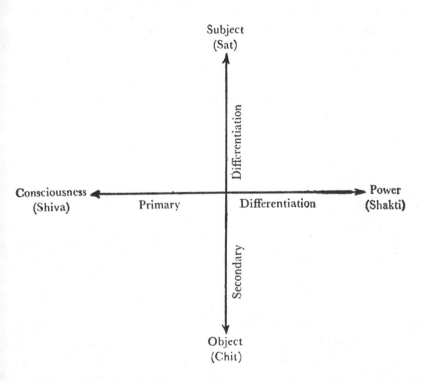

of the Triple Logos, or the Triple Monad, or the triple individuality or the triple personality is merely a reflection at different levels of the hidden and subtle triplicity which is present in the Unmanifest in its three aspects of (1) The Absolute (2) *Śiva-Śakti Tattva* and (3) the Unmanifest Cosmic

Logos or *Maheśvara-Maheśvarī Tattva.* This is on the side of consciousness or subjective Reality. On the side of power or objective Reality we also find the same triplicity reflected again and again on the lower planes. Thus the Divine worlds are triple (Ādi, Anupādaka and higher Ātmic). The spiritual worlds are triple (lower Ātmic, Buddhic and higher mental). The temporal worlds are triple (lower mental, astral and physical). The existence of these triple counterparts in the realms of consciousness and power or spirit and matter or *Puruṣa* and *Prakṛti* is inevitable if the Ultimate Reality in its primary and secondary differentiations divides into two opposite polar Principles.

The two aspects of the Unmanifest, one pertaining to its oneness and the other to its triplicity, can be brought out simultaneously to a certain extent by representing it as a cross as shown on the previous page.

In this diagram we have the intersection of two straight lines representing the primary and secondary differentiations. These differentiations are of a polar nature but the products of these are fundamentally different as shown above. The following points may be noted about this cross which is meant to represent the totality of the Unmanifest in its triple aspect:

(*a*) This double polarity arises from the point of intersection which represents the Absolute in its aspect of the One.

(*b*) Though the two polarities which are the result of the primary and secondary differentiations are represented by straight lines in the above diagram we must not make the mistake of thinking that they involve any kind of separation in space. The Unmanifest transcends the Manifest and so is above time and space. To imagine that any kind of polarity in the Unmanifest involves separation in space will be absurd from the philosophical point of view. The conception of a polarity which is above spatial relationships and which functions in a point and from a point is one of the subtlest though fascinating concepts which we have to deal with in the realm of philosophy. It is difficult to grasp but if our intuitive faculty and the higher mind are trained to deal with these subtle concepts concerning these transcendental realities we may be able to obtain a glimmer of the truth. Anyhow, whether we are able to gain a glimpse of the underlying truth or not, let us remember that the symbolic representation through straight lines hides an extremely subtle truth.

(c) Not only have we to conceive this polarity above the realm of space and functioning about a point but we have also to conceive it as the result of an internal redistribution in one and the same Principle which produces contrast or potential without the introduction of anything from outside or affecting the wholeness and self-sufficiency of the Principle. It is possible for us even on the physical plane to conceive something with a uniform distribution of some kind of energy resolving into two or more states with different distributions of the same energy and without involving any addition or subtraction of energy in the limited field. For example, a surface illuminated uniformly by white light can be divided into different portions with differing distribution of light. In this case the total amount of light remains the same but the element of contrast appearing as light and shade is introduced. To take another example, water contained in a cistern can be distributed into two cisterns placed at different levels. Here we have the same amount of water but the difference in the two levels gives us potential energy which can be utilized for doing work. Similarly, electrical potential can be created by redistribution of electrons on the surface of a conductor. Here again the total amount of electrons remains the same but the redistribution produces electrical potential which can be used for doing work. This question of production of contrast or potential by internal redistribution has been dealt with more thoroughly in another chapter. So all that we have to do here is to understand how such a thing is possible and whether the principle can throw some light on the nature of the Unmanifest.

(*d*) If we have grasped the significance of what has been said above, we shall see at once that the principle referred to in the last paragraph can throw some light on the nature of the polarities or contrasts produced in the primary and secondary differentiations in the Ultimate Reality. *Śiva Tattva* may be considered to have more of Reality or Reality at a higher potential while *Śakti Tattva* may be considered to have less of Reality or Reality at a lower potential. Light contains darkness and darkness contains light potentially. For, it is a question of relativity. There can be no absolute light or absolute darkness except as ideal limits. Similarly, positive and negative electrical charges are matters of relative states and the potential difference between two charged objects will determine in which direction the current will flow. The Principle which contains more of Reality, as it were, and shows the attributes of subjective consciousness and positive will is called Śiva while the Principle which contains relatively less Reality and shows the attributes of objectivity and negative power is called Śakti in Hindu philosophy.

It is for this reason that in the *Śiva Tattva* power is considered to be inherent but present in *niṣkalā* or inactive state and on the other hand, in the *Śakti Tattva* consciousness is considered to be inherent but present in the background. Both contain both but in relative degrees, though the differences in functions make them appear poles apart. It is this fact of relative reality which constitutes the polarity of *Śiva-Śakti Tattva* and lies at the basis of the mysterious relationship existing between Śiva and Śakti. Even when this *Tattva* descends lower into the realm of manifestation and consciousness begins to function through the mind and power becomes *sakala* or active, this mysterious and intimate relation between consciousness and power and their respective expressions is maintained everywhere.

(e) What has been said above with regard to the result of primary differentiation is also true with regard to the result of secondary differentiation though in a different sense. In the case of the *Mahesvara-Mahesvari Tattva* which is the result of secondary differentiation of the Ultimate Reality the polarity is of a different kind and results in the appearance of subject-object relationship which is the basis of the Mind-Principle. Perhaps the use of the word ' polarity ' for this relation between subject and object is not quite appropriate for we associate the word 'polarity' in Science with phenomena involving forces of different kinds. The contrast between the two components in the subject-object relationship does not involve forces and energies in that way. But it is a relation in which there is the existence of opposition and mutuality between the two components, in which there is merely an internal redistribution of contents as it were, and nothing is added to or subtracted from the totality of the Whole, and so the use of the word 'polarity' may be allowed.

The *Mahesvara-Mahesvari Tattva* or the Cosmic Mind-Principle which has been referred to as the Unmanifest Cosmic Logos is the seat of Cosmic Ideation. It is in that dark and incomprehensible realm that the manifest universes which follow one another in eternal succession take shape as a result of the mental activity of the Cosmic Logos. Although we use words like ' mind ' and ' ideation ' in relation to this activity we should not make the mistake of considering it similar to ordinary mental activity. In fact, it is more spiritual in its nature than the highest spirituality which we can conceive of or experience. The use of these words for this subtlest Divine activity is justified only because its reflections in the realm of manifestation give rise to those phenomena which we consider as mental.

The subject of Cosmic Ideation has been dealt with in detail in other chapters and it is not necessary to go into it here except to point out a few salient ideas which throw some light on the nature of the Ever-Unmanifest.

The Unmanifest is an integrated state. It has been shown in another chapter that an integrated state is a very peculiar condition in which all possible kinds of differentiated states are present potentially but none of them is present actually. They are not only present potentially but they can emerge from that state at any time whenever and wherever the necessary conditions are fulfilled. This idea is very important in considering the nature of Cosmic Ideation in the realm of the Unmanifest. We should be careful not to regard the Cosmic Mind as a stack of blue prints containing the series of universes which follow one another eternally in the alternation of *Śṛṣṭi* and *Pralaya*. This will not be an integrated state like sunlight but a differentiated state like the spectrum of sunlight. No number of separate things, however numerous they may be, can constitute an integrated state. Although an infinite number of universes can continue to emerge from the Mind of the Cosmic Logos they cannot be there already in the form in which they will appear in time and space or even in their spiritual form. To suppose this will amount to denying even to the Cosmic Logos the freedom to create and the question will arise: 'What is the ultimate source of the universe? Surely not the Absolute.'

The concept of the integrated state will enable us to understand not only how the Great Creator is free to create the universes but should be able to create an unending series of universes owing to the integrated state of His Consciousness. God cannot be bound by His creations as He would be if all His plans were already there in some form. The universes are coming out of the Unmanifest as a result of free Divine creative activity though the Logoi working in the lower fields of manifestation have to work according to the great Plan which is the result of this activity.

This does not mean, as appears to many, that the Solar Logoi are bound in Their creative activity. We get this impression because we imagine the Solar Logoi to have a separate and independent existence from that of the Cosmic Logos. As a matter of fact, they are merely facets of that Reality which we refer to as the Cosmic Logos, and the Divine Plan finds expression through them in the same way as the work of a bank is carried out through all its branches scattered throughout the world. The Cosmic Logos, according to the Occult Doctrine, is a Principle and on the lower planes may be considered as the manifest Reality behind all the solar systems functioning in the universe.

So we see that the primary and secondary differentiations in the Ultimate Reality bring about only a partial differentiation and the Realities which result from these differentiations are still integrated states though of a lower order than the super-integrated state of the Absolute. It is for this reason that they can provide the basis for inexhaustible potential Cosmic Power and potential Cosmic Ideation. It is only when manifestation takes place that pure integrated Consciousness differentiates into states of mind of different degrees of subtlety and potential integrated Power differentiates into specific powers, each such power being related to its own level of mind and function of consciousness as shown in the symbology of the *Devīs* and *Devatās* of Hinduism. So in the manifested state we have *Citta* (mind) instead of *Citi* (consciousness) and *Prakṛti* instead of Śakti (conscious Power). Both *Citta* and *Prakṛti* belong to the realm of manifestation and are differentiated states. Both are capable of activity and can thus serve as the primary instruments of the manifested states. But we should not forget that we are dealing here with general principles in distinguishing the Unmanifest from the manifest state. In the realm of manifestation and therefore relativity, everything is relative and what may be considered as integrated and potential will depend upon its level of manifestation and the relation of this level to levels which are higher and lower.

It will also be seen from what has been said above that the secondary differentiation in the Unmanifest is very closely related to the primary differentiation. In fact, they appear almost as two aspects of the same process. The element of Consciousness in the primary differentiation becomes the perceiver or seer (*dṛṣṭā*) or the basis of the subjective phenomena in manifestation. The element of Power provides the objects of perception and becomes the basis of the objective phenomena (*dṛśyam*). The seer functions through the mind or *Citta* and the seen through *Prakṛti* or the root of so-called matter according to Sāmkhyan terminology. Although, therefore, the secondary differentiation is different in nature, it may be considered as merely an extension of the primary differentiation. It is for this reason that in Hindu philosophical and religious thought the *Śiva-Śakti Tattva* and the *Maheśvara-Maheśvarī Tattva* are taken almost as synonymous. There is no hard or fast line of demarcation between them though it is necessary to distinguish between them from the philosophical and if I may say so from the scientific point of view.

In fact, in the involution of the different levels of Reality right from the Absolute to the physical plane it is difficult to separate the different levels by water-tight compartments. It is the same Reality which gradually, and step by step, brings out its less subtle aspects, one by one, and yet remains the same underlying Reality in all these aspects, as hinted at in the famous Hindu philosophical maxim 'Verily, all this is Brahman'.

In considering the involution of the Ultimate Reality into the lower aspects or states we should remember that when involution into a lower state or level takes place the higher state or level does not disappear or become non-existent. If that happened then on complete manifestation nothing would be left except the last derivative or the densest state in the chain: Reality → Consciousness → Mind → Matter. What happens may be expressed as follows:

The Ultimate Reality is involved partially in Consciousness but still one aspect of it remains unaffected. At the second stage Consciousness changes partially into Mind but still one aspect of it is left unaffected. At the third stage Mind changes partially into so-called Matter but still one aspect is left unaffected. So when the whole process has been completed we have all the four levels of Reality present and functioning simultaneously, co-existing as it were, the lower supported by and existing in the substratum of the higher. This kind of relation of the different levels of Reality may be represented to some extent diagrammatically as follows:

We see thus that Matter floats and functions in a sea of Mind, Mind functions in a sea of Consciousness and Consciousness functions in the Void or Plenum of the Ultimate Reality. This picture of the whole process of manifestation enables us to see very clearly the truth of the Occult Doctrine that in spite of the infinite variety

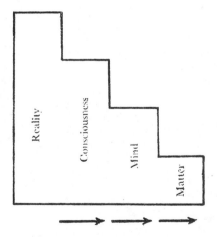

and levels of existence in manifestation there is only one Ultimate Reality from which every aspect is derived and in which all aspects of manifestation without exception are contained. The whole universe, manifest and Unmanifest, literally springs from, floats and functions in the Absolute. At the time of *Pralaya* the manifest is withdrawn into the unmanifest and at the time of creation the manifest is projected from the unmanifest, the unmanifest pertaining to that particular level remaining unaffected.

It will also be seen from what we have learnt about the unmanifest state that its essential nature at any level is shown by the fact that it remains in the background, unseen, and does not appear in the field of manifestation or takes a direct part in its activities and processes. It is the energizing and guiding force behind these activities and provides the necessary power and plan for them and yet remains hidden behind these activities and works through its outer agents. This holds true at all levels and in case of different entities, for, manifest and unmanifest are relative terms. Thus the Ātma in the case of Individuality is the unmanifest and remains hidden and works through the Buddhi and Manas. Maheśa in the Logos or *Īśvara* is the Unmanifest and functions through Viṣṇu and Brahmā. The Absolute in the Ever-Unmanifest is the Ultimate Unmanifest and works through the *Śiva-Śakti Tattva* and *Maheśvara-Maheśvarī Tattva*.

CHAPTER VI

THE MANIFEST LOGOS

(Īśvara)

IT was pointed out in the chapter dealing with the Unmanifest Cosmic Logos that after every *Mahāpralaya* involving the dissolution of the universe, the manifest Cosmic Logos may be considered to emerge from the unmanifest and to prepare the ground for the manifestation of a new universe by creating cosmic planes. This creation after each *Mahāpralaya* lays the foundation of a new universe and on the ground thus prepared are laid the foundations of the innumerable solar systems which come into being during the period of manifestation. The solar planes of each solar system are made independently out of the material of the cosmic planes and, when a universal dissolution takes place at the time of a *Mahāpralaya*, all the solar systems disappear automatically, for, they depend for their very existence on the cosmic planes.

It may be mentioned here that *Pralayas* or dissolutions of manifested systems are of different categories according to the unit which is affected. There are the minor *Pralayas* affecting only globes and chains but the two most important are the solar *Pralaya* when the whole solar system with its globes and chains comes to an end, and the *Mahāpralaya* when the whole universe is dissolved and passes into the unmanifest. The period of a *Mahāpralaya* or the " Great Night " according to Hindu calculations is 311,040,000,000,000 solar years when the universe rests in Brahman. How time is calculated in a *Mahāpralaya* is an intriguing question into which we cannot enter here.

The Solar Logoi are like the rays of the Cosmic Logos as the Monads associated with a solar system are like the rays of its Solar Logos. As the sun rises in the east with all its rays in the morning, so does the Cosmic Logos manifest after the dark night of a *Mahāpralaya* with all the Solar Logoi as His rays. And each Solar Logos brings with Him out of the Unmanifest all the Monads which will be associated with Him during the coming *Mahākalpa*, the period of manifestation. This is on the highest plane and as the successive planes are formed and the vehicles become ready they begin to function in their respective spheres.

We are not going into this question of Cosmogenesis at all. We are concerned here with the nature and functions of the manifested Logoi and the Monads. But before we go into this matter it is necessary to clarify our ideas about the relations existing between the Cosmic Logos, the Solar Logoi, and the Monads associated with them. As we have seen, all these have the same origin, status and essential nature and differ only in the degree of unfoldment and their functions in the manifested universe, although these differences are so tremendous that it is difficult even to imagine how this is possible.

It has been pointed out above that the Monads are like the rays of their respective Solar Logoi who in their turn are like the rays of the Cosmic Logos. The relation between the physical sun and its rays is one of the mysteries of modern science and this mystery merely reflects the still more profound mystery of the relation between a Monad and Solar Logos on the one hand and the relation of a Solar Logos and the Cosmic Logos on the other. All these mysteries may be considered to be merely different aspects of the eternal mystery of the One and the Many.

In view of this mutual relationship of the three—the Monads, Solar Logoi and the Cosmic Logos, is it possible to link them up in some manner and represent this linking by means of a diagram? Such a linking will integrate into one concept the three basic realities which are manifesting in the universe, visible and invisible, and which though different are yet the same. The diagram given below is an attempt to show not only how the spiritual links between the Cosmic Logos, Solar Logoi and Monads may be represented to bring

FIG. 7. The Cosmic Logos, Solar Logoi and Monads

out the fact that they are One and the many at the same time, but also how their vehicles of consciousness are related on the form side.

The above diagram symbolizes the following facts:

(1) While the Solar Logoi are directly linked with the Cosmic Logos, the Monads are directly linked with their respective Logoi and only indirectly with the Cosmic Logos. This fact is of great significance because it shows that the Monad can contact the consciousness of the Solar Logos directly; but the consciousness of the Cosmic Logos only through the consciousness of his Solar Logos.

(2) The second point to be noted is that each Monad who has descended into manifestation has also a world of his own within the world of the Solar Logos. His set of vehicles on all the solar planes constitute his world on the form side, and the different levels of the mind rooted in the consciousness of the Logos on the life side. His world is a world within the larger world of the Solar Logos, as the solar system is a world of the Solar Logos within the still larger world of the Cosmic Logos.

(3) The figure also shows radiating lines from the centres representing the Monads because each Monad is a potential Logos and when the Monad reaches the high status of a Logos, the Monads who now exist potentially within him shine forth like rays of the new sun which has appeared. The reader will see in this proliferation of Monads an analogy with many similar phenomena on the physical plane. For example, every tree after it attains its full stature produces seeds which have the capacity to germinate and grow into similar trees and this process repeats itself *ad infinitum*.

(4) The mystery of the relation between the Monad and the Solar Logos is one of the greatest mysteries of life—the final secret mentioned in *Light on the Path*, which is imparted at the time of Liberation or *Jivanmukti*. The crux of this mystery lies in the simultaneous existence of the oneness and

separation between the Monad and the Solar Logos at the same time. It will be seen from the diagram how the unravelling of this mystery on attaining Self-realization will not only reveal the nature of his relationship with the Logos of the solar system, but will also give the Monad a faint glimpse into the analogous relation of the Solar Logos with the Cosmic Logos, for both are essentially the same and differ only in the differences of level, tremendous though these differences of level must be. Everywhere we find these reflections of reflections. The study and experiences of these lower reflections help us in gaining a glimpse into the nature of the realities which they reflect. And we should not forget that very frequently the experiences, which we take to be the realities themselves, are mere reflections or perhaps reflections of reflections. It is not given to human beings to realize the ultimate truths of existence, though many, misled by conceit and ignorance, think and claim that they have done so.

With this preliminary consideration of the relation between the Monad, Solar Logos and Cosmic Logos which has cleared the ground we may now proceed to the consideration of the nature and functions of the Triple Logos. Since we are concerned with our own solar system and the Solar Logos who presides over it, we shall confine ourselves to the nature and functions of a Solar Logos though these in some remote and mysterious manner must also reflect the nature and functions of the Cosmic Logos according to the occult maxim " As above, so below ".

The most significant point we have to note about the Solar Logos is His triple nature. Before dealing with these three aspects in detail and their functions and correlations with the phenomenal side of Nature let us dwell for a while on the question how this triple nature has arisen. For the consideration of this derivation of the Three from the One will not only throw some light on the nature of these aspects and their relation to one another, but also on the large number of triplicities which we find everywhere in the realm of manifestation.

The derivation of a triplicity from a unity is rooted in and can be understood from the relation of the Self and Not-Self which has already been referred to very briefly in dealing with the question of Cosmic Ideation in the realm of the Unmanifest. The Self is whole, complete, self-sufficient, perfect and Self-existent and is called *Sat* in Sanskrit. In this *Sat* a differentiation can take place owing to the inherent power present in It to project something outside Itself, and yet within Itself, which brings about a kind of opposition or polarity between the Self and what has been projected and which we may call the Not-Self. This aspect of the Self which is present now as Not-Self is called *Cit* and the aspect which represents or is related to their relationship is called *Ānanda* in Vedanta philosophy although the use of the word *Ānanda* is most inappropriate and deceptive. For, *Ānanda* in its usual connotation of bliss is a by-product or derivative of this relationship and does not represent fully the aspect of this relation between the Self and Not-Self. But since this word is deeply entrenched in our philosophical thought we have to take it in both the senses and continue to use it also for the relation between the Self and Not-Self or the middle term connecting *Sat* and *Cit*. The relation between the Self and Not-Self, or between *Sat* and the product which appears in the Self as a result of the *Cit* aspect coming into play, is not unlike the relationship between the consciousness of an individual and a mental picture which may appear in his mind whereby the picture goes out of the whole and integrated consciousness, and a subject-object relationship is established between the two. The picture has become the object and the mind has become the subject and the perception of the picture by the mind is the relation which binds the two. As a matter of fact, the relation established is between the consciousness behind the mind and the picture, but, since the mind is the medium through which the consciousness usually functions, we may for all practical purposes consider the mind as the subject. The differentiation of the Self and Not-Self from *Sat* is analogous and brings into play the triplicity of *Sat, Cit, Ānanda* which lies at the basis of the triple aspect of the Logos. The important point to note is that *Sat* contains the other two aspects *Cit* and *Ānanda* as the perceiver includes the perceived and perception. It is, therefore, self-sufficient and independent and remains independent and self-sufficient even when the Not-Self has separated from it. The Not-Self or the product of *Cit* aspect, on the other hand, is not self-sufficient. It is dependent upon and is supported by *Sat* and can become absorbed again in *Sat*. It cannot exist independently, as a picture in the mind of an artist cannot exist unless the artist puts himself partly into the picture in the form of constant attention directed to it. The moment the attention is withdrawn the picture disappears. As regards the third term *Ānanda*, which connotes the relation between *Sat* and *Cit* or Self and Not-Self, it is obvious that this also should depend upon *Sat* and must disappear when the Not-Self is re-absorbed in the Self.

The question may arise how the Self can remain whole and perfect when the Not-Self has separated from It. The problem is similar to that of the appearance of the manifested universe from the Unmanifest leaving the Unmanifest whole and perfect, and has been put very beautifully in the famous mantra of *Bṛhadāraṇyaka Upaniṣad* " THAT is Perfect Whole, THIS is Perfect Whole, because THIS has come out of THAT; when THIS Perfect Whole is taken out of THAT Perfect Whole, what remains is also Perfect Whole." We cannot enter into this interesting question here.

The relation of *Sat-Cit-Ānanda* aspects of Divinity discussed above will enable us to understand easily the essential relation of the three aspects of the Logos to one another.

The Logos of a solar system ideates a world in the Divine Mind which becomes the basis of the form side of the solar system. This aspect of the Logos corresponding to Not-Self is called Brahmā, or the Third Logos in Theosophical literature. But a world ideated in this manner cannot remain independently without its being ensouled by the Logos, just as a picture in the mind of an artist cannot remain without the artist ensouling it with his attention. The created world ensouled by the Logos is called Viṣṇu, the indwelling Life, or the Second Logos in Theosophical literature. This corresponds to the *Ānanda* aspect which is the relating principle between *Sat* and *Cit* or Self and Not-Self. But as will be shown later, this process of ideation being a process in consciousness and not matter, does not affect the Logos Himself. He remains as He was, though supporting and pervading the manifested solar system over which He presides. " Having created this world and ensouled it I remain," as Śrī Kṛṣṇa says in *The Bhagavad-gītā*. So, that aspect of the Logos which remains unaffected and independent of the world He has created is called Maheśa or the First Logos in Theosophical literature. It is the Transcendent Aspect, as Viṣṇu is the Immanent Aspect and Brahmā the Imprisoned Aspect of Divinity, if I may use such a term. The first is related to pure Consciousness, the second to Life and the third to Form.

One of the most striking facts in the whole field of manifestation is the presence of a large number of triplicities in various spheres of life. All these triplicities will be found on close examination to be rooted in this triple nature of the Logos. Let us consider briefly a few of these triplicities which we find in Nature because they throw light on the nature and functions of the Logos Who presides over a manifested system.

Let us take first the important functions of creation, preservation, and regeneration. These are the well-known functions of the Third, Second and First Logos or Brahmā, Viṣṇu and Maheśa, and many people think that they are the only functions connected with the three aspects of the Logos. Even in considering these functions we have to go a little deeper and not think that the creative function comes to an end when the world has been created and the destructive function comes into play only at the time for dissolution. These functions are being exercised all the time and everywhere. Take the human body for instance. There are taking place continuously and simultaneously creative, preservative and destructive processes, side by side, and it is the perfect adjustment of these forces which keeps the body alive and in a healthy state. In fact, so fine and exquisitely balanced is this adjustment that to study and see it in action is to be convinced that the most consummate Intelligence and Wisdom lie at the basis of the universe, provided our intuition is functioning and our mind is not prejudiced and obsessed with the materialistic outlook. It is the Life and Consciousness of the Logos which pervades the universe in His three aspects, and this alone can account for the marvellous intelligence and wisdom present in every sphere of natural phenomena.

The word 'destruction' does not give a correct idea of the function of Maheśa. It is true that destruction plays a very important and definite part in life everywhere, but it should not be viewed in isolation and should be considered as a part of a more comprehensive function which may best be described as regeneration. Death or destruction is generally nothing but the removal of something which has served its purpose and is standing in the way of further progress or unfoldment. It generally provides a better instrument or opportunity or environment for further advancement. It is thus a necessary part of the progressive evolution of bodies and the unfoldment of consciousness, and should be considered as complementary to the functions of creation and preservation. Viewed in this light it is not less necessary or beneficent than these two functions. It is perhaps for this reason that the destructive function of the Logos is separated from the more comprehensive and beneficent regenerative function of Maheśa and symbolized by Rudra.

I think it will enable us to understand the functions of the three aspects of the Logos if we arrange some of the well-known triplicities under three heads to bring out the correspondences between them.

BRAHMĀ	VIṢṆU	MAHEŚA
(Third Logos)	(Second Logos)	(First Logos)
Creation	Preservation	Regeneration
Form	Life	Consciousness
Known	Knowing	Knower
Electricity	*Prāna*	*Kundalini*
Rajas	*Sattva*	*Tamas*
Cit	*Ānanda*	*Sat*

We have already dealt with the triplicities of creation, preservation and regeneration, and life, form and consciousness. Let us now take another important triplicity, that of electricity, *prāna* and *Kundalini*. These are three distinct types of forces working in the human body and Science with all its detailed study of the human body knows something only about one, namely electricity, though it suspects the presence of another force which is vaguely referred to as vitality. But to the occultist these three forces are quite definite, real and capable of being seen and manipulated objectively. The most important thing to remember about these forces is that they are not interconvertible, but are really three different types of energies which are being poured out from the sun and are appropriated by the human body for its various functional activities. Each of these forces exists in several forms. Thus electricity can be transformed into mechanical energy or heat and vice versa. *Prāna* can exist in five varieties, and different forms of *Kundalini* are also known, though occult literature does not give details about these for obvious reasons.

Though people familiar with occult literature know about the existence of these three different types of forces, many do not know that they are derived from, and related to, the three aspects of the Logos and are instruments of their respective functions in the human body. Thus electricity and its variants are related to Brahmā, *Prāna* to Viṣṇu, and *Kundalini* to Maheśa. These relations of the three types of forces to the three aspects of the Logos follow from the functions of the three aspects of the Logos in the manifested system. Brahmā is the Creator and, as has been pointed out above, is related to the form side of Nature. All changes in the human body of a material nature depend upon and are brought about by electricity and other related forces familiar to Science. Viṣṇu is the Preserver related to the life side of the human body, and the five types of *Prāna* are responsible for, and underlie all life processes which are going on in the physical body and make it a living organism in contradistinction to an insentient aggregate of matter and force. *Prāna* also lies at the basis of sensation and without its association with a sense-organ the vibrations received by the organ remain ineffective and are not converted into sensation. The relation of *Prāna* to Viṣṇu, the Indwelling Life, is thus obvious both in His function of preservation as well as perception. The third force, *Kundalini*, is derived from Maheśa and among all living organisms is found only in the human body. This is so because the functioning of the First Logos in a body begins only on individualization, when the causal body is formed. It is with the connection of the Monad with the physical body and the descent of this eternal element into the causal body that man enters that unending cycle of evolution which has no limit. The previous stages in the animal kingdom serve merely as a preparation for this stage.

The functioning and unfoldment of consciousness in the human body depends upon *Kundalini*, the power of Maheśa, from the earliest stages but it is only in the final stages of the unfoldment that *Kundalini* is aroused, and the mechanism of *Suṣumnā* and *Cakras* is utilized for developing the supramental states of consciousness. But this subject, by its very nature, has to be kept shrouded in mystery on account of the dangers which are inherent in manipulating these subtler forces. It is only when a *Sādhaka* is ready otherwise and has the necessary qualifications that knowledge concerning the manipulation of these forces is imparted to him.

We could take one triplicity after another and trace its relation to the three aspects of the Logos but it is not possible to do this here.

It will be seen from what has been said above that Brahmā, Viṣṇu and Maheśa are not three Persons but three aspects of the Logos in the exercise of His three different functions. The tendency to consider these three aspects as three Persons is so strong that we have constantly to remind ourselves that there is only one Logos and not three Logoi in one. But, though there is really one Logos in His three aspects, these aspects find expression on three different planes, one lower than the other: Maheśa on the Ādi plane, Viṣṇu on the Anupādaka plane and Brahmā on the Ātmic plane. This difference in the medium of expression for the three aspects does introduce some difference in the expression of the three aspects. So, while the three aspects are the same, they are not yet quite the same.

We may conclude the consideration of this subject by pointing out the distinction between the Unmanifest Cosmic Logos who is called *Maheśvara-Maheśvari Tattva* and Maheśa who is the Presiding Deity of a manifested system. The former has been seen to be a universal unmanifest Principle

like the *Śiva-Śakti Tattva* and is the hidden source of
Cosmic Ideation and Plans for all manifested systems of all
categories. The latter is a manifest but hidden Deity on
the Ādi plane who presides over a manifested system, and,
deriving His power and plan from the universal Principle,
brings into existence a manifested system over which He
rules from behind the scenes. It is Viṣṇu, or the Second
Logos who functions actively and actually exercises all the
powers.

It has been said above that the Unmanifest Cosmic
Logos is the source of Cosmic Ideation, and it is from this
source that a manifest Logos brings His plan for the manifested system He is to bring into existence. Since the manifested Logos also has to Ideate and unfurl His plan, as it were,
it may be asked what is the difference between the two
Ideations. This difference can be illustrated very effectively
by the process which is employed in the development of a
photographic plate. When a photographic plate is exposed
to light for taking a photograph it is affected in a very subtle
manner by the light acting on the sensitive plate, but there
is still no image of any kind present on the exposed plate.
It is only when the plate is developed by putting it in a solution
of chemical substances that the image of the scene photo-
graphed appears on the plate in the well-known form of a
negative. And yet, although no image is visible in the exposed
plate before it is developed, we know that it must contain a
subtle image of some kind which is an exact duplicate of the
image in the negative, for otherwise the developer could not
bring out the image in the plate. This phenomenon can
throw some light on the relation of potential Cosmic Ideation
of the Unmanifest Cosmic Logos and the Ideation of a manifest
Logos which precipitates actually a manifested system according to the plan He has brought from within the realm of
the Unmanifest.

CHAPTER VII

THE MONAD AND THE LOGOS

(ĀTMĀ AND PARAMĀTMĀ)

THE relation of the *Jīvātmā* and *Paramātmā* or the individual soul and God is one of the mysteries of manifestation and a problem of philosophy. It cannot be conceived, it cannot be explained, but it can be realized within the depths of one's consciousness. In fact, it is considered to be the last secret which is imparted to a human being, and which liberates him from the bonds of human limitations and illusions and makes him a *Jīvanmukta*. But the fact that a mystery is beyond human comprehension does not mean that we should not think about it, and should not try to understand it as far as this is possible within the realm of the intellect.

People who talk glibly about the futility of efforts to understand, as far as this is possible, these transcendent realities of the spiritual life are not aware of the fact that it is not possible to know anything completely and really, even the simplest things which they handle and deal with every day. For everything is rooted ultimately in the One and, therefore, unless we know the Whole we cannot know any part truly and in the correct perspective. So the only consistent attitude which such people can adopt is to keep silent, cease to wonder, and abstain completely from making any effort to understand anything, least of all things pertaining to the inner life.

A little thought will show the absurdity of this attitude and the static condition of the mind to which it is bound to lead. It is because people wondered about the mysteries of life and keenly sought solutions of these deeper problems of life that they were led to probe into their minds, and developing the necessary techniques for investigating the phenomena of the mind, ultimately succeeded not only in unravelling the deeper mysteries of life but also in discovering the Reality which constitutes the heart of these mysteries.

Although we now know something theoretically about these mysteries as a result of the discoveries by those great pioneers in this field, every individual has to pass through these phases of wondering, thinking, seeking to understand, and adopting practical methods of investigation before he can unravel these mysteries of the inner life by direct realization. Trying seriously to understand these mysteries intellectually is merely a first and necessary step in the search, and provided we do not stop there it is bound to lead to the other successive steps. So if one finds himself adopting and advocating this attitude of thoughtless resignation toward the problems of life, let him ask himself whether this outwardly philosophical attitude is not a cloak to hide sheer mental laziness and indifference towards these vital problems of life which ought to worry him.

The relation of *Jīvātmā* and *Paramātmā* has been explained by means of many kinds of similes. Each of these similes brings out only one aspect of this relationship and does not fit in with the other aspects. It follows therefore that, if we examine some of these well-known similes which are used for this purpose and combine the different ideas which they respectively contribute toward the understanding of this important problem, we may be able to understand this relation to some extent as far as this is possible with our present limitations.

The relation of the Logos to the Monads is compared to that of the sun and its rays. While this simile brings out the fact that the Monads are all rooted in the Logos and derive from Him their life and consciousness, it suffers from the serious defect that it does not indicate the microcosmic nature of each Monad which makes the Monad unfold and ultimately become a Logos himself. A ray is a mere emanation and although it is part of the sun and derived from the sun, it has no potentiality to grow into a sun.

Another simile frequently used is that of a fire and the sparks which come out of it. This brings out the identity of the nature of the Logos and the Monad; and also to some extent the microcosmic nature of the Monad, for it is possible to convert a spark into a roaring fire by blowing upon it after placing it in a suitable environment. In fact, in the fourfold *Bhūta-śuddhi mantra* which is considered to be one of the most significant and profound *mantras* describing the whole process of the gradual merging of the individual consciousness with Divine Consciousness, this blowing upon the spark of the Monad by the Logos is described in the fourth *mantra* in the following graphic manner:

" *Om Parama Śiva suṣumnā-pathena mūlaśṛingātam, ullasa, ullasa, jvala, jvala, prajvala, prajvala, so 'ham, hamsah, svāhā.*

Om Supreme Śiva! blow upon, blow upon, inflame, inflame, illumine, illumine (the spiritual spark immersed in the) the mountain of matter along the path of *suṣumnā*. May the realization indicated by the maxim 'I am THAT, THAT am I' be accomplished.

The defect in this simile is that it does not show a constant continuing relation between the Logos and the Monad. Once the spark has gone out of a fire it has separated from it finally and does not maintain any relation with it which can make it grow continuously. But the Monad is a part of the Logos, is attached to Him during the whole course of his unfoldment in the solar system, appears with Him at the beginning of manifestation and becomes *laya* with Him at the time of *Pralaya*.

Perhaps the most suggestive simile used for the relation between the Logos and the Monad is that of a tree and its seed. The most striking resemblance between a seed and the Monad is the presence in both of the potentiality to grow gradually into the likeness of their parents from which they are derived. The seed grows into the likeness of the tree from which it has come when it is sown in the earth; and so does the Monad when it is sown in the soil of *Prakṛti* or matter. The former also needs the light of the physical sun for its growth, and so does the Monad need the internal pressure of the Divine Life to make it unfold all its Divine possibilities on the lower planes. This simile also like the previous ones is defective in some respects. For instance, a seed is derived from the tree into the likeness of which it grows, but the Monad is not derived from the Logos Who provides him only with a field for his unfoldment. He is derived from the *Śiva-Śakti Tattva*. Again, the seed like a spark does not maintain any constant and continuous relation with the tree from which it has come. It becomes independent of the tree.

It will be seen from the few hints which have been given above that the relation of the Monad with the Logos is very complex even when considered intellectually. Perhaps, if we think over the various similes which have been used to illustrate this relationship, we may be able to build up a concept which comes nearer the truth.

The relation of the Monad and the Logos, important and interesting as it is from the purely theoretical point of view, is of far greater significance in the field of *Sādhanā*, in understanding and organizing effectively the technique of Self-discovery. For according to the Occult doctrine, the

Reality which is the object of Self-discovery is hidden within the heart of each aspirant, and before he embarks on the voyage of Self-discovery he must at least have an intellectual map of the seas he is going to explore. It is true that there are no roads and lanes to guide us unerringly and safely to our goal, but if we have a map, it at least helps us to keep in the right direction, and to know what and where are the obstacles we are likely to meet, and how to get over them. But a map is a map and should be assessed at its real value and not be considered as a picture of the thing which we want to explore.

The whole of Reality in Its infinite depths or levels is hidden in its completeness and full splendor within each individual soul. That is why there is no limit to the level of knowledge we can gain, the degree of unfoldment we can attain. If we are to enter this realm of infinite depths we ought to have a clear and general idea of its different levels and the realities which correspond to them. If we have a correct perspective, this will prevent us from jumping to hasty and immature conclusions when we have certain experiences or attain to certain levels of consciousness. It will correct the tendency to over-simplification which goes with insufficient knowledge, and to some extent will prevent us from going off the track owing to conceit or mistaken notions.

It is true that the realities which we seek to explore are beyond the range of the intellect; but this does not mean that we cannot have and should not have a clear intellectual conception of their nature, mutual relations and the stages of progress which correspond to them. Everything has its use and place; the difficulty lies in not assessing its value properly. This is also true of intellectual knowledge.

It is possible to quote examples of people who, without making an effort to lay the foundations of intellectual knowledge, started their search and succeeded in reaching their goal. This would seem to indicate that it is really not necessary to acquire all this knowledge before undertaking the voyage of Self-discovery. This knowledge may be useless in the case of those mature souls who come with a tremendous momentum from past lives and are thus qualified to plunge directly into the divine adventure. But in the case of the ordinary and even fairly advanced *Sādhaka* it appears to be necessary. Otherwise, the whole problem of Self-discovery remains obscured by a nebulous cloud of vague ideas which not only does not provide any inspiration or encouragement to the aspirant, but also prevents him from organizing his efforts effectively. Let us use our common sense and not be carried away by emotional impulses.

Though all states of consciousness right up to the Ultimate Reality are hidden, layer after layer, behind the Centre of our consciousness and can be reached theoretically, the problem is not as easy and natural as it appears on the surface, because the whole process of unfoldment of consciousness and evolution of vehicles is involved in it. These inner states of consciousness are not distant in the sense of physical distance but by virtue of their subtlety. A state of consciousness or reality may be nearest in the sense that it is hidden within the very core or Centre of our being, and yet be infinitely distant by its being extremely subtle, beyond the reach of our highest consciousness. Distances are of many kinds. The distance which can be measured by physical means is only one of them and is the lowest aspect of remoteness. There is the distance of lack of sympathy on the emotional plane. Two people may be living together and yet be at an enormous distance from each other by their lack of affinity, while two others may be extremely near to each other while living poles apart. Then there is the distance of the lack of response which operates on the mental plane. A thought is distant from us according to the difficulty of our responding to it. If our mind cannot respond to it, we are really very distant from it though it may be present in our mind in the form of a formulated idea. But the subtlest kind of distance is in the realm of consciousness. This kind of distance depends upon our ability to suppress all intermediate levels of mental action and fuse our consciousness with the reality which we want to know by direct perception.

As this kind of distance is of great importance to us in the task of Self-discovery let us try to understand it by means of an illustration. Suppose a yogi sits down to meditate and wants to reach a particular level of consciousness, e.g. the Ātmic consciousness which is hidden beneath the astral, mental and buddhic levels. If he is an Adept he can instantaneously stop the activity on all the intermediate levels and can rise immediately to the Ātmic level. This is what an Adept does when he wants to be centred in his Monadic consciousness. The Ātmic level may thus be considered to be very near the level of His physical consciousness. The arrangement and relation of the different bodies and the corresponding levels of consciousness are just the same in the case of the ordinary man who tries to meditate. But the intervening levels of his mind are an insuperable barrier in his case, and therefore, the Atmic consciousness, though it is the very core and centre of his being also, is very distant from his personality.

It is in this sense that we must understand distances between us and these tremendous expressions of the One Reality which we denote by words like Solar Logos, Cosmic Logos, Śiva-Śakti, etc. All these Realities are no doubt hidden in the deeper levels of consciousness of every individual soul who has the Divine spark within him; but these Realities are so subtle compared to other expressions of Reality with which we are familiar that the nearer they are to the Centre of our being the more distant they become by reason of their transcendental subtlety.

How near an aspirant is to his goal is a question he might well ask, because very few people can know the potentiality hidden within themselves by virtue of the unfoldment which has already taken place in previous lives and which has merely to be recapitulated in this life. In such a case the progress up to the stage reached in the previous lives is generally very rapid unless there are some special obstacles or *Karma* causing temporary obstruction.

Patanjali gives in one *sutra* a criterion to determine how near one is to the goal which he has set before himself in the realm of his inner being.

This *sutra* is: *tīvra-samvegānām āsannah* (I. 21)

'It is nearest to those whose desire is intensely strong.'

So here we have a definite means to determine our potential for success in this realm—the intensity of desire. By the intensity of desire we can in a way measure the distance from our object and to a great extent also our capacity to gain that object. For intensity of desire is nothing but an outward index of our inner potential upon which our progress depends. And when that potential reaches a certain high level of intensity all barriers are broken down and we and the object of our search become one. It is just like a bolt of lightning which strikes across the intervening air when the potential difference between the charge of electricity on the cloud and on the earth crosses the critical limit. We will see, therefore, that an intense desire is a kind of harbinger of the experiences to come later in our life. That is why *mumukṣhutva* or intensity of desire is one of the four qualifications on the Path of Liberation.

But we must try to understand these things carefully and not come to any hasty and immature conclusions. It is true that our progress and capacity are indicated to a great extent by the intensity of our desire; but the intensity of desire is not an invariable factor in our lives. It may shoot up very rapidly if there are *samskaras* or previous *Karma* holding us back when these *samskaras* are exhausted. We generally have to intensify this desire gradually by adopting the right means of doing so, but the factor of the unpredictable in life is always there. So there is no cause for pessimism in the case of those whose desire is not sufficiently strong in the present.

No one can really know his potentiality and his future until he has tried and not even then. For we may continue to try again and again and fail every time and then suddenly find that success is in our grasp. The only sensible attitude to adopt on this Path is to continue to strive to the utmost, patiently and perseveringly, hoping for the best and being prepared for the worst. It is this kind of attitude and endeavor which spells success in the long run. After all, no one can take away from us our birthright to know the Reality within us; and if we are really sincere and serious about these things time seems to matter less and less as we progress. It is only when we are not serious and truly interested in these things that time hangs heavy on our hands, and we ask all kinds of artificial questions but do not really care if they are answered. When we ask a question sincerely with regard to spiritual matters it is answered generally though not through words but through an experience which makes the question unnecessary.

It may appear as if I have been discussing matters which are not really connected with the subject under discussion. But deeper thought will show that this is not so. The discovery of the Reality within us is the most important aspect of the relation between the Monad and the Logos to which all other aspects are subordinate, and therefore discussion of the factors which are involved in this discovery is of the greatest importance to every aspirant.

Let us now come back to the subject and consider the relation of the Monad and the Logos from a different point of view. Those of us who have carefully studied the doctrines of the Ancient Wisdom, and have understood the nature of the manifested universe to some extent, will see that, despite the multiplicity of planes and states of mind and consciousness, there are really only three worlds existing side by side inter-penetrating one another. These are (1) the world of matter, (2) the world of mind and (3) the world of pure conscious-ness. The worlds of matter and mind exist in several states of density or subtlety; while the world of pure consciousness is one homogeneous undifferentiated Reality. Our mind is so taken up by the multiplicity of planes and sub-planes that it fails to realize that in reality there is only one world of matter of different densities. Similarly, although the mind does exist in several degrees of subtlety there is only one world of the mind. These different degrees of subtlety are produced by the differentiation of consciousness as a world of colours is produced by the differentiation of white light. Pure consciousness exists only as a homogeneous integrated state, like white light before it enters a prism and is dispersed by it into different colours.

If this idea has been grasped it will be seen that the three worlds mentioned above are the very basis and substance of the manifested universe. The world of matter provides the stimula-tion and a mechanism for the mind to work with and is there-fore the real basis of the objective universe. The world of consciousness provides the very substratum of the whole mani-fested universe and is also the ultimate basis of the subjective side of manifestation. The world of the mind springs forth from the interaction of the two worlds of consciousness and matter. Being derived from both these worlds it partakes of the nature of both and is thus dual in its character acting both as subject and object. As the centre of consciousness recedes inwards, the boundary between the subjective and objective recedes progressively towards the Centre, and what was subjective becomes objective in its turn, until only the Subjective remains.

In this triple world of matter, mind and consciousness are scattered all the Monads who are rooted in the world of consciousness, and are functioning in the world of matter through a complete set of vehicles on all the planes. The mental world of each Monad, in all its complexity and diversity and grades of subtlety, is produced by the interaction between his underlying consciousness, and the world of matter around him through the instrumentality of his bodies on the different planes.

It will be seen from what has been said above that the relation between the Logos and the Monad can be studied from three different points of view, i.e. from the point of view of the vehicles, from the point of view of consciousness and from the point of view of the mind. We shall deal with the relation with respect to the bodies and consciousness in the next chapter when we consider the total constitution of the Monad. Here we shall confine ourselves to the relation between the Logos and the Monad with respect to mental phenomena alone, using the word mental in its widest sense and including all degrees of subtlety in which the mind can exist below the realm of pure Consciousness. For, the world of the mind is the only world which the ordinary man knows really, and it is only this world in which our relation to the Logos is experienced directly. The other two worlds we know only by inference and intuition until we are in the realm of the white Light of Reality and can see this Light as the source of both mind and matter.

Now, the important point to note in considering the world of the mind is that this world, in which we live and which alone we are aware of directly, is the result of the combination of two sets of phenomena which are interwoven but which we can separate to some extent if we do a little introspection. One set of phenomena is produced by the impact of the world around us on our mind, and the other set by the activity of our individual mind itself. The rising and setting of the sun and other natural phenomena, as well as the movements of people and things in our environment, produce a series of mental images which are independent of the activity of our own mind. But these images are mixed up with the images produced by our own mind, independently of the external world. So we see that these two sets of images, each having a different source, combine to make our total mental world throughout our life, generally without our being even aware of this fact.

What is the source of these two sets of mental images? If we think carefully about the matter, we shall realize that the source of the former is the consciousness of the Logos, Who through the Universal Mind has produced the manifested world, which produces a constant impact on all individual minds. The source of the latter is the consciousness of the Monad who has a set of vehicles functioning on all the planes. These two streams of white light, passing through the prism of manifestation, produce their respective beams of coloured lights on the other side, and it is the mingling and interaction of these two beams in the field of our consciousness which produce our composite and complex mental world.

As this idea is rather subtle and difficult to grasp, one can imagine two beams of white light having different sources and different intensities passing through a prism simultaneously and emerging on the other side as a mixture of two beams of coloured lights. The coloured beam derived from the infinitely stronger source is the Universal Mind; and the coloured beam derived from the much weaker source is the individual mind of the Monad working on the different planes.

We may consider another interesting inference from this experiment. Suppose the beam of coloured light from the weaker source representing the Monad is suppressed by some means in any realm of manifestation. What will happen in such a case? Only the beam of coloured light derived from the stronger source representing the Universal Mind will remain in its purity, unpolluted by the other beam. This is *Sabīja Samādhi* whereby we realize the reality of any object in the world of Relativity. Only the Universal Mind which contains all these relative realities remains and the yogi, whose individual modifications of the mind or *citta-vrittis* have been suppressed, knows directly the reality of the particular object as it exists in the Universal Mind.

Let us now go one step further and imagine the centre of consciousness passing through the prism and emerging on the other side in which there is only the undifferentiated white light. What will happen then? There is only white light on that side, and the white light of the weak source can mix with the white light of the stronger source without producing any pollution or debasement. There cannot be two varieties of white light though there can be two intensities. So the realization of the Monad on his own plane of pure consciousness which is above the plane of the mind is direct, unobscured and pure, even though there are two sources of white light existing side by side. The consciousness of the Monad mingles with the consciousness of the Logos and yet is separate and we have duality in unity. This is the *Nirbīja Samādhi* which leads to *Kaivalya* or Liberation. These are subtle ideas which will require deep thought and reflection but if one can grasp them even partially he cannot but be filled with wonder and exaltation of spirit.

CHAPTER VIII

THE MONAD

(ĀTMĀ OR PURUṢA)

THE relation of the Monad with the Logos has already been discussed in the previous chapter. We saw that this relation could be truly known only through an inner realization in which the Monad is established in his true nature which is the same in essence as the nature of the Logos. As far as intellectual comprehension is concerned we considered a few similes each of which brings out some aspects of this mysterious relationship, but is found deficient in other respects. We also considered the mental phenomena which result from the interaction of the Universal Mind and the individual mind and produce our respective mental worlds. We shall now pass on to the consideration of the Monad as a centre of Divine life and consciousness in the three aspects of body, mind and consciousness and try to gain some comprehension of his true nature as well as that of his expressions on the lower planes of manifestation.

The first point we have to note is that the Monad is triple in his nature like the Logos, and the triplicity of his nature is reflected even in his expressions on the lower planes of manifestation. This triplicity is not a special attribute which the Monad shows like the Logos. It is a part of the microcosmic nature which he has inherited from his Divine Parents. So let us first dwell for a while on the microcosmic nature of the Monad, to understand what it signifies and how it finds expression in innumerable ways in his expressions on the lower planes.

The relation of a macrocosm with a microcosm is a very interesting question, not only because it throws light on many natural processes and phenomena but also because it enables us, through the help of analogy, to infer certain attributes or principles pertaining to the macrocosm. Many concepts which we find in the field of Science have been unnecessarily deprived of their most profound significance on account of this lack of knowledge concerning the relation between the microcosm and macrocosm.

A scientist sees and studies many natural processes empirically and is struck by the wonderful potentiality and intelligence which seem to underlie these processes. But he stops there and does not ask the natural question: ' why '? And so he is never able to understand the inner significance and beauty of the process. Knowledge which has been gained through Occultism throws light on the inner driving and guiding forces which underlie all natural phenomena and processes, and thus makes our conceptions of natural phenomena far more meaningful, rich and beautiful, although they may lack the dry and detailed information which generally forms part of scientific knowledge.

Before we proceed further let us ask the question: What is a macrocosm? We may say generally that it is a manifestation of any kind which involves a definite structure, the structure being vitalized and activated according to a set of laws working uniformly and invariably in all its spheres and aspects. The whole living mechanism is guided and controlled by a single unit of life or consciousness, and follows a uniform and predetermined pattern in its growth and modes of expression. What is a microcosm? It is a smaller unit of the same kind but in an undeveloped state. It contains, in a potential form, all the powers and capacities which can be developed by a process of evolution in an environment which provides the necessary conditions of growth, and under the pressure of an indwelling life which provides all the motive power and plan for that growth. A seed, as we have seen, is a good example of a microcosm although it does not illustrate the microcosmic nature of the Monad in every respect.

In considering the relationship existing between a microcosm and a macrocosm, it is necessary to remember that it is the underlying principle or life embodied in the outer form, which is reflected in the microcosm; and that the outer structure may or may not show any points of resemblance in a particular case, though this happens frequently. If we go behind the outer structures and examine the principles, potentialities and tendencies inherent in the outer form, we shall always be able to see a strong resemblance between the functions and modes of expression of the macrocosm and the microcosm.

An illustration will make this point clear. A human being is a microcosmic representation of a solar system. In both cases there is a centre of consciousness operating and functioning through a set of vehicles and guiding the vehicles in their functional activities. If we take the physical solar system and the physical body of man there is hardly any resemblance between the two, but there is a functional resemblance which will startle anybody who studies it for the first time.

It is not necessary to deal here in detail with this question but a few facts which show the microcosm-macrocosm relationship between the Monad and the Logos may be pointed out:

1. In both cases there is an eternal Centre of consciousness functioning on seven planes through a set of seven vehicles. In Hinduism they adopt a fivefold system of classification because the highest two planes are considered Divine and not really in manifestation.

2. In both cases the vehicles are functioning within larger and subtler planes which provide the basis and the field for evolution—cosmic planes in the case of the Logos; solar planes in the case of the Monad.

3. In both cases the lower vehicles undergo a more frequent alternation of manifestation and dissolution than the higher ones.

4. The sun pumps vitality and other types of energy throughout the solar system, as the heart pumps the vital blood throughout the physical body.

5. Not only does the Monad show a triple nature like the Logos but even his limited expressions in the form of the individuality and personality show this triple nature, and function generally as a microcosm in relation to the Monad.

We could take aspect after aspect of this interesting relationship between the Monad and the Logos but it is not necessary to go into further details here. We are concerned chiefly with the constitution of the Monad.

The total constitution of man has been dealt with very thoroughly in Theosophical literature and much interesting and detailed information is available about this subject of such vital interest to students of the Divine Wisdom. The following salient features of man's total constitution may be noted:

1. In spite of the multiplicity of vehicles and great differences in the nature of manifestations through them, the consciousness functioning through them is one and the same.

2. As we go from the periphery to the centre, the vehicles become less and less material and complex, and consciousness becomes increasingly predominant and all-inclusive.

3. Although the different vehicles of a particular Monad are on different planes, and the manifestation of consciousness

working through them differs from plane to plane, they function in sets of three. Consciousness working in each set as a
whole is a unity, although this unity is subordinate to, and
is contained within the larger unity of the next higher manifestation. This fact is illustrated in the following diagram
which shows the constitution and mutual relation of the three
components of our total constitution—the personality, the
individuality and the Monad.

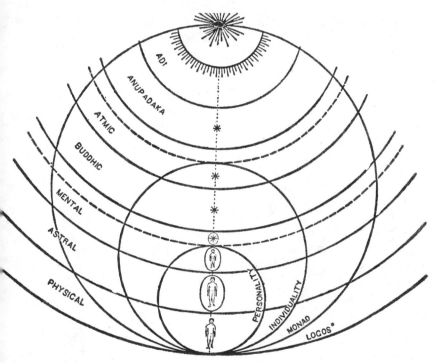

FIG. 8.   The Monad, the Individuality and the Personality

4.   The lowest component of our constitution, the personality, is that limited human consciousness which works
through the physical, astral and lower mental bodies, and
therefore changes completely with every new incarnation.

5. The next higher component is the individuality, also called the Ego or Higher Self, which works through the causal, Buddhic and Ātmic vehicles. He represents the spiritual element in man and is the immortal Self who endures from life to life, and gradually unfolds all the mental and spiritual attributes and powers from within himself during the long period of human evolution.

6. But even this immortal Self who is the spiritual element in us is not the highest aspect of our nature. Within him abides the eternal Monad, the *Puruṣa* of the Sāṃkhyan philosophy; that mysterious Being whom we cannot really understand though he is the very core of our being. The Ego is immortal, and though he has an immeasurably long life as compared with the personality, still, because he came into existence at a particular time with the formation of the causal body, he too, sometime or other, must also cease to be. But the Monad is above time and lives in the eternal. It is he who is one in essence with the Solar Logos and having his root on the Ādi plane and the Centre of consciousness on the Anupādaka plane overshadows and influences the individuality on the Ātmic plane. What appears as evolution and unfoldment of the individuality on the lower planes is, in some mysterious manner, eternally present within the Monad and is unfolded in some way which we cannot understand.

After this brief review of the total constitution of man we might deal with a few important problems regarding the nature of the Monad. It has already been pointed out in a previous chapter that the unfoldment of the Monad has no limit. "The soul of man is immortal and its future is the future of a thing whose growth and splendour has no limit," as has been stated in *The Idyll of the White Lotus*. The ultimate destiny of the Monad is to become a Solar Logos; and even as a Logos his consciousness continues to expand on the cosmic planes in a manner which is utterly incomprehensible to us.

The question arises: if the consciousness of the Monad is to expand *ad infinitum* and to approach, but never to reach the Consciousness of the Cosmic Logos, what about the doctrine of the complete merging of the individual consciousness with the Divine Consciousness, which is taken for granted in Hindu philoscphy and religion as well as in other religions? The phrase used in *The Light of Asia* is ' The dew-drop slips into the shining sea!' suggesting that the consciousness of the liberated person merges with the Ultimate Reality on attaining Nirvāṇa; and the individual uniqueness developed in the unfoldment of the consciousness is completely lost for ever. For, obviously we cannot get back a drop from an ocean, after it has been allowed to mix with the water of the ocean.

Now, all the facts revealed in the Occult doctrine point to the eternal continuance of the individuality with its uniqueness. The very word *eternal* used for the Monad would be meaningless if at any stage in the unfoldment of his consciousness the individuality was completely and irreversibly merged with a Universal Principle. It is a well-known doctrine of Occult philosophy that, at the time of a *Mahāpralaya*, all the Logoi and Monads become reabsorbed in the Unmanifest and again emerge when the manifestation of a new cosmos takes place. If the Monads can pass into the Unmanifest and come out again into manifestation on the birth of a new cosmos, it is obvious that they retain their individual uniqueness in the Unmanifest even during the period of a *Mahāpralaya*. So the doctrine of complete mergence of the individuality from which there cannot be its re-emergence in the world of manifestation is quite untenable and must be given a decent burial once for all.

Then, how are we to reconcile the continuation of the individuality with its uniqueness with the destruction of the ' I ' consciousness which seems to be a necessary condition for Self-realization? I think the paradox can be easily understood on the basis of the assumption that the individuality can exist in infinite grades of subtlety like everything else. As the unfoldment of consciousness proceeds, the coarser forms of individuality with their undesirable concomitants are shed, one after another, and the subtler forms emerge with the expansion of consciousness and the enlargement of the circle which limits our life and love. This process can continue *ad infinitum* as the following diagram illustrates to some extent.

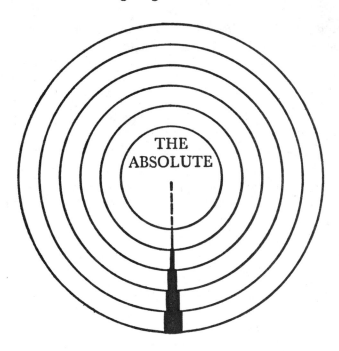

FIG. 9.   The Progressive Attenuation of ' I ' Consciousness

We see in this diagram a number of concentric circles one within the other, and a radial line connecting the centre with the outermost circle. Now, if the thickness of parts of the radial line between the successive circles beginning with the outermost, represents the coarseness of the individuality, we see how this thickness can go on decreasing as the radial line approaches the centre. We know what is the limit which a line which progressively becomes thinner and thinner approaches—an ideal line which has no thickness at all, but only direction. An *actual* line can, according to mathematics, only approach this limit more and more without ever reaching it.

We may imagine that the ideal portions of all the radial lines which represent different Monads are present in the Unmanifest, and that all these ideal lines, which are the continuations of the actual lines in manifestation, meet at the ideal centre which represents the Absolute. As it is possible to have an ideal line without thickness, so it should also be possible to have individuality without egoism or any of its subtler forms in the higher worlds. Therefore, individual uniqueness and utter egolessness are perfectly compatible and it is not necessary to assume the complete destruction of individuality in order to attain a state in which consciousness embraces everything in a manifested system.

It will be seen that it is not the radial lines which can impose a limitation on a centre because they leave the centre free to expand *ad infinitum*. It is the circumference which imposes limitation on the centre. This circumference can be considered to become larger and larger as the radial line representing the individuality of the Monad approaches the ideal limit of zero thickness. When the circumference expands to infinity the line becomes an ideal line in the realm of the Unmanifest.

So, by this simple mathematical analysis which is symbolic in character we can resolve the paradox of the co-existence of individual uniqueness with an ever expanding consciousness which ultimately embraces the whole cosmos in the last stage.

The same kind of mathematical symbol and analysis will also throw some light on the problem of the co-existence of Oneness and Manyness in the Divine Consciousness. In fact the two problems are merely two aspects of the same problem. Let us imagine a centre from which innumerable radial lines diverge, as shown in Fig. 10.

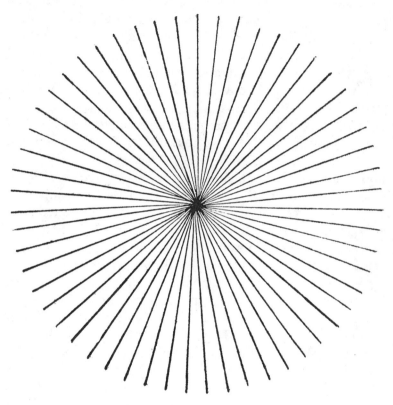

FIG. 10. The One and the Many

Does the figure indicate Oneness or Manyness? Both. If we consider only the centre it indicates Oneness. The moment we leave the centre it indicates Manyness. The further we move away from the centre the more do the radial lines diverge, indicating greater and greater separation in consciousness. A closer examination of the figure will show that there is a still subtler Oneness than the Oneness in the centre

and that this over-all Oneness includes the Manyness also.
For, if the figure is considered as a whole, including both
centre and radial lines, it is still the representation of the
One Reality. The above example shows why a knowledge
of mathematics was required for initiation into the mysteries
of the Pythagorean schools.

A very interesting and intriguing aspect of the problem
revealed by this figure is the mergence of the many points
which approach the centre along the radial lines meeting
in the centre. How can an infinite number of points each
approaching along a separate line be accommodated in
the centre without being thrown out of the dimension in
which they are proceeding? Here we see the marvellous
nature of a point which has zero dimension and can therefore
accommodate any number of points entering from worlds of
any number of dimensions. And since this point of zero
dimension represents the Absolute this mathematical analysis
brings out another aspect of the Absolute, as not only the
harmonious synthesis of all principles, *tattvas*, etc. but also
a harmonious and mysterious integration of all the Monads,
with their infinite variety of individual uniqueness.

We see thus that the individual uniquenesses of Monads
with their infinite variety are merely the differentiated aspects
of the Ultimate Reality. The Absolute is thus not only
the harmonious synthesis of all the principles, *tattvas*, etc.
which constitute the paraphernalia of manifestation but also
the harmonious synthesis of all the fragments of the Spirit
which is Eternal and above manifestation. This is the final
and ultimate synthesis which justifies the sacred maxim:

Sarvam khalv idam Brahma—' Verily, all this is Brahman.'

Another question which requires careful thought is the
doctrine of Sāṃkhyan philosophy that the *Puruṣa* or the
Monad is a mere witness or spectator of the drama which is
being played by *Prakṛti* for his instruction. This is one of

the weak points of the philosophy and the idea is considered to have been introduced in the philosophy for the sake of philosophical consistency. But in trying to keep the philosophy in harmony with the needs of logic its expounders have done a greater violence to reason than assigning an active role to the *Puruṣa* would have done.

The question whether the *Puruṣa* is a mere passive witness of the drama which is being played round him and for him, or also has the complementary active role is easily answered if we examine the process of evolution of bodies and unfoldment of consciousness. From the earliest stages both the active and passive functions go side by side. Thus we have the *jñānendriyas* and *karmendriyas* in the physical body as instruments of the cognitive and conative functions of consciousness. Then later on when the consciousness is transferred to the spiritual planes as a result of Yogic practices the two powers which are simultaneously developed in the advanced stages of the practice are *Pratibhā* and *Vikaraṇabhāva*, non-instrumental perception and non-instrumental action. At a still higher stage when the *Puruṣa* attains *Kaivalya* or Self-realization both Omniscience and Omnipotence appear as a result of this realization. Still further along the path of the unfoldment of consciousness when the Monad becomes a Solar Logos, He is not only the *Sarva-sākṣi* or the All-pervading Witness of everything in the solar system, but also the active Ruler or *Īśvara* of the solar system. Where then in these series of progressive unfoldments, in which the active and passive functions always go side by side, is there room for the Sāṃkhyan doctrine of the *Puruṣa* being a mere witness of what is taking place around him? Even in the case of the Absolute to whom any active function or action cannot be attributed we have to assume the absence of both the functions and not only one of them, because in It all opposites are harmoniously blended to produce a Void or perfectly neutral state.

In spite of this overwhelming evidence and the needs of reason and common sense the validity of the Sāṃkhyan doctrine is taken for granted and it is being promulgated century after century. So enamoured do we become of ideas that we are loath to discard them even when we find them untenable. Academic philosophy continues to play with ideas because it has moved away from the true ideal of philosophy which should be the search for Truth. Modern philosophy is becoming more and more bogged down in a welter of futile and artificial elaboration of philosophical concepts and the only way in which it can be redeemed is by again placing the pursuit of Truth as its ideal and aim.

Another interesting question we may consider before closing the subject is: Who is Liberated? We have all along been talking of Liberation as the present goal of human evolution and it is pertinent to ask after considering the constitution and nature of the Monad what Liberation really means. Is it the personality which is liberated from the bonds of illusion and human limitations when *Jivanmukti* is attained? Obviously not, because the personality is a mere shadow, a temporary expression of the Ego or the Individuality in the lowest three worlds for gaining experiences of various kinds and developing certain faculties which become a permanent part of the immortal Ego who functions through *Ātma-buddhi-manas*. After its work is over it gradually disappears completely without leaving any trace except the essence of its experiences and a memory of its past existence in the mind of the Ego.

Then, is the Ego or *Jivātmā* Liberated on attaining Enlightenment or Nirvāṇa? Superficially considered, we might attribute this attainment to the Ego because he is relatively a permanent entity and endures through all the series of his incarnations as personalities. But we have to remember that the Ego is also only relatively permanent because whatever has a beginning in time must also have an end in time. The

Ego comes into existence when individualization takes place and there must be a time when his life also comes to an end. When this takes place will depend upon the path chosen by the Monad after attaining Self-realization or liberation from the bonds of matter. If his work needs the bodies on the spiritual planes, the outer form of the Ego continues to remain in existence merely as an instrument of the Monad on these planes. If the work, on the other hand, is on still higher planes the lower bodies are dropped temporarily or permanently according to the work which has to be done. But since the Monad has ultimately to become a Solar Logos, the Ego must also disappear at one stage or another.

We see thus that the Liberation is really not even for the Ego but for the Monad. It is he who was involved in manifestation and it is he, therefore, who after the evolution and unfoldment has been completed, must get liberated from the subtlest illusions and limitations of manifestation. But as he is Eternal and not in time, and on his plane is always aware of his divine nature, in spite of involvement on the lower planes, we should be careful to understand the significance of Liberation in the case of such a being. It really should mean that the part of him involved in manifestation realizes its true nature, can exercise the powers which accompany such realization, and becomes one with the part which was always free and aware of his divine nature. We have seen already in chapter V that when a Principle is involved in a lower state of manifestation only a part is involved, the rest remaining free.

The personality and the Individuality associated with a Monad are not independent entities but only partial expressions of the Monad on the lower planes, a projection of his consciousness into these planes. When Self-realization takes place, it fuses these three elements far more intimately into a unity of consciousness which was not present before. So, the personality and the Individuality also share this realization to the extent of their capacity and as long as they last. We may say, therefore, that although it is neither the personality, nor the Individuality which is Liberated they nevertheless share in the fruits of Liberation as long as they last.

Allied to the question ' Who is Liberated? ' is the other question ' Who brings about Liberation? ' Here again it is obvious that it is not the personality which can do so; for a thing which is involved in illusion and tremendous limitations cannot get out of these limitations solely by its own efforts. All it can do is to aspire upwards and bring down the forces and guidance which lead to Liberation. It can co-operate in this work or cause hindrance, but not much and not for long. For, when the proper time has come and the Monad wills to be liberated, the puny personality cannot stand against his will. ' Then with pain and desperate cries from the deserted lower self he will return,' as stated in *Light on the Path.*

The same remarks apply to the Ego in a different sense. As he is not involved in gross illusions and limitations like the personality he does not cause serious resistance to the will of the Monad. But the upward urge and drive really come from the Monad even in his case. If a magnet is moved below a sheet of paper on which iron filings are scattered, the iron filings seem to move of their own free will, but we know that it is the magnet from which the motive power is really derived.

CHAPTER IX

INDIVIDUALITY, INDIVIDUAL UNIQUENESS AND RAY OF THE MONAD—I

It is necessary for the aspirant to study carefully the Occult doctrines regarding the three attributes of the human soul which form the title of this chapter. Unless his ideas with regard to them are clear and well-defined his efforts in the task of mastering his lower nature are likely to be misdirected and lead to waste of time and energy. He ought to know what is possible and what is not possible and how what is possible can be achieved.

A great deal of confusion is prevalent with regard to these important questions on account of the conflicting ideas current about the nature of the human soul and the inability on the part of the student to distinguish between the false and the true. Many of these ideas are based on the uncertain speculations of academic philosophers or religious beliefs found in orthodox creeds. They are not based on knowledge of facts concerning the realities of life. Such knowledge is available only to Occultists who have investigated thoroughly the deepest problems of life, have discovered the truths underlying them by direct experience within the depths of their own mind and consciousness and have tried to communicate this transcendent knowledge to others as far as this is possible through the medium of language. Reliable knowledge concerning the nature and destiny of the human soul can therefore be found only in Occultism or doctrines which are based on Occultism.

One always feels hesitant in using the word occultism for this accumulated Wisdom gathered through the ages by a long line of mystics and occultists and preserved intact and undebased by infallible methods which need not be discussed here. The word occultism has very unpleasant and frequently wrong associations in the mind of the average educated man of today and stands for dark practices such as witchcraft, voodoo, telepathy, mind-reading, seances, black magic and the murky, suspicious atmosphere associated with them.

These practices are not based on superstition as many sceptical and naïve people assume without studying and investigating these things. There is a basis of some truth in these phenomena and practices based on them though there is also a great deal of fraud and charlatanism and superstition associated with them. But the important fact to keep in mind is that true Occultism, the Sacred Science which stands for real and transcendent knowledge of the highest truths of Nature and the practice of the purest spirituality and altruism, has nothing to do with the psuedo-occultism with which it is confused. And those who are seriously trying to understand the deeper problems of life should not allow these prejudices and misconceptions which exist in the public mind with regard to so-called occultism to stand in the way of their examining and studying genuine Occultism. For, to do so would mean cutting themselves off from the only source of true and reliable knowledge regarding the deeper secrets of Nature and the unfathomable nature and glorious destiny of the human soul. The only alternative to this knowledge is the uncertain and indefinite knowledge provided by academic philosophy and orthodox religion or wandering in the desert of rank materialistic philosophy or agnosticism in a futile search for the waters of life which lure the seeker like a mirage. This may appear like a tall claim for true Occultism but the enquirer is not asked to take things on blind faith. Let him examine this claim with an open mind and come to his own independent conclusion. Truth has nothing to fear from the most searching scrutiny provided the scrutiny and enquiry is motivated by a genuine and earnest desire to know the truth.

Before we go deeply into this interesting subject it would be worth while explaining very briefly in a general way what is meant by individuality, individual uniqueness and the ray of a Monad as understood in Occultism.

Individuality may be considered as that centre in the human soul which acts as an indestructible focus through which the mind and consciousness function and the potentialities hidden within it gradually become active powers. Both the origin and the ultimate destination of a Monad are shrouded in a mystery and hidden from our view, but as far as we can see downwards and upwards we see a Monad existing and evolving endlessly to greater and greater heights of knowledge and power. That Eternal centre of consciousness round which the life of a Monad revolves and evolves, ever changing, ever growing, may be called his individuality. It ever remains the same and yet never remains the same.

Individual uniqueness may be defined as that fundamental nature in each Monad which determines for all time his expression and evolution in manifestation and distinguishes it from the expression and manifestation of all other Monads. As all Monads are essentially of the nature of Reality, what distinguishes one Monad from another Monad can be only the modes of expression or manifestation and the different paths which are followed in the unfoldment of his consciousness and powers. Each soul must evolve according to the law of its being and must express the pattern of its eternal nature in terms of time and space. This law by its very nature must be inviolable and the pattern inexhaustible so as to provide for the unending and ever new experiences. The

tremendous nature of this eternal pattern hidden within each
Monad can be judged from the fact that each Monad is
destined ultimately to become a Solar Logos in the course
of his unending unfoldment and to continue even further
His own unfoldment in the unimaginable realms of the cosmic
planes. All these expressions which arise from and conform
to his eternal pattern really constitute his individual
uniqueness.

Although all Monads are individually unique, still, it has
been found that they can be divided into seven groups according to the modes of their expression and the different paths
followed in the unfoldment of their consciousness and powers.
In other words, they may be said to belong to seven types,
the Monads belonging to one type showing certain common
characteristics in the lower stages of unfoldment and playing
similar roles in the drama of manifestation when they have
evolved to a higher stage. These seven types or groups into
which all Monads are divisible in spite of their individual
uniqueness are called ' rays '.

After having obtained a general idea with regard to the
above three fundamental attributes of the human soul let us
now go deeper into the subject and try to understand their
inner significance in the light of the Occult doctrine and with
the help of facts discovered by Science. For, the realities of
spiritual life are reflected in the phenomena of the physical
plane and we can enlarge our knowledge of the former by
studying the latter.

As the question of ' rays ' is closely connected with that
of individual uniqueness we shall first consider the relation
between the two. In order to understand the nature of the
two and the relation which exists between them nothing is
more helpful than the study of the phenomenon of dispersion
of white light by a prism. This differentiation as we all
know produces a spectrum of coloured lights which are visible
and the spectrums of infra-red and ultra-violet radiations

which are invisible but can be detected by suitable means. Confining ourselves to the visible spectrum for the moment we can represent the differentiation or dispersion of white light by the diagram given in chapter I (Fig. 1).

Science tells us that though there are seven colours in the visible spectrum, all different from one another, (violet, indigo, blue, green, yellow, orange, red) there are really only three primary colours and the seven colours are produced by the different combinations of the three according to the septenary law indicated by the numbers 1,2,3,12,13,23,123. We have three primary colours in the spectrum (blue, red, yellow) three colours produced by the mixture of two primary colours (green, orange, violet) and one colour produced by the combination of all three primary colours (indigo). There is a slight discrepancy in the nature of this seventh colour but we need not enter into this mystery here.

Science also tells us that although we see separate colours spread out in the spectrum it is really a continuous band of electro-magnetic vibrations merging into one another. There are no gaps separating one vibration from a contiguous one or an irregularity indicating a transition from one colour to another. Each of this series of vibrations is indicated by a number called a wave-length, but this is so only for the sake of convenience in identifying them and measuring them exactly. The wave-lengths are based on an arbitrary unit adopted as a standard of measurement and a different unit will give another series of wave-lengths. Actually, the vibrations cannot be separated from one another and we may thus suppose that an infinite number of vibrations having characteristic wave-lengths are arranged in a series in the visible spectrum alone. The whole phenomenon is a mystery which Science has not been able to unravel so far.

We are not concerned here with the nature of these vibrations and the mystery which surrounds them. We are concerned only with the fact that the band of coloured lights constituting the spectrum is basically nothing but a continuous series of vibrations, each vibration having its own individual wave-length which characterizes it and can thus identify it. So that the moment we mention a wave-length we know to which part of the spectrum it belongs and what colour it can produce when it strikes the human eye.

We should also note that the seven colours in the spectrum which are derived from the three primary colours are a purely mental phenomenon produced in the mind and these divisions and classifications do not exist in the vibrations themselves which form a continuous series. If we consider the vibrations objectively as mathematical entities we see no transition from one colour to another colour or division into seven groups of colours merging into one another. The objective and subjective aspects of the phenomenon may be represented by the following figure in which the continuous progressive series of vibrations and the corresponding colours are shown side by side.

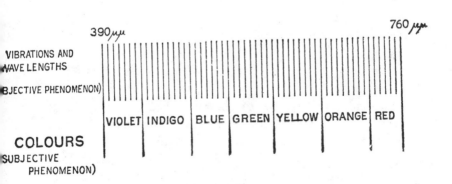

We see from what has been said above that an infinite number of light vibrations, each with its characteristic wavelength is divisible into seven groups derived from the primary colours according to the septenary law. We also see that the fact of individual uniqueness of vibrations is more fundamental and goes deeper. Each vibration is first unique and

then belongs to one of seven groups according as it affects
the human eye.

The above light phenomenon is almost a perfect reflection
or illustration of the two truths which form part of the Occult
doctrine, namely, that each Monad is individually unique and
unlike any other Monad; and each Monad belongs to one
of seven groups or rays which determines his character in
the widest sense of the term and the nature of the role he will
play in the drama of manifestation during the long and almost
unending course of his spiritual unfoldment. It is true that
this role is confined within our own solar system in the early
stages of his unfoldment but we have to remember that he
has ultimately to become a Solar Logos and play a far more
tremendous role in the vaster drama of the universe. We can
also see, as in the case of the analogous light phenomenon,
that the individual uniqueness of the Monad is a primary
truth and the classification into seven groups or rays, as
these groups are called, is a secondary truth if we may put
it in this way.

What is the basis of the classification into seven groups or
rays? Or, to put it in other words, how do the seven rays
differ from one another? There is a mystery surrounding this
question but I think a reasonable solution of the problem can
be found on the basis of the three aspects of consciousness
which are denoted by the Sanskrit words *Sat-Cit-Ānanda*.
Wherever we find a group of seven things we should always
look for a group of three primary things from which the
seven things are derived by different combinations of the
three things according to the septenary law. We noted in
the case of the seven colours of the spectrum that these colours
are related to consciousness and are of a subjective character.
There is nothing in the vibrations themselves to justify their
division into seven groups. It is when the vibrations affect
consciousness and are converted into sensations that they can
be divided into seven groups. So we have to look for a basis

of this grouping into seven colours or seven rays in the realm of consciousness and correlate them with the three aspects of consciousness. If this is done then the seven rays should be based on the following seven combinations of *Sat, Cit, Ānanda* according to the septenary law:

1.	*Sat*	4.	*Sat-Cit*
2.	*Cit*	5.	*Sat-Ānanda*
3.	*Ānanda*	6.	*Cit-Ānanda*
		7.	*Sat-Cit-Ānanda*

The first three rays according to this classification should be the expressions of pure *Sat, Cit, Ānanda* respectively and the Monads belonging to them should therefore exhibit the qualities of these aspects very markedly because there is no admixture with other aspects. The next three rays are based on a mixture of two aspects, and Monads belonging to them should therefore show the qualities of both the aspects, sometimes one and sometimes the other gaining predominance. But as there is admixture with another aspect neither of the two aspects can be present in a marked degree. In the last ray all the three aspects of consciousness are blended and so qualities associated with them must be present in a fair degree and may become predominant by turns. But none of the aspects can be expected to be expressed in a marked degree.

There are some people who are so overwhelmingly characterized by love of power, the thirst for knowledge or a highly emotional nature that one can be almost certain that they belong to one of the first three rays. In others two aspects seem to be blended so well that it is difficult to say which of them rules their life. All that can be said is that the third aspect is markedly weak. They can be taken to belong to one of the mixed ray groups. In the case of the last ray all three aspects are present in a harmoniously blended state but one may become somewhat prominent temporarily according to circumstances. Those belonging to this ray are the people who are most difficult to classify.

The above explanation of the origin of rays and the classification of Monads in the seven groups corresponding to the seven rays is scientifically and philosophically sound and all questions concerning rays may be studied in the light of what has been said, instead of arbitrarily correlating rays and superficial temperaments of individuals without any basis of reason or facts of the inner life. It is in such things that mathematics can help us and serve as a guide in coming to correct conclusions with regard to the mysteries of our inner life.

The idea that it is possible for Monads to change their rays, though found in Theosophical literature, appears to be philosophically unsound and should not be accepted without definite and cogent reasons in support of it. The ray of a Monad must by its very nature be inherent in the eternal nature of the Monad and cannot be affected by changes or necessities of situations arising during the course of unfoldment. The idea probably arose when certain individuals with a particular temperament had to adopt a line of activity not in consonance with their temperament and it was assumed that they had changed their ray.

It should also be noted that the ray is a characteristic of the eternal Monad and not of the temporary Individuality or personality although it may be reflected in these expressions of the Monad. It is only when the personality and Individuality have become sufficiently purified and subservient to the Monad and begin to express him that his ray can be considered to find real expression on the lower planes. It is absurd to identify and find correspondences of rays with human weaknesses, temperaments and idiosyncrasies. These are passing phases and characteristics we gather during the course of our evolution and then shed as we evolve further.

The same thing can be said about individual uniqueness. Individual uniqueness like the ray is also an attribute of the Monad and not of the Individuality (*Ātmā-Buddhi-Manas*) or the personality. These are temporary expressions of the Monad which are needed in the earlier stages of evolution and are dispensed with in the highly advanced stages, though we do not know definitely when. The individual uniqueness of the Monad begins to influence the course of his evolution from an early stage, but this influence is not very pronounced and does not become a definite force until the Monad has acquired a definite control over his vehicles and can express himself through them in an effective manner. In the earlier stages there is so much to be learnt of a general nature that specialization of functions and faculties is not possible. We see this even in an ordinary educational system. The student is given a general education in the earlier stages of his educational career and the field of his knowledge becomes narrower as he advances in knowledge and develops his mental faculties. It is only towards the end of his career that he specializes in one subject and tries to master it as thoroughly as possible. He tries to be an expert and become individually unique as it were. Although individual uniqueness begins to find partial expression in the case of highly evolved souls it probably begins to flower only when the soul has liberated itself from the illusions and limitations of the lower life and becomes an Adept.

One lesson of practical importance which we ought to learn from our knowledge about individual uniqueness is not to try to imitate other people in unfolding our mental or spiritual nature. If we do so we create an artificial mould for receiving the creative forces which flow from within. On the other hand if we try to be ourselves we let those forces create their own channels and receptacles. These are bound to be more effective because they are produced naturally and do not lead to any kind of distortion. They will not only be more effective but they will also help to bring out our individual uniqueness progressively. How many people thwart their Higher Self by trying to imitate carefully the excellence

which they see in some other person, not letting their innate
abilities find a natural expression. There is no harm in deriving inspiration from other people in such matters. The trouble
comes in when we adopt their methods of work or modes
of living *in toto*. Then we stifle our real nature and thwart
our natural growth. And instead of being true and natural
expressions of our Selves we become bad imitations of others.
Sooner or later this artificial mould we have created has to be
demolished to allow the creation of a vehicle which will
express our Self—our individual uniqueness in that particular
sphere.

What then is individuality? We find that the Monad is
unfolding eternally according to his individual uniqueness.
But there is no permanence in any phase of this unfoldment.
The expression of the Monad according to his individual uniqueness is constantly changing in the realm of time and space.
There are only two things in this constant change which do
not change. One is the centre through which this expression
is taking place. This centre always remains separate from
other centres and is Self-existent or indestructible. The other
changeless thing is the eternal pattern which is the basis of
individual uniqueness and determines the nature and direction
of this eternal unfoldment in time and space. So we see that
a Monad is a centre of pure Consciousness or Reality through
which his individual uniqueness manifests in an ever-changing
or unfolding series of expressions. Besides these changeless
attributes of his eternal nature there is nothing which is not
involved in constant change. His individuality can therefore
be considered to be an expression of his individual uniqueness
at a particular point in time and space. Like the present
moment which is an ever-moving partition between the past
and the future, it has a momentary existence. But in the
actual unfoldment which takes place in the realm of time
and space it appears to remain the same for some time and
thus to have a continuity of existence or stability. It is this

particular expression in a certain period in which the change is too small to be noticeable which we generally call the individuality of a person. But from what has been said above it will be seen that though the change is not noticeable it is still there.

CHAPTER X

INDIVIDUALITY, INDIVIDUAL UNIQUENESS AND RAY OF THE MONAD—II

WE now come to the question of individual uniqueness, its nature, its origin in the Absolute and the presence of the individual uniquenesses of all the Monads in a perfectly harmonized and integrated state in the Absolute. As has been pointed out elsewhere the individuality of a Monad becomes attenuated progressively as consciousness recedes toward its centre and it becomes *ideal* in the Absolute. The Monads may thus be considered to be present in the Absolute in a non-differentiated ideal condition which makes it possible for an infinite number of Monads to be eternally emerging from the Absolute, getting involved in manifestation and then merging again in the same non-differentiated condition of the Absolute after going through the process of unfoldment. The whole process of manifestation may thus be seen to be an eternal cycle of the One becoming the Many and the Many becoming the One. Let us now consider in some detail some interesting aspects of this cosmic phenomenon taking place in the Unmanifest in order to understand more clearly our nature and destiny as Monads. This may enable us to see ourselves in a more correct perspective and avoid the fear and insecurity we feel when we regard ourselves as puny creatures desperately fighting for our individual life and survival in a vast universe of frightening realities.

Let us start this enquiry by considering first the relation of the One and the Many. This relation may be represented symbolically by the following diagram which shows at a glance many important aspects of this relationship.

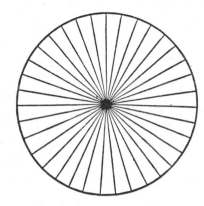

FIG. 12.   The One and the Many

One interesting aspect of this relation is the co-existence of Oneness and Manyness in several stages such as the following.

(a) In the first stage we see that a centre of consciousness represented by a point on a radius is in the realm of manyness and separateness. As it approaches the centre it also draws nearer to all the other units of consciousness represented by the radii and at the centre becomes one not only with the centre but with all the other units of consciousness. *The Manyness gives place to Oneness at the centre.*

(b) The second stage of co-existence is seen in the simultaneous existence of Oneness and Manyness at the centre. In this stage we see Oneness not merely as a culmination or end of Manyness but as *an over-all Oneness which also includes the Manyness.* If we look at the diagram as a whole it is one and includes both the centre and all the radii. In this it is not a question of the Oneness being an alternative to Manyness but the Oneness and Manyness together constituting a deeper Oneness.

(c) There is a third kind of Oneness which goes beyond even the second stage and this is the ultimate Oneness in which all the Monads with their different individual uniquenesses become merged in an integrated state. In this state they do not exist as separate entities just as the infinite number of individually unique vibrations with their specific or characteristic wave-lengths in the visible spectrum become merged in white light and do not exist in white light as separate entities. This ultimate kind of Oneness is a very interesting philosophical and scientific conception because it throws some light on the nature of the Ultimate Reality and some of the ultimate questions which are connected with this Reality.

In order to understand this integration of the individual uniquenesses of an infinite number of Monads into one undifferentiated state of the Absolute let us refer to the diagram given above. We see in that diagram a limited number of radii coming out of the centre and separated by gaps between them. The number of radii which symbolize the Monads is limited because only a limited number of Monads however great their number (infinity of a smaller order) can appear in a manifested system. Even the universe in its cosmic aspect does not manifest all the Monads at the same time. For, a universe according to the Occult doctrine is a recurrent phenomenon in the eternal alternation of *Sṛṣti* and *Pralaya* (manifestation and dissolution) and each universe however stupendous it may appear must therefore be a limited expression of the Absolute. Every time a new universe is created a number of Monads emerge from the realm of the Unmanifest to start their long journey in the realm of manifestation.

Now suppose the number of radii in the figure increases progressively. How many can be accommodated in the figure theoretically? Obviously, an infinite number because each radius is an ideal line without any thickness. We shall not be able to accommodate an infinite number of radii actually because each radius has a certain width or thickness and this thickness will make the adjacent radii to merge with one another. But if we increase the size of the circle progressively we shall see that an increasing number of radii can be accommodated though they may appear to merge nearer the centre of the circle.

Though there is no limit to the number of radii which can be accommodated in this manner we can see easily that the figure containing the increasing number of radii is approaching a limiting form. What is this limiting form? Obviously, it is that of a continuous superficial circle with no gaps between the adjacent radii. In the limiting form the infinite number of separate linear radii of one dimension become a continuous superficial unbroken circle of two dimensions. So, in the limiting or ultimate condition the infinite number of linear radii are nothing but a superficial circle in which none of the radii is present as a separate entity.

In the above process we have proceeded from Manyness toward Oneness, from the differentiated state to the integrated state and we have seen that an infinite number of separate radii can in the ultimate limiting condition become one continuous circle in which all the constituent radii are present but in a condition in which none can be seen separately or distinguished from another. It is possible, obviously, to reverse the process and see the other side of the coin, as it were. This will mean that a superficial continuous circle can be broken up or differentiated into an infinite number of radii. It can be the source of any number of radii emerging from the centre *ad infinitum*.

It is not necessary now to say anything further with regard to the significance of the above mathematical relationship and its bearing on the relationship which exists between the Monads and the Absolute. It shows how the infinite number of Monads which continue to emerge from the Unmanifest as universe succeeds universe in the eternal alternation of *Sṛṣti* and *Pralaya* can be nothing but the differentiated expressions of the Absolute. *Their number can be infinite and inexhautible because they are derived from a super-integrated state.* They may be considered to be present in the Unmanifest simultaneously, eternally and to emerge in manifestation in succession, in time. They may be considered to be One in the Absolute and to become Many in manifestation. They lose their individual uniqueness only in the undifferentiated wholeness of the Absolute and assume it when they descend into manifestation. The individual uniqueness does not really disappear in the Absolute but the individual uniquenesses of the infinite number of Monads are blended so harmoniously and perfectly that none can be seen separate from the others. They are all there just as all the vibrations corresponding to the spectrum of coloured lights are all there in the white light *in a mysterious integrated condition in which they are present and yet not present.*

This is the mysterious paradox of Being and Non-Being. Whatever aspect of existence we take, its opposite aspect may also be considered to be present in the Absolute. So, from the intellectual point of view everything which can be posited about the Absolute has its opposite also in the Absolute as has been pointed out in many texts of the Upanishads and other occult treatises. This is not philosophical hair-splitting or quibbling. It is an imperfect statement in terms of the intellect of one of the highest mysteries in existence. If we can get even a very partial intuitive glimpse of the tremendous, almost unbelievable truth hidden behind this philosophical conception it will illuminate in a flash many abstruse doctrines of Occultism.

We must however be on our guard against considering the integrated state as a kind of repository of all the constituents which appear on differentiation. If that were true then the integrated state would be nothing but a summation of the constituents which appear on differentiation. In that case the one integrated state and the many differentiated constituents would be at the same level, as it were, of the same category; but this is not the true conception of the integrated state. It is a condition which is different from the differentiated state although it contains the differentiated constituents potentially. We saw in the case of the mathematical example of the circle and its radii that in the integrated state we have a figure in two dimensions while in the differentiated state it is a figure in one dimension. This difference in dimension makes all the difference and illustrates the difference between the two states.   It is this difference which makes the integrated state the potential container of all possible differentiated states which is truly inexhaustible.

The difference can be illustrated by a simple example. If we have a white sheet of paper of infinite dimensions we can cut out from it *any* number of pieces of all shapes and sizes as we need them.   But if we try to keep together all these pieces of different sizes and shapes the stock will not be inexhaustible and we shall not to able to get from it pieces of *any* shape or size.

The above conception of the integrated and differentiated states will also be seen to throw further light on the question of the nature and origin of the Monads and the nature of manifestation. If the Absolute is a perfectly Super-Integrated State existing eternally in the heart of the manifested universe and the infinite number of Monads who appear and play their respective roles in it exist in a perfectly integrated state in the Absolute then involution-evolution is merely a cyclic process centred in the Absolute.   Monads appear continuously and endlessly from that Ultimate Reality, being involved and passing downward into manifestation then reversing their direction, evolving upwards through different stages of Logoic manifestation until they disappear again into the undifferentiated and Unmanifest state of the Absolute. They emerge from an undifferentiated state and ultimately disappear into the same undifferentiated state.   It is this undifferentiated or integrated state in which the reversal of direction takes place.   It is the Mystery of Mysteries which the human mind is unable to penetrate.

Seen in this light the whole phenomenon of manifestation is only a play or *lilā* of God. Using His *Cit-Śakti* in Cosmic Ideation He manifests through the universe He has created both as the One and the Many and when the play is over withdraws the universe into Himself again in His undifferentiated state during the period of *Pralaya*. The Monads in their totality may be considered merely as His differentiated aspect. Without these centres of consciousness to help in organizing the play and witnessing it, the play would obviously be impossible and meaningless. I have put the mystery in the form of an idea which appears anthropomorphic but let us try to go beyond the poetic imagery and grasp the underlying philosophical concept which means really that there is nothing in the universe both in its subjective and objective aspects except the Ultimate Reality of the Absolute. Even the Monads are merely the differentiated aspect of His infinite, inexhaustible, subjective nature appearing as different and separate centres of consciousness with their own identity and individual uniqueness in manifestation and being one and indistinguishable in His ultimate unmanifest state. This relation of the Absolute and the Monads is reflected again and again in the phenomena of the lower planes, in the relation of an archetype with its infinite number of individually unique expressions, in the expression of an individuality in innumerable personalities, in the differentiation of white light into innumerable vibrations of coloured lights. All these phenomena throw light from different angles on the mysterious relation of the One and the Many.

It has been pointed out in the chapter on 'The Unmanifest Cosmic Logos' that the highest Occult doctrines and the relation of different aspects of Reality to one another lead to the conclusion that the origin of the Monads is to be traced to the *Śiva-Śakti Tattva*, the Sanskrit equivalent of the Father-Mother Principle mentioned in *The Secret Doctrine*. The concept of the integration of Monads in the Absolute shows clearly why all the Monads should owe their spiritual birth to these two Ultimate Positive and Negative Principles in existence. In the Absolute all the Monads are present in the undifferentiated or integrated condition and no Monad exists

as a separate entity.   Now, as we have seen, the next lower
aspect of the Unmanifest is the *Śiva-Śakti Tattva*.   It is only
when the Absolute descends, as it were, into this dual polar
state that the possibility opens for the integrated Monads to
separate and emerge into the differentiated state.   For, unless
there is a ray of separate consciousness there can be no separate
Monad.   And there can be no separate ray of consciousness
unless there is a sheath to separate it from the other rays.   So
there must be at least potential matter to separate off potential
rays of consciousness from one another.   This is what the
Śiva-Śakti Tattva provides.   Everything in this dual *Tattva* is
potential in its nature as has been pointed out in the chapter
on the subject.   But this potential state is adequate for the
potential existence of the separate Monads.   The Monads
begin to manifest and function at a much lower level in the
realms of manifestation but they can exist as separate entities
at least potentially in the *Śiva-Śakti Tattva*.   Śiva and
Śakti are thus logically our spiritual Father and Mother and
we must trace our ancestry to these two Divine Positive and
Negative Principles instead of to monkeys as materialists
would have us believe.   It is really pathetic to see the modern
intellectual man insisting that he is descended from apes on
the basis of the uncertain evidence of fossils and ignoring the
evidence of all great mystics, occultists and spiritual teachers
who proclaim emphatically and unequivocally his Divine
origin.   He not only insists on it as a scientific possibility but
is proud of his simian origin.   No wonder then that we find
in this modern civilization based on this materialistic philosophy such an extraordinary glorification of animal propensities.   If we believe that we are descended from apes is it
not natural that we shall show a great deal of tolerance for
the manifestation of animal propensities?

   If there is only one Reality and the Monads are merely
centres of consciousness in that Reality questions like those of
freedom of will and predestination, or the apparent injustice

involved in assigning different roles to different Monads in the drama of manifestation, all such philosophical questions, doubts and paradoxes are resolved naturally. They are based on the false assumption and illusion that the Monads are fundamentally different from the One Reality. Where is the question of the freedom of will of an individual Monad if he is one of the many centres through which the Supreme Will is being carried out in the unfolding drama of manifestation? It is not even that the will of the Monad is subservient to that of the Supreme Will. The One and the Many together constitute the Ultimate Reality and as seen above are merely two aspects of that Reality. So the Will which finally prevails in manifestation is the Will of the One *and* the Many taken as a whole and not of the One alone. God does not impose His Will on His children. They are not automatons who like robots carry out the orders of their master mechanically. They are part of Him and share His power. But they can share this Power only to the extent to which they have evolved. They can exercise their individual will conjointly with the will of the other Monads who are evolving side by side and with the Supreme Will which co-ordinates and regulates the activities of the different Monads. It is these two limitations which are inherent in the very nature of things and which will be seen to be natural and necessary, which impose restrictions on our will as Monads. But just as the children of a king can share the power of the king and exercise their will within the limits imposed by common interests, so the Monads can share Divine Power and exercise their individual will as they unfold their spiritual faculties and can work in co-operation with others for the good of all. How great is the power of an individual Monad when he comes of age is seen in the case of a Solar Logos. But for the unevolved individual there is hardly any freedom to do what he likes except the freedom to do wrong and learn the lessons which are needed through suffering. This is the only way in which an unevolved Monad can exercise his limited freedom and, evolving his mental, moral and spiritual faculties, gradually enlarge his freedom.

The misconception of apparent injustice involved in playing different kinds of roles by different Monads is also based on the illusion that the Many are separate from the One while in reality they are differentiated aspects of the Whole and so their roles in manifestation are necessarily complementary. Of course, the injustices of life which common people resent owing to their vision being confined within the span of a single life can be explained very easily by the law of Karma, according to which every one reaps what he has sown. But there is a different kind of apparent injustice which appears to be involved in the difference in the roles which different Monads have to play in manifestation. Some seem to evolve in a steady regular manner and though there are bound to be ups and downs there is nothing which seems to show the existence of a distorting force in their life which introduces complications of all kinds. The course of lives in the case of other Monads seems to be under a curse from the beginning and they appear to be destined to evolve through a series of lives marked by so-called evil and violent disturbances which accompany evil. It is probable that if we view these series of lives in the long perspective we shall find the law of compensation at work and so no real injustice will be seen to have been done to any Monad. But apart from this aspect of the question if we look at the problem from the point of view of the same Reality finding expression both through the One and the Many the question of injustice does not arise at all. If all the Monads are individually unique and have to play their respective roles in the drama of manifestation it is inevitable that some will have to play roles which appear better than others from the lower point of view. Anyone can see that in the vast drama of manifestation an infinite variety of roles is needed and must be taken by different

Monads according to their individual uniqueness and consequent aptitude. From the point of view of the whole it does not matter who plays the different roles. It is how the roles are played which is important. When an ordinary play is put up different parts are assigned to different people. One plays the part of a beggar, another that of a king. Does the person who plays the part of a beggar consider himself unjustly treated? No! The whole play is one joint undertaking and its success depends upon each playing his own part perfectly.

It will be seen therefore that the idea of injustice arises when a particular individual isolates himself from the whole and considers himself as a separate unit of consciousness with his own limited interests apart from those of others. The very idea of injustice disappears when he rises to a higher level and sees all life as expressions of the One. The idea of injustice is thus due to a limited vision and though it is natural to have such ideas and be influenced by them in the earlier stages of evolution we can see at least intellectually where the error lies.

So let us ponder these questions carefully and clarify our ideas sufficiently to be able to get above the sense of injustice and such other feelings which may be embittering our life and marring our usefulness in the Plan. We cannot have the tremendous privilege of sharing the Divine Life and being part of the Ultimate Reality without sharing the responsibilities which such a privilege involves. We have ultimately to play our individually unique part in the Divine Plan and should not only be prepared to play that part expertly but should not mind the training which we have to go through in order to be able to do so. The personality not knowing the Divine nature and destiny of the Monad and caring only for the present temporary enjoyments frets against this schooling but wisdom lies in learning our lessons properly and as quickly as possible for we have to learn them sooner or later.

CHAPTER XI

THE RELATION OF THE MANIFEST
AND THE UNMANIFEST—I

THAT there is an unmanifest Reality hidden behind the manifest universe is a well-known doctrine of Occultism. This idea is also implicit in the various conceptions of God which we find in the great religions of the world, though it may not have been elaborated and embodied in a definite philosophical doctrine. We have already considered some aspects of the unmanifest Reality in dealing with the concept of the Absolute, *Siva-Sakti Tattva*, the unmanifest Cosmic Logos and the Monads. We have also been given in Occult literature some knowledge about the manifest and the various processes and laws which underlie the manifested world. One of the major contributions of Occultism in the world of thought has been to clarify and enrich our ideas about the manifest universe, both visible and invisible. As Science studies and adds to our knowledge of the physical world, so Occultism investigates and adds to our knowledge of the invisible worlds which are hidden within the physical. Both these sources of knowledge are important for us and are in a way complementary. Occultism helps to enlarge our horizon and enables us to see the extremely limited nature and significance of knowledge gained through modern Science. Science provides precise knowledge of natural phenomena, enables us to see how Nature works and thus enables us to grasp more easily and fully the Occult concepts and doctrines regarding the invisible realms of Nature.

These two worlds, the unmanifest and the manifest, are generally considered as two independent realities of existence, and most men keep them separate in their mind without seeing any relation between them. To most of them the unmanifest world is synonymous with God and the manifest world with the tangible physical world with which they are familiar. Between these two worlds lies a nebulous region in which they expect to spend their life after death and which they regard with a mixture of hope and fear. Whether there is a relation between these two worlds does not occur to them, or even if it does, they consider it a purely philosophical question in which only academic philosophers need be interested.

The relation between the unmanifest and the manifest or between God and the universe is one of the perennial problems of philosophy, and people have been thinking and wondering about this ultimate question since times immemorial. Much of this thought is speculative in character and, though of interest to the mere academic philosopher, is not of much use to the seeker after Truth who is not interested in ideas as ideas but as signposts to the Reality which is the object of his search. Since we are considering all these questions from the point of view of the seeker after Truth we shall confine ourselves to those conceptions of the relation between the manifest and the unmanifest which are based on Occult doctrines. These doctrines may have the outward appearance of philosophical systems but they are really based on the direct experience of those who have penetrated into the realities of existence and found the Truth. They are not to be taken as mere theories for explaining the ultimate truths of existence but as attempts of those who *know* these truths to convey them to those who do not. Let us see what light the intellect can throw on this important though extremely subtle question.

The relation between the unmanifest and the manifest can be considered in its two general aspects. One aspect has to do with the essential nature of the manifest and the other with the ultimate mechanism which connects the unmanifest and the manifest.   We shall discuss at some length the nature of the mechanism which connects the unmanifest and the manifest later and shall first consider briefly the question of the essential nature of the manifest and in what respect it differs from the unmanifest.

The whole question of the essential nature of the manifest and its relation to the unmanifest has been put most beautifully in a nutshell in the famous *mantra* of *Bṛhadāraṇyaka Upaniṣad* which is given below.

Om pūrṇamadaḥ pūrṇamidam pūrṇāt pūrṇam udacyate
Pūrṇasya pūrṇamādāya pūrṇam evāvaśiṣyate.

It is impossible to translate into English this profound *mantra*, every word of which is replete with the deepest significance and throws light on the ultimate truths of existence.   Translated literally it means ' That (the Unmanifest) is whole and perfect, This (the Manifest) is whole and perfect, because this whole has come out of that whole.   Even on taking out this whole from that whole what remains is still whole.'

The *mantra* therefore hints at the following truths which have a direct bearing on the fundamental question which we are considering, namely the relation of the unmanifest and the manifest.

(1) The manifest universe is whole and perfect like the unmanifest because it has come out of the unmanifest.

(2) This appearance of the manifest from the unmanifest does not affect the wholeness and perfection of the unmanifest.

Let us first give a little thought to the meaning of some words in the *mantra* before we discuss the significance of the *mantra* as a whole.   Let us first take the word *pūrṇa* which has been repeated over and over again in the *mantra* to emphasize the truth which it represents.   It has a wide range of meanings some of which are conveyed by such English words as whole, complete, entire, full, perfect. The idea which is sought to be conveyed in the present context includes all these meanings and many more. It is difficult to express the idea fully because it really seeks to sum up in one word the nature of the Reality which is not only the unmanifest but also the manifest. How can we convey to the human mind through language, much less a single word, the nature of that Reality which is not only beyond imagination but beyond the reach of the subtlest thought and about which it is said:

Yato vāco nivartante aprāpya manasā saha.
'From where speech returns along with thought without having found It.'

The words 'This' and 'That' are frequently used in Hindu philosophy to denote the manifest and the unmanifest respectively. These pronouns are used because they do not qualify in the slightest degree the realities which they are meant to indicate and leave the question of their nature free. They simply point to these realities and do not associate them with any kinds of attributes. This kind of reference may appear justifiable in the case of the unmanifest which is indicated by the word 'That'. But 'This' refers to the manifest and the question may be asked why the indefinite pronoun 'This' is used in this case. It is true that the manifest has attributes but it exists at so many levels and has so many facets that no word can indicate its multifarious nature. The use of the pronoun 'This' enables us to eliminate the question of its nature altogether and leaves us free to consider it in any aspect we want.

Let us now consider the profound significance of the *mantra* as a whole. It really contains two separate ideas: The first idea refers to the wholeness and perfection of both the unmanifest and the manifest. The second points out that the appearance of the manifested universe from the unmanifest does not in any way affect the wholeness and perfection of the unmanifest. Both the ideas are really inter-dependent but as they appear different outwardly we shall consider them separately.

The perfection, wholeness and harmony of the un-manifest has been dealt with already in chapters dealing with the unmanifest Reality. Although we cannot have any conception of that perfection and wholeness we can easily see how that Reality by logical necessity must have these attributes if the word ' attributes ' can be used in this special sense, in relation to the unmanifest. The *Upaniṣads* and other Hindu scriptures are full of references to the perfection and wholeness of the unmanifest Reality and so no doubt are the scriptures of other peoples. This perfection and wholeness are naturally beyond the comprehension of the intellect but, even so, these descriptions and conceptions represent the highest and most profound attempts of the human mind to formulate in language what is and will ever remain the object of wonder and eternal search in the case of humanity.

The *mantra* given above, however, points out not only that the unmanifest is *pūrṇa* but also the manifest. In view of the imperfection and disharmony which we find every-where in manifestation, especially at the lower levels, it is difficult to believe how the manifest universe can also be *pūrṇa* like the unmanifest. It is true that as we go deeper into the inner realms of existence we find that disharmony and imperfection decrease progressively and we seem to be approaching a Reality which is perfect in every way. Still, the fact remains that the manifested universe cannot be called *pūrṇa*, and the statement that it is *pūrṇa* like the unmanifest requires explanation. The tendency to accept everything given in the scriptures and philosophical systems without question is so ingrained, and so sedulously fostered by the orthodox pundits in religion and philosophy, that we do not

question statements even when they are contradictory and
fly in the face of reason and commonsense. This is really the
result of mental laziness or the misconception that such questioning amounts to disbelief or even heresy. Questioning of
this sort not only shows a healthy and alert mind but is
necessary if we want to go deeper into things instead of
always being satisfied with skimming on the surface. We
can continue to swim all our life on the surface of the
ocean and will never find anything except what is present
on the surface. It is only when we dive in, that we can
come in contact with the treasures which are hidden in
the ocean. Questioning is the diving board of the human
mind.

Now, here is a statement which is patently not in conformity with facts as we see them. Who can call this manifested universe with which we are familiar, which is full of
imperfections, disharmonies, conflicts, incompletenesses, which
is always changing and characterized by death and decay,
who can call this universe perfect and whole? And yet
there must be millions of people who have read over and
over again this famous *mantra*, and never questioned what the
statement means. For, the declaration given in the *mantra* is
not untrue or incorrect, a product of poetic fancy which has
no relation with the facts of existence. It is true, the most
fundamental truth which underlies the manifested universe.
But we have to look at the question from the deepest point
of view and not superficially in its literal or obvious
meaning.

Before we try to go deeper into this question let me give
a few aphorisms from the Hindu scriptures which point to
the same truth, and show that the idea given in the above
mantra is not an isolated statement but permeates the whole
field of Hindu philosophical and religious thought. It is the
most important though least understood doctrine of Hindu
philosophy and religion.

(1) *Brahmaivedam viśvam.*

'Verily, this universe is nothing but Brahman (Reality).'

(2) *Sarvam khalv idam Brahma.*

'Verily, all this is Brahman.'

(3) *Ātmaivedam sarvam.*

' All this is only the Self.'

If the manifested universe appears the opposite of what it has been declared to be in the *mantra*, it is obvious that we should try to understand in what sense it is considered to be whole and perfect like the unmanifest Reality from which it is derived.   It is considered to be *pūrṇa* in the sense that it is nothing but a modification of Consciousness which is the basic Reality of the manifested universe.

The use of the word modification in relation to Brahman or the Supreme Reality which is considered above change is no doubt incongruous and philosophically untenable, but we have to use some word to indicate this subtle and incomprehensible change in the changeless which brings about the appearance of the universe in that Reality.   Śaṃkarāchārya used another conception, that of *Māyā* to describe or account for this change.   According to his *vivarta vāda* as opposed to the *pariṇāma vāda*, referred to above, the manifested universe is a mere illusory form in Brahman.   But all these different conceptions with regard to the nature of the change which brings about the appearance of the manifested universe are concerned with the nature of the change, which is obviously beyond the comprehension of the human mind.   There is no difference of opinion with regard to the fact that the manifested universe is derived from Brahman.   Our ideas with regard to this difficult though fundamental question will become clarified if we illustrate it by means of a few similies.

Let us recall an experiment which has been referred to before.   Suppose we have a glass tank which is filled with clear water and there is an arrangement for churning the water with increasing speed. A high powered electric bulb is suspended in the centre of the tank and can illuminate the water. If the light is turned on, the electric bulb can be seen clearly through the still and transparent water. The water remains invisible as long as there is no motion. Now turn on the motor for churning the water. As soon as the churning starts the bulb appears in a distorted shape and the water can be seen owing to the refraction of light emanating from the bulb. When the churning reaches a certain speed the water begins to form patterns which appear and disappear rapidly in the water and a point is reached when the bulb is lost in these dense patterns formed by the water, and the rapidly changing illuminated patterns alone can be seen. Now slow down the motor. The whole process is reversed until the water becomes quite still and the bulb can be seen clearly and without distortion as before.

We will see in the above experiment that there are only three basic things involved, the light, the water, and motion, and yet the motion of the water brings about such a remarkable change in the observed phenomena. Without motion there is only the light and the invisible water. With motion, the light, although it itself remains unchanged as before, is lost to the sight of those who are in the churning water, and they can see only the patterns of the water formed by its motion. When the patterns subside the water becomes invisible and the electric light which illuminated those patterns alone can be seen. This gives a fairly good idea of the universe from the point of view of Sāṃkhya. The *Puruṣa* or the unit of consciousness gets involved in *Prakṛti* or matter owing to the mental patterns formed by the three *guṇas* as a result of the motion. He cannot see his own real form owing to the light of his consciousness being imprisoned in these mental patterns. When the mind becomes tranquil and harmonized, and the agitation caused by desire even in its subtlest form gradually subsides, the *Prakṛti* regains its *Sāmyāvasthā* or harmonized condition, the mind though still present, loses its obscuring and distorting power and the *Puruṣa* sees himself in his true form, *Svarūpa*, as a centre of the light of pure consciousness independent of *Prakṛti*. He has freed himself from the illusions and limitations of *Prakṛti* and is a liberated or Self-realized individual. And he is able to remain aware of his Real nature even when functioning in the realm of the unreal. This is the object of his descent into the lower worlds in order to unfold his consciousness and powers.

Let us now go a step higher and take another simile to illustrate the doctrine that the manifested universe is merely a modification of Consciousness using the word consciousness in its highest sense of Reality. This view corresponds to the still higher Vedāntic conception of the universe.

Suppose we have a perfect sphere made of solid gold. The sphere is perfect in form and substance as far as material things go. Now, we take this sphere and out of it make a number of articles, some beautiful in design and useful, others ugly and capable of being misused. One could make a rod of gold and kill a person with it. This fragmentation of the sphere has destroyed its perfection as a form, but has it affected its perfection as a substance? No. All the articles, beautiful and ugly, useful and dangerous, are still pure gold as a substance and have all the perfection of pure gold in them. It is only the forms of the articles which are different, and, owing to the different appearances and functions, appear beautiful or ugly, good or evil. All the things are not only made of the same substance, gold, but also retain fully the perfection of the substance from which they are made.

Similarly, pure Consciousness or *Brahma Caitanya*, when It ideates and projects this manifested universe in all its different grades and infinite variety of forms, is present in every part and every form of the manifested universe as a basic substance, using the word substance here not in the sense of material but as a basis of the different forms. For, as gold articles are made of, and partake of the nature of gold, in spite of their different forms and functions, so the mental universe formed in the Divine consciousness by Divine Ideation is of the same nature as Brahman or the Reality from which it is projected. The ideated images are not different and apart from the ideator. They are part of him and cannot remain separate and independent of him.

You may say that this is all right as far as the Divine images on the highest Divine planes are concerned. They are made of pure consciousness and are of the same substance as consciousness. But what about the lower levels of manifestation in which the mind appears to be the basic substance? Is the mind at all its levels of the same nature as consciousness? Yes. Just as the patterns produced in water which is being churned are not different from the basic substance water, although they appear to have a separate existence of their own, so the mental worlds at all levels are not different essentially and substantially from the consciousness from which they are derived. They are phenomena in consciousness or of consciousness, and though temporary and imperfect are of the same nature as consciousness.

Another very suggestive simile is that of the ocean and icebergs formed in it. The ocean is really formless, but change of temperature condenses some of the water to ice and thus icebergs are formed. Forms are produced from the formless without any change of substance or essential nature. The chief advantage in using this simile is that it shows that forms are produced from the formless by lowering the temperature or tempo of movement. The progressive condensation of consciousness into different levels of mind or density of matter may be considered as the slowing down of the dynamism of Reality which manifestation really is. The Real differs from the unreal or the relative not in any essential aspect, but only in the progressive condensation into less real or more relative states. For, in the Total Reality which is the Whole and out of which nothing can exist, there is the possibility of only one kind of change, into more real and less real states. This produces the needed contrast just as in a uniformly illuminated surface which is self-contained we can have light and shade only by having more light and less light by redistribution.

This is the fundamental conception which we should try to grasp if we are to understand clearly the relation between the unmanifest and the manifest. This is the only way in which the intellect can comprehend the derivation of the manifest from the unmanifest, and also the essential perfection and wholeness of the manifested universe in spite of its apparent imperfections and incompleteness. The perfection and wholeness are related to the basic substance and not to the imperfect and infinite number of forms which are derived from that basic substance—consciousness. The basic Substance called *Sat* is the reality of manifestation. The forms are illusory, temporary mental images created by *Cit* or the power of ideation which is also inherent in *Sat*. We shall deal with this aspect of the question in greater detail in the next chapter, but unless the underlying fundamental idea is clear in our mind it will be difficult to understand the corollaries which are based on it.

CHAPTER XII

THE RELATION OF THE MANIFEST AND THE UNMANIFEST—II

In the last chapter we tried to consider in what sense the perfection or *pūrṇatā* of the manifested universe is to be understood. Its perfection consists in the fact that it is derived from the Divine Consciousness, is *Brahma Vṛtti* or a phenomenon in consciousness. As such it is perfect and whole in every part or at every point, just as ornaments made from gold have the properties and perfection of gold in every part, nay in every point. If an author sits down and begins to think out a novel, the various characters and situations which are present in his mind are to some extent objective and seem to have a separate existence, but the basic fact in the whole phenomenon is that they are all mental. They are of mental stuff if I may say so. And as his mind is in its turn a modification of his consciousness and is based on his consciousness they are essentially phenomena in consciousness and of the nature of consciousness.

Having thoroughly understood this aspect of the question let us now pass on and consider the other aspect referred to in the *mantra* quoted in the last chapter. How does the appearance of the manifested universe in the unmanifest affect the wholeness and perfection of the unmanifest? Usually we see in the realm of material phenomena that if anything goes out of a thing which is whole, the latter becomes incomplete and loses its wholeness. If anything goes out of a thing which is perfect and harmonious the latter loses its perfection and harmony. We might feel inclined to apply this law operating in the realm of material things to the appearance of the manifested universe from the undifferentiated, whole and harmonious Reality, and might think that the unmanifest Reality is whole and perfect when there is no manifestation, and loses its wholeness and perfection as soon as a manifested universe appears in it. It is to warn us against this natural misconception that the second part of the above *mantra* states unequivocally that, when the manifested universe appears in that Supreme Consciousness, it is not affected and does not lose its wholeness and perfection.

So here we have another paradox and should try to resolve it as far as this is possible through the instrumentality of the intellect. As has been pointed out several times, the paradoxes of the higher life are the result of the incomplete vision of the intellect and can be resolved in the true sense only in the light of the spiritual consciousness when the intellect is transcended. But since we have to work in the realm of the intellect let us see whether similes, etc. cannot help us to gain some partial insight into these truths which appear paradoxical to the intellect. Before we proceed to discuss the question in detail let us take an illustration from the field of Science to show that manifestation need not necessarily affect the wholeness of the unmanifest.

Fig. 1 given in chapter I shows the dispersion of the white light of the sun into a spectrum of colours by a prism. The light breaks up into light of different colours on passing through the medium of glass. On one side of the prism is the world of white light and on the other a world of colours. So here we have a phenomenon of the co-existence of the undifferentiated and differentiated states of light. Does the differentiation of white light by the prism affect or destroy its wholeness or integrated state? Obviously, not in the light before it enters the prism. What about the light which has been dispersed by the prism? The white light is still there, but it is not present now in its integrated state, though it is present in its fullness. The whole of the white light is still present in the spectrum, but it is present in a differentiated state. Every single vibration which was present in the white light is still present in its differentiated form, and so in a 'way, the fullness and completeness of the white light is still present in the spectrum. Nothing has been lost, nothing has been deducted. This fact can be proved by combining the spectrum again into white light. The reason why the incident white light is not affected by passing through a prism is, of course, that it is a dynamic phenomenon capable of renewing itself. If you take a limited source of energy with a certain potential and you transform a part of that energy into some other form, you not only change the portion which has been transformed, but you also affect the potential of the whole system. But if the source of energy is infinite and inexhaustible the system remains unaffected by the transformation.

Let us now consider the statements given in the *mantra* in the light of the phenomenon just referred to. We may note the following points.

1. The unmanifest and the manifest are both integral aspects of the Ultimate Reality.

2. Both are whole (*pūrṇa*) but in a different sense. While the unmanifest is *pūrṇa* as an integrated whole, the manifest is *pūrṇa* as a differentiated whole. The manifest is the same as the unmanifest substantially and essentially, as gold articles are the same as a sphere of gold, or as the spectrum of coloured lights is the same as white light, both being light.

3. Manifestation means differentiation, and differentiation means the absence of the integrated state. So, when there is manifestation one aspect of Reality is present in the differentiated state while the other remains in the integrated state as before. But since there can be nothing

outside and independent of the Ultimate Reality the manifest and the unmanifest in their totality still constitute a whole.

We are apt to overlook the fact that if the ultimate reality is the Ultimate Reality we conceive it to be, there can be nothing outside it, and so nothing can go out of it. And if nothing can go out of it, it cannot lose its wholeness even according to our physical standards. A whole can become incomplete only if something is taken away from it and if nothing can be taken away from it, it must always remain whole though in a different form.

We have already considered the concept of the Absolute and it has been shown that the Absolute corresponds to that state of Reality which is always perfectly integrated, and perfectly harmonized, and eternally the same. All aspects of Reality below that of the Absolute suffer from some degree of differentiation and therefore cannot be the same as the Absolute. Even the *Śiva-Śakti Tattva* which is the very basis of the manifested universe and remains always unmanifest is really below the Absolute, although this *Tattva* or Principle is frequently taken as synonymous with the Absolute or Parabrahman in Hindu religion and philosophy. But we are considering these things here from the philosophical point of view, and must differentiate between these different aspects of Reality to clarify our ideas with regard to the relations between the manifest and the unmanifest. The *Śiva-Śakti Tattva* is to be considered at a lower level than the Absolute because it is the result of the primary differentiation into the root of consciousness called Śiva and the root of power called Śakti. Polarity by its very nature means the absence of perfect integration and even this highest Principle must therefore stand below the perfectly integrated state of the Absolute.

The perfectly differentiated state of Reality is represented by the Logos who contains or embodies within Himself all the *tattvas* (principles) and powers which are the basis and the

instruments of the manifested system over which He presides.
He needs all these powers and principles for running the
machinery of the manifested system and they must therefore
be present in a differentiated form.   Without these differentiated principles and powers He would be as helpless as a
painter who is required to make a painting only with white
paint.   There can be no contrast of light and shade, no
variety due to different colours. Similarly, no manifestation
of Divine attributes in all their variety and beauty is possible
without the separation of different principles and powers from
the undifferentiated and unmanifest state of the Ultimate
Reality.

Below the Logos stand different hierarchies of beings who
embody these separate, differentiated principles and powers
within themselves in different degrees and combinations.
They represent the different colours of the spectrum derived
from the white light of the Ultimate Reality.   But they are
not independent of one another.   They are related to one
another as the colours of the spectrum are related to one
another and in their totality form a harmonized whole.   This
fact may not be apparent in the extremely complicated and
multifarious activities of a manifested system, but it is there
and must exist from the very nature of things.   And the proof
of this lies in the fact that when a period of manifestation is
followed by a period of *pralaya* all these principles, etc. are
again reabsorbed into the unmanifest in a harmonized
state, just as the spectrum of white light can be transmuted
again into white light by passing it through an inverted
prism.

It is in some such way that we can try to understand
the relation between the unmanifest and the manifest as
depicted in the *mantra* quoted above. Of course these similies
and illustrations are not anything but crutches for our intellect,
but if they help us to gain a partial glimpse into these realities
there is no reason why we should not utilize them.

In the above paragraphs we have discussed the relation between the unmanifest and the manifest in its general aspect. But as the manifest is a very complex phenomenon having many levels of mind and matter of different densities, we have to account not merely for the appearance of the manifest from the unmanifest, but also for the appearance of all those fundamental derivatives which are derived from the One Reality. Unless we can account for these derivatives, and derive them as it were, from consciousness, the doctrine that there is only one principle which is the basis of both the manifest and the unmanifest, will remain unconvincing. For matter, energy, states of mind, are the things with which we are familiar and which we can partly understand, and they do not appear to be the products of such an intangible and mysterious thing as consciousness. In order that we may take them even tentatively as products of consciousness we should know at least theoretically the links which connect these various derivatives. We must have at least a general idea of how these fundamental and obvious realities of our life are derived, one from the other. It is only then that the Occult doctrine embodied in the maxim " All is Brahman ", will have any meaning for us.

The problem referred to above is really the problem of the relations existing between Reality, consciousness, mind and matter. This is a very important and complex problem which will be dealt with in detail in Part II. But since we are dealing here with the relation of the unmanifest and the manifest we should try to get at least a general idea of the links which connect the basic realities of existence referred to above. This will prepare the ground for a more thorough study of the subject later on.

If there is only One Reality or Ultimate Principle in existence it follows that all other realities of a lower order are derived from that basic Reality. Thus it is this Reality which must become consciousness. It is consciousness which must become mind. It is mind which must become matter, or to put it more correctly must appear as matter.

We have already considered in an earlier chapter on the concept of the Absolute the derivation of Consciousness from the Ultimate Reality. In the Absolute there is perfect equilibrium of all opposites and integration of all principles which by their differentiation provide the instruments for running the machinery of a manifested system. The primary differentiation of the Ultimate Reality leads to the appearance of two Realities which are polar in nature and which are called Śiva and Śakti in Hindu philosophy, and the Father-Mother principle in *The Secret Doctrine*. Śiva is the root of consciousness and Śakti that of power: all manifestations of consciousness are derived from Śiva and those of power from Śakti. So the first link in this chain of derivation is the appearance of Consciousness from the Absolute. The Absolute by its very nature is a void or plenum and cannot contain the principle of awareness which implies duality of a sort.

We must be careful when discussing these extremely subtle conceptions not to consider these different aspects of the unmanifest as different realities separate from one another or one inside the other. It would indeed be absurd to divide Reality itself into separate principles when we are trying to show that there is only One Reality in existence, and that consciousness, mind and matter are its derivatives. These transcendent principles are to be considered merely as different aspects of a Reality which appears to the human intellect in different aspects on account of its different functions. These differences are to be taken very lightly and intelligently and we should not have the attitude of a biologist who dissects an animal and tries to lay bare its different anatomical parts. These conceptions relate to the deepest and most sacred mysteries of existence which are utterly beyond the human mind and which we dare probe into because they are within us and the very root of our own existence.

So the first link of the chain we are considering is that between the Ultimate Reality and the first and highest Principle of existence, the root of consciousness referred to as Śiva. We use the word consciousness in a very wide and loose sense and should not confuse ordinary expressions of consciousness with the Śiva principle from which it is derived. In a way consciousness is present wherever there is mind and is the basis or the medium in which the mind works. But this consciousness which is associated with the mind and forms the background of the mind will be found on examination to be nothing but a kind of vague and general awareness, and is quite different from the pure Consciousness working in its own realm above the realm of the mind, and called *Sat* in Sanskrit. True, this pure integrated Consciousness is the root of the mind and provides the field in which the mind works but it is independent of and above the realm of the mind. It is above the subject-object relationship which gives rise to the mind principle and so we cannot really comprehend it.

Then we come to the second link in the chain, that which connects consciousness and mind. How is the mind derived from consciousness? We have already seen in the chapter on ' The Unmanifest Cosmic Logos ' that the secondary differentiation into the Self and not-Self forms the basis of Cosmic Ideation. The Self which is pure Consciousness called *Sat* in Sanskrit, is pure Being or self-existent Truth devoid of or rather transcending the subject-object relationship. In this pure Being another differentiation takes place as a result of the *Cit* aspect coming into play whereby the purely integrated state of Consciousness is replaced by a dual state which is characterized by what is called the Self-not-Self relationship. In ' That ', ' This ' appears as hinted at in the famous *mantra* we have discussed above. It is true that in this initial stage of Cosmic Ideation this universe is still in a nascent state, but it is the parent or source of the manifested universe which unfolds in time and space when creation takes place.

This subject-object relationship appearing in pure Consciousness is the basis of mind of all grades of subtlety. True, in the unmanifest Cosmic Logos, it is not yet the mind as we know it down here but only the root of mind from which all grades of mind from the highest to the lowest are derived. It is the mind principle if we may use such a phrase. For, Cosmic Ideation which takes place in this mind principle is essentially a mental activity however subtle and beyond mental comprehension it may be. It is when manifestation takes place that this mind principle, the medium of Cosmic Ideation, descends lower into the field of manifestation and assumes the different grades of mind which we deal with in yogic psychology and experience in our ordinary life.

Again, we must be careful not to regard this highest level of the mind as something nebulous, vague, indefinite, as it appears to the limited intellect, its instrument on the lowest planes. We are apt to forget that we are looking at these highest realities of existence from the lowest realms of illusion and limitations. To us these realities appear vague, nebulous and unreal while their shadows down here appear full of life and real. But the truth is just the opposite. Deep down in our own consciousness where the intellect cannot penetrate are the realities of life. What we consider and feel as realities on the surface of our ordinary, physical life are only their shadows or rather shadows of shadows.

So this pure mind principle in the unmanifest which is the root of the mind in manifestation should, like its parent pure consciousness, be considered not as something vague and unreal, but as the very quintessence of real and dynamic existence or being. The realism and dynamism is so intense and utterly beyond our mental comprehension that it appears to us like an unreal dream, just as sound when it goes beyond a certain pitch appears as silence.

Then we come to the last link in the chain, the relation between mind and matter. This link is naturally present and functions in the realm of manifestation, the field of mind and matter. This is the link which is the most difficult to understand although we are most directly and intimately concerned with it. Our outer life functions in the realm of mind and so-called matter, and we have become used to regard and treat these two things as separate and belonging to two different categories—mind as something intangible and subjective, and matter as something tangible and objective.

It is not possible to go here into this interesting but complicated question. It requires an analysis of our psychological states and the illusions under which the mind works. It requires a study of the subject-object relationship at its lowest level. It requires a knowledge of psychology, philosophy and technique of Yoga. Here it may be merely pointed out that the clue to the link between mind and matter is to be found in the nature of the perception by the mind of a world outside itself. What we perceive as an external world outside us is merely an ever-changing mental image within our own mind. We "see" a series of mental images within our own mind with the light of our own consciousness, but the mind projects these mental images outside us by a process which is called *Vikṣepa*. So these things appear to be outside us and to have an independent reality of their own, while they are nothing but the products of our own mind within the point of our consciousness. The process is analogous to the *seeing* of a panorama outside us when we use our physical eyes. The mind is joined to the tiny retinal image formed in the eye and lo! a world of forms and colours seems to appear outside us. The whole external panorama is really contained and centred in that retinal image, illuminated by the mind or to be more exact, consciousness.

The above does not throw any light on the nature of the stimulator which produces the mental images in our mind and which we generally describe as matter. All that can be said here is that the mechanism which stimulates the mental images in our mind is also mental in its essence. That is why it is able to affect the individual mind and produce these mental images. Like can affect like and not otherwise. This problem is a complicated one and has been dealt with in detail in Part II under the heading 'Glimpses into the Nature of Matter'.

CHAPTER XIII

THE RELATION OF THE MANIFEST AND THE UNMANIFEST—III

WE have already dealt with the essential nature of the manifest and the unmanifest and the relation between the two in the previous two chapters. There are certain other aspects of this relation which are of considerable interest to the student of Occultism and we may now consider them briefly in order to gain a clearer comprehension of this subject.

A question which will arise naturally in the mind of the student who has studied the previous two chapters is: Where is the dividing line between the manifest and the unmanifest? This question is not easy to answer because the process of manifestation is really a projection of an Ultimate Reality from within outwards and this projection is not a simple one-stage process. The same process is repeated in a general way over and over again with the result that we have a repetition and reflection at different levels of the same realities and principles. It is true that with each reflection and repetition there are tremendous changes in the nature of phenomena and a progressive obscuration of the Real by the unreal. But since all these are expressions of the same Reality and the underlying principles and processes are fundamentally the same a very subtle kind of similarity exists between the different levels of manifestation. So it is difficult to say where the boundary between the manifest and the unmanifest really lies.

The relation between the Manifest and the Unmanifest is somewhat analogous to that between the subjective and objective. As consciousness recedes towards its centre what was subjective before becomes objective and it is difficult to say where the line of demarcation between the subjective and objective lies. All such difficulties are due to the fact that manifestation means relativity and everything in manifestation is relative. Only the Absolute is absolute.

Although it is difficult to fix the dividing line between the manifest and the unmanifest, still, let us at least try to understand this interesting question. Theoretically, each level of consciousness right from the root of consciousness to which we refer as the *Śiva Tattva* to physical consciousness is a stage in the progressive manifestation of the Ultimate Reality. So the Absolute is really the only perfectly and completely Unmanifest Principle in existence. In the *Śiva-Śakti Tattva* there is differentiation into Consciousness and Power and if we think over the matter carefully we shall see that in this primary differentiation the first step has been taken towards manifestation although it does not bring forth the universe actually into manifestation. A further step in the same direction is taken in the secondary differentiation when the Self-not-Self relation is established in Reality and the Cosmic Mind, the seat of Cosmic Ideation, comes into being. But even this does not bring about manifestation.

It is only with the appearance of an *Īśvara* or Logos with His three aspects of *Brahmā*, *Viṣṇu* and *Maheśa* that Divine Ideation in contradistinction to Cosmic Ideation begins to take a practical shape and a manifested system begins to unfold in terms of time and space. It is at this stage that the universal becomes the particular, the potential becomes kinetic. And so the boundary between the unmanifest and the manifest may be most reasonably fixed between the Ever-Unmanifest, and the manifest Cosmic Logos, the presiding Deity of a manifest universe. It is the manifest Cosmic

Logos in His triple nature who brings into existence the cosmic planes and makes it possible for the Solar Logoi to create the solar planes and bring into existence their respective solar systems. It is the manifest Cosmic Logos who brings from the dark realms of the Unmanifest the cosmic Plan for His universe which is then worked out by the Solar Logoi in Their respective solar systems during the period of a *Mahākalpa*.

It is necessary to remember that the Unmanifest Cosmic Logos is only a Principle while the manifest Cosmic Logos is a Person Who may be considered as the presiding Deity and the Ruler of the whole universe in manifestation. Although He has no central energizing body in the physical universe corresponding to the physical sun in a solar system, the cosmic planes in their totality may be considered to be His body and there is no doubt that tremendous forces and energies flow from Him into the universe and provide life to the whole cosmos. Science has accumulated a great deal of knowledge with regard to these things but it knows really very little because the whole phenomenon of cosmic manifestation is too vast and stupendous and the intellect of puny man is too limited and illusion-bound to be able to comprehend it. But the discovery of cosmic rays and radiations from the recently discovered quasars shows that there are tremendous sources of energy existing in the universe even on the physical plane which it is impossible to account for except on the basis of the Occult doctrine. The wild and naive guesses of modern scientists with regard to these things show not only their lack of humility and obsession with the materialistic philosophy of life but go to confirm the validity of the well-known dictum ' there are none so blind as those who *will* not see '.

Although the line of demarcation should logically be drawn between the Ever-Unmanifest and the realm of the manifest Cosmic Logos as pointed out above there are some difficulties in accepting this conclusion without any reservation.

The highest planes of manifestation, both cosmic and solar, are planes of Divine or Logoic manifestation and are considered above the cataclysmic changes of *Sṛṣṭi* and *pralaya*. They are called ' Eternal ', a word with very ambiguous meaning but certainly including the idea of continued existence. This means that even when a *mahāpralaya* takes place they must continue to exist in some form and the Logoi who function in them must continue to live their eternal life even though they have been deprived of the lower worlds over which They presided.

Some light may be thrown on this question by taking into consideration the three types of worlds mentioned in the Hindu scriptures. These are called (1) *Kṛta* (result of construction) (2) *akṛta* (transcending the realm of construction and (3) *kṛta-akṛta* (having the attributes of both (1) and (2). The worlds belonging to the first category exist only for one day of *Brahmā* the Creator, those belonging to the third category for one hundred years of *Brahmā*, while worlds included in the second category are above the realm of construction and destruction, i.e. they are ' eternal '. This means in other words that the worlds belonging to the first and third category are subject to *pralaya* or dissolution while those belonging to the second category are not. Although it has not been stated in so many words all Occult references to this question point to the fact that solar *pralaya* affects the lowest three worlds of manifestation (physical, astral and lower mental) while a *mahāpralaya* involving the whole universe brings about the dissolution of the next three higher worlds (higher mental, *Buddhic* and lower *Ātmic*) also.

If this is correct then we can also with some justification place the line of demarcation separating the unmanifest and the manifest between the Divine worlds (*Ādi, Anupādaka* and higher *Ātmic*) in which the consciousness of the Logoi functions and the five-fold worlds created by Them at the time of creation. When the five-fold created universe is dissolved in a *mahāpralaya* and there is nothing left on the lower planes in which the Cosmic Logos can function it can be reasonably assumed that His consciousness withdraws into the highest three cosmic planes along with that of all Solar Logoi for this period until another universe is created. On the other hand, in the case of a solar *pralaya* the Solar Logos withdraws into the highest solar planes (*Ādi, Anupādaka* and higher *Ātmic*) until he reincarnates in a new solar system in the same continuing universe. These longer and shorter periods of withdrawal for a Solar Logos from the lower planes of manifestation are reflected in the case of a *Jivātmā* or the Individuality in the longer and shorter periods of withdrawal during death and sleep respectively. These withdrawals in case of Logoi during different kinds of *pralaya* may be represented diagrammatically as follows:

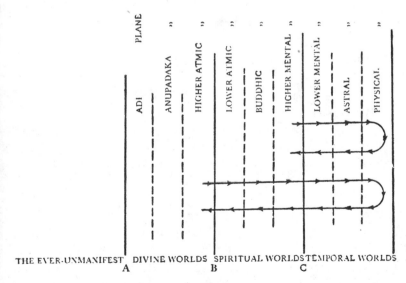

Solar Pralaya and Mahāpralaya

The line at **A** represents the boundary between the Ever-Unmanifest and the manifest but the lines at **B & C** may also be considered lines of demarcation between the unmanifest and manifest as pointed out above. These lines correspond to different levels of manifestation and at each of these stages manifestation becomes denser on the form side and the Reality which manifests becomes more obscured and limited than in the previous stages.

We have been considering in the above paragraphs the macrocosmic aspect of the relation between the unmanifest and the manifest. Let us also briefly refer to its microcosmic aspect. Any one who has understood the relation of the Monad, Individuality and the personality will see at once that the dividing line between the unmanifest and the manifest can be placed with equal justification where the expression of the Monad changes into that of the Individuality and again into that of the personality. For, all these three expressions of the Monad act as one entity on three planes in which they function and each expression acts as the unmanifest towards the next lower expression. Thus the Individuality may be considered as the unmanifest in relation to the personality. It is from the Individuality that a succession of personalities emerge and are again absorbed in the Individuality at death, just as a manifested system comes out of the unmanifest at the time of creation and disappears into it at the time of dissolution. A similar, though not identical relation holds between the Monad and the Individuality and a comparison of this relation with its macrocosmic counterpart will be found interesting.

So we see that the unmanifest and the manifest are relative terms and the line of demarcation can be drawn at different levels. We are not able to decide definitely where the boundary lies not because there is no boundary but because there are several boundaries and at each of these the more subtle expression of Reality may be considered as the unmanifest in relation to the less subtle expression which follows. So all that we have to do in this matter is to understand the problem and leave the question of the boundary between the unmanifest and the manifest open.

Let us now turn to a question which frequently troubles a class of students who have acquired a pseudo-philosophical outlook and who begin to ask ultimate questions before they have learnt to question life seriously and study its deeper problems with real earnestness. I mean the ultimate question: Why this manifestation?

The concept of the Absolute as a perfectly harmonized and integrated State which appears like a Void to the intellect but is really a Plenum, which is a complete, self-sufficient, perfect, Whole and, therefore, without any kind of deficiency and need of fulfilment, this concept of the Ultimate Reality which exists eternally at the heart of the universe raises the question: why should there be any manifestation at all. This is what is called an ultimate question which is beyond the realm of the human intellect. It is solved or rather resolved in the depths of one's consciousness when the seeker after Truth has penetrated far into the realms of Reality and come face to face with it. But since we are studying intellectually the philosophical import of the relation between the unmanifest and the manifest let us give a little thought to this question to remove at least some of the gross misconceptions which may be lurking in our mind with regard to it.

The explanations frequently given to explain away this philosophical difficulty are generally worse than useless, bordering on the silly sometimes. To say, for example, that God wanted to put up a show for His entertainment or He wanted companions and so multiplied Himself in the form of innumerable souls is really to attribute to God characteristics and weaknesses above which even a *Jivanmukta* must rise before he is able to gain a glimpse into the Reality which we popularly refer to as God. Obviously, the answer lies somewhere else and must be at a much deeper level, if there can ever be an answer to such an ultimate question.

Let us examine the idea of a perfectly harmonized, self-adjusting, self-sufficient Ultimate Reality and see whether we cannot find in it a clue which can give us a glimmer of the truth and enable us to hold our soul in patience until we can know it directly within the deepest recesses of our own consciousness. The Will to manifest is a force with an outward thrust from the centre to the periphery. It can obviously be neutralized by an inward thrust from the periphery to the centre, the two together producing a perfectly neutralized and harmonized state in which the Will to manifest is perfectly balanced by the Will to demanifest if I may use such a word. What is this opposite force? Obviously, the Will to withdraw into the Centre at the time of *pralaya*. So, *Sṛṣṭi* and *pralaya* are a pair of opposite forces which perfectly balance each other in the Absolute and produce the phenomena of manifestation and dissolution by periodic alternation at different levels of manifestation. This explanation has at least the merit of rationality even though it cannot be considered as an answer to the ultimate question. For further explanation the student should study the chapter on Cosmic Rhythm.

In dealing with the relation of the unmanifest and the manifest we may also consider the nature of the mechanism through which the unmanifest becomes the manifest. This is a difficult subject but if we are able to grasp the idea that such a mechanism exists and also gain some comprehension of the general nature of this mechanism it will suffice for our present purpose. Manifestation in its infinite degrees of subtlety and variety is too vast and complicated a phenomenon to be comprehended by the limited human intellect except in the most general manner. Thousands of scientists with highly trained intellects and working with the most complicated and delicate instruments have been engaged for centuries in studying the outermost shell of the manifested universe which we refer to as the physical world and their idea with regard to its nature, in spite of this stupendous effort, is very superficial, partial and erroneous fundamentally. Their knowledge with regard to certain aspects of the physical world is no doubt very remarkable and reliable and has enabled them to do many wonderful things but their conception with regard to the essential nature of the universe comes nowhere near the truth. This is partly due to the stupendous nature of the task and partly to the erroneous philosophy of materialism which they have arbitrarily adopted as the basis of their search for Truth. They not only insist on laying the utmost emphasis on physical life and its phenomena but deny or ignore the existence of other aspects of life which are not physical and cannot be investigated by purely physical means.

These superphysical aspects of life and the universe have been investigated by methods which are essentially scientific though not physical by a large number of highly evolved individuals who are called *Mahātmās* or Adepts of Occultism. The results of these researches in the deepest realms of manifestation are available, though not to the general public. They can be known and verified by direct experience by those who are prepared to go through the necessary training and make the necessary sacrifices. It is this vast body of true and mostly transcendental knowledge which is referred to as true Occultism and it is fragments of this knowledge in its general aspects that we find scattered here and there in the great religions of the world and some esoteric schools of medieval and modern times.

It is necessary to remember that methods of Occult research are fundamentally different from those of physical research and it is only through them that it is possible to know the real nature of the manifested universe in its totality in spite of its complexity and vastness. For, the various processes and phenomena of the manifested universe, both visible and invisible, undergo a subtle and progressive transformation and integration and merge ultimately into One Reality. This enables those who are able to penetrate into the deeper recesses of their consciousness and come into touch with the different levels of this Reality, to acquire an integrated view of these processes and phenomena at those levels and to gain integral knowledge which in its differentiated form is too complicated and vast to be grasped by the human mind. It is only through such integral knowledge that the universe in all degrees of subtlety and infinite variety can be known with certainty and in its wholeness without possibility of any error. It is such knowledge, gaining which everything can be known in its essence and reality, that is in the possession of Adepts of true Occultism and it is through this technique and knowledge alone that the mechanism of manifestation can be studied and known with certainty. The methods of physical research and intellectual reasoning are too crude and superficial for this kind of work and as long as modern scientists and philosophers insist on confining themselves to these methods they have to remain content with the scrappy and uncertain knowledge of the physical world and complete ignorance of the wonderful worlds of increasing splendour and reality which are hidden within the outermost shell of the physical world.

Although this knowledge with regard to the mechanism of manifestation exists in its fullness in the custody of the highest Adepts of Occultism only hints with regard to its existence and nature have so far been given out to the world outside. This is partly because it is of a transcendental nature and beyond the comprehension of the human intellect and partly because of the possibility or rather the certainty of its misuse in the conditions prevailing in the world at the present time. It is only when an individual possessing the necessary qualifications and trained inner faculties, dives into his own consciousness that he can acquire this knowledge and know the innermost truths of existence.

But whatever hints have been given out with regard to these inner mysteries of existence they are of sufficient importance and value to be considered carefully and deeply by all students and aspirants so that the intellectual edifice of the philosophy of Occultism may be as meaningful and complete as possible. It is no part of wisdom to reject or ignore this partial and unsatisfactory intellectual knowledge because we cannot have the full and real knowledge. The student of Divine Wisdom tries to understand whatever knowledge is available and then presses forward into the deeper knowledge which lies behind. The knowledge which has been given out to the world at large constitutes the lowest rungs of the ladder which leads, step by step, to full and real knowledge and we must place our feet on the first rung of the ladder and make an effort to climb before we can hope to reach the top. A man must learn to swim before he can dive and an aspirant must learn to understand and master these intellectual concepts and try to penetrate into them before he can have real knowledge.

We have used the phrase ' mechanism of manifestation ' to indicate the totality of those agencies which are involved in the process of manifestation. This should not give the impression that these agencies are of a mechanical nature and necessarily involve matter of different degrees of subtlety. Some of these agencies like the different planes of the universe, cosmic and solar, do involve matter in the widest sense of this term, though it has been shown elsewhere that this so-called matter is merely a mental phenomenon from the highest point of view. But there are certain agencies involved in manifestation which are not associated with matter in any form. Time, Space, Point, Illusion, etc. which also form part of the total mechanism of manifestation cannot be considered material even in its subtlest sense. In fact, agencies like *māyā* or Illusion which lie at the very basis of manifestation are not even objective. They are of a subjective nature and therefore, more difficult to understand than the objective agencies like the planes of manifestation. We see thus that the phrase ' mechanism of manifestation ' includes a large variety of agencies of different kinds, which though related to one another fundamentally, yet appear quite different in expression to the intellect. An effort has been made in subsequent chapters to consider in a general way some of these agencies involved in manifestation in the light of the Occult doctrines as well as the knowledge of modern Science. The latter enables us to understand these subtle ideas according to the occult maxim " As above, so below ".

In understanding this total mechanism of manifestation it is also helpful if we have some idea of certain fundamental processes of a general and universal nature such as Involution and Evolution, Differentiation and Integration, etc. A few of these processes have, therefore, also been dealt with in some of the chapters. It should be remembered however that this is a vast and complicated subject enbracing the whole field of manifestation, visible and invisible, Real and unreal, and so our knowledge at best can only be fragmentary and super-ficial. But even this very limited knowledge will be found to be illuminating by the student of the Divine Wisdom and help him to understand the Occult Doctrine better. Further research in these fields is needed to make the Occult doctrines more interesting and acceptable to the intelligent and educated man of today and to complete the edifice of the philosophy of Occultism as far as this is possible in the limited realm of the intellect.

CHAPTER XIV

INVOLUTION AND EVOLUTION

THE highest conceptions of the Occult Doctrine imply that the fundamental urge of the individual Soul to find the Truth which is hidden within it, is an urge to find itself. Or, in other words, the seeker and the Sought are really one. This paradoxical truth suggests that evolution is a cyclic process without a beginning or end. We may not be able to imagine or understand that cycle in its completeness but we can appreciate intellectually the logical necessity of this conclusion. We can see the downward and upward streams of involution and evolution like the movements of the escalators which are used in underground tube stations in some cities. We see the upward movement on one side and the downward movement on the other side. But how the process is reversed at both ends is not clear to us, because the reversing mechanism is hidden from our view. In the same way we do not know where and how the two descending and ascending streams of life join. This is really an ultimate question which like many such questions is rooted in the origin of things and is thus beyond the realm of the intellect.

What is the significance of this urge in every Soul or *Jīvātmā* to find itself? I think the significance of the doctrine that the *Jīvātmā* and *Paramātmā* or the Soul and the Over-Soul are essentially one is not fully understood. It means that the Consciousness of *Paramātmā* or the Whole Reality is really at the back of the consciousness of every *Jīvātmā*. The

Centre of life and consciousness through which each *Jîvâtmâ* functions is formed by the progressive covering, step by step, of this Reality by the limitations and illusions which are inherent in manifestation. It is a question of the Whole Reality becoming limited or constricted progressively, into the Monad, then into the individuality, and lastly into the personality. The reverse process of Self-realization which means the progressive removal of the limitations and illusions releases the consciousness and makes it spring back, step by step, into conditions of greater freedom, power, knowledge and bliss until the part expands into or is again united with the Whole.

In involution the Reality functioning through a Divine centre becomes progressively involved in manifestation and the free and unlimited consciousness becomes more and more constricted and limited. In evolution of the human soul the consciousness imprisoned within the personality is progressively released from these limitations and expands, step by step, into that original unfettered state from which it had descended. It thus completes a full circle, although we are not able to see the upper part of this circle which is hidden in the darkness of the Unmanifest.

Is there any limit to the expansion of consciousness and the number of vehicles through which it finds expression in the cosmos? Looking at the problem from the physical point of view we find on the basis of facts gathered by modern astronomers that the cosmos is not only unlimited but that the existence of innumerable nebulae in space shows that countless solar systems are in the process of being formed all the time. So there will be no dearth of vehicles when the Monads who are evolving as human beings at present, will in the far distant future become Solar Logoi and need solar systems for their expression.

As regards the expansion of consciousness, again, there seems to be no limit to such expansion. We come down from the Unmanifest, and after passing through all the stages of evolution and unfoldment again disappear into the Unmanifest, thus apparently completing a full cycle. We can with great difficulty visualize this expansion through the human and super-human levels up to the stage of a Solar Logos, but what happens after that is utterly beyond our intellectual grasp. But though these higher stages are beyond our comprehension we can through the help of similes and scientific illustrations try to gain a glimpse into the general nature of this cycle of involution and evolution. We can see only a few arcs of this gigantic circle here and there. Let us see whether we can mentally construct the whole circle with the help of a simile.

How consciousness starts its downward journey from the *Śiva-Śakti Tattva* and after going through the long cycle of involution and evolution again returns to It, can I think be best understood by considering the formation of rivers and their relation to the ocean. The ocean is the great reservoir of water on this globe. The heat of the sun partially converts this water into vapour, which forms clouds and then falls as drops of rain or snow. These give rise to rivers which after flowing over the land for some distance again fall into the ocean. The whole cycle is repeated over and over again continuously and keeps the rivers flowing on the surface of land. The ocean, however, remains the same, unaffected by these changes.

Now, we can consider land as the manifested universe and ocean as the Unmanifest Reality or *Śiva-Śakti Tattva*. The Father provides the water or consciousness. The Mother or *Prakṛti* provides the land or the field for manifestation on which the water falls and forms separate rivers. The rivers flow through different areas of land and after their long journey reach and merge in the ocean. Their water is the same as that of the ocean. They are separate as long as they are on land. They are one when they join the ocean.

We have been referring to involution and evolution as the downward and upward streams of life but of course as we know, the movement is really not upward and downward, but outward and inward, from the centre to the periphery and back from the periphery to the centre. Consciousness emerges from the Centre of Reality into the realm of manifestation, penetrates deeper and deeper into materiality, and when it has reached the limit of materiality it begins to withdraw again to the Centre carrying with it the fruits of evolution and the knowledge and powers which have been developed or unfolded in the long journey.

Narrowing down our view and considering the expression and unfoldment of consciousness in the human stage we find that the expression is extremely limited in the beginning owing to the undeveloped condition of the material and mental mechanisms. As these mechanisms evolve, the mental manifestations become fuller and subtler and approach more and more the nature of pure consciousness. Ultimately, the mental manifestations are gradually transformed into manifestations of consciousness and function in the realm of Reality from which they are derived.

I like to imagine this involvement and liberation of consciousness in the following manner which can be illustrated very effectively by means of cinematographic projection. Imagine an area of brilliant white light extending in every direction to infinity. Now visualize that in this expanse of white light a point appears. The moment this point appears the whole expanse of white light is blotted out and everything becomes dark except the point of light. Then this point begins slowly to expand and colours of all kinds begin to appear in the circle. The expansion goes on and the dark periphery round the circle is pushed further and further away from the centre and the lighted area becomes larger and brighter. Ultimately, the circle shutting out the darkness becomes infinite in diameter and the original unlimited expanse of light replaces the darkness, but with a difference. There is the centre, and this centre is an additional focus through which the love, knowledge, power and wisdom of God can find unrestricted expression.

We have been considering the whole question of involution and evolution so far from the point of view of the microcosm, the involvement of a single Monad in manifestation and his liberation from the bonds of illusions and limitations after going through the evolutionary process. Let us now deal with the question very briefly from the point of view of the macrocosm. According to the Occult doctrine the whole manifested universe is the result of the involution of consciousness after the production of matter of different degrees of subtlety. To say that consciousness or Reality gets involved in matter would not be quite in keeping with this doctrine because matter is not anything independent of the Reality which it involves, but is itself a derivative of that Reality. Perhaps we should put it this way: that one aspect of consciousness or Reality produces matter, another aspect prepares the vehicles for the functioning of consciousness and a third aspect uses these vehicles thus prepared for its expression. This is the work of the Third, Second and First Logos respectively according to the Theosophical terminology.

If we look at the universe in this manner we see that it is essentially nothing but consciousness and the aphorism *Brahmaivedam Viśvam* which means " Verily, this universe is nothing but Brahman," is then seen in its true significance. Of course, there is one philosophical view that consciousness and matter are two separate, independent and eternal realities, but this dualistic point of view of Sāṃkhya is considered to be lower and a necessary step towards the highest monistic point of view of Vedānta referred to above. We are really facing here one of the paradoxes of spiritual life which the intellect finds so difficult to comprehend, but we shall deal with this interesting question later on.

The conception that the whole manifested universe in all its different states of subtlety down to the physical plane is the result of the involution of consciousness *as matter and not in matter*, and is thus a phenomenon of pure consciousness, is so startling that many people find it not only difficult to comprehend but difficult to believe. But this doctrine is not as unbelievable as it appears at first sight. The fact is that the various factors involved in the consideration of this question have not been clearly stated, the links in the chain of reasoning have not been pointed out and the student is left to make what he can of the doctrine which seems to fly in the face of all commonsense and facts of our ordinary experience. He takes this doctrine as he takes so many other things on authority, but in most cases doubts keep lurking in his mind and prevent him from taking it seriously. So it remains a pious belief, an idea for religious propaganda as in the case of most Hindu religious teachers, or a speculative doctrine of philosophy as in the case of most academic philosophers. There are very few people who take it sufficiently seriously so that it becomes an effective and inspiring ideal to guide their search for Reality.

This relation of Reality, consciousness, mind and matter is a very difficult and subtle question and we shall deal with it later, but I would like to put forward in this context one or two ideas which we may think over carefully, so that when we do take up this question our mind is better prepared to deal with it effectively.

The first idea which we may consider is this: In order to produce the universe as an objective reality which can be perceived as something outside the perceiver, subjective-objective relationship is established in consciousness producing two streams out of itself, one the basis of the subjective phenomena and the other the basis of the objective phenomena.

the one related to the perceiver and the other to the perceived. These two streams, both derived from consciousness, descend plane by plane until they reach the physical plane and terminate in the *indriyas* or sense-organs, and the *bhūtas* or the agents which stimulate the sense-organs. It is at the junction of the *bhūtas* and *indriyas* that the subjective and objective streams meet. So it is in these two conceptions of *bhūtas* and *indriyas* that we have to look for the nature of the two streams of consciousness, and the clue to the doctrine that the universe is a phenomenon in consciousness or of consciousness.

There are two aphorisms in the *Yoga-Sūtras* of Patanjali which are very significant and have a special bearing on this important question. These are the *sūtras* on *Bhūta-Jaya* (III-45) and *Indriya Jaya* (III-48) for the mastery of the *bhūtas* and *indriyas* respectively.

" Mastery over the *Panca-Bhūtas* by performing *Saṃyama* on their gross, constant, subtle, all-pervading and functional states (III-45)."

" Mastery over the sense-organs by performing *Saṃyama* on their power of cognition, real nature, egoism, all-pervasiveness and functions (III-48)."

If we examine these *sūtras* on *Bhūta-Jaya* and *Indriya-Jaya* and consider the different steps whereby the *bhūtas* and *indriyas* are transcended, as well as the powers which develop as a result of this transcendence, we can see clearly the various steps through which integral consciousness gives rise to subjective-objective phenomena on the lower planes. It is a difficult concept to grasp but if we read the commentary on these *sūtras* and think over the underlying ideas it is possible that we may get a glimmer of this most significant truth which is hidden within them. Once we grasp the underlying idea the whole field of thought on this question will be suddenly illuminated and we shall begin to realize that the doctrine incorporated in the sacred maxim " Verily, all this is Brahman " is after all not so absurd as it appears on the surface.

Involution and evolution will be seen to be two opposite forces working in the realm of manifestation. The first is centrifugal in character, i.e. from the centre to the periphery. The second is centripetal, from the periphery to the centre. Here again we have an example of separation of the One Reality into two opposite forces which tend to balance each other and to maintain the harmony and balance of the whole. A deeper view of the two processes will show that involution is accompanied by an increasing differentiation, and evolution by an increasing integration. When consciousness moves from the Centre to the periphery it undergoes increasing fragmentation. The sense of separateness becomes more and more marked and reaches its maximum at the level of the physical. In the reverse movement from the periphery to the Centre the process of integration begins, the sense of separateness decreases progressively and disappears on reaching the Centre.

Before closing this subject I would like to deal with one more question which is connected with evolution and which puzzles the student of Occultism. It has been pointed out before that the process which results in evolution and which involves time and space, as we know it, cannot be applicable to a Monad or a Solar Logos, because they live in Eternity and their consciousness is above time and space. What is the nature of the process taking place on the Divine planes which corresponds to evolution on the lower planes? Some people call this process " Becoming ". But a thing is not understood by giving it a name, especially a name with a very vague connotation. This process cannot be anything like evolution because in some way which is incomprehensible to the human intellect, the perfection which we are to achieve, is already present in the realm of the Eternal as indicated by the Occult maxim " Become what you are." It is also reasonable to suppose that the state of consciousness in which the Monad lives after he has completed the cycle of human evolution on the lower planes cannot be exactly the same as it was when he started his journey in the lower worlds of illusion. Some change of a very fundamental character must have taken place though it is difficult to visualize what it is. The mere fact that the Monad after gaining Liberation from the lower worlds enters upon another journey which ends in his becoming a Solar Logos shows that his consciousness is also capable of unfolding in spite of the fact that it is Eternal. Why should we assume that living in the Eternal means necessarily living in changelessness? The ultimate source of change is not the *Īśvara* of a solar system but the Cosmic Logos, the source of Cosmic Ideation, and so everything below the consciousness of the Cosmic Logos must be going through some kind of change. It may not be the kind of change which we can visualize or comprehend and may be governed by different conditions which we cannot understand, but if unfoldment of consciousness is involved, if higher states of consciousness are progressively attained, it is difficult to understand how this is possible without some kind of change.

The idea that there are subtler states of Time and Space than those with which we are familiar will help us to resolve this paradox. The Monad is above the time and space with which we are familiar but he is still under the sway of subtler kinds of Time and Space. That there are such subtler kinds of Time and Space is well known to students of Hindu philosophy and Occultism. In Hindu philosophy we have not only *Kāla* but *Mahākāla*, not only *Ākāśa* but *Mahākāśa*. If there are subtler states of Time and Space there must be subtler kinds of change based on these states. And the unfoldment of consciousness in the case of Self-realized Monads and *Īśvaras* of solar systems must be based on these subtler kinds of changes taking place on the cosmic planes.

So it seems we have to revise our ideas about all these things, Time, Space, unfoldment, Eternity, etc. The real trouble lies in our taking all these things in an absolute sense. Naturally, the deductions which we draw from such defective premises must lead us into blind alleys and create paradoxes and enigmas of our own making. If we understand clearly that all these things are relative and have different degrees of subtlety, most of our philosophical problems and difficulties will be resolved. Everything below that Ultimate Reality to which we refer as the Absolute must be relative. Otherwise, why do we refer to It as the Absolute?

CHAPTER XV

REFLECTIONS OF REFLECTIONS

WE have seen in the chapter on " Involution and Evolution "
that manifestation means an outward thrust of consciousness
from the centre to the periphery and back to the centre again.
Since potential consciousness needs a medium for expressing
and unfolding its potentialities when it descends into manifestation, its descent is preceded by the formation of a manifested
system of different grades of matter and mind. It is on this
field and through the mechanisms which it gradually evolves
for itself that it unfolds its potentialities and the powers and
faculties which are hidden in them.

How the field for manifestation is prepared by the Logos
and how the individual Monads associated with Him evolve
their individual mechanisms for their unfoldment is dealt with
in great detail in Theosophical literature. Perhaps one of the
most valuable contributions of the Theosophical movement in
modern times is to give to the student of Occultism a clear
idea of the *modus operandi* of manifestation. There is not much
in this knowledge which has been thus given which is quite
new; what is new is the systematic method and clarity of
presentation. Much of this knowledge has always been
available, especially in the literature of the ancient religions
like Hinduism. But it was present in most cases in the
form of unintelligible doctrines and statements. Theosophy
has brought order, clarity, system and a rational outlook
into this confusion, and enabled the earnest student to

acquire a clear and systematic idea of the processes and laws which underlie the manifested universe, both visible and invisible.

This does not mean that we know everything or have a clear comprehension of those realities which are, and will ever remain, beyond the reach of the intellect. But what can be known is known with some degree of clarity and definiteness. I think there is some confusion in the minds of many students of Occultism on this question. The fact that many of the realities of the inner life are beyond the comprehension of the human mind does not mean that we should allow our mind to remain in a state of confusion with regard to them—a cloud of vague and nebulous ideas. When we say that the realities of the spiritual worlds are beyond the realm of the intellect what we mean is that the intellect cannot have a direct perception of those realities which is possible only when the intellect is transcended and consciousness can know the realities by becoming one with them—knowing by fusing, as we say. But the intellect can go up to a certain limit in gaining knowledge of these realities, however restricted that limit might be. And within this limit or realm it can work either with clarity, precision and definiteness, or allow the mind to remain in a chaotic or nebulous condition. It is this latter condition which the earnest student of Occultism should try to avoid if he wants to have a sound base of intellectual knowledge on which a satisfactory edifice of Divine Wisdom can be raised. We do not come nearer to these realities by leaving the mind in a hazy and nebulous condition with regard to them.

Some people think that by having clear-cut and definite ideas we are really conditioning the mind and such a mind is unable to perceive or reflect the realities of life within itself. This idea is again, I think, based on a misconception. A mind which has confused and vague ideas about any reality is as much if not more conditioned than a mind which has clear and definite ideas. Vagueness and indefiniteness is not the same thing as *citta-vṛtti-nirodha* or the freedom of mind from modifications of any kind which is achieved in *Samādhi*. The former is the result of mental laziness, lack of clear thinking and avoidance of concentrated effort to tackle an intellectual problem effectively. The latter is the result of the most rigorous discipline of the mind and yogic training which is required for the practice of *Samādhi*. The two conditions are thus poles apart and diametrically opposed to each other.

The proper attitude and course to adopt in this matter is to have a clear idea with regard to the limitations of the intellect and how far we can go in our approach to these realities through the instrumentality of the intellect and within that limit to use the intellect as rigorously and effectively as possible. Under these conditions our ideas and conceptions, however clear and definite they might be, do not become a hindrance in our effort to know the truths of the inner life directly and really. For, it is much easier to make a disciplined mind which has clear-cut and definite conceptions *niruddha* or without modifications than one which is full of vague and nebulous ideas.

I have digressed from the subject to discuss this important matter here because it is these doubts and misconceptions lurking in our mind which prevent us from attacking the problem of acquiring intellectual knowledge with vigour and enthusiasm. I myself am very conscious of the limitations of such knowledge and its uselessness unless we transmute it into Wisdom and direct knowledge of Truth. But I am not one of those who believe in raising the edifice of Divine Wisdom without any foundations or on foundations of sand. I believe that only on a sound foundation of intellectual knowledge can the temple of Divine Wisdom be constructed, and only into such a temple can the Monad descend and do his work.

One very interesting phenomenon which we find in manifestation is the reflection at lower levels of the realities which exist on the higher. The same realities which are found on the higher planes are seen in expression on the lower planes. The same processes which underlie the phenomena of Nature on the spiritual planes are seen at work on the temporal planes. The same laws which govern the unfoldment of consciousness and evolution of bodies in the spiritual realms are seen to be applicable to the unfoldment of mind and bodies on the lowest planes. This important fact which has been observed by adepts of Occultism who are familiar with phenomena of both the higher and the lower worlds has found expression in the well-known occult maxim " As above, so below ".

When I use the word " same " in this context I do not mean exactly the same. The reflection of the higher into the lower is not like the reflection of a building standing on the shore of a lake. It is not that the phenomenon or the process or the law is repeated in exact detail, but only the principle or the essential features of the particular law, or the process in question. We use the word " reflection " for want of a better word to indicate this subtle reproduction on the lower planes of what happens on the higher. The word " shadow " would perhaps be a more appropriate word to indicate the similarity of the lower to the higher. In a shadow play we see only the forms and actions of the players on the screen in outline, and cannot get any idea with regard to the other features. Sometimes the shadows are very deceptive and give an entirely wrong idea of the thing which they represent. Thus a circular thin disc held at right angles to the screen will give a line and not a circle. A large object can cut off completely a smaller object further away from the screen. So the interpretation of the shadows and the inference of the realities from the shadows which they cast on the screen is not an easy matter, and great care is needed in arriving at correct conclusions. Similarly, it is not easy to get a reasonably correct idea about the realities of the higher worlds by seeing their shadows down below. But if we cannot go behind the screen and see for ourselves what is happening there, well, the shadows do provide a faint idea of those realities. So, it is in this broad and general sense that the maxim ' As above, so below ' ought to be understood.

Another point we may note in this preliminary consideration of the subject is that though there are seven planes on which the manifested solar system functions, there are really three worlds in which consciousness functions, the Divine, spiritual and temporal, if I may use this last word for the lowest three planes taken together, namely, the physical, astral and lower mental. These three worlds correspond to the three worlds in which the Monad, individuality and personality function as shown below:

ÂDI		
ANUPÂDAKA	DIVINE	MONAD—*ÂTMÂ*
ÂTMIC		
BUDDHIC	SPIRITUAL	INDIVIDUALITY—*JÎVÂTMÂ*
MENTAL		
ASTRAL		
PHYSICAL	TEMPORAL	PERSONALITY—*JÎVA*

I have dealt with this question of the division of the planes into three separate groups elsewhere and it is not necessary to go into it again here. My purpose in referring to it in this context is to show that although the number of planes is seven we have really to deal with three worlds only, each world functioning on three planes as shown above. It is the splitting of the Âtmic and Mental planes into two groups of subplanes which makes this possible as will be seen from the above arrangement.

Now, if we are broadly dealing with three worlds which may be called Divine, spiritual and temporal, we can expect to have two reflections of the same reality, one from the

Divine into the spiritual, and another from the spiritual into the temporal. The second reflection which will really be a reflection of a reflection will naturally be more blurred, indistinct and further removed from its reality than the first.

Since our consciousness is confined to the three temporal planes—physical, astral and lower mental—and under the present conditions has to function through the physical brain, one can see at once under what great handicaps it has to work. Reflections of reflections is all that we can see in this dark and dingy world in which we are confined at present. No wonder we cannot see around us much of divinity and the expression of the spiritual life unless we can see and contact these realities from within, with the spiritual faculties which we have developed within ourselves. And one can also see why it is difficult for us to understand the realities of the higher life even though they are reflected everywhere around us. If a thing has been reflected twice from two dark and imperfect mirrors we will not be able to recognize it even if it is on the physical plane. Then how can we hope to perceive the transcendent and glorious realities of the inner planes when the mirrors of our mind within us are dark and murky with desires and thoughts and impurities of the lowest kind?

It is because the realities of the higher and subtler planes are reflected into the lower planes that the study of scientific laws and phenomena on the physical plane is of some help to us in drawing certain conclusions regarding their counterparts on the higher planes, and understanding them to some extent. It is true that we have to be very cautious in drawing such inferences for reasons I have given above and it would be very difficult to derive much benefit of this nature from the study of scientific laws and phenomena but for one fact. This fact is that Occultism has also placed at our disposal a certain amount of knowledge with regard to the subtler planes. No doubt this knowledge is sketchy, incomplete and very difficult to comprehend. But when we study these real things along with their shadows on the physical plane we are able to understand the facts and laws of Occultism and also those of Science much better. The broad and general knowledge of Occultism helps us to understand the significance of scientific facts. The detailed and precise knowledge of Science helps us to understand the *modus operandi* of the laws and processes which are a part of the Occult knowledge. That is the reason why similes and illustrations taken from the field of Science are so helpful in illuminating the doctrines of Occultism.

Take for instance the phenomena of light on the physical plane. The more you study the behaviour of light the more you are struck by the similarity of these phenomena to the modes in which consciousness functions. One somehow gets the impression that light is nothing but the expression of consciousness on the physical plane. Such things offer a very fruitful field for research to students of Occultism. If they go into these questions deeply I am sure they can throw much light on the doctrines of Occultism and make them far more acceptable to the modern educated man. Dr Besant has put the whole idea in a nutshell in the following words taken from *A Study in Consciousness*:

> For all that happens down here is but the reflection in gross matter of the happenings on higher planes, and we may often find a crutch for our halting imagination in our studies of physical development. ' As above, so below.' The physical is the reflection of the spiritual.

We may also recall in this connection the special relation which exists between the Ātmic plane and the physical plane. On account of the inversion which takes place when the spiritual world of Ātmā, Buddhi and Higher Manas, is

reflected in the temporal—physical, astral and lower mental
—the Ātmic plane is reflected in the physical and so the
phenomena of the physical plane have a particular significance in understanding the nature of spiritual consciousness
functioning on the Ātmic plane.

After these preliminary considerations let us now consider a few cases of these reflections which take place from
the higher to the lower. Theosophy, by giving us some
definite knowledge with regard to the phenomena of the
higher planes, has provided the student of Occultism with
many striking instances of the similarity between these phenomena and the phenomena we observe on the physical plane.

Let us take the growth of a tree on the physical plane
and compare it with that of a soul on the spiritual planes.

(1) When the seed is sown in suitable soil and natural
forces begin to work upon it, it sprouts and begins to grow by
the play of sunshine, air, etc. above the surface of the earth,
and water, minerals, etc. below the surface of the earth.   It
absorbs nutriment through the leaves from the atmosphere
and through the roots from the soil.

Similarly, the seed of the human soul is sown in the soil
of the lower planes when the causal body is formed and the
Spirit or a ray of the First Logos or *Śiva-Tattva* descends
into it to start it on its long cycle of evolution and unfoldment.   The soul descends into the lowest three planes again
and again, and grows steadily as a result of the experiences
which it gains from without and the budding of its potential
faculties from within.

(2) Every year in autumn the tree sheds its foliage,
withdraws the sap into the trunk and assimilates the extra
nutriment which it has absorbed during the year.   Then
comes spring, the tree puts forth a new foliage and the whole
cycle is repeated again and again.

In the same manner when the incarnation of a soul
comes to a close it sheds its lowest three bodies, one after

another, withdraws the essence of its experiences during the last incarnation into the causal body and assimilates it for its growth and unfoldment of potential faculties. When this work has been completed it descends again into the lower worlds with added powers and faculties, and the cycle of reincarnation is repeated in the same manner.

(3) When the tree becomes mature it begins to flower and form seeds which on sowing in the soil form trees of the same species and this process of proliferation is unending.

Similarly, when a soul reaches the spiritual maturity of a Solar Logos we find the process of proliferation taking place at the spiritual level. Innumerable Monads emerge with the Solar Logos and begin to evolve in the field of the solar system which He provides. The same thing happens on a limited scale and at a much lower level in the case of the physical body which begins to proliferate as soon as it reaches maturity and thus provides physical vehicles for the incarnation of other souls.

We could consider so many other similarities between the growth of a tree and that of a human soul. But it is not necessary to do so here. Enough has been said to show how clearly the growth of the human soul on the spiritual planes is reflected in the growth of a tree on the physical plane. Even the inversion of the spiritual planes when they are reflected in the temporal planes can be seen in this reflection. The Tree of Life called Aśvattha has its roots above and hangs downwards. The tree on the physical plane has its roots below and grows upwards.

These similarities provide not only interesting examples of the maxim 'As above, so below', but can be utilized for enlarging and enriching our knowledge with regard to processes and phenomena on the spiritual plane by a thorough and intelligent examination of their counterparts on the physical plane. Of course, we cannot draw very reliable conclusions merely from these analogies, but they can provide clues for research along different lines and may lead to substantial additions to our knowledge of the subtler realms.

Let us now take another example of this reflection of the realities of the higher planes into the lower planes, namely, the reflection of the triple aspect of the Monad first into the realm of the individuality and then still lower into the realm of the personality. This double reflection may be represented as shown below:

Divine World	Sat	Cit	Ānanda	Monad
	↓	↓	↓	
Spiritual World	Spiritual Will	Knowledge	Bliss	Individuality
	↓	↓	↓	
Temporal World	Desire	Thought	Pleasure	Personality

It will be seen from the above that in the Divine world the three aspects are present in their pure, infinite and integrated form. In the spiritual world these aspects separate as different functions but self-sufficiency characterizes all of them, i.e. no external aid or stimulus is needed for their expression. In the still lower realm of the personality the functions or expressions become crude as it were, and dependent upon external stimuli. The self-sufficiency and awareness of their being derived from their Divine source is lost. But in spite of this degradation and difference in external expression we can see that the essential nature of the derivatives is the same as that of the original aspects of the Divine from which they are derived. We cannot expect anything better when we are dealing with reflections of reflections.

The fact that the lower forms of expression are reflections or derivatives of their corresponding higher counterparts, and hide the higher forms within them is brought home to us in another way. If we suppress the lower forms the corresponding subtler forms emerge and begin to function. By suppressing lower personal desires spiritual will is developed. By suppressing lower concrete thoughts (*citta-vṛtti-nirodha*) knowledge of realities of the spiritual planes is developed. And by renouncing sensual, emotional and intellectual pleasures, bliss or *Ānanda* is developed.

We should also note that the finer forms of the triple aspects on the spiritual planes are characterized by self-sufficiency, while the cruder forms depend for their expression and growth on external aid and stimulation. Thus spiritual will acts without any ulterior motive. Its action is not determined by external attractions and repulsions. It is Self-determined and therefore free. This is the real freedom of the Spirit, and not the opportunity to satisfy one's personal desires and whims which is generally mistaken for freedom by ignorant people. A slave in external bondage may be really and completely free if he has no personal motives or desires, while a so-called free man may be a real slave if he is dominated by his desires and prejudices.

Similarly, real knowledge is independent of external aids such as collection of facts and data, reasoning, thinking, etc. It is based upon direct perception and cannot be falsified or modified by external changes and pressures. Thought on the other hand is dependent on external aids and associations, is affected by prejudices and may be completely falsified by emergence of new facts on the mental horizon.

The same relation holds between pleasure and bliss. Pleasure depends upon external stimuli, physical, emotional or mental. It can change into pain by change of circumstances. It can lead to pain, in fact always leads to pain in the long run as explained in the well-known *Sūtra* (II-15) of *Yoga-Sūtras of Patañjali*. Bliss on the other hand is independent of external stimuli or circumstances. It wells up from within without any external stimulation or cause, when the individual is pure and harmonized, and in contact with its source, namely, the *Ānanda* within himself.

CHAPTER XVI

DIFFERENTIATION AND INTEGRATION I

(INTEGRATION IN THE SEPARATE REALMS OF SPIRIT AND MATTER)

WE have already dealt with the relation of the unmanifest and manifest and seen that both are different aspects of the One Reality. A more comprehensive study of the manifest state shows that there are some fundamental processes underlying this state and a study of these processes enables us to gain a deeper understanding of the nature and mechanism of manifestation. We have already dealt with two such processes in the chapters on *Involution and Evolution* and *Reflections of Reflections*. In this chapter we shall discuss another of these fundamental processes whose study enables us to gain a deeper insight into the significance of some Occult doctrines.

We have been referring frequently to integration and differentiation in a general way in different contexts. Let us now go a little more deeply into this problem and see whether the scientific phenomena involving integration and differentiation can throw some light on the mysteries of manifestation. Let us first ask the question what is integration and differentiation?

Differentiation may be broadly defined as the separation or breaking up of an integrated whole into its constituent and inherently related parts. It is not simply the breaking up of anything in any manner.   The shattering of a china vase on falling to the ground is not differentiation.   Dismaning a machine is not differentiation.   But the dispersion of white light by means of a prism is.

Integration is the opposite of differentiation.   It is the fusion into a harmonious whole of parts or constituents which are continuous and inherently related to one another.   When the constituents are blended harmoniously in real integration they all disappear in the integrated state and none of them can be distinguished in the integrated state.   A new state has appeared.

It is possible to have partial integration of a sort by combining some constituents.   Thus if light of four colours of the spectrum is combined we shall have coloured light which contains these four colours in an integrated form but not white light which contains no colour at all.   So we see that the characteristic of real and complete integration is that there is nothing in the integrated state of the condition which is present in the differentiated state.   If there is, even partially, then the integration is not real or complete.   This fact is of great significance in understanding the relation between the unmanifest and the manifest.

Some interesting aspects of integration and differentiation and their usefulness in throwing light on the phenomena of Nature and accomplishing certain remarkable results in the field of Science are understood when we study the technique of integral and differential calculus in higher mathematics.   But as few people have this knowledge we shall confine ourselves to those aspects which can be understood by a layman.   The whole field of manifestation offers opportunities for studying this dual process of integration and differentiation.   Let us consider a few examples of this process which are of great importance to the student of Occultism.

The differentiation of white sun-light into spectrums of visible, infra-red and ultra-violet radiations by means of a glàss prism is a wonderful phenomenon which throws light on many fundamental doctrines of Occultism. Its special importance is due to the fact that light has a very close relation with consciousness, is in fact an expression of consciousness on the physical plane in a very mysterious manner. The behaviour of consciousness, for this reason, is almost duplicated in many spheres of light phenomena. We can therefore draw certain inferences with regard to the nature of consciousness and understand the phenomena of consciousness by studying carefully their reflections in the field of light phenomena according to the Occult maxim 'As above, so below'. We have already discussed differentiation and integration in relation to light on several occasions in various contexts and need not dwell on this phenomenon. Let us pass on to other phenomena based on vibration.

There are a large number of physical phenomena known to modern Science which are based on vibrations of different kinds such as sound, X-rays, radio-waves, etc. These vibrations differ from one another not only in their essential nature but also in their wave-lengths, each kind of vibration existing as a continuous series of wave-lengths within certain extreme limits and having different properties. It is thus possible to prepare a table in which these different kinds of vibrations are arranged in a series according to the range of their characteristic wave-lengths. Such tables are frequently given in text-books of physics and one can see from such tables not only the enormous range of the wave-lengths of these vibrations but also the gaps which exist between vibrations of different kinds. These gaps will probably be filled up in due course with further extension of scientific knowledge.

The study of such tables shows not only that each type of vibration exists as a continuous series of wave-lengths but also points to the possibility of all these different types of vibrations being derived from the differentiation of an integrated vibration in which they are contained in a potential form just as the three types of vibrations in infra-red, visible and ultra-violet spectrums are contained in white sun light.

This is not, however, a mere possibility but a fact according to the Occult doctrine. There is according to Occultism a mysterious integrated state of vibration from which all possible kinds of vibrations can be derived by a process of differentiation. This is called *Nāda* in Sanskrit. It is a vibration in a medium called *Ākāśa* which may be translated as 'space' in English. But the conception of *Ākāśa* in Occultism is quite different from that of Science. It is not mere empty space but space which, though apparently empty, contains within itself an infinite amount of potential energy which can find expression in all kinds of vibrations needed in a manifested system. This infinite potentiality for producing vibrations of different kinds in any intensity or amount is due to the fact that at the back of *Ākāśa* or hidden within it, is consciousness. Consciousness alone can produce out of itself *any* amount of energy. According to Science energy cannot be created. It can only be transformed from one form into another or degraded from a higher to a lower level. This is no doubt true of physical phenomena. But obviously, this limitation cannot exist in the case of consciousness and mental phenomena which are derived from it and based upon it. Consciousness is self-determined, integrated and free and can thus produce out of itself an infinite amount of energy through the medium of the mind. That is why the ' spaces ' in which worlds of different degrees of subtlety function are called *Cidākāśa* or ' mental space '. As this point has been discussed at length in the chapters on ' Time and Space ' we need not elaborate it here. All that is necessary to note here is that the different kinds of vibrations taking place on the physical and superphysical planes are the differentiated forms of *Nāda*, a super-integrated vibration in *Ākāśa* which is essentially mental in nature.

We have discussed above very briefly the Occult doctrine according to which the infinite variety of vibrations which we find in Nature are derived from a superintegrated vibration. These infinite number of differentiated vibrations lie at the basis of sensuous perceptions or sensations of different kind and are related to them mathematically as has been pointed out elsewhere. As the different properties of objects which we cognize through our sense-organs are related to these underlying vibrations mathematically in this manner it follows that these properties or *dharmas* are also differentiated aspects of some principle in manifestation. This principle is the well-known *Prakṛti* of Sāṃkhya philosophy which is therefore called *Dharmi* or the potential container of all *dharmas* or properties. According to Sāṃkhya philosophy all properties through which we cognize the objective universe around us are derived from three fundamental properties or *guṇas* called *rajas, tamas* and *sattva*—just as all innumerable colours which we can perceive with our eyes are derived from the three primary colours of the spectrum—blue, red and yellow. *Prakṛti* is thus nothing but the *sāmyavasthā* or balanced and integrated state of the three *guṇas* in which all *guṇas* or properties are present potentially and none actually.

Here then we have really another example of integration and differentiation not at the level of matter or vibration but at the level of the mind, for perception of properties is a function of the mind though the stimulation comes from matter and vibrations. The conception of *Prakṛti* as an integrated state of the *guṇas*, which contains all *guṇas* in a potential state and from which any *guṇa* or property can emerge if the proper conditions (the particular combination of the three *guṇas* based on harmonious motion, irregular motion and no motion) are present will thus be seen to be in perfect accord with our scientific ideas regarding the nature of integration and differentiation.

In the conception of *Prakṛti* as the integrated state of the *guṇas* (*dharmas* depend upon different combinations of the three *guṇas*) we have gone up from the level of matter or vibration to the level of the mind which is the product of the interaction of Spirit and matter. Is it possible to go up still higher and show that the same process of integration and differentiation is at work in the realm of the Spirit or pure consciousness? Is it possible to show that the Many or the individual Monads are merely differentiated aspects of the One Reality? Let us see.

It has been pointed out already in a previous chapter that all states of consciousness right from that of the personality to that of the Cosmic Logos are hidden one within the other in a continuous manner behind the physical consciousness working through the human brain. All these states may be considered to be centred round the *Mahābindu* or the Great Centre from which manifestation of the cosmos takes place. The unity of the spiritual consciousness which is finding expression through the Cosmic Logos, Solar Logoi and the Monads can be represented diagramatically by Fig. 7 given in Chapter VI and all the Solar Logoi and the Monads may be considered as raying out from the centre representing the Cosmic Logos. In this figure each Solar Logos and the Monads who are evolving with Him are shown separate to bring out the partial independence of the solar systems in the cosmos. But essentially all the Solar Logoi and Monads are rays of the manifest Cosmic Logos and the different worlds in which they respectively function are based ultimately on His Consciousness.

In considering the question of integration and differentiation in relation to pure consciousness nothing helps us to gain a glimpse into the relation of the One and the Many as mathematical symbolism. In order to understand how mathematical symbols can be utilized for this purpose let us first consider the relation of a circle to the radii which can be drawn from its centre to the circumference as shown in the following figure.

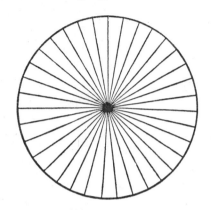

As has been shown in Chapter X the number of radii in such a circle can be increased progressively and the figure approaches a limiting value which is a superficial circle. The superficial circle is the whole, the limiting form when an infinite number of radii are integrated by a mathematical process. To put it simply for the layman we may say that the full superficial circle is an integrated form of an infinite number of separate radii or expressing it in the reverse manner the radii are the differentiated parts of the whole circle.

An interesting aspect of the relation existing between a circle and the radii which radiate from its centre is that it is impossible to say whether it is a whole circle or its constituent radii which can be infinite in number. It is both. Looking at the figure in one aspect it is one. Looking at the same figure in another aspect it is the many. To say that it is one would not be correct for it would mean we are ignoring the many constituent radii which are inherent in the whole. To say that it is the many would again not be correct for it would mean ignoring the whole which is inherent in the constituent parts. The state of wholeness and that of being separate parts or the one and the many are thus complementary and one cannot exist without the other.

And yet the problem is not as simple as stated above. There is a mystery surrounding it which eludes intellectual grasp. The mystery lies at the border where the one-dimensional linear radii disappear into the two dimensional superficial circle. We are unable to ' see ' intellectually the transition from the one state to the other. We see the one or the other but not the relation of the two.

Those who have gone deeply into the philosophical problem of the One and the Many will see in the relation of the whole superficial circle and the constituent linear radii an almost perfect reflection of the Great Mystery which surrounds the relation of man and God. That is why the circle with the infinite number of radii radiating from its centre is a natural symbol of this relationship. And because mathematics is the basis of manifestation the various aspects of this relationship in the realm of manifestation are reflected in the mathematical relationship of the circle and its radii and from a careful study of the mathematical symbol we can draw some interesting conclusions with regard to the realities which they represent according to the occult maxim ' As above, so below.'

It should also be noted that the mystery of the One and the Many has many aspects and levels of manifestation. Considering the realm of pure Spirit alone we see that it has at least three levels. The highest level pertains to the relation of the Cosmic Logos to the infinite number of Solar Logoi who are manifesting throughout this vast and apparently limitless universe. The consciousness of the Cosmic Logos provides the field for the manifestation of the Solar Logoi, in which the consciousness of the Solar Logoi unfolds in its unending journey toward the ever unattainable state of the Absolute. It is also on the base provided by the cosmic planes that the Solar Logoi build their individual worlds functioning through the solar planes.

The second lower level pertains to the relation of a Solar Logos with the Monads who are associated with Him in the manifestation of a solar system. This relation is a reflection of the relation of the Cosmic Logos with the Solar Logoi and all aspects of the latter must have their counterparts in the former though we may not be able to trace them with our present limitations. But we can at least see that the Consciousness of our Solar Logos provides the field in which the Monads of the solar system unfold their consciousness, that the cosmic planes are reflected in the solar planes and that the individual worlds of the separate Monads are built upon and function within the solar planes.

The third lowest level pertains to the relation of a Monad with the Monads who will be associated with him when the former attains the status of a Solar Logos and is able to provide a field for the latter. This relation is still unmanifest for the field for its expression is not yet ready. It lies in the lap of the far distant future. But it is as real as the other two relations referred to above. For, it is rooted in the Eternal and must manifest as inevitably as the parts of the earth which are temporarily in darkness must be lighted up when the earth turns round and faces the sun. For manifestation is not a process of construction and destruction. It is essentially a process of projection in the realm of time and space of those realities which already exist in their true forms in the Eternal.

The student will see from what has been said above that the dual and complementary processes of integration and differentiation are at work not only in the realm of matter and mind but also in the realm of the Spirit. All manifestations of a spiritual nature are differentiated forms of the One Spirit. These sparks from the One Fire separate more and more as they descend lower and lower in manifestation and then begin to draw together and integrate into closer and closer relationships as they draw nearer to the Central Fire. But they never touch the Flame as pointed out in *Light on the Path*. All these different types of differentiation and integration in the realm of matter, in the realm of mind and in the realm of consciousness or Spirit are symbolized by an inverted Tree of Life which is called *Aśvattha* in Sanskrit. This symbol represents not only both the processes simultaneously but also shows their mutual relationship.

Fig. 13. Aśvattha

The above figure represents the manifested universe hanging upside down and rooted in the unmanifest. In a tree the smaller branches join together into progressively larger branches until we reach the fork where bifurcation takes place. Above this is the one trunk which hangs from the roots hidden in the ground. The student will see for himself how aptly the inverted tree symbolizes not only the progressive

integration of minor principles or *tattvas* into more comprehensive principles but also the relation of the unmanifest and
the manifest.   He can work out the correspondences between
the branches etc. of the inverted tree and the different principles operating in the realms of the unmanifest and the
manifest and will be fascinated by the closely analogous
relationships.

The nervous system in the human body is also like an
inverted tree rooted in the brain.   And since the nervous
system along with the brain is the essential physical vehicle
of man on the physical plane through which mind and consciousness function and the rest of the body merely serves to
maintain the nervous system, we see how the realities underlying manifestation are reflected again and again at different
levels and in different spheres of manifestation.

There is one more idea to be noted in considering super-
integration.   This super-integration is the total result of many
integrations taking place at different levels and in different
spheres.   Some of these integrations are accomplished by the
harmonious blending of a number of things in a series as in
the integration of coloured lights in a spectrum into white
light.   Other integrations take place through the reabsorption
in the reverse order of a series of derivatives derived from one
another in a definite order.   Thus we have the reabsorption
of *pṛthvī* (solid) into *jala* (liquid), *jala* into *vāyu* (gas), *vāyu*
into *agni* (radiation) and agni into *ākāśa* (space), the parent
of the five *tattvas*.   In this kind of integration we have a
kind of reversion to a higher or subtler state or *tattva* and
the disappearance of the lower state in the reverse order in
which they had appeared on manifestation.

What is the difference between the two kinds of integration? We see that in the case of the first kind of integration
the components which are integrated are at the same level of
manifestation while in the case of recessional integration
referred to above the level of manifestation changes at each

step. The idea can be best understood by looking at the diagram given above. We see that in the tree the leaves integrate into twigs, the twigs into branches, the branches into the fork and the fork into a single trunk. Now, each of these parts of the tree represents a level of manifestation and forms a kind of link in the series of derivatives derived from the main trunk.

Such a recessional integration may also be considered to take place when the senses are reabsorbed in the mind, the mind in *Buddhi*, the *Buddhi* in *Ātmā* and the *Ātmā* in *Paramātmā* as indicated in *Śloka* I—3—13 of the *Kaṭhopaniṣad*.

Without taking into account the nature of the process involved in recessional integration it is difficult to understand the conception of the Super-Integrated State or how it can be brought about from such a bewildering variety of things existing in manifestation. The idea will also throw some light on the essential nature of *pralaya* which may be considered as a withdrawal of consciousness from a lower to a higher state of manifestation through the process of recessional integration.

CHAPTER XVII

DIFFERENTIATION AND INTEGRATION II

(INTEGRATION OF SPIRIT AND MATTER IN ONE ULTIMATE PRINCIPLE)

IN the last chapter we dealt with the process of differentiation and integration in relation to matter and Spirit and the product of their interaction—mind. But we assumed that these two basic realities of manifestation, Spirit and matter, are essentially separate and independent and considered the process of differentiation and integration in relation to them as separate categories. Those who are familiar with the two important systems of Hindu philosophy, Sāṃkhya and Vedānta, will recall that Sāṃkhya considers Spirit and matter, or *Puruṣa* and *Prakṛti*, as two eternal, independent and ultimate principles in existence. It not only considers Spirit and matter as independent principles but regards Spirit as consisting of innumerable units or independent centres of consciousness called *Puruṣas*. Vedānta on the other hand is monistic and according to it there is only One Ultimate Principle in existence in which not only all *Puruṣas* or Monads are seen as differentiated aspects of the One Spirit but Spirit and matter themselves are seen to be two aspects of One Ultimate Reality.

Occultism considers both these doctrines as true from different points of view. It is natural that in the evolution of philosophical concepts concerning the nature of the universe and the realities underlying it we should first arrive at the penultimate stage before reaching the final ultimate stage. The Sāṃkhyan system represents the penultimate stage while Vedānta goes to the extreme limit and tries to present the ultimate Truth of existence in which even the two basic realities of existence—Spirit and matter—are seen to be two aspects of one and the same Ultimate Reality.

But we must not forget that Sāṃkhya and Vedānta are both philosophical systems based on the intellect and suffer from the limitations and disadvantages of intellectual presentation of spiritual truths. Both of the systems bristle with all kinds of inconsistencies and paradoxes which are inevitable when we try to see these highest truths through the instrumentality of the intellect and present them to others through the still more limited and ineffective medium of language. The value of these two doctrines is based not on the fact that they are brilliant philosophical concepts which satisfy our innermost spiritual longings and intuitive perception of the right and the true. It is based upon the fact that they are essentially true and in accordance with the experiences of all great occultists and mystics who have been able to penetrate into the deepest realms of mind and consciousness and realized through direct experience these transcendent truths of existence. Truth when it is known by direct experience is so utterly different from what it appears in the form of intellectual concepts that one may doubt the utility of such philosophical systems. But we must not forget that a philosophical system or Occult doctrines are not to be taken as a substitute for Truth as is often done by mere scholars. They are to be taken as mere signposts to indicate the direction in which we have to proceed in order to realize the Truth within the recesses of our own mind and consciousness. Their value lies not in enabling us to know the Truth through the intellect, which is impossible, but in providing us with a map of the inner realms of the mind which we have to traverse in order to reach our goal. A map is not meant to give us true knowledge of the country which it represents. Its value lies in serving us as a guide in the discovery of that country. All that matters is that it should indicate the relative positions of the physical features of the country correctly and enable us to avoid going off the track in our search for the goal. It is in this sense that Sāṃkhya and Vedānta are of value to the seeker after Truth. They indicate to us how we have to organize our search, what are the obstacles, and how we have to proceed in the direction of greater and greater integration until we find that all minor truths of existence are different aspects of the Ultimate Truth, of the One Reality which by progressive differentiations produces this drama of the manifested universe.

We have seen already in the previous chapter how mathematical symbolism helps us in gaining a glimpse into the mystery of the One and the Many. We have seen how a superficial circle of two dimensions can be differentiated into an infinite number of radii of one dimension, all rooted in the same centre, and can thus symbolize the emergence of an infinite number of spiritual Monads from the One Spirit. The reverse process which leads from the Many to the One involves the integration of the consciousness of the apparently separate and independent Monads or *Puruṣas* into the one, undifferentiated Reality which is whole and perfect. This integrated state of all spiritual fragments of the One Spirit is the real *Puruṣa*, the ultimate spiritual essence of consciousness which is One yet Many.

We also saw how Sāṃkhya philosophy starting from the side of mind and matter tried to bring about an integration of all kinds of material forces and states of mind in the concept of *Prakṛti* which is a state in which all material forces and the corresponding mental states are integrated and harmonized so perfectly as to leave nothing but a void, a principle in which no force or property exists as such but all kinds of forces and their corresponding mental properties exist potentially, to emerge into manifestation when the right conditions present themselves. The concept of *Prakṛti* will thus be seen to represent the integration of all material forces using the word matter in its widest and subtlest sense and including expressions of mind as well.

The integration of Spirit in the concept of the *Puruṣa* and that of matter in that of *Prakṛti*, the two ultimate polar opposites in manifestation, raises the question whether it is possible to go one step further and bring about the final conceptual synthesis of *Puruṣa* and *Prakṛti* or Spirit and Matter in One Ultimate Reality. The very fact that the two penultimate principles *Puruṣa* and *Prakṛti* are polar opposites points to the existence of an Ultimate Principle from which they are derived. For, we always find in Nature that behind every pair of polar opposites there is hidden a principle which fuses together and unifies at a deeper level the two polar opposites. This fusion and unification is not only theoretically possible but becomes inevitable because the two principles are polar and opposites.

The dualistic conception of Sāṃkhyan philosophy therefore leads naturally and inevitably to a monistic conception in which the polar opposites of Spirit and Matter are seen as products of the primary differentiation of the One Reality which must be Ultimate because the two elements which it harmonizes and unifies are themselves penultimate and the products of progressive integration along two separate channels. Such a conception is found in the philosophy of Vedānta. It will be seen therefore that the monistic philosophy of Vedānta is not an accidental off-shoot of philosophical thought but represents a natural culmination of the evolution of philosophical thought in the intellectual search for an ultimate principle underlying all forms of existence.

The fact that Vedānta is a natural product of the evolution of philosophical thought should not, however, lead us to think that it is a mere philosophical system embodying a clever guess regarding the essential nature of the universe as most philosophical systems are. The real general purpose of philosophy is the search for the Truth underlying the universe in which man finds himself and to pursue this enquiry earnestly with a serious purpose of finding that Truth. It is not to play with philosophical concepts and ideas as an intellectual pastime which modern philosophy is tending to become in an increasing measure. When this search for Truth is motivated by real earnestness and there is a dynamic spiritual urge behind it, it not only leads to the rapid evolution of philosophical thought but also transfers the effort of an individual from the realm of purely intellectual enquiry into the realm of spiritual experience and realization. He cannot remain satisfied with mere ideas and concepts. He wants to know the Truth. The reason for this fundamental change in attitude toward the great problems of life is, of course, the coming into play of his intuitive faculty. He becomes really aware of these deeper problems of life and cannot therefore remain content with merely intellectual solutions. He is thus obliged to enter the path of Yoga and discover these truths of the inner life by direct experience. These discoveries made by occultists and mystics then inevitably react upon the current of philosophical thought and direct it gradually into the right channels. The philosophical thought therefore begins to reflect more and more the Truth which was the object of the purely intellectual enquiry. This accounts for the fact that it is only where philosophy and religion grow together and not in separate compartments that they can have a dynamic approach to life's problems and avoid degenerating into intellectual futility on the one hand and the blind following of a creed on the other.

We should, however, not forget the limitations of the intellect. No system of philosophy or religion can contain the Truth itself. At best they can present certain aspects of Truth from a particular standpoint. Some of these presentations are more in harmony with Truth than others, more useful than others, but they are all imperfect and relative. Truth transcends them all and can be realized only by direct experience in different degrees within the depths of our own consciousness.

We have therefore to hold our philosophical concepts and religious doctrines lightly, as mere attempts at expressing on the intellectual plane what is really beyond the intellect and can be realized only when the intellect has been transcended. If we remember that the differences which we find in the doctrines of different systems of philosophy are due to the differences of points of view we shall be able to avoid the error of adopting a partisan attitude in these matters and be able to see these systems in the correct perspective as different facets of the Greater Philosophy of Occultism which includes and harmonizes all points of view.

As an illustration we may take the two systems of Sāṃkhya and Vedānta with which most aspirants are familiar at least in a general manner. Those who are familiar with the literature on the subject will recall the bitter controversy which has characterized the development of thought along these two lines. Academic philosophers in India have been debating for centuries whether the Sāṃkhyan or the Vedāntic conception of the universe is the correct one, as if the two conceptions were mutually exclusive. Most of them have adopted a partisan attitude and tried to prove that the system which they advocate is true and the other false.

And yet any one who is not prejudiced and examines the two systems of philosophy can see that they represent the penultimate and ultimate views of the universe as we look at it within the deepest recesses of our own consciousness. A simple diagram given below will make the point clear.

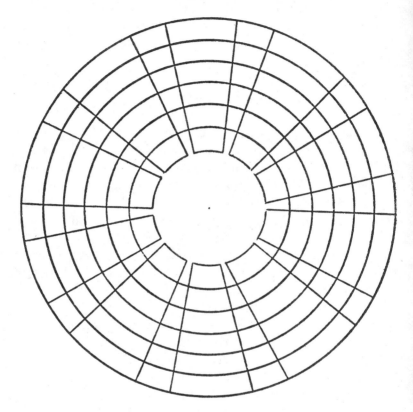

Fig. 14.   Dualism and Monism

The figure represents a number of concentric glass globes illuminated by a central light. The smallest globe which is translucent contains on its surface a number of very small holes or circles which are transparent and allow the light from the centre to pass through the surface of the globe in the form of pencils which produce their corresponding patches of light on all the globes.

Now, the point to note in this diagram is that within the innermost globe the light emanating from the centre is one, and the same light when it goes out from the innermost globe is broken up into a number of separate pencils of light. The breaking up of the one light into many lights is produced by the mechanism of the innermost globe. In fact it is possible not only to break up the one light into many lights but also to impart to the different pencils of light the character of individual uniqueness by changing the shape and size of the holes in the innermost globe.

The above figure illustrates to some extent how the same Reality can appear as one undivided consciousness or as an innumerable number of separate units of consciousness which are essentially of the same nature but have different external expressions. Which particular view of Reality will appear valid will depend upon the point from which it is seen. If it is seen from any point within the innermost globe it will appear as one Ultimate Principle—the *Parabrahman* of Vedānta. If it is seen from any point outside this globe it will appear as a number of *Puruṣas* or Monads who are involved in illusion on account of association with *Prakṛti* and can free themselves from this bondage by withdrawing from the realm of *Prakṛti* and knowing their essential nature. This is the view of Reality presented to us by Sāṃkhya. Can we really say that there is any real contradiction between the two views? Are they not two views of the same Reality depending upon the depth in consciousness from which that Reality is seen?

The above diagram also illustrates the fact that when we see the One Reality as the many *Puruṣas* or Monads it is not the One Reality which is broken up into separate fragments. The separation is illusory and is due to the vehicles or *upādhis* with which it is associated or the sheaths in which the rays of the Spiritual Sun are enclosed. A common simile which is used to illustrate this point is the multiple images of the sun produced by a number of mirrors. Millions of images of the sun may be produced in this manner but they do not affect the sun which produces those images. The images also partake to some extent of the character of the sun. The image produced by focussing the light of the sun by a concave mirror is a miniature sun with intense concentration of light and heat but it does not affect the sun which produces these images.

If we go a little deeper into the matter and consider the nature of the *upādhis* or vehicles we find that even these are not different from the One Light which they appear to divide into separate fragments. It has been pointed out elsewhere that according to the latest discoveries of modern Science matter is nothing but condensed or bottled-up light (called radiation). So the globe of glass which seems to divide the light is also nothing but light in a condensed form. This experiment given above will thus be seen to illustrate not only the unification of different centres of consciousness called *Puruṣas* in Sāṃkhyan philosophy into one undifferentiated Consciousness but also the integration of this over-all Consciousness with Matter or *Prakṛti* into the One Ultimate Principle of Vedānta.

We have seen in the previous chapter on differentiation and integration how mathematical symbolism helps us in gaining a glimpse into the mystery of the relation of the One and the Many. But in that chapter we considered the Spiritual and the material side of the problem separately, how the innumerable Monads evolving in a manifested system are differentiated aspects or fragments of the One Spirit, the Essence of Consciousness. The form side of the manifested universe which we generally refer to as Matter was considered separately and it was shown that *Prakṛti* is an integrated state of the *guṇas*. Thus Matter is in a way one half of the manifested universe, the polar opposite of Spirit. In Hindu philosophy we refer to these two eternal and ultimate principles in existence as *Puruṣa* and *Prakṛti*. These two ultimate principles are according to *The Secret Doctrine* also merely two aspects of the One Ultimate Reality. The monism of Vedānta and not the dualism of Sāṃkhya therefore represents the ultimate Truth of existence.

We have already dealt with the philosophical aspect of this question. Does mathematical symbolism also throw any light on this question as it does on the integration of the Monads into the One Spirit? For, if it can be shown that this final synthesis or integration of Spirit and Matter or *Puruṣa* and *Prakṛti* is in accordance with and is reflected in mathematical relationships we shall feel surer of our philosophical doctrines. There is a certain quality of certainty about mathematical demonstrations which we do not find in any other kind of demonstration. And so if we can place any truth on a mathematical foundation we feel surer of its validity than in any other way.

In order to utilize mathematical symbolism for representing the final integration of Spirit and Matter all that we have to do is to go a little deeper into the symbol which represents the integration of Spirit and relate it with another symbol which may be used for the integration of Matter. Figures (*a*) and (*b*) given below are mathematical symbols which naturally represent the differentiation of Spirit and Matter respectively. We need not enter here into an elaborate discussion of the reasons for symbolizing Spirit and Matter in this manner. Mathematical postulates do not require any proof because they are self-evident and the usual methods which are adopted to prove them do not seem to increase their validity to any marked extent.

But we might mention in passing that Spirit is free, unbounded, centralized, capable of limitless expansion and is One and the Many at the same time. So it can be symbolized aptly by an infinite number of unbounded lines meeting at a centre as shown in the figure on the left. Matter on the other hand is an agent of restricting freedom, imposing limitations and capable of existing in an infinite number of degrees of subtlety. So it can be symbolized aptly by an

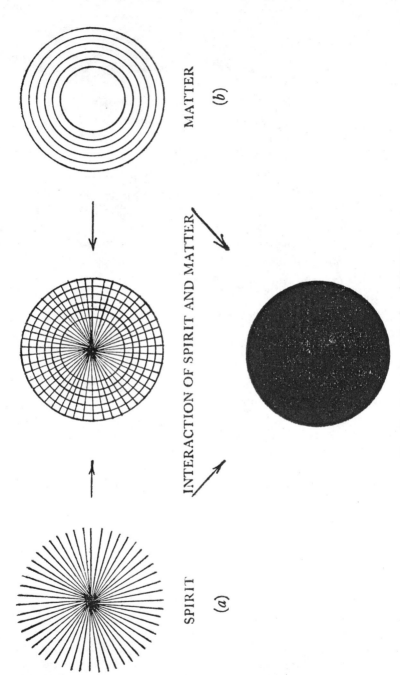

SPIRIT
(a)

INTERACTION OF SPIRIT AND MATTER

MATTER
(b)

Fig. 15. Integration of Spirit and Matter

infinite number of concentric circles as shown in the figure on the right. The central figure is only a combination of the two figures and therefore represents the coming together or interaction of Spirit and Matter which is what manifestation really is. The central figure will thus be seen to be the most appropriate symbol of manifestation representing in an integrated mathematical form all the essential aspects of Spirit and Matter. But its most remarkable feature is that it shows in an effective manner that the two polar and opposite principles of Spirit and Matter are derived from or are aspects of One Ultimate Principle. In order to understand how this is possible let us take the two figures representing Spirit and Matter separately and integrate their respective constituents. Or, to put the same thing in simple non-mathematical language let us find out the limiting value of the figures when the number of constituent units becomes infinity. Taking the figure representing Spirit we can see at once that if we increase the number of radii *ad infinitum* it will tend to become a superficial circle with the centre at the point where all the radii meet. Since the radii are lines with no thickness no number of them even if it is infinite can make a complete superficial circle but the figure will tend to become a superficial circle as the number of lines approaches infinity. This is expressed by saying that if we increase the number of radii *ad infinitum* the limiting value is a *superficial* circle. The actual figure will approach the limiting value more and more nearly but never reach it. The limiting value of any variable quantity in mathematics is obtained by the mathematical process of integral calculus and is a very definite thing from the mathematical point of view. There is no vagueness or uncertainty about it. It represents a definite fact of existence. One thing we have to note particularly about this limiting value of the figure represented by the black circle at the bottom is that it is a thing in a higher dimension. For, it is a superficial circle of two dimensions while the constituents from which it is derived are all lines with one dimension. So when the figure representing Spirit attains its limiting value it goes into a higher dimension, as it were. It is no longer a combination of lines but a continuous surface containing no lines. The two states are in a way mutually exclusive.

Let us now take the figure representing Matter and apply the same process of integration to the concentric circles which constitute it. The circles in this case represent as pointed out above the infinite number of planes of different degrees of subtlety which can emerge from the bosom of *Prakṛti*, the infinite substratum of all kinds of matter having different properties. We can see at once that as we increase the number of circles *ad infinitum* they will tend to approach a limiting value more and more nearly but never reach it. What is this limiting value in the case of an infinite number of concentric circles representing the limitation of consciousness by Matter? The same superficial circle which was found to be the limiting value in the case of the figure representing Spirit. So we find that the limiting value in the case of the two figures which are so different and which represent mathematically the polar opposites, Spirit and Matter, are identical.

The significance of this identity is obvious. It implies that the same Ultimate Reality differentiates along two different lines to produce on the one hand an infinite number of Spiritual Monads and on the other hand an infinite variety of material planes for ensheathing and evolving these Monads. The complementary nature of Spirit and Matter is thus inherent in the very nature of manifestation and can be traced to the very source of manifestation, namely, the Unmanifest. As long as there is separation in the realm of consciousness, or there is individuality, there must be matter to separate off one unit of consciousness from another, however subtle this matter might be. Even in the case of Solar Logoi in whom the awareness of unity must be at its highest, there must be a thin film of matter or a subtle veil of *Māyā* to separate off the consciousness of one Solar Logos from that of another and to make it possible for each Logos to be individually unique and to function separately. Without matter to separate off expressions of consciousness there can be no Monads, no Solar Logoi, no *tattvas*, no planes, no manifestation, in short only the perfectly harmonized, perfectly blended and integrated state of the Ultimate Reality which we refer to as the Absolute.

In the mathematical symbolism discussed above we have chosen a two dimensional figure to illustrate the integration of Spirit and Matter in One Ultimate Principle. But we all know that a two dimensional superficial circle is a cross section of a sphere in three dimensions and a sphere is a kind of cross section of another figure corresponding to a sphere in four dimensions and so on. On each plane the relation between the integrated form and the corresponding differentiated forms remains the same and reflects the relation of Spirit and Matter on the plane. So these figures should not be considered as mere symbols but as mathematical representations of spaces of different dimensions which exist on different planes of manifestation, being three dimensional on the lowest physical plane. All these spaces are rooted in and derived from the Ultimate Space or *Mahākāśa* by differentiation as explained in the chapter on ' Time and Space II '. If the student studies the chapter on ' Theos, Chaos and Cosmos ' in the second volume of *The Secret Doctrine* in the light of what has been discussed in this chapter he will find it easier to grasp the inner significance of what is written in that chapter. He will see that both Theos and Chaos, or Spirit and Matter, are rooted and contained in an integrated state in the Ultimate Space or *Mahākāśa* or the Void of the Absolute and it is by the differentiation and subsequent integration of Spirit and Matter that manifestation takes place and a Cosmos is evolved.

CHAPTER XVIII

MATHEMATICS AS THE BASIS
OF MANIFESTATION

IT is fashionable these days in scientific circles to represent everything in mathematical terms. If we can somehow put any law or phenomenon of Nature in the form of a mathematical equation we think we have brought it within the realm of scientific knowledge and put it on a scientific basis. To a certain extent this effort to reduce everything in Nature to mathematical terms is justified because the basis of manifestation is mathematical. The relation between mathematics and the phenomena of manifestation has long been known and expressed in various ways. Pythagoras called God a Geometrician, and in more recent times the same idea has been put by Sir James Jeans in the statement that 'God must be a mathematician.'

Fundamental truths of Nature are based on mathematics and are reflected in mathematical relationships. The most spectacular demonstration of this fact was made in the formulation of the Theory of Relativity. Einstein, sitting in his room with a pencil and some paper, and not even stepping into a laboratory, discovered some of the most fundamental truths with regard to the physical universe. Some of these truths were incorporated by him in the form of a simple formula $E = -mc^2$ which led to the discovery of atomic energy. This discovery has not only revolutionized the fundamental conceptions of Science but brought about far-reaching changes in our life. The Theory of Relativity appears to have given almost a new direction to our civilization and to have created problems which are a challenge to our current outlooks and modes of thinking.

Now, it is not only truths of the physical world which are reflected in mathematical relationships, but also those of the subtler worlds. By this it is not meant that they can necessarily be reduced to mathematical formulae but that these truths can be grasped to some extent by the intellect with the help of mathematics without direct realization in one's consciousness as is done in Yoga. It is true that such a knowledge is bound to be skeletal or like a map. It gives only the relations and not the contents of the realities which it represents. These latter can be known only by direct experiences on the higher planes. But this mathematical knowledge is knowledge which can be relied upon, because the conclusions of mathematics are infallible and utterly dependable. The only difficulty is in the interpretation of these conclusions which may or may not be correct and may completely vitiate the conclusion. For being without content and of a general nature they can be interpreted in different ways. That is why such conclusions are always tested by actual experiments before they are accepted. Einstein's theory was not considered valid until it had been tested by experiments made by astronomers and physicists.

That the physical universe is based on mathematical laws will be seen easily if we remember that all phenomena are essentially of the nature of vibrations or motions of different kinds. Every vibration in the ultimate analysis is a mode of motion which can be represented by a mathematical formula. Since the *bhūtas* (Elements), which affect our sense-organs and produce the five kinds of sensations through the instrumentality of the sense-organs, are dependent upon vibrations of various kinds they are really in the ultimate analysis merely mathematical qualities. Every sensation is produced by a vibration and is mathematically related to the vibration. For example, light of a particular wave-length will produce the sensation of a particular color, sound of a particular wave-length will produce the sensation of tone of a particular pitch. Some sensations may be produced by a complex group of vibrations but these can be analysed and can always be reduced to mathematical terms. That is why sensations are called *tanmātras* in Hindu philosophy. The Sanskrit word *tanmātra* means literally ' the measure of that '. Sensations are measures of reality in its objective aspect, and we can actually represent them by mathematical formulae. We can contact reality in its objective aspect only through them as proved by Science. The whole physical universe in its objective aspect which we perceive through our sense-organs is thus reducible to a set of mathematical formulae.

That the whole of the manifested universe in its physical and superphysical aspects must be based ultimately on mathematics follows from the very nature of the Ultimate Reality. If undifferentiated Consciousness is the only Reality at the basis of the universe and all the phenomena are merely modifications of Consciousness or in Consciousness, it follows logically that all phenomena and noumena as well must be nothing but *relations* in that underlying Consciousness. And since mathematics is the science of pure relations it must underlie all the truths of existence and must reflect those truths in every sphere of life. The pure undifferentiated Consciousness can be compared to pure water in a perfectly still condition and the perception of phenomena by the mind to the patterns produced in the water when it is churned in different ways and with different speeds. If pure water is being churned in a tank and we consider the essential nature of the infinite variety of innumerable patterns of water we shall find that there is nothing else in existence but water and *relations* between its different parts. *There can be nothing else.* And these relations between the different parts of the water which find expression in an infinite variety of patterns are all based on mathematics and can be defined by mathematics.

Only the Absolute is absolute and not relative. All else in manifestation below that State is strictly relative and since mathematics is the science which deals with relations of every conceivable type it must be the very ultimate basis of manifestation. Because the Absolute is also the womb of this relative manifested universe and is the ultimate source from which the universe comes forth it should be possible to represent the Absolute also by the ultimate reality of mathematics. What is this ultimate reality of mathematics? Zero! Zero is the undefinable, unknown, potential container of all figures and so of all mathematical relationships. It is the womb of mathematics, containing the very essence of all possible relationships with which we deal in the science of mathematics. It is for this reason that it alone can serve as a symbol of the Absolute.

Mathematics deals only with pure abstract relations without taking into consideration the contents of those things which are related to one another. It is obviously, therefore, concerned with the world of the Relative and not with that Ultimate Reality which we refer to as the Absolute. It gives us the foundation principles upon which the manifested universe in all states of subtlety is based, but it cannot touch the Absolute, for, in the Absolute those different parts or aspects which are related in manifestation become so completely integrated and perfectly harmonized as to appear a void to the intellect. So, all the laws and formulae of mathematics which are applicable to the manifested state must also become integrated into a state of No-Relation or No-number, as this state is called in *The Secret Doctrine*. But this No-number or No-relation represented by the zero is not a void in the ordinary sense. It contains all the laws and relations of mathematics within itself in an exquisitely harmonized though incomprehensible condition. From this No-number or

No-relation can be obtained by differentiation or derivation all those laws of pure mathematics which regulate the relations of things in manifestation.   Upon these derived laws of mathematics in their totality, whether discovered or still undiscovered, is based the whole structure of the manifested universe in all its aspects and parts.   It is according to these laws that the Great Architect of the universe plans and erects the universes through which He manifests.

It will be seen from what has been said above how and why mathematics can provide us with valuable clues in investigating, understanding and representing the mysteries of Occultism.   In trying to understand the nature of Reality in manifestation through the instrumentality of the intellect we can derive help from mathematics because it is the science of pure relationships devoid of any content and can throw some light on the relations of different aspects of manifested Reality to one another.   Let us be quite clear in our mind what this means.

We cannot *know* Reality in its different aspects and different levels except through direct perception, which means the fusion of the individual's consciousness with the Divine Consciousness.   But we can know the relations between these different aspects and levels of Reality because these relations *are reflected in the facts and laws of mathematics.*   The difference between the two kinds of knowledge is very similar to the difference in the knowledge of a country gained by going and seeing it directly with our own eyes or by looking at its map.   There is really no way of knowing a country truly except by going to it and seeing it with our own eyes and coming in direct contact with it.   But we can get some idea of the country, though of a different nature, by looking at its map.   A map or a diagram can give an idea only of the relations of the different parts of a thing which it represents.   It is a symbol, but a symbol of things as they exist in relation to one another and not as they are in reality.   In a way a map or a diagram sometimes gives a better idea of a composite and complicated whole than seeing it directly or through pictorial representation. For it can give a general idea of the whole as well as the parts in relation to each other, while seeing it directly or through pictorial representation gives only a partial view of a particular aspect at a time. A man who sees and studies a map of Kashmir gets a better idea of the natural features of the country than a person who goes there and sees things one after another in a haphazard manner as a tourist. But of course, the map will not give him the slightest idea about the beauty of the scenery and the life of the people.

It is necessary to have a clear idea with regard to the limitations and advantages of symbolic representation of Occult truths through diagrams or in other ways if we are to utilize these properly for investigating and understanding those truths. The limitations have been pointed out above. These are mainly two: one is that we can get an idea in this manner only of the relations between different aspects of reality, and not of their real nature; the other is that we have to be careful in representing and interpreting correctly the conclusions which we arrive at in this manner. It is here that intuition comes in and becomes a necessary factor in our studies or investigations. For, while the conclusions arrived at in the field of physical science can be interpreted adequately and correctly with the help of the intellect alone, because they deal with non-sentient blind forces of Nature, the conclusion with regard to the realities of mind and consciousness cannot be left to the intellect alone. They require the light of intuition which comes from the realms of consciousness.

In spite of these limitations there is no doubt that mathematics can be of great help in investigating, representing, and understanding the truths of the inner life; it can provide us with a map of the country which we shall later explore unaided within ourselves. The value of a map under these conditions cannot be overestimated; it may not help us directly but at least it helps us in having a correct perspective and keeping to the right course, and not losing our way. A military commander who has to carry out operations in a country is provided with a map of the country and not picture post cards. This is the function of philosophy in tackling the problem of Self-discovery and Self-realization. It gives us a sort of map of the country which we have to explore.

Let us now discuss very briefly the significance of numbers, for mathematics is ultimately based upon numbers, and all numbers should therefore have some relation with the basic realities of manifestation. If we examine the series of numbers beginning with 1 we find that they increase from 1 to 9, and then after that the numbers begin to repeat themselves in various permutations and combinations as shown below:

0,	1,	2,	3,	4,	5,	6,	7,	8,	9,
10,	11,	12,	13,	14,	15,	16,	17,	18,	19,
20,	21,	22,	23,	24,	25,	26,	27,	28,	29,
30,	31,	32,	33,	34,	35,	36,	37,	38,	39,
90,	91,	92,	93,	94,	95,	96,	97,	98,	99,
100,	101,	102,	103,	104,	105,	106,	107,	108,	109,
110,	111,	112,	113,	114,	115,	116,	117,	118,	119,

$$--- \ --- \ --- \ --- \ --- \ --- \ --- \ --- \ --- \ --- \ \infty$$

. The evolution of all numbers from the number one is an interesting mathematical problem but we are not concerned with it here. All that we need note here is that there are only nine fundamental numbers, 1—9 and their derivatives, flanked by two intriguing mathematical entities O (zero) and ∞ (infinity) which are really no numbers. These eleven mathematical entities which seem to have a specific identity of their own are, therefore, not only the basic realities of mathematics but must somehow represent the basic realities of existence and their relations to one another. The correlation of these eleven mathematical entities with the realities which they represent is an interesting problem, and research in this field will be very rewarding, for, it will throw new and interesting light on the nature of these realities and the relations which exist between them. But even with the little knowledge which Occultism has placed at our disposal we can see the tremendous significance of these numbers and their correspondences with the fundamental realities of existence, both in the unmanifest and the manifest state. The Occult doctrines fit in very nicely in this scheme of correspondences, and, if there are any gaps or discrepancies, a thorough investigation of these will be of great help in throwing further light on the mysteries of these realities. In the scientific study of any problem nothing is more useful than the exceptions and discrepancies which sometimes crop up in the working of a natural law. It is through the investigation of these exceptions and discrepancies that new vistas of knowledge and lines of enquiry open up before the investigator.

We have already referred very brrefly in the chapter on the concept of the Absolute to the intriguing and to a certain extent unpredictable characteristics of zero which make it eminently suited for representing the Absolute in the world of mathematics. The zero contains within itself potentially all mathematical quantities and relationships that can possibly be imagined, each + quantity being balanced by its exactly opposite − quantity. It is not, therefore, a symbol of *nothing* but *everything* present in a harmonized and balanced state. It is a symbol of *No-thing* for it does not contain any quantity as such, yet all quantities are present in it potentially, and can be drawn from it as need arises. The zero is thus a natural symbol of the Absolute. A careful investigation of its properties may enrich our concept of this Reality.

Let us now descend from the realm of *No-number* or zero into the realm of numbers. Here obviously 1 is the starting point, for all numbers are made up by the successive addition of 1 as shown below:

$$1, 1+1=2, 2+1=3, 3+1=4, 4+1=5, 5+1=6, 6+1=7,$$
$$7+1=8, 8+1=9, \text{ etc.}$$

We see thus that one is the fundamental number, the father of all other numbers, all of which can be derived from the proliferation of one. And since one, unlike zero, is also in the realm of manifestation it must represent that level of Reality which is the very basis of manifestation, that Principle in which is rooted the tendency or the power to manifest. What is this level of Reality or Principle? In order to be able to answer this question we have first to consider two facts. One is the primary differentiation of the One Reality into the *Śiva-Śakti Tattva*. This *tattva* or principle being the primary dual *tattva* must obviously be represented by the number 2. This means that there must be another level of Reality between zero and 2, which corresponds to the number 1 in the fundamental series of numbers: 0, 1, 2, 3, 4, 5, 6, 7, 8, 9. The symbolization of the *Śiva-Śakti Tattva* by a bi-focal ellipsoid also presupposes the presence of another *tattva* corresponding to a sphere, for an ellipsoid can form only by the separation of the centre of a sphere into two separate foci of an ellipsoid. As an ellipsoid presupposes the existence of a sphere from which it is derived, as ' two ' pre-supposes the existence of ' one ' from which it is derived, so a bipolar dual *Śiva-Śakti Tattva* or $+$ and $-$ Principle presupposes the existence of a non-polar unitary *tattva* or Principle from which it is derived.

The second fact we have to consider is that in the concept of the Absolute as a harmonious synthesis of all opposites, and an integration of all *tattvas* there is no place for a centre. It must be an undifferentiated state which we generally indicate by the word *nirviśeṣa* (without distinction). A centre means centralization, and centralization means partial distortion and deviation from the perfectly uniform undifferentiated, *nirvikāra* (undistorted) state of the Absolute. And yet without a centre there can be no manifestation. Even the primary differentiation of the *Śiva-Śakti Tattva* requires the presence of a centre which can then separate into two foci. This second fact also, therefore, points to the existence of a level of Reality which comes between the uniform undifferentiated Absolute and the dual *Śiva-Śakti Tattva*. This level of Reality must be a centralized reality but non-polar, unlike the *Śiva-Śakti Tattva*. It must contain within itself the principle of individuality and the potentiality of manifestation, for without a centre of individuality there can be no manifestation. It is this level of Reality which is represented by the number 1.

So when we talk of the One we do not refer to the Absolute but to this aspect or level of Reality which comes between the Absolute represented by zero and the *Śiva-Śakti Tattva* or the Father-Mother Principle represented by 2. Let us not try to identify this Reality by any specific name and refer to it merely as the One for the time being. We see in the above illustration the value of mathematics in helping us to arrive at definite conclusions with regard to these things which are beyond the realm of the intellect. If our conceptions of the Absolute and the *Śiva-Śakti Tattva* are correct, then the existence of a Reality coming between these two and corresponding to number one in the mathematical series 0, 1, 2, 3, etc., becomes inevitable. This Reality corresponding to number one can be considered as an aspect of the Absolute but we shall not go into this question here.

The level or aspect of Reality corresponding to the number 3 is obviously the Triple Logos who is the very basis of a manifested system. His triple nature, as has been pointed out in a previous chapter, is the result o the appearance of the subject-object relationship which brings into action His *Chit* (Mind) aspect, the basis of Divine Ideation. All triplicities, which we find in Nature everywhere, are derived from the triple nature of the Logos, are reflections of His Life and Consciousness, as has been pointed out already in chapter VI.

It is not possible to discuss here in detail the correspondences between the fundamental numbers from 0 to 10 and the different levels of Reality which they represent, but the following chart gives some hints with regard to this interesting question and may be taken tentatively by the student for further thought and enquiry. The significance of numbers and the powers and potencies associated with them is a subject of very wide scope with which many Western occultists are familiar. It is not only of theoretical interest but forms the basis of many occult arts.

We have not dealt with the significance of geometrical figures in this chapter. Many examples of geometrical symbolism will be found in different parts of the book.

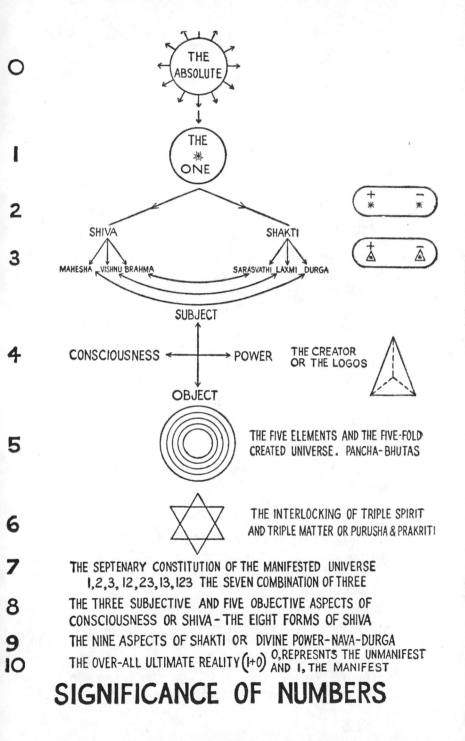

SIGNIFICANCE OF NUMBERS

CHAPTER XIX

DIVINE PRINCIPLES AND FUNCTIONS (TATTVAS)

ONE of the most profound and subtle concepts of Hindu philosophy is that of *Tattvas* or fundamental principles of existence. Like so many other doctrines concerning the basic factors involved in manifestation it is difficult to grasp its real significance and most people who are familiar with it have only vague and general ideas as to what *Tattvas* really are. It is natural that a concept of such fundamental nature should be referred to by many scholars in various contexts but very few have tried to explain clearly the real significance of *Tattvas* and their place in manifestation. An enumeration of *Tattvas* with sometimes a vague indication of their nature is all that is generally given. Since these lists vary widely and are sometimes contradictory this produces further confusion in the mind of the student.

It must be admitted that the conception of *Tattvas* is extremely subtle and so difficult to grasp that there is nothing to be surprised at in its remaining a vague and little understood doctrine of Occult philosophy. But it is not beyond the capacity of the human intellect to grasp it in its general sense and to relate it with the other concepts of a fundamental nature. The real difficulty in understanding any particular doctrine lies in the fact that all doctrines of the Occult philosophy are closely related and based upon a few fundamental conceptions. And unless we have a clear idea about these doctrines as a whole and know their relation to one another it is difficult to see what place any particular doctrine occupies in this system and thus to understand its real significance and relation to the whole.

This is a general principle which is applicable not only to the study of the philosophy of Occultism but to any science or art. If our ideas with regard to the fundamental principles of any science or art are clear and definite we not only have a firm grasp of the whole field of knowledge in a general way but are able to understand and assimilate any new and detailed knowledge in that field easily. But people generally get so much involved in the study of details that they are unable to distinguish between the essentials and non-essentials, between the fundamental principles and the mass of detailed information in which these principles are embedded.

It is true that knowledge in every field is increasing at a tremendous rate and specialization is therefore becoming more and more necessary. But specialization has its disadvantages and dangers. It tends to make people narrow-minded, mechanical and lopsided. The kind of specialization which has been described humorously as ' knowing more and more about less and less ' has become inevitable in the development and application of scientific knowledge, although even in this field the leaders of thought are always those who have a firm and clear grasp of fundamental principles and can use and co-ordinate the specialized knowledge of specialists and technologists working in teams for their larger purposes.

Important though this distinction between the essentials and non-essentials is for the student of Science, it is even more necessary for the student of Divine Wisdom to distinguish between fundamental principles and detailed knowledge of facts and to make a definite effort to acquire first a clear idea with regard to the basic principles and their relation to one another. The domain of Divine Wisdom is so vast and fathomless that unless he does this he will find himself floundering in a mass of unrelated and mostly useless ideas and lose his bearings completely. The erection of the intellectual edifice of Divine Wisdom should be like the construction of a skyscraper. We should first prepare the steel frame of fundamental principles and it is only when this work has been completed that we should with great discrimination begin to acquire and fill in the detailed knowledge which serves to embody and illustrate the fundamental principles.

Much of this detailed knowledge is not of great use for the serious aspirant because it cannot be utilized by him in his direct search for the truths of Divine Wisdom. All knowledge gathered from external sources and based merely on the intellect, though necessary for the development of the mind, suffers from the defect that it is partial, distorted and at best represents a view of a particular truth from a particular point of view. It has, therefore, to be taken tentatively, lightly, as an aid in the search of that Truth of truths which is enshrined in our own heart and in which all the relative truths hidden beneath all intellectual knowledge are contained in their reality and purity. That is why the ancient Seers have always exhorted us to concentrate all our efforts on finding ' THAT, knowing which everything is known '. The pursuit of intellectual knowledge for the true aspirant is justified only in so far as it helps him to organize effectively the search for this supreme Truth. And he will find if he considers the matter carefully that this basic intellectual knowledge which he really needs is that immutable and eternal steel frame binding together in a harmonious whole the fundamental doctrines of the Divine Wisdom. The light of Wisdom which illuminates this edifice of intellectual knowledge is far more important than its size.

After this digression let us now come to the subject in hand. The word *Tattva* is generally translated as ' a fundamental principle of existence ' in English but the word ' principle ' does not at all convey the profound and rich significance of the Sanskrit word. The word is derived in

Sanskrit from the root *tat* which means 'that' and *Tattva* therefore means 'thatness'. In this derivation from the word 'that' lies the clue to its real and profound meaning.

We find in the manifested universe innumerable objects. Apparently, most of these objects seem to be unrelated and to have no particular function to perform. But the real fact is that in a cosmos which is based upon Divine Consciousness and pervaded by Divine Life there can be nothing which is not without its function and which is not related to other things in some manner, though on account of our limited vision we may not be able to see these hidden relations and functions. All things must be related and all things must have their unique function.

If this is so, then tne whole universe can be considered in one of its aspects as a network of functions which are being performed at different levels through different agencies and instruments and which make it possible for the whole machinery of the universe to run efficiently and smoothly. If we take any machine like a clock or the human body and examine its working we shall find that it embodies a number of functions which are performed in perfect co-ordination hrough a number of instruments or parts. Each function is related to the other functions and has its own instrument or organ through which it finds expression. Now, a manifested universe or any other smaller unit of manifestation such as a solar system is like a running machine, though a machine which is unimaginably complex and vast in its nature. There must be, therefore, a number of hidden but necessary functions being performed behind and through the outer visible, ever-changing and moving structure. These functions must be of infinite variety and must be performed according to definite laws of Nature working at different levels with mathematical exactitude. The recent developments in Science, for instance those connected with the developments of space-crafts and missiles have shown how exactly the laws which lie at the basis of the physical universe work, a fact which enables scientists to regulate and manipulate their movements with a precision which appears astounding.   But this precision in the working of these laws is not confined to the physical universe as orthodox Science naively assumes.   It holds good in every realm of phenomena—mental, emotional and moral.   It is in this respect that the knowledge and attitude of occultists differs fundamentally from that of orthodox scientists.

It is these Divine aspects and functions of different kinds which find expression in the manifestation of a universe that are referred to as *Tattvas*.   For what is a function essentially? It is the manner in which a thing works or gives expression to its *essential* nature.   Divine functions are thus the different manners in which the One Reality works and gives expression to the different aspects of its Infinite nature to accomplish different kinds of objects in manifestation.   The word *Tat* or THAT is used here in its highest sense as referring to the One Reality and not to ordinary things.   When used in reference to ordinary things the word used for the essential qualities is not *Tattva* but *Dharma*.

This ' thatness ' has both a static and dynamic aspect. In its static aspect it constitutes the essential nature of a thing.   In its dynamic aspect it constitutes the essential function or mode of expression of the thing.   Both these aspects are included in the conception of *Tattvas*.   Both these aspects are related to each other, for, naturally, the functions which a thing performs will depend upon its essential nature and the particular aspect of its nature which will come into play will depend upon the particular function.

This dual nature of *Tattvas* can be best understood by considering the nature of *Dharmas* or ' thatness ' in relation to ordinary things in manifestation.   The properties and functions of anything in Nature will be seen to be the static and dynamic aspects of its essential nature.   When we see the nature of a thing in repose, as it were, distinguishing that thing from all other things we are dealing with its ' properties '. When the thing plays its appointed role in Nature based upon its peculiar properties we are dealing with its functions. The word *Dharma* in Sanskrit covers both these aspects of the essential nature of anything, properties as well as functions.

Another interesting fact we have to keep in mind with regard to *Tattvas* is that though their essential nature remains the same always, their expression differs according to the level at which they are functioning and the sphere in which they find expression. The differences in expression are sometimes so great that it is hardly possible to recognize the same *Tattva* hidden behind the different expressions. And yet a careful mental analysis or intuitive insight will enable us to see easily the same *Tattva* in action behind expressions which seem to have nothing in common outwardly.

Let us take the function or expression of a particular well-known *Tattva* like *Agni* to illustrate the above point and to throw further light on the nature of *Tattvas*. *Agni Tattva* may be crudely translated as the ' Principle of Fire '. What is the essential nature of fire? To burn any substance and reduce it to the irreducible minimum constituents under a particular set of circumstances. If we take impure gold and heat it at a high temperature all the dross is burnt away and pure gold is left behind. If we burn coal all the carbon is burnt off and an ash, the more permanent constituent of coal is left behind. This is the ordinary kind of fire with which we are all familiar. But there are other kinds of Fire which do not seem to have any well-known external characteristics which we generally associate with fire and yet on closer examination will be found to have the essential characteristic of removing the non-essential parts of a thing and leaving the essential. There is, for example, the gastric fire or *Jatharāgni*. This ' gastric fire ' according to the philosophy of *Hatha Yoga* disintegrates the food we take and reduces it to its essential simple elements which can be assimilated by the body for its normal functioning. There is the *Jnānāgni* or the Fire of Wisdom which burns up the illusions of the lower life and *Avidyā* or ' Ignorance ' and leaves only the knowledge of the Real.

It will be seen that in all the above cases the essential function of the *Agni Tattva*, namely, to remove the non-essential and leave the essential, is present although the processes through which this function is fulfilled may be outwardly so different as to apparently have hardly anything in common. So, in studying the nature of any particular *Tattva* we have to ignore the mechanism or process through which the *Tattva* fulfills its function or expresses its quality and have to concentrate our attention on the essential function or quality. It is only in this way that we can trace the *Tattva* at different levels and in different spheres of expression.

Agni is one of a group of five *Tattvas* called *Pañca Tattvas* or *Pañca Mahābhūtas*. One of the functions of the *Pañca Tattvas* will be considered in detail in discussing the mechanism of sense-perception and it will be shown that they are the stimulating agents in the production of sensuous images in the mind through the instrumentality of the five sense-organs. It must be remembered, however, that this function connected with the phenomenon of sensation is merely one of the functions of the five *Tattvas*. Actually they are Cosmic Principles which play a very fundamental and comprehensive role in manifestation, a role which is too profound and complicated to be comprehended by us.

Since these *Pañca Tattvas*—*Pṛthvi* (earth), *Jala* (water), *Vāyu* (air), *Tejas* (light) and *Ākāśa* (space)—are not mere abstract Principles but conscious Principles, they are called *Devatās* or *gods* in Hindu philosophy and invoked in different ways in ceremonies for bringing about certain specific results in consonance with their respective natures. They function through various hierarchies of nature spirits etc. of various grades and are related to different types of natural forces.

On account of the intimate relation of consciousness and sound their powers can be invoked and the corresponding forces brought down through particular sounds which have the specific potencies hidden in them. For example, in *Tantrik* practices the five syllables called *Bija-akṣaras* (Seed-letters) which are frequently used in various mantras, etc. are *Ham, Yam, Vam, Lam* and *Ram*. But the subject is too complex and surrounded by mystery for an ordinary student and all that he should aim at is to acquire a general but clear idea about the nature and functions of these five Principles generally referred to as the Five Elements.

One of the most remarkable instances of tracing this subtle connection between the highest and the lowest expression of a *Tattva* is provided by the following significant maxim of Hindu philosophy which is concerned with the highest *Tattva* in existence, namely, the *Śiva-Śakti Tattva*:

Saṃkaraḥ puruṣāḥ sarve striyāḥ sarvā Maheśvari

The above Sanskrit maxim translated literally into English means:

' All men (expressions of) Śaṃkara (Śiva) and all women are (expressions of) Maheśvari (Śakti) '.

This may appear to the casual student a strange and almost blasphemous statement but it is really a wonderful method of unequivocally asserting the Divine origin and nature of man and indicating the essential nature of the relation between the sexes. We have only to recall the fact that when individualization takes place and the human soul is born in the realm of manifestation, as it were, a ray of the First Logos descends into the newly formed Causal body and it is the presence of this highest Divine element in man which makes it possible for the human soul to evolve *ad infinitum* and ultimately become a Solar Logos. Outwardly, man is like other animals, only more evolved in every respect, but inwardly, he is fundamentally different from all animals because he contains within himself the Divine element derived from Maheśa while this is absent in the case of animals. And this Divine element is nothing but the *Śiva Tattva*, the highest *Tattva* or Principle in existence.

The differentiation between men and women in the maxim referred to above further enhances its significance and aptness. Although the human soul has no sex, its being clothed in a male or female body does make a difference in the expression of the soul through the personality. We all know that there are natural differences in the attitudes, expressions and functions of men and women. These differences on closer analysis will be found to be related to the fact that men are the temporary expression of the positive principle in Nature and women of the negative principle. It is also this fact which accounts for the subtle polarity existing between men and women which finds its crudest and most obvious expression in the realm of sex. Since the polarity is derived from the differences in the physical body it is natural that wherever there is strong identification with the physical body, the polarity will be felt in its grossest form, namely sex. That is why we find in this materialistic civilization with its extraordinary emphasis on the physical life such a great preoccupation with sex. As man advances in evolution and gradually rises above his physical nature his interests are transferred to the emotional and mental levels and the expression of the polarity changes in its nature accordingly. But the polarity cannot disappear altogether because it is derived from that subtle and incomprehensible polarity existing between the *Śiva* and *Śakti Tattvas*.

It has been pointed out above that all philosophical concepts and Occult doctrines are ultimately related to one another and can be seen in their correct perspective and significance only when viewed as a whole. It is for this reason that we should have a clear and comprehensive even though sketchy idea of the Occult philosophy as a whole in order to understand any one of these concepts. In the case of no other doctrine is this fact brought home more forcibly than the doctrine of *Tattvas* which is based upon the most fundamental doctrine of Occultism, the doctrine that the whole universe seen or unseen, is based upon and is the expression of the Ultimate Reality. Unless we understand this fundamental truth clearly, we cannot really comprehend the extremely subtle conception underlying the Hindu doctrine of *Tattvas*. This fundamental truth which is expressed in the philosophical maxim ' Verily, all this is Brahman ' has been dealt with in different contexts elsewhere and we need not enter into the question here again. Let us just try to see how the doctrine of *Tattvas* is related to the above doctrine and follows from it almost as a corollary.

If the whole manifested universe in its totality is of the nature of mind and is based upon and derived from the One Reality which for ordinary purposes may be considered to be the same as integrated Consciousness, then it follows that there can be nothing else in manifestation except the One Reality in Its different aspects and the innumerable functions which are needed for keeping the universe in the manifested state. All things which we perceive being ultimately of a mental nature and being derived from one basic Substance, Consciousness, what else can there be except functions of that Reality related to Its different aspects. Through the exercise of these innumerable Divine functions it should be possible to produce all kinds of modifications in that Consciousness which make the manifested universe what it is—a glorious, vast, incomprehensible mental phenomenon. This is an extremely subtle conception which is rather difficult to grasp by those who come across it for the first time and are puzzled by its apparent absurdity. But if one ponders it and gets even a faint glimpse into the truth which underlies the conception, one is enchanted by its philosophical splendour, even though it is merely a conception on the plane of the intellect and not a realization within the realm of consciousness.

As the idea is difficult to grasp let us take the help of a simile which has been used elsewhere in another context to illustrate another idea. Such repetitions are inevitable when we have to utilize the same simile, on account of its aptness, for throwing light on different aspects of the Occult doctrine and helping in the comprehension of subtle ideas. Let us imagine a tank of transparent glass which is full of clear water in which there is suspended a lighted electric bulb and there is a hidden arrangement for churning the water with different speeds. If the water in the tank is churned with sufficient speed by means of an electric motor the electric bulb will disappear from view and all that we will see is an infinite variety of ever-changing patterns in the water which are lighted up by the light issuing from the now invisible bulb.

If we examine this phenomenon carefully we shall see that the existence of the patterns depends ultimately only on two things—the water in the tank and the motion imparted to it by the invisible electric motor. Now, water as a substance or substratum is a constant and unchanging factor in the phenomenon and the infinite variety of ever-changing patterns therefore depend upon the only other factor involved in the phenomenon, namely, motion. Of course, the seeing of the patterns will depend also upon the light from the bulb and the mind which perceives the phenomenon but we are considering the phenomenon here only in its objective aspect.

We see thus that an infinite variety of patterns can be produced by motion associated with a basic medium and the nature of each pattern depends upon the kind of motion imparted to the medium. Underlying each pattern must be a particular mode of motion which can be expressed in mathematical terms. In the language of mathematics this can be expressed by saying that the patterns formed in the water are a function of motion, i.e. they depend upon the motion underlying them and vary with the nature of this motion. We see thus that an infinite variety of patterns which are of an objective nature can be produced by an infinite variety of motions which in themselves have no objective existence and are mere mathematical functions. All that we need is the basic medium—water in this case—associated with an infinite variety of functions which can be expressed in mathematical terms.

The student will see at once in the above phenomenon and its *modus operandi* a faint reflection of the manner in which the infinite variety of mental phenomena constituting a manifested universe can be derived from pure consciousness having and exercising an infinite number of functions through motions of different kinds. The basic substance is nothing but consciousness and the whole universe which is of purely mental nature is derived from that consciousness through modifications and movements of the mind, which in the realm of mind correspond to patterns and movements of water in the above illustration. So, all that is needed to create, preserve and destroy a purely mental universe is integrated consciousness as the basic Reality and the required number of functions of that Reality to produce an infinite variety of mental phenomena through the differentiation of that consciousness into different states of mind. Each function carries out its appointed task (which is inherent in it) and though it is rooted ultimately in the Absolute it creates for itself the necessary vehicles and the necessary channels for expression in its descent into lower and lower realms of manifestation. It is these basic functions which in their totality lie at the basis of the manifested universe and run its machinery with the help of motions of different kinds that are called *Tattvas* in Hindu philosophy.

When we come to the question of the number and nature of these *Tattvas* we naturally find that it is impossible to enumerate or classify them. The functions needed in running the vast and complicated manifested universe must necessarily be so large in number and variety as so to defy enumeration or classification though the Purāṇas give the approximate number of *Devatās* symbolising these functions of Reality. Only a few important *Tattvas* are referred to in the literature of Hindu religion and philosophy and the rest are taken for granted. The *Śiva-Śakti Tattva*, the *Īśvara Tattva*, the *Pañca Tattvas* etc. are some of the most important *Tattvas* though many others are mentioned in different contexts.

As has been pointed out in *An Introduction to Hindu Symbolism* the *Devatās* of Hindu religion are nothing but the symbolic representations of these Divine functions and the corresponding *Devis* are the symbolic representations of the powers which make the exercise of those functions possible. The study of the symbology of the well-known forms of *Devis* and *Devatās* will give us some insight into the nature of these Divine functions and powers and enrich our conception of Godhead in a wonderful manner.

One very important point to note in this connection is that since these *Tattvas* are functions of Divine Consciousness they are not mere abstract functions but *Conscious Principles.* The function is exercised not only through appropriate vehicles at different levels but is guided by Divine Intelligence at the highest level. It is this underlying, all-pervading Divine Consciousness which not only makes the exercise of the innumerable functions in the universe possible but also co-ordinates the exercise of these functions in various spheres. There is perfect co-ordination, harmony, intelligent direction and control everywhere in Nature because there is one over-all Divine Consciousness exercising all these functions.

The orthodox scientist observes this wonderful phenomenon but with a shrug of his shoulders turns aside and does not even bother about seeking an explanation. He thinks that merely saying that these things are 'natural' is a sufficient explanation.   And yet he claims to be a rationalist!

The Occultist recognizes the presence of Divine Consciousness in the form of Intelligence at the back of all natural phenomena and regards all natural processes as being carried on under the direction of this Intelligence through the agency of various Divine hierarchies of different grades acting along different channels.   Each member of these hierarchies is the embodiment of a function, has a vehicle through which the function is performed and has consciousness and power at its back as its guiding and energizing force.

Because there is consciousness and power at the back of these Natural forces it is possible to invoke them for gaining particular ends which come within their respective provinces. Such invocation and utilization of these Natural forces forms part of the occult arts which are practised in different parts of the world by those who have acquired the necessary knowledge and technique.   These practices can be divided into a wide range of occult arts according to the nature of the forces invoked and the motive which underlies such invocation.   But we are not concerned here with these occult arts but with the fact that Consciousness pervades, energizes and regulates all natural phenomena because the manifested universe is derived from and is based upon Divine Consciousness.

CHAPTER XX

THE GREAT ILLUSION—I

(MĀYĀ)

ACCORDING to the highest conceptions of Hindu philosophy the manifested universe is nothing but a product of Divine Ideation and the individual worlds of souls are the result of the impact of this Divine Ideation on individual minds. The illusion which is implied in taking our individual world as something independent of the Divine World is called Māyā. Most people who have studied this doctrine think that it is merely an ingenious hypothesis adopted to account for some of the transcendental doctrines of Hinduism, which are also generally considered as matters of philosophical speculation. They do not realize that illusion pervades all human life and it is our lack of discrimination or *aviveka* which prevents us from becoming aware of it. If they are sufficiently hard-headed they think that it is absurd to imagine that we are living in a world of illusions. Is not the world around us made of hard tangible objects? Are there not definite laws which govern the behavior of these objects? Has not man conquered Nature to some extent and produced all these wonderful inventions? Surely, it is madness to suppose that all this patently real world around us exists in the framework of a Grand Illusion imposed upon man from inside or outside.

This argument is really very plausible and the ordinary man can really be excused for accepting it and continuing to live his illusion-bound life as if it were the only real life in existence. But the whole argument begins to crack and disintegrate when we examine facts based on scientific knowledge and probe into phenomena of human life with a keen intelligence. Then we are able to *see* at least mentally that we are involved in illusions of the grossest kind on every side although we are not really aware of them. We may not be able to understand the doctrine of Māyā, but we can at least understand ordinary mental illusions and if we find that we are involved in such illusions, the ground is prepared for giving some thought to the doctrine of Māyā with an open mind. So let us first examine some of these patent illusions in which we are involved and of which we are blissfully unaware.

I would like to deal first with a few illusions which scientific knowledge has helped to reveal. The modern man is generally inclined to think that facts are not facts unless they bear the hall-mark of scientific approval. It is an irony of Fate that Science which laid the foundations of modern materialism has also provided those facts which have really demolished scientific materialism. Scientists may not be aware of this fact but this is so because their outlook is purely intellectual, lacking in that intelligence which comes from the light of Buddhi.

We shall begin with some facts which astronomers have supplied us. Let us take first the physical universe which they have studied so thoroughly with the help of their powerful telescopes. They are very proud of the knowledge which they have gained in this manner, and in one sense it is a remarkable achievement. But in another sense it appears like a cruel joke which Nature has played on them. Let us see how.

Astronomy presumes to give us a picture of the physical universe around us. It has shown that it is much larger and more populated than what it appears to us when we look at the sky at night. There are billions of stars of all sizes, some in the process of formation, others in the process of disintegration. The distances which separate us from these stars are stupendous. The 100″ telescope at Mount Wilson can photograph stars 500 million light-years away. The 200″ telescope at Palomar can photograph stars 1,000 million light-years away. The nearest star in galaxies other than our own is millions of light-years away. A light-year is the distance which light travels in a year at the rate of 186,000 miles a second. So one can understand the tremendous distances which separate the stars from one another and from us.

The astronomers are certainly giving us scientific facts, for telescopes and photographic cameras are not supposed to lie. But what are these facts which they give us? Do these facts give us a picture of the physical universe as it exists? Not at all. If light takes millions of years to reach us from the vast majority of stars, then the picture of the physical universe which astronomy presents to us is not the picture of the universe as it exists at present, but as it existed millions of years ago. What the universe is like now will become known to us millions of years hence. Even when we look at the heavens at night with our naked eye, we do not see any star as it exists at present, for the light which is reaching us at the moment left the nearest star about fifty years ago. For all we know, the whole galaxy of which we are a part and which alone we can see at night (with the exception of our sun) may have disappeared long ago without our knowing anything about it. Light waves which left the stars in this galaxy thousands and millions of years ago will continue to strike the earth and dupe the astronomers, who will be looking for and photographing these stars which ceased to exist long ago. One has only to look at these facts intelligently and with an open mind to realize the great illusion in which we are involved with regard to the physical universe which we presume to know so well and which the astronomers claim to reveal to us with all the exactitude and certainty of scientific investigation.

Let us now pass from the realm of the infinite to that of the infinitesimal. Here again it is Science which has revealed to us the great illusion under which we live our lives. What appear to us as solid tangible objects around us are composed of atoms and molecules and vibrations playing between them and the molecules and atoms composing our sense-organs. The atoms and molecules are practically empty space. The actual amount of matter in these objects is extremely small. It has been calculated that if all the empty space in the molecules and atoms composing a human body is eliminated, the body will be reduced to a mere speck of dust so small that it can be seen only with a magnifying glass. So it is mostly the movements of points with unimaginable speeds in space which are the basis of this seemingly solid, tangible and apparently real physical world around us, and the material world in the sense in which we understand it does not exist at all.

Modern physics has gone one step further in demolishing the material basis of the physical universe and in the light of the latest theories, the conception of matter as consisting of atoms and molecules seems almost obsolete. I cannot do better than quote in this connection the last paragraph of Chapter III from *The Mysterious Universe* by Sir James Jeans.

To sum up the main results of this and the preceding chapter, the tendency of modern physics is to resolve the whole material universe into waves, and nothing but waves. These waves are of two kinds: bottled-up waves, which we call matter, and unbottled waves, which we call radiation or light. The process of anni- hilation of matter is merely that of unbottling imprisoned wave-energy and setting it free to travel through space. These concepts reduce the whole universe to a world of radiation, potential or existent, and it no longer seems surprising that the fundamental particles of which matter is built should exhibit many of the properties of waves.

In the light of the above statement by a distinguished scientist, it is difficult to escape the conclusion that scientific materialism of the orthodox type is dead, and that we are face to face with a mystery of the most profound nature. We are much nearer to the Occult view of the universe as based on vibration or *Nāda* which only a few decades ago was considered fantastic by modern Oriental scholars and scientists. We are however not concerned here with materialism but with the question of the great illusion in which we are involved with regard to the nature of physical objects which we take to be so real and among which we spend our lives.

If there is no material or substantial basis for the physical universe, if it is based only on waves and nothing but waves according to modern physics, how do we see this wonderful world of forms, colours, sounds, etc. around us? Science has no answer to this question because it does not recognize the existence of subtler worlds of the mind and consciousness hidden within the physical world of atoms, molecules and waves. The fact that it has no answer to this very pertinent question, and what is more amazing, is not interested in the question, shows how utterly unintelligent, narrow and one-sided its approach to the problem of life is. It would be hard to believe if it were not a fact that such a large number of people who are intellectual enough to produce a radio, an aeroplane or a spacecraft could be so lacking in real intelligence as not to be disturbed at all when they found that the material world on which they had built their philosophy of life disappears into nothing but waves in ether. They do not even ask where this apparently real world around them comes from if there is nothing material to account for it.

They just go on pursuing their aim of investigating this phantom world consisting of waves and nothing but waves. If we need a striking illustration to show the difference between mere intellect and intelligence derived from the Buddhic faculty, here it is.

In order to find an answer to the question posed above, it will be necessary to go into the mechanism of mental perception through the sense-organs. We shall then see not only where the world in which we live comes from, but also the great illusion underlying the perception of an external world through our sense-organs. As this is a question of very great importance both for the student of psychology and the aspirant, we shall go into it in some detail.

We all think and feel that we are living in a world of real tangible objects—touching, seeing, smelling them directly. But it is not necessary to go into any subtle philosophical enquiry or psychological analysis to convince ourselves that we are really living in a mental world which is in our own mind and the objects which we touch, see and smell are merely our own mental images, which have been projected outside by some mental process. These mental images are no doubt stimulated in our mind by some agencies external to the mind; but the first important fact to realize is that we are perceiving our own mental images and not the external objects we take them to be. There is nothing in the external physical world even remotely corresponding to the objects as we see them. There are only, as we have seen above, atoms, molecules and vibrations playing between them.

Let me make this point clear by taking a concrete example. Suppose you take an orange in your hand. You see it, you smell it, you feel it, and so you naturally think you are in contact with a real orange. But what are the scientific facts involved in the phenomenon? The light vibrations from the so-called orange strike the eye, are carried along the nerves to the corresponding brain centre and produce in the mind the visual image of an orange. The object which has produced this image has neither form nor colour. It is a mere aggregate of a number of atoms and molecules reflecting light rays which fall upon it. It is these reflected rays or vibrations which strike the retina and are carried along the nerves to the brain centre. Similarly, the other sensuous impressions which are provided by the orange are merely vibrations which strike the corresponding sense-organs and produce in the mind impressions which do not exist in the object itself. Our mental image of the orange contains these different sensuous components contributed by different sense-organs fused by the mind in a composite image.

So it is necessary to realize the first truth or illusion of sensuous perception: that what we perceive outside are not the objects outside us but mental images in our own mind produced by an external world of mere atoms, molecules and vibrations.

The second point we should very carefully note in this connection is that the different components of the mental image, i.e. form, colour, smell, etc. produced in the mind are all supplied by the mind and are not derived from the external object. The object merely sends certain types of vibrations to our sense-organs and these stimulate the corresponding sensuous impressions in the mind. It is the mind which brings out of itself all the sensuous impressions of form, colour, etc. The molecules of sugar do not possess any sweetness. The molecules of chlorophyll are not green. The atoms of gold are not yellow. The chemical molecules of chloroform do not contain any odour. All these qualities are supplied by our mind. As the mental image in our mind is nothing but an aggregate of five kinds of sensuous impressions, it follows that the object which we see in the external world independent of us is nothing but a product of our own mind stimulated by the external, *unknown*, stimulating agent. I have called this external stimulating agent unknown deliberately.

Although we consider the objects in the external world to be made up of atoms and molecules, we do not really know what atoms and molecules are. According to the quotation of Jeans given above, matter is nothing but bottled-up radiation, which really means that we do not know what it is.

The fact, that the objects which we think we see in the external world are the products of our own mind in the form of mental images, is confirmed by the fact that we can reproduce them from memory. A highly imaginative artist can form a mental picture from memory which does not differ appreciably from the mental impression produced by direct contact with the object. We can not only recall an object from memory, but also construct it by the power of our imagination without any basis outside the mind. It may be said that in such cases the different elements or constituents of the image are derived separately from previous sense-contacts and the mind merely puts them together in a new combination. But this does not take away from the fact that the object in the mind is of purely mental origin.

We should also remember that the *saṃskāras*, or memory impressions left in the brain or the mind by previous sensuous impressions, are merely dead or insentient complex aggregates of atoms and molecules and cannot be expected to produce by themselves the mental images by the power of memory or imagination. It is the contact of the mind with these impressions which is essential for the production of such images in memory or imagination. Without such contact they are just like files in an archive with no one to read the records. The mind is thus an essential factor in all such phenomena and this again confirms the fact that the objects of perception are merely mental images in our mind though stimulated directly by external objects or indirectly by the records stored in our memory.

Let us go a little further into the nature of these two types of stimulations, i.e. (1) by direct contact with external objects; and (2) by indirect contact with impressions stored in the brain or higher vehicles of consciousness. We have seen already that the mind of the individual is an indispensable factor in such perceptions, and that the stimulation can be provided, either by external objects or by the impressions left in the vehicle by previous contact with objects.

But a closer analysis will show that these two sources are not enough to account for all the mental images and experiences produced in the mind. They certainly are the source of the mental images in the earlier stages of evolution, but as the mind develops it can work independently of these sources and bring out, as it were, from within itself entirely new kinds of experiences. It is difficult to analyse and separate these experiences derived from within from those which have their origin outside; but anyone who has given some thought to the working of the mind and tried to dive into its deeper recesses, gradually realizes that the mind contains within itself potentially everything and can bring out anything from within as its power to dive inward develops. The dependence on direct sensuous perception and impressions left from previous experiences is found only in the early stages of mental development and when evolution has reached a certain stage they can be dispensed with to a great extent. The *Prātibha Jñāna* or non-instrumental perception referred to in the *Yoga-Sūtras* points clearly in this direction and shows that the mind in its essential nature is independent of the senses and external objects and requires these only in the earlier stages of its growth.

It is seen frequently in the study of the evolutionary processes that certain organs or other factors appear at a certain stage in the process to help in the evolution of certain faculties of the mind or body and when these faculties have been developed sufficiently the organs or factors become more or less redundant and are either discarded or relegated to another function. In Yogic psychology the senses are considered to be merely the instruments of the mind, the extension of the mind into a number of separate channels of communication, or tentacles through which it contacts or affects the external world. This is a view of the mind and the senses, which is far nearer to reality than the view which regards sensations as the basic reality, and the mind as a product of sensations received through the sense-organs. The simile of the queen bee and other bees in the hive, which is frequently used in Yogic psychology to indicate the relation of the mind and the senses, is meant to show that the senses are not only extensions of the mind, but are subordinate to the mind, merely serving its purposes and growth and by no means forming the basis of the mind.

If the senses and sense-organs are viewed in this light we get a more correct view of the mind, and consequently a more correct view of the universe, for the latter is based on the former. We cannot understand the nature of the universe without understanding the nature of the mind, because the universe arises from consciousness and is of the same essential nature as mind. And as the all-inclusive, all-apprehending mind with its unlimited possibilities is nothing but a differentiated form of consciousness, it will be seen that pure Consciousness or Reality is that substratum in which all mental potentialities lie hidden, and from which all possible mental creations can be made. It is all a question of unfoldment of consciousness and the development of powers which accompany such unfoldment. The Logos, in whom consciousness is fully unfolded, can create a solar system while an undeveloped Monad can create only his little world through the personality.

Consciousness is thus like white light which contains in an integrated form all the colors of the spectrum which can be brought out of it by proper conditions. Or rather, it is like the total radiation from the sun which includes not only white light containing all colors in a blended combination, but also infra-red and ultra-violet vibrations and energies. In this simile the supra-mental levels correspond to the ultra-violet (finer) vibrations; the sub-conscious levels to the infra-red (coarser) vibrations; and the conscious levels to the visible spectrum in the middle. An unlimited and unexplored region of the mind extends on both sides of the conscious mind with which the ordinary man is familiar. In Yogic practice these unexplored but far more real and subtle realms of the mind containing all the secrets of life and consciousness are explored and mastered, and even the nature of pure consciousness can be known. This is true Self-realization. It is then that we realize that all this manifested universe is mind or consciousness, for mind is not essentially different from consciousness as colored lights are not essentially different from white light.

The above discussion regarding the nature of the total mechanism of mental perception may appear like a digression from our main theme, namely, the illusion involved in sensuous and mental perception, but it was necessary to clarify this point and trace the various links which connect the pure consciousness at the Centre of our being, and the sense-organs which are the outposts of this consciousness at the periphery of the physical body. Without a general idea of these links, we cannot really understand the great illusion which is involved in sensuous perception which makes us see outside what is really within our own mind; which makes us interpret the inner world of our own mind as an external world containing tangible and real things of infinite variety. But one has to ponder these things and go deeply into the matter to grasp their real significance.

One might ask the very pertinent question: What about the world of atoms, of molecules—or whatever is the basis of the external physical world—which stimulates the formation of the mental images through the instrumentality of the sense-organs? What is the nature of this world and where does it come from? For such a world, whatever its nature, must exist if it produces definite mental images in the minds of all the individuals who live in it, and especially, because it produces many experiences which are common to all the individuals. We all see the sun rising in the east every morning. We all feel its heat when we expose our bodies to its rays.

The question posed above is a very important one, but it is not relevant to our present theme and we shall not go into it here. It involves the most fundamental question of philosophy, namely the relation between Reality, Consciousness, Mind and Matter and will be considered later in Part II. So let us assume that there is a world outside our mind which produces in our individual minds our common experiences and let the question of its nature remain unanswered for the present.

CHAPTER XXI

THE GREAT ILLUSION—II

(Māyā)

In the previous chapter we have discussed a few illusions in which we are involved and of which we are quite unaware. These illusions may be considered of an objective nature, i.e., they consist in seeing things which do not exist as we see them. For example, we think that we are looking at the present physical universe when we turn our gaze towards the stars at night, but what we are actually seeing is the universe as it existed thousands and millions of years ago. For, the light with the help of which we see the stars, left those stars thousands and millions of years ago and has been travelling ever since through empty space to reach us now. And what is the total length of time during which all these observations have been made by astronomers? About two hundred years. And yet they think that they know the physical universe and are on the point of solving its great mystery.

Again, we think we are looking at solid tangible objects with form, colour, hardness, etc. all about us, but what are they? Only atoms and molecules which are practically empty space with a few points moving with unimaginable speeds and widely separated from one another. Surely, no one can argue that we are not all involved in illusions of the grossest kind, though we are utterly unaware of them. These things are not based on speculations of philosophers or doctrines of Occultism which anybody can challenge. They are based on hard scientific facts, as hard as any facts can be.

Let us now take another class of illusions which I may call subjective. These are really based on our lack of thought or discrimination and not on any new fundamental facts which have been discovered by Science. It is really these common illusions which are responsible for our complete immersion in the life of the world and our inability to extricate ourselves from its temptations and allurements.

Let us take the illusion of pleasure derived from contact with external objects. Anyone who has even an elementary knowledge of physiology knows that this pleasure is felt owing to nervous currents aroused in our own body by chemical changes of different kinds induced by external stimulants or internal psychological states. For example, when we eat any food which we relish, the chemicals present in the juices affect the taste buds and the nerves susceptible to odours and these arouse certain sensations which are carried by the nerves to the corresponding centres in the brain, and the mind becomes aware of the sensation. But, instead of seeing the stimulation of the nerves as the cause of the sensation, the mind projects the sensation on the object which stimulated the nerves and considers that object as the source of the pleasure which is felt. But what are the facts? Firstly, the seat of the sensation is in our own body. It is the stimulation of the nerves which causes the sensation. Secondly, the pleasure derived from sensation is not present in the sensation itself, it is present in the mind. Exactly the same sensation which was felt to be pleasurable can become painful under a different condition of the mind. A man who is very fond of tinned fish will begin to hate tinned fish if his son dies of food-poisoning on taking tinned fish. Obviously, the condition of the mind determines the pleasure and so the source of the pleasure must lie deeper within.

This fact is brought home to us very clearly when we begin to study and watch our mind. We find that we may be surrounded by all kinds of luxuries and means of enjoyment, but, if we are internally disharmonized and disturbed, we remain frustrated and unhappy and all that we can get perhaps from the external sources of pleasure is a little pleasurable physical sensation. If, however, we purify and harmonize the mind and put it in tune with our higher nature then all these external things may be taken away from us and yet we will feel a fountain of joy playing within us all the time, without rhyme or reason. All this shows that the source of pleasure, joy, happiness, *ānanda* is really within us although things in the external world may in various degrees stimulate the mind temporarily and produce the illusion that they are the source of these pleasurable sensations or states of mind.

And yet how we run desperately after all kinds of objects hoping to extract from them whatever little pleasure they are capable of yielding at the physical, emotional or mental level. Billions of living creatures are subjected to all kinds of cruelties and slaughtered to provide momentary, pleasurable tickling for our palates. Millions of innocent creatures are trapped and made to die horrible deaths so that their furs may provide a little pleasurable sensation of warmth and softness around the neck of fashionable ladies. Millions of gallons of alcohol are consumed to provide a few moments of exhilaration to dissatisfied and unhappy minds. So this illusion underlying sensuous pleasure is not as innocent as it may appear at first sight.

I could take many other similar illusions, like the illusion of power, which makes us think that we are the source of power instead of mere centres or instruments through which His power flows for a time. The illusion of intellectual knowledge which makes us take mere ideas for truth. The illusion of the physical body which makes us think that we are the body, and when the body grows old we grow old and when the body dies we die. The illusion of wealth which makes us think that by having a big bank balance we can ensure our security and comfort. The illusion of name and fame which makes us engage in certain pursuits in the vain hope of becoming famous and leaving a name which shall endure for ever. The illusion of nationality which makes us think that a person living on the other side of an imaginary line drawn arbitrarily is not a human being but an enemy who must be killed without compunction.

Now, the object of bringing all these illusions to our notice is to show that illusion pervades our life and the fact that we are not aware of it does not mean that it does not exist. Some of these illusions are of such a nature that we can become conscious of them if we examine the working of our mind carefully. Others go deeper and we become aware of them only when our consciousness rises to subtler planes. And there are still others of a more fundamental character like those of Time and Space of which we become aware only when we transcend the realm of the mind and our consciousness functions in the realm of Reality.

But we are not concerned here with the question how illusions can be transcended. We are concerned with the question whether or not illusions of various kinds play a very fundamental and constant role in our life. When the subject of *Māyā* is discussed among people who have not gone deep into the matter they are apt to regard it merely as a philosophical doctrine which has nothing to do with real life and about which therefore they need not be concerned. People in the West especially who are proud of being realists look upon the doctrine of *Māyā* with great suspicion, for it seems to strike at the very root of their realism. They are inclined to discuss it as an ingenious hypothesis invented by Hindu philosophers to substantiate their philosophical doctrines.

If it can be shown that illusion pervades our whole life even according to scientific knowledge upon which we place so much reliance, then I think the ground is prepared to consider seriously the doctrine of *Māyā* which is an integral part of the Occult philosophy. We shall then be inclined to consider it seriously and also be able to understand it more easily and thoroughly. For these different types of illusions which I have referred to in the previous pages are merely different aspects at different levels of that fundamental Illusion which we refer to as *Māyā* or *Avidyā* (Ignorance). If we can understand, to some extent, some of these lower manifestations or aspects of the Great Illusion it may perhaps be possible for us to gain a glimpse into that fundamental Illusion from which they are all derived.

Let us now come after this rather lengthy introduction to the consideration of the main subject, the nature of Māyā or the Great Illusion, and the means of transcending it. I cannot do better than begin the consideration of this subject by quoting a stanza from the well-known book in Sanskrit *Durgā-Sapta-Shati*. This stanza occurs in one of the hymns addressed to Durgā by the *Devas* after that *Devi*, representing the Great Divine Power underlying manifestation, had helped them to overcome the forces of evil. The stanza is given below:

> *Tvam Vaiṣṇavī Śaktir anantavīryā*
> *Viśvasya bījam paramāsi Māyā*
> *Sammohitam Devi samastametat*
> *Tvam vai prasannā bhuvi muktihetuḥ*

You are the unlimited Divine Power of Vishnu, the Effective Cause of the manifested universe called the Great *Māyā*. You have put this whole manifested universe under the spell of your Illusion. And it is you only, who being pleased, can give us freedom from this Illusion while we are still living on this earth.

This is the highest conception of this Divine Power of Illusion which underlies manifestation and which keeps the Monads involved in manifestation until their unfoldment has been completed and they are ready to be liberated from this Illusion by realizing their real Divine nature. But we have to gain a glimpse into the deeper significance of the words in order to appreciate the grandeur and beauty of the idea embodied in this stanza.

Let us begin the consideration of the subject by asking the question: What is this Power of Illusion which is referred to as *Māyā* in Hindu philosophy? People who have not properly studied and thought over this question have generally got an entirely wrong conception about *Māyā*. They think it means that the world in which they live is an unreal thing like a dream and there is nothing real corresponding to the mental images which are produced in the mind of the individual who perceives this objective world. This is not at all the conception of *Māyā* in Hindu philosophy. The example of illusion which is usually given and which has become hackneyed to a degree is the mistaking of a rope for a snake in the dark. This illustration is very apt and gives a correct idea about the nature of illusion involved and that is why it has been used for thousands of years. The essential idea involved in the conception of Māyā is ' seeing a thing incorrectly ', or ' taking it to be what it is not in actual reality '. Now, in the example given, when a man sees a rope as a snake in the dark it is not that there is nothing corresponding to the snake which is present in his mind for the time being. There is—the rope which has produced the false impression of the snake. The illusion lies in taking the harmless rope as a deadly snake. If we see the rope as a rope we see it correctly and there is no illusion.

Now, the universe we live in is an expression or embodiment of Divine consciousness when we ' see ' it from the

Centre of our being. But we do not see it as an embodiment of Divinity or modification of pure Consciousness. We see it as a vast, unknown, hostile environment in which we are fighting for our individual existence. There lies the fundamental illusion which is called *Māyā* and which is responsible for our involvement in this manifested world. The moment we begin to see truly this world as nothing but Brahman as indicated in the sacred maxim ' Verily, all this is Brahman ', the illusion disappears for we then see the world as it is in Reality. The outer world remains the same in form (we do not see a new external world as a liberated individual) but it is seen in a different light, as an expression or embodiment of Divinity. It is seen as God made manifest. What is there to be afraid of then ?

The same essential mistake characterizes every type of illusion in which we are involved. We see the thing not as it is in reality but as something quite different. We see ordinary time as ' duration ' independent of the mind, while actually it is nothing but a succession of mental images in the mind. We see ordinary space as something empty—with length, breadth and thickness—while actually it is merely a mental conception in the mind produced by so-called objects external to the mind. We see the panorama of the world unfolding outside us while it is merely the impression created in our mind by the unfolding of the Divine Mind or Divine Ideation as it is generally called. In all these cases there is *something* which causes all these various types of false impressions in the mind but that something is not what we take it to be. In most cases we cannot know what that something is, which produces these wrong impressions in our mind. But there is something behind those mental impressions. It is not all imagination, the stuff which dreams are made of. The illusion therefore consists not in seeing something where there is nothing but in seeing something different from what it is really.

The above paragraphs give in a nutshell the conception of *Māyā* as propounded by teachers of Vedānta, like Śaṃkarāchārya. I have tried to avoid all philosophical subtleties and technical terms, and put the idea as simply as possible. It will be seen from what has been said above that the general principle, namely, 'taking a thing to be what it is not in actual reality,' holds also in all cases of minor illusion which we have discussed in the previous pages. Of course, the word *Māyā* or the Great Illusion is used strictly for that fundamental illusion which makes us see the manifested universe as something different from Brahman and which is the cause of our bondage. But the other forms of illusion to which we are subject are not essentially different from the fundamental illusion mentioned above. They differ from the fundamental illusion not essentially but in having a more limited scope and in being easier to overcome. For example, while the illusion created in our mind when we mistake a rope for a snake in the dark can be removed merely by bringing in a light, the removal of the fundamental illusion which makes us see the universe as something different from Reality requires the treading of the path which leads to Liberation.

It may also be pointed out here that no external or internal material change is required in our getting rid of any illusion of this kind. It is all a matter of perception or seeing things in a new light. But this 'seeing' is not of the nature of intellectual comprehension, but of realization which is quite different. The former, i.e. mere intellectual comprehension, does not free us from the illusion and the effects which follow from the illusion, the latter, namely realization, does. If a child mistakes a rope for a snake in the dark it will be of no avail telling him that it is merely a rope. He will continue to be afraid of the rope and refuse to go near it. But bring in a light and he realizes his mistake immediately and will pick up the rope without any hesitation. Similarly, it is no

use our having an intellectual comprehension that all this
manifested universe is nothing but Brahman. We will still
be afraid of death and decay and suffering of various kinds.
We will still strive for our individual ends and fight for our
separate existence. We will still have a limited outlook.
But a *Jīvanmukta* who *knows* that ' all is Brahman ' sheds
fear completely. Death, decay and suffering become meaningless to him for he knows that they affect the vehicles only
and he is not affected at all by them. He has no individual
ends left. His outlook becomes universal. All this is possible
because he has realized the truth of his Divinity and oneness
with God and his knowledge is not merely intellectual. So
all this intellectual comprehension which we are trying to
gain with regard to these fundamental truths should be considered merely as a stepping stone or a stage in our journey
towards our final goal. It should not engender complacence
but should make us intensify our efforts to transmute our
intellectual understanding into realization of these truths
which are different aspects of the one Truth.

As we are considering the Great Illusion as an instrument
of manifestation let us dwell for a while on the function of
Māyā in manifestation and the manner in which this function
is exercised. Again, I must point out that this is really a
question beyond the scope of the intellect. For only he who
has transcended *Māyā* can know what it is and how it works.
When we are considering this question on the plane of the
intellect we are looking at the problem, as it were, from
below or from this side of the veil which separates the unreal
from the Real. We can only know how it appears to the
intellect in the light of knowledge which Occultism has placed
at our disposal.

One obvious function of *Māyā* is to make it possible for
the Monads to descend into the lower planes of manifestation,
and, after going through the evolutionary cycle, to emerge
from those planes as Self-realized individuals who are not

only aware of their Divine nature and purpose, but can also function on and are masters of the lower planes through which they have evolved. It seems that the whole process of evolution on the lower planes is a necessary part of their unfoldment, though why it should be so cannot be grasped by the intellect, being part of the ultimate mystery of human life. But perhaps we can understand to some extent why it should be necessary for the Divine power of Illusion to come into play in order that the Monads may descend into the lower planes and go through the evolutionary cycle. In order to understand how Māyā serves as an instrument of manifestation let us first recall very briefly a few Occult facts connected with the descent of the Monads into the lower planes.

When creation takes place and a new solar system is born, the Logos brings down with Him the Monads who will be associated with Him during the ensuing *kalpa* or period of manifestation. These remain in His consciousness as long as the lower planes are not yet ready to receive them. In that state they are one with Him and conscious of their Divine nature, but unable to function on the lower planes. A very small number of the Monads who have already evolved to a high stage in the previous *kalpas* can function on all the planes when they become ready to receive the Monads, and these serve as *adhikāri puruṣas* like *Manus*, etc. The others descend into the lower vehicles when these vehicles are ready for them and under the guidance of their Divine Teachers evolve slowly on these planes until they themselves become Self-realized individuals who are now masters of these planes.

Now the question arises: why should the Monads who are living on the Divine planes at-one with the Logos and therefore fully conscious of their Divine and blissful nature, descend into the lower planes to undergo the limitation and suffering which evolution on the lower planes undoubtedly involves? As external compulsion does not seem to have any place in the scheme of spiritual evolution and man seems destined to become perfect by internal choice rather than external compulsion. The Divine power of Illusion appears to be utilized for inducing the Monads to descend into the lower planes and as a result of this illusion, the desire is born within them to have the experiences of the lower planes. It is this desire which is called *Trishnā* in Buddhism which involves them in evolution on the lower five planes, and which continues to keep them in bondage until the purpose of evolution has been achieved, i.e., they have become perfect and masters of the lower planes and fit to be re-united again with the Divine consciousness as Self-realized and Self-determined individuals. So Māyā has to be considered not as an arbitrary power which God uses for fooling us but as a necessary force which has to be exerted to make our evolution and perfection possible. Otherwise, who would come down from those Divine planes where Bliss reigns to these lower planes where there is so much misery and suffering, and who would engage in all kinds of pursuits which are necessary for the development of our faculties!

It may be asked: how can God exercise this kind of power on such a large number of individuals evolving in His solar system? That the power of illusion can be exercised is now a well-established scientific fact. Hundreds of hypnotists are using this power as a matter of routine especially in the field of medicine. They can make their subjects see anything and feel anything which they will that they should see and feel. The power of illusion can be exercised more generally and effectively on the subtler planes. In fact every neophyte who begins to function on the subtler planes has to learn how to distinguish realities from illusions created by the Brothers of the Shadow, and to guard himself against these illusions.

If ordinary individuals can exercise the power of illusion on a small scale, why should it not be possible for the Lord of a solar system to exercise it on a large scale? In fact every power which we find present in a microcosm is present in its unlimited form in the Macrocosm. And so there is nothing incredible in this great power of Illusion which the Logos exercises in various ways. This power is exercised not only in a general way as we have seen above, but also on special occasions, when the forces of evil get out of control and those who are the centres of evil influences and disturbances are lured to their own destruction by all kinds of illusions created in their mind. The *Purāṇas* are full of allegorical stories illustrating the use of the Divine power of Illusion in this manner.

We should not, however, interpret such stories literally and thus anthropomorphize God. These stories do not mean that God is watching human beings and devising special means to bring about the destruction of all things which are based on unrighteousness or *adharma*. The ultimate failure and destruction of all such evil is brought about automatically by the progressive clouding of Buddhi or the discriminative faculty which leads the evil-doer into courses of action which are self-defeating and self-destroying. As the universe is based on truth and righteousness, the failure of what is untrue and unrighteous is inherent in the very nature of things and is brought about by Nature in due course of time.

CHAPTER XXII

INTEGRATED 'SOUND'

(NĀDA)

WE have seen that manifestation is brought about through the agency of certain instruments like Time, Space, Illusion, Point, Sound etc. We have discussed Illusion already and shall now take up for consideration Sound or *Nāda* as it is called in Hindu philosophy. The word sound should be considered in this context not in the usual sense of vibrations which affect our ears, but in the much larger sense of all kinds of vibrations which are found in Nature or can be produced artificially, both on the physical and the super-physical planes. The essential nature of a vibration may be simply defined as a transmission of energy through space without involving any forward movement of the medium through which the transmission takes place. There is rhythmic movement in the medium as the waves pass through it but the medium remains unaffected otherwise. Science has made us familiar with many types of vibrations, such as those of sound, light, X-rays, radio-waves, and the gamut of these vibrations has not only an enormous range but is almost without any big gaps. A table giving the nature and frequency of these different types of vibrations is found in most text-books of Science dealing with radiation.

Occultists who have been able to develop their super-physical faculties and have investigated the phenomena of the superphysical planes have found that vibrations play an even

more important role in the phenomena of the superphysical
planes. On these superphysical planes, as on the physical,
the perception of external objects depends upon the interaction of the object and the vehicle, through the vibrations
playing between them. Thoughts, feelings, emotions are
found to be essentially of the nature of vibrations in the matter
of the subtler planes, although they also give rise to forms
which can be seen objectively. Investigations made in the
field of psychical research have shown conclusively that phenomena such as those of telepathy or thought-transference are
possible, and the vibratory nature of thought has thus been
partly demonstrated.

While the very important part played by different kinds
of vibrations in natural phenomena is recognized by the
ordinary educated man of today, he will find it difficult to
believe that vibration in its subtlest sense forms the very basis
of the manifested universe. The universe is created by
vibration, is maintained by vibration, and at the time of
Pralaya or dissolution is destroyed by vibration. And yet this
is the Occult doctrine with regard to the ultimate constitution
of our universe both in its physical and superphysical aspects.
This doctrine is generally accepted in one form or another
by the great religions of the world as shown by mystic statements such as:

> In the beginning was the Word, and the Word was
> with God, and the Word was God.

In fact, the very word used for the Presiding Deity of a manifested system in Theosophical literature is Logos, or the
Word. In Hinduism this aspect of Reality is called *Shabda
Brahma*, *Shabda* meaning Sound in its most comprehensive
sense, and Brahma is the Reality underlying the universe.

Of course, this doctrine was not taken seriously by people
who were not prepared to accept anything as truth which
had not been investigated by modern scientific methods and

obtained the seal of scientific approval. How could this vast
and complex universe with an infinite variety of phenomena
and containing hard and tangible objects of all kinds be based
on such an intangible and immaterial thing as a vibration,
they argued, and especially, how could a single integrated
vibration be split up into an infinite variety of vibrations
which we have undoubtedly found in different fields of natural
phenomena. The idea appeared obviously absurd and was
regarded as one of those arbitrarily assumed doctrines in
which the literature of Occultism and ancient religions
abounds. And yet, see to what conclusion Science, after half
a century of the most careful and intensive research by
thousands of scientists of the topmost rank, has arrived. I
am giving below a quotation from chapter three of *The Mysterious Universe* by Sir James Jeans, a book which has become
famous and is considered almost as an authority on the latest
theories of modern physics by the layman.

> To sum up the main results of this and the preceding
> chapter the tendency of modern physics is to resolve
> the whole material universe into waves and nothing
> but waves. These waves are of two kinds: bottled-up
> waves, which we call matter, and unbottled waves
> which we call radiation, or light. The process of
> annihilation of matter is merely that of unbottling im-
> prisoned wave-energy and setting it free to travel
> through space. These concepts reduce the whole uni-
> verse to a world of radiation, potential and existent,
> and it no longer seems surprising that the fundamental
> particles of which matter is built should exhibit many
> of the properties of waves.

The above quotation will be seen to be almost a perfect
restatement of the Occult doctrine regarding the basis of the
universe in scientific terminology. That Science should
come so close and so quickly to this idea which had been

proclaimed thousands of years ago by Occultists on the basis of their investigations into the inner realms of Nature, shows the validity and reliability of the Occult methods of investigation, and the unwisdom of rejecting the Occult doctrines simply because they do not seem to agree with the facts so far discovered by Science. It is true that the scientific conclusions are concerned only with the physical universe while the Occult doctrine encompasses the whole universe, seen or unseen, but if the doctrine has been corroborated with regard to the physical universe which is the grossest and most material, there is no reason to doubt its validity with regard to the subtler realms of Nature which are known to be far less tangible though more vivid than the physical.

Let us first consider a few simple scientific experiments which tend to show that the fundamental idea of the universe being based on an extremely subtle integrated vibration is not as absurd as it appears on the surface, and there are many phenomena in Nature which show how this is possible.

We may first take the question of how an integrated vibration which outwardly appears very simple can contain within itself in an integrated form an infinite number of vibrations which appear when the integrated vibration is differentiated or separated into its constituent vibrations. Let us take white light as it comes from the sun. This light as we know can be differentiated or separated into its constituents by passing it through a prism. As a result of this dispersion it gives us an infinite number of vibrations which are present in the ultra-violet, visible, and infra-red spectra. These vibrations differ from each other not only in their wavelengths but also in their physical, chemical and physiological properties and are capable of producing a large variety of phenomena on the physical plane.

Now, if it is possible to have an integrated vibration of this nature which, though simple outwardly, contains within itself an infinite variety of vibrations of a particular kind, there is no reason why it should not be possible to have a super-integrated vibration that contains within itself in an integrated form vibrations of all categories which may be found on different planes and different spheres of phenomena. There is no reason why it should not be possible to have a super-integrated vibration including not only all vibrations of a physical nature but also those which constitute thoughts, feelings, and subtler expressions of consciousness on still higher planes. There is nothing in the principle of integration which makes it necessary to consider it as applicable only to a limited range of vibrations.

It should be remembered, however, that the conception of the universe being based on a super-integrated vibration is not to be taken as a mere hypothesis in the scientific sense. In Science a hypothesis is put forward to account for a group of phenomena and to direct further research in the field of those phenomena. The hypothesis may or may not be true. If new facts are discovered, which make the hypothesis untenable, it is either suitably altered or discarded and a new hypothesis more in harmony with all the known facts takes its place. The fundamental doctrines of Occultism are not to be taken in that way. It is true that for the ordinary student they are merely like scientific theories which help him to understand the realities of life more easily and fully. They cannot be verified by him by personal experience for the time being. But they are not unproved assumptions. They have been verified and found valid by all those Adepts of Occultism who have unfolded the necessary capacities for this purpose. That is why we also refer to them as truths of the inner life though for the ordinary student they can be considered merely as doctrines. The purpose of treading the Path of Occultism is to transmute this intellectual knowledge of the doctrines into direct knowledge of the truths, and thus get out of this realm of the intellect in which doubts, uncertainties and errors have full sway.

We shall now pass on to another question, the production of forms from vibrations. For, the universe as we know it contains not only vibrations but also an infinite variety of forms, and unless we can demonstrate that vibrations can produce these forms, it will be difficult to understand how the whole universe which is full of forms can be based on vibration and nothing but vibration. Of course, the perception of form is a mental phenomenon and is, as has been shown elsewhere, based on consciousness; still, the appearance of the mental image with a form requires something external. This something is nothing but an aggregate of atoms and molecules according to Science, and a particular combination of the *gunas* (qualities) according to Sāṃkhyan philosophy. So what we have really to demonstrate is that vibration can create certain aggregates of particles which produce in the mind mental images with well-defined forms.

Here again experiments made in the field of Science are of great help to us. The fact that vibrations can produce forms of well-defined patterns can be demonstrated by a very simple experiment. All that one needs is a drum, a bow and some sand. The parchment head of the drum is a vibrating surface and if a bow is drawn across the edge of the drum it makes the parchment vibrate. The note which is given out by the vibrating surface depends upon many factors such as the tension of the parchment, its thickness, area, etc. Now, if one scatters some sand on the surface of the drum and then draws the bow across the edge of the drum the sand is thrown up by the vibration of the drum, but when it falls down it is not evenly distributed on the surface but forms beautiful patterns which are called Chladni's figures after their discoverer. The nature of the geometrical figure which is formed varies as the bow is drawn across different points of the circumference, and in this way a large variety of patterns can be obtained. What happens really is that the vibrations of the parchment make the sand assume definite geometrical forms, and since the vibrations are different when different points of the drum are bowed, the patterns produced are also different. We should remember that the sounds produced by musical instruments or the human voice in this manner are not single notes but contain many harmonics, and it is the different combinations of these harmonics which produce these different patterns of beautiful design. Other powdered substances besides sand could be used in the experiment in order to increase its delicacy, but the experiments with sand are spectacular enough and show in a remarkable and simple manner how vibration can create forms of different kinds.

Many experiments have been made both in India and in Europe to show that musical sounds are capable of producing forms. These musical vibrations as well as the forms produced by them can be made visible to the eye by ingenious experiments, by throwing the images on a screen. In this way we can see how sound is capable of making the most elaborate forms such as those of trees, flowers, ferns, etc.

Sound can not only build forms but can also destroy or disintegrate them. The experiment in which it is possible to shatter a glass by subjecting it to the impact of its fundamental note is well known. We can determine the fundamental note of the glass by half filling it with water and drawing a bow across its edge. If we produce the same note on an instrument in which the sound can be made to increase in intensity gradually, the sound which is transmitted to the glass will make it vibrate more and more strongly until the glass is shattered completely.

In discussing how vibration can build or destroy forms I have taken examples from the realm of physical phenomena, firstly, because we are inclined to believe and to be impressed by what we can see and touch and hear, although the physical senses are the most deceptive sources of knowledge unless the information which they give is checked by reason. We see the sun going round the earth but reason tells us that it is a pure illusion created by the revolution of the earth on its axis. We see ourselves surrounded by solid and apparently impenetrable objects but Science tells us that we are living in a world which is mostly empty space, and that our body is also mostly empty space. We look up at the sky at night and think we are seeing the stars. Nothing of the kind. We are merely looking at the physical universe as it existed thousands and millions of years ago, for, the light which is reaching us now left those stars thousands and millions of years ago. For all we know the whole physical universe indicated by the twinkling stars may have disappeared in the meanwhile and we may be looking at an empty sky!

Secondly, I have taken illustrations from the field of physical phenomena because, if we can show that the comparatively heavy matter of the physical plane can be moulded into definite forms by vibrations, it is easier to believe how the much lighter matter of the subtler planes can take different shapes under the impact of the much finer vibrations of those planes. Clairvoyant investigation of phenomena on these subtler planes has shown how easily the matter of those planes takes different forms under the impact of our thoughts and feelings which are of the nature of vibrations on these subtler planes. It is not necessary to labour this point any further, and we can see at least how it is possible that the whole universe with all its complexity can be based on different kinds of vibrations which are all derived from a super-integrated vibration.

I now come to a very interesting property of a mathematical point which is the centre of an enclosed sphere. This property shows how a super-integrated vibration of the nature referred to above can act from a centre in a manifested system and energize the whole system automatically. It can provide every type of vibration at every point of the manifested system and the potentiality of every kind of form which may be needed to express a particular phase or stage of life.

For, as we have seen above, vibration has the capacity to
bring into existence form, and if every type of vibration is
potentially present at every point of space, this means that
every kind of form can come into existence anywhere provided
the necessary conditions are present. This is exactly the
conception of *Prakriti* in Sāṃkhyan philosophy which provides the theoretical background of Yogic technique.

The following figure represents an enclosed glass sphere
with the centre, and illustrates the reflection of light waves
from the inner surface of a silvered glass sphere as pointed out

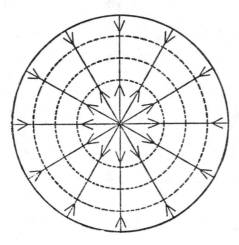

already in another con-
text on page 33. If un-
der these ideal condi-
tions we introduce a
point of light at the
centre, the light will
radiate in all directions
along the radii of the
sphere and · the wave
front will be an expand-
ing sphere starting at
the centre and expand-
ing continuously until it
strikes the surface of
the enclosing sphere. As
the inner surface of the sphere is silvered all the rays of
light travelling along the radii of the sphere will be reflected
back on themselves following the same path which they took
in the outward expansive movement. The result of this
perfect reflection from the inner surface of the sphere will be
that the light wave front which was an expanding sphere
will be converted into a light wave front which is a contracting sphere converging towards the centre. Now at the centre
a very interesting thing occurs. Those who are familiar with
the behaviour of light waves can see that the contracting light

wave front which is converging towards the centre will, on reaching the centre, as it were, turn inside out upon itself and again be converted into an expanding wave front as before. The whole process of expansion, reflection, contraction, and passing through the centre will be repeated over and over again with unimaginable speed, for light travels at the rate of 186,000 miles per second and this is the highest speed which, according to the Theory of Relativity, is attainable by any object in our universe. If the sphere is perfect in form and the inner surface properly silvered there will be no defect or loss introduced in the process of reflection and the whole process can continue *ad infinitum*. The net result of this process going on within the enclosed sphere will be to fill the whole sphere with the light introduced at the centre and keep it filled with that light as long as the enclosing sphere remains.

The behaviour of any kind of radiation from the centre will be the same as that of light. If, therefore, we introduce a point of sunlight at the centre, the whole sphere will become filled with sunlight. So, in introducing a point of sunlight at the centre we are really filling the whole globe with sunlight and keeping it filled with sunlight indefinitely and automatically. Now, sunlight contains potentially all the vibrations which are present in the visible, infra-red, and ultra-violet spectra derived from sunlight. At any point within this sphere any of the vibrations which are contained in these spectra with an enormous range of vibrations can manifest under proper conditions, for all of them are present potentially at every point though in an integrated form. Light of any colour, any infra-red radiation, any ultra-violet radiation can instantaneously manifest at any point within such a sphere.

Let us compare the wonderful phenomenon described above with our Occult conception of a manifested system such as a solar system, which, according to the Occult doctrine, is an enclosed system with the Consciousness of the Presiding Deity or the Logos functioning from the centre of the manifested system. Such an enclosed manifested system is called *Brahmāṇḍa* or the Egg of Brahmā, as the Creator is called in Hindu philosophy. The phenomenon referred to above shows not only how the Consciousness of the Logos of a solar system pervades the solar system and is present at every point in the solar system but that His very Life expressed through *Nāda*, or the integrated vibration or the Word, is present also at every point in the solar system over which He presides. And since *Nāda* is a super-integration of all possible kinds of vibrations which can find expression in the solar system on all the manifested planes, this means that His Life and Power are not only present at every point in His solar system but can manifest as needed or as the existing conditions permit this. Just as the diffused light of the sun shining over a landscape, itself remains invisible but brings out from the objects present in it all kinds of colours and forms according to their nature, so the Consciousness and Life of the Logos pervading the solar system, itself remains invisible, but brings out from all the objects, animate or inanimate, an infinite variety of expressions which are characteristic of the manifested universe. And this Life and Consciousness is present potentially in every human being, for a human being is a Spirit and therefore essentially of the same nature as the Logos. And it is this Life and Consciousness which every human being can contact and put himself in rapport with in an increasing measure by a gradual unfoldment of his inner faculties and powers. Surely, to know that such a full Life and transcendent Consciousness exists within us, and yet to do nothing seriously to draw nearer to It and to draw upon It means that, though we profess these things, we do not really believe in them.

CHAPTER XXIII

THE POINT—I

(Mahābindu)

A POINT is a well-known mathematical entity or conception but its wonderful properties have been only very partially investigated by mathematicians who cannot think of any more than three dimensions in relation to space. The most extraordinary properties of a point can be studied and understood only when we consider them in relation to the subtler worlds of more than three dimensions which interpenetrate and exist within our familiar world of three dimensions. This is no doubt a subject which is difficult to study but a general idea about dimensions can be obtained by a layman by examining the nature of the lowest three dimensions with which we are familiar. The general principles of higher dimensions can then be understood to some extent in a very general way by means of analogies.

Let me first point out very briefly a few extraordinary but little-known properties of a point before we enter more deeply into the subject and try to understand these properties and their significance for the student of Occultism and the aspirant.

(1) The most wonderful property of a point is that it can serve as a meeting ground of any number of planes of different dimensions. In fact it is the only mathematical entity which can serve as a sort of common door for entering a number of planes which interpenetrate one another.

(2) A point is the basis of space. A point moving in any direction develops a line. A line moving in any direction, except its own, develops a surface. A surface moving in any direction except its own plane, develops a solid, and so on for objects of higher dimensions. We can thus say tentatively that space of any number of dimensions develops out of a point and is really nothing but a derivative of a point. We shall see later that it is this fact which enables consciousness to pass into a world of any number of dimensions through a point.

(3) A point is the mathematical representation in terms of space of the meeting ground between the manifest and the unmanifest. It is at a point that the manifest disappear into the unmanifest, or vice versa, the unmanifest emerges into the manifest. This holds true not only for the meeting ground of the Real and the unreal but for every plane. The forces from a higher plane as well as consciousness emerge on the next lower plane at a point and vice versa. In the case of the spiritual vehicles the point or centre is the vehicle itself, but in the case of the temporary vehicles the point is hidden at the centre of the vehicle and the forces or consciousness are, as it were, dispersed throughout the vehicle.

(4) One of the most fascinating facts we know about the nature of a point is that consciousness can penetrate into it *ad infinitum* without movement of any kind and come into contact with deeper and deeper aspects of Reality or worlds of increasing subtlety. The mystery of this penetration of consciousness into itself is, like all such mysteries, beyond the comprehension of the ordinary human mind, though we can get a glimpse into it when we have understood the nature of a mathematical point. It is because a point is of 0 dimension that it is possible to penetrate through it into worlds of any number of dimensions, positive or negative.

(5) Another intriguing fact we can infer about the nature of a point is that any number of points can co-exist within

one another, or to put it in other words a point can contain within it an infinite number of points. As a result of this property it is possible for any number of spiritual entities living in their respective mental or spiritual worlds to function from a common centre and to share a common state of consciousness.

(6) As a point can be the only meeting ground between the manifest and the unmanifest, manifestation always takes place through a point. We should always remember that consciousness can function only from a centre or a mathematical point, both in its passive role of perception and active role of action. On this fact rests the whole Occult doctrine of manifestation and cosmogenesis. It should not be difficult to understand that Reality being above time and space should be able to express itself only through a point in the realm of space, and the moment in the realm of time. All space is reduced ultimately to the mathematical ideal point. All time is reduced ultimately to the point of time which we generally refer to as *Kṣaṇa* or moment.

(7) As pointed out above, the point is the meeting ground or door leading from the world of the unreal to the world of the Real, or from the world of the mind to the world of pure Consciousness. On the one side of the point is the world of Reality or pure Consciousness, on the other side the multi-dimensional worlds of the mind, created by the mind and existing within the mind. He whose consciousness is established in the point is therefore in contact with both the worlds. He is standing, as it were, at the threshold of existence. When he looks within, beyond the point, he is aware of the Reality which lies at the basis of the manifested worlds of the mind. When he looks outside he is conscious of all the worlds created by the mind. The vision which can be obtained from this Point or Centre of manifestation is therefore unique.

The few statements made above even though they may not be quite intelligible show the fundamental role which the point plays in manifestation, and the importance of studying its nature thoroughly if we want to understand as far as possible the process of manifestation. The projection of the worlds of manifestation from the Unmanifest, the expression of consciousness in the worlds of manifestation as mind, the functioning of mind, all these problems can be understood only when we have a clear grasp of the nature of the point and can see how consciousness and mind can function only through a point. Let us therefore study to some extent the properties of a point and see how these facts throw light on some of the fundamental doctrines of Occultism. Of course it is not possible to understand these things fully through the instrumentality of the intellect, but I think we can get a glimpse into them and this will be enough to show that we are dealing here with mysteries of a fascinating nature and of fundamental importance.

References to the Point which is called *Bindu* in Sanskrit are very common in Hindu occult literature. *The Secret Doctrine* also mentions the point in connection with many Occult doctrines, but the idea behind it has not been elaborated or explained. Take, for instance, the following opening lines of the Proem written by H. P. Blavatsky in the first volume of *The Secret Doctrine*.

"An archaic Manuscript—a collection of palm leaves made impermeable to water, fire, air, by some specific and unknown process—is before the writer's eye. On the first page is an immaculate white disk within a dull black background. On the following page, the same disk but with a central point. The first, the student knows, represents Kosmos in Eternity, before the re-awakening of still slumbering Energy, the Emanation of the World in later systems. The point in the hitherto immaculate disk, Space and Eternity in Pralaya, denotes the dawn of differentiation. It is the

Point in the Mundane Egg, the Germ within it which
will become the Universe, the All, the boundless
periodical Kosmos—a Germ which is latent and active,
periodically and by turns."

An extraordinary description of the appearance of the
manifest from the Unmanifest through a point.

Why has a point such an important role to play in the
mechanism of manifestation? Because of its mathematical
properties. Those who have even an elementary knowledge
of the theory of dimensions know that dimensions play a very
fundamental part in the structure and perception of all kinds
of objects, and since this universe according to the Occult
Doctrine is a play of consciousness, dimensions of space determine the play of consciousness and mind through the mechanism of manifestation.

Science recognizes only three dimensions of space for all
practical purposes. A lot of mathematical work has been
done on the fourth dimension of space, but since our physical
consciousness works in three dimensions, and Science does not
recognize the existence of worlds subtler than the physical,
the conclusions drawn with regard to the fourth dimension
are considered to be of pure academic interest. Mathematically it is possible to have objects not only of four dimensions,
but also of any number of dimensions but such objects are
supposed to have only a theoretical existence and are considered to be of no significance in real life. We should, however, be careful not to confuse the fourth dimension of space
with the fourth dimension of time in the Theory of Relativity.
In order to fix any event in space and time Einstein based
his Theory of Relativity on three dimensions of space and
one of time, but this fourth dismension of time has nothing
to do with the fourth dimension of space referred to above.

The fourth and higher dimensions of space are recognized
for practical purposes only in Occultism because occultists

know of the existence of worlds subtler than the physical, and also that consciousness functions in these subtler worlds in a greater number of dimensions of space than the three with which we are familiar on the physical plane. The phenomena of these subtler worlds are of a different nature from those of the physical. It is not possible to describe or explain in terms of three dimensions any of these phenomena and occult powers which are hinted at in the third section of The *Yoga-Sūtras* of Patanjali, but anyone who has studied the subject knows the extraordinary nature of these phenomena and the occult powers by means of which they are observed or brought about.

The scriptures of the world which are based on revelation or the experience of seers also declare unequivocally the existence of superphysical worlds and the extraordinary nature of experiences which are possible when consciousness rises into these subtler realms. The orthodox and generally thoughtless followers of these religions accept and take all these things for granted, and never wonder how these things could be on the basis of the laws of Nature with which we are familiar on the physical plane. All these things would be impossible if the subtler world were similar to the physical world and were governed by the same natural laws which operate on the physical plane.

To question these things is considered a sign of heresy and so no questions are asked and no explanations given of the most extraordinary things which are a part of the revealed doctrines. Everything is taken as a matter of course and man is left to guess what will happen when he crosses over into the life beyond death. As the prospect is not very bright and has been made particularly gloomy for the wicked by those who want to keep a firm hold on their followers, the common man does not even try to guess. He just keeps himself busy with the pleasures and pursuits of this world. Enough for him are its attractions and diversions and he can now depend upon

Science to provide new ones in an ever-increasing measure. He can leave the problems of the other world to the few cranks and visionaries who, in his opinion are not realists, but live in an imaginary world of their own. He is the realist who knows how to live in the present, and, without asking any questions about the past and future, is prepared to lay down his life when death comes and snatches it away from him.

Now, the fact of the matter is that most of these extraordinary things about which we are told, either in revealed religions or in Occultism, are not fairy tales but facts of experience for those who can develop special faculties or states of mind and become aware of these subtler worlds or states of consciousness. And the extraordinary nature of the phenomena or states of consciousness on these subtler planes is due to the fact that consciousness functions on these planes in different numbers of dimensions of space and measures of time. I do not want to use the word " dimension " in relation to time in order to avoid any confusion. I have used the phrase " measures of time " to indicate that varying quality in relation to time, which is suggested by the word " dimension " in relation to space. As consciousness recedes into its subtler levels, dimensions of space vary *pari passu* with measures of time, and on each level the dimension of space is matched by its counterpart, the corresponding measure of time. Both may be considered to become rarefied progressively until the centre of consciousness passes through the point of manifestation and emerges into the world of the Unmanifest.

The peculiar role of a point in manifestation is due to the fact that it has zero dimension. As we all know a line has one dimension, a surface has two dimensions and a solid has three dimensions, while a point, from which all these geometrical entities may be considered to have been derived, has zero dimension. Now, zero is a very intriguing entity in mathematics and its behaviour in mathematical calculations is most unpredictable and mysterious. In brief this may be expressed by saying that it can mean " anything from nothing to everything ". Its nature is potential and this potentiality includes practically every mathematical quantity except infinity represented by ∞ symbolically. Zero and Infinity, or 0 and ∞ are polar opposites. The infinite potentiality of zero is shared by zero dimension and the point which has zero dimension has therefore the capacity to contain potentially worlds of all dimensions of space. This means that worlds of any number of dimensions can start from and be based on a point. Or, to put it in another way, any number of worlds of any dimension can be projected from a point and can be entered into through a point.

Some of the implications of the above-mentioned properties of a point in Occultism may be formulated as follows:

(1) Although a manifested system contains several planes of different numbers of dimensions it can be based upon a point.

(2) A centre of consciousness functioning in a point of zero dimension can be aware of everything, can energize everything and can control everything in such a manifested system which has been projected from it. Such a centre from which a manifested system is projected and controlled is called a *Mahābindu* in Sanskrit, and means the " Great Centre or Point ", and the subtlest consciousness functioning through it is of course that of *Maheśvara*, the Cosmic Logos, the Presiding Deity of the cosmos in its totality.

(3) Since the Solar Logoi and Monads have also to function through multi-planar and multi-dimensional worlds, their consciousness must also function through points or centres. Each fully developed spiritual entity functioning through such a centre is aware of everything and can control everything in the manifested system projected from his consciousness.

Since some students may find it difficult to understand how a spiritual entity functioning through a point can be simultaneously in touch with all the planes of different dimensions we may dwell here for a while on this question.

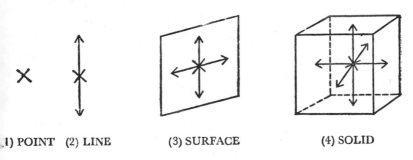

1) POINT   (2) LINE   (3) SURFACE   (4) SOLID

The above diagram represents the three stages in the development of a point into a line, a surface, and a solid. If we represent the vibration of a point as shown in (1) as representing the capacity to function in a particular dimension, it will be seen from the above figure that a point can vibrate simultaneously along the line as shown in (2), along different lines in the same plane as shown in (3), and along different lines in three dimensions as shown in (4). Now, the point retains its central position in taking upon itself these increasingly complex roles, and we can see that even when the number of dimensions is increased it will be able to maintain its position and vibrate in all the directions permissible for a particular dimension.

Since we have assumed that the vibratory capacity in the above diagram represents symbolically the capacity of a centre of consciousness to function in a world of a particular dimension—and the assumption appears to be justified—we can see how the unique position of a point in relation to different planes enables it to serve as a vehicle of consciousness on all the planes of the system manifested round that point.

If anyone finds the above mathematical illustration difficult to understand he can consider the whole question in this way. Suppose there are a large number of roads meeting at a crossing or a junction as shown in the diagram. Anyone standing at the centre **O**, not only gets a simultaneous view of all the avenues, but can enter directly any avenue he likes from the position he occupies. But it is different in the case of a person who is standing at a point A, on a particular road. In the first place he can see only those objects which are situated on that road. The objects on the other roads cannot be seen by him. In the second place, if he wants to go to some place situated on any other road he must first go to the junction of all the roads and then proceed along that particular road. So we see that the junction has a unique position in relation to the roads which meet at it. It provides free access and a simultaneous view of all the roads. Similar is the position of a point in relation to the planes of different dimensions which are formed by the mental projection of a manifested system from that centre, or the point through which the consciousness of the Logos functions. Any one who can reach or establish himself in that central point by diving into his own consciousness, unites his consciousness with the consciousness of the Logos and is

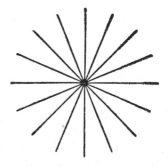

thus able to attain a simultaneous though partial view of the solar system.

Not only can he obtain a simultaneous view of all the planes of the solar system but also of the individual worlds of the Monads who are evolving in the solar system. This will be clear by merely looking at the figure on the right.

While one is on any point on a radial line he can see only along that line, *i.e.*, only into the world of that particular Monad. But being at the centre will enable the individual to see along all the lines simultaneously. The central point has therefore a unique position.

CHAPTER XXIV

THE POINT—II

(Mahābindu)

We saw in the last chapter that a point, on account of its being of zero dimension can be the basis of a manifested system containing any number of planes of any number of dimensions. We also saw that consciousness functioning through such a point is not only aware of everything but can control everything in the manifested system which has been projected from it through such a centre. It is in this way that the manifested systems, presided over by the Cosmic Logos, the Solar Logoi and the Monads, are all centred in a point and the consciousness of the Presiding Deity of the system functions through that point.

If the consciousness of each spiritual entity is centred in a point—and there are obviously an infinite uumber of such entities in the manifested universe, right from the Cosmic Logos to the youngest Monad—does it mean that these centres of consciousness are scattered throughout the vast space in which the physical universe seems to function? How then can consciousness be considered above space? How can these different units of consciousness have a common basis of underlying Reality? How can the infinite number of solar systems scattered throughout the universe be pervaded by the consciousness of the Cosmic Logos, and energized and controlled by Him? These are questions which naturally arise in the mind of the student if we integrate the different planes through which each unit of consciousness functions in one common centre, and do not integrate these different centres of consciousness into one common centre. The Occult conception of the relation existing between these different units of consciousness is based upon all these different centres of spiritual consciousness being centred in one Common Centre which we have referred to previously as the *Mahābindu* or " The Great Point ".

But the Occult doctrine of all these different centres being rooted in a common centre will mean that an infinite number of points can occupy the same position, or can be contained in the same point. This again raises a very intriguing mathematical problem. A careful consideration of the problem will, however, show the student that though the state of a number of points occupying the same position in space or being contained in a point is not imaginable, it is mathematically possible. Let us see how.

The following figure represents a number of straight lines meeting at a point 0.

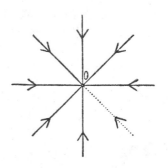

An ideal straight line is made by the projection of a point in one direction. The point in its movement to make the straight line occupies successively every possible position on that line, and so we can also imagine a straight line as a succession of points on the line situated at infinitely small distances from each other. Now try to imagine all the points, which by their movement produce the intersecting straight lines, withdrawing towards the point of intersection. What will happen in the ultimate stage when each point reaches its end? Each line is a separate entity and has its own point which traces it. This point cannot disappear into nothing when it reaches its ideal end. It must be present ideally and potentially at its terminus. But we have supposed that an infinite number of lines meet at the point of intersection. So all the points, which have traced these separate lines, must be *ideally* present at the point of intersection. Please note the word "ideally" for in this lies the clue to the mystery. So, theoretically, the point of intersection can contain within itself an infinite number of points which have traced heir separate lines in the same plane. One might say that there is only one point at the centre, and the multiplication of points takes place after the central position is left. This will mean that the central point has divided itself into an infinite number of points which trace the different lines, and the same anomaly will thus appear in a different form. We are thus dealing here with a paradox which always appears when a mystery of the spiritual plane is sought to be comprehended by the intellect in terms of the intellect. The mathematical paradox we have dealt with above really represents the mystery of the One and the Many, i.e. the co-existence of oneness and separateness.

We could, of course, consider the same question from the point of view of the third dimension by imagining a number of concentric spheres contracting to their respective centres. Each sphere will be reduced to *its* own centre and so these different centres will be contained in the common centre of all the spheres. Here again we have the same situation—a number of points co-existing in the same common point.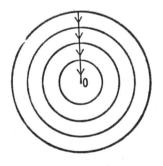

We have seen from the above examples that the existence of a number of different points co-existing in a common point is theoretically and mathematically possible and therefore there is nothing absurd in the idea of the centres of consciousness of an infinite number of spiritual entities like the Solar Logoi and Monads being rooted in the Common Centre or the *Mahābindu* of the Cosmic Logos.

The paradox of a number of points occupying the same position in space is seen in the correct perspective when we understand the true nature of ordinary space. Ordinary space from the highest point of view is an illusion. It is not something independent of the mind which conceives it. It is the result of the mental projection in the realm of the mind of a world from a centre of consciousness.

When an individual projects a mental image from the realm of consciousness such a projection can take place only through a point, because consciousness as we have seen is multi-dimensional, and can be projected in the form of its mental modifications only through a point. The mental worlds which are projected are worlds of different dimensions but not their source, consciousness, which as we have seen contains potentially all dimensions and can therefore be projected only through a point. Dimensions can come into play only when the threshold of the point is passed, and pure consciousness emerges into the realm of the mind on this side of the threshold, just as colors can come into play only when white light passes through a prism and emerges on the other side of the prism.

We have seen above how it is possible for an infinite number of spiritual entities to function in the realm of the mind from a single centre. Each entity, whether He is a Solar Logos or a Monad, projects His own independent mental world and functions in that world although He is rooted in a common centre. The common centre in the case of the Monads is the Centre of the Solar Logos to whom he is attached, and in the case of the Solar Logoi, the Centre of the Cosmic Logos. So ultimately all centres of consciousness will be seen to be concentric with the Centre of the Cosmic Logos.

It is necessary to distinguish between the attachments between monads and their Solar Logos on the one hand and the Solar Logoi and the Cosmic Logos on the o t h e r , because each Solar Logos provides a separate field for the mental worlds of the Monads who are attached to Him. It is on His consciousness f u n c t i o n i n g through the solar planes that the

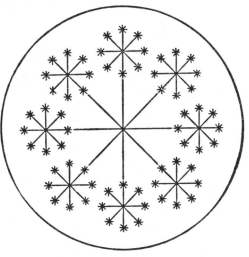

Monads build their own independent worlds, as the Solar Logoi functioning through the cosmic planes build their independent worlds on the consciousness of the Cosmic Logos. Again we see that the consciousness of the Cosmic Logoi is the ultimate basis or substratum of all the worlds created by the Solar Logoi and Monads as shown in the diagram given above.

The question may arise how these infinite number of mental worlds created by the Monads and Solar Logoi can function from the same centre without interfering with one another. Here again mathematics can help us. Mathematics may not help us to visualize the vast panorama of an infinite number of worlds functioning from the same centre and on the basis of the same consciousness, but it can help us to understand how this is possible.

The following diagram represents a number of circles or spheres having a common centre. Anyone can see that it is posssible to draw an *infinite* number of circles with a common centre.

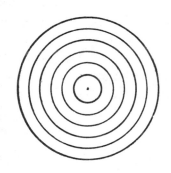

Practically, it may not be possible to do so without adjacent circles merging into one another, but theoretically this is possible. In practice the circumference of each circle must have a certain thickness however thin may be the lines which are drawn, and it is this thickness which will bring about the ultimate merging of one circle with another. But, *in theorv* each circumference is an *ideal* line with no thickness at all and it is this ideality of the lines which makes it possible for us to have an infinite number of circles having a common centre. Besides this there is no limit to the length of the radius of the concentric circles, and so an infinite number of circles can be drawn with a common centre.

Not only can we have an infinite number of concentric circles but no circle can cut or interfere with another circle however close they might be. Again we have to remember that we are dealing with ideal circles whose circumferences are ideal lines with no thickness at all, and it is this fact which accounts for their non-interference. In actual practice, if we try to draw an infinite number of circles in a limited area, a stage will come when the circles are so close together that they will overlap or merge with the adjacent circles, but this is impossible in the case of *ideal* circles.

If two *ideal* circles with a common centre overlap or interfere with each other it means that they are exactly the same and indistinguishable. So we see that it is possible for two circles to interfere with each other if they have the same radius. If they have the same radius they are identical and indistinguishable. It is also not possible to have two concentric circles whose circumferences are partly in common. Either the circles are exactly the same or entirely independent and different. We should try to grasp the significance of this fascinating mathematical fact which is self-evident and easy to understand. For it embodies in mathematical form the mystery referred to in the above question, namely: How can an infinite number of mental worlds function in the same consciousness from a common centre? They cannot interfere with one another and that is how an infinite number of manifestations are possible in the Cosmos, all contained in the Consciousness of the Cosmic Logos, and all functioning from the *Mahābindu*, " The Great Centre or Point ".

A centre surrounded by a number of concentric circles which continue to expand *ad infinitum* is the nearest and most appropriate symbol of unfolding consciousness and gives very aptly in an integrated form an idea of some of the most fundamental realities of manifestation and the dynamic processes involved in manifestation. Of course, a diagram should not be expected to represent fully these profound facts of existence, but it can sometimes help us to understand and even to visualize to a certain extent these realities of the spiritual worlds.

The reason why mathematical symbols can sometimes represent very aptly the realities of manifestation lies, of course, in the fact that the basis of manifestation is ultimately mathematical. For there is only One Reality or the Absolute lying at the basis of manifestation and everything else is relative and therefore expressed in terms of relations established in that Reality. Now, mathematics is the science which deals only with relations. It does not deal with actual things at all but only with relations between these things. That is why the world of the relative is based on mathematics, and it is only the Absolute who is beyond the realm

of mathematics. Even Science which investigates only the
phenomena of the physical plane is finding that the basis of
the physical phenomena is ultimately mathematical, and there
is a trend now in scientific circles to reduce all these phenomena to mathematical terms. Unless a natural process or
scientific law can be expressed in mathematical terms it is
not considered to be perfectly scientific.

If the manifested universe is ultimately based on mathematics it is natural that the realities of this universe, seen or

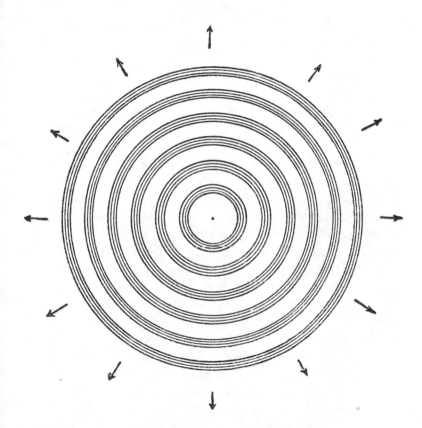

Fig. 16. Continuous and Unlimited Expansion of Consciousness

unseen, should be best symbolized by mathematical symbols.
It is natural that we should be able to understand the deeper
mysteries of the spiritual worlds with the help of mathematical
diagrams. Not only diagrams but numbers should play a
very important role in this work. And as is well known,
numbers and diagrams have not only a symbolic significance
but have potencies which are utilized by occultists to gain
certain ends.

Let us take the above diagram to illustrate how the
realities of manifestation both in their static and dynamic
aspects can be expressed through mathematical symbols.
The following points should be noted:

(1) The diagram consists of a number of concentric circles
arranged in a number of groups, each group consisting of
a number of circles so close together as to give the impression
of a ring. If, however, each ring is resolved by magnification
it will be found to contain a number of circles very close
together.

(2) The number of concentric rings can be infinite, as
well as the number of circles in each ring. Since each circle
is ideal it is mathematically possible to have an infinite
number of circles in a ring of any width. Of course the
number of concentric rings which can be arranged around a
common centre can also be infinite if the size of the rings
goes on increasing *ad infinitum*.

(3) All the rings and the circles associated with them
can expand continuously, though not necessarily uniformly.
This fact is indicated by the arrows. It will be seen
that there is no limit to the expansion of the rings and the
circles associated with them. It has already been pointed
out above that no two circles can overlap or cut each other,
though, if they are expanding at different rates, they may
overtake and pass other circles.

The above figure represents very effectively the following
facts of manifestation:

(1) The separate rings (or a group of circles separated from another group) with an infinite number of circles included within each ring, symbolize the Solar Logoi, and the circles included in each ring symbolize the Monads who are associated with the particular Logos. Each ring is a separate unit, and in its totality represents the consciousness of a Solar Logos. But it is resolvable into an infinite number of separate circles, each circle representing a Monad.

(2) When a Monad becomes a Solar Logos the corresponding circle may be considered to separate from the parent ring and form an independent ring of its own. This ring now differentiates in its own turn and is found on resolution to contain an infinite number of circles representing the Monads who will be associated with the newly born Solar Logos. This process can go on *ad infinitum* theoretically.

(3) The whole diagram of infinite radius *in two dimensions* which includes within it all the rings and circles obviously represents the Cosmic Logos. The whole area of this infinite circular diagram is the field of consciousness provided by the Cosmic Logos for the unfoldment of the Solar Logoi and Monads. The common centre of all the circles is the *Mahābindu*, the Great Centre or Point from which the consciousness of the Cosmic Logos projects the manifested universe containing everything. It should be noted that, while the infinite circle representing the Cosmic Logos is a two dimensional figure, the circles representing the Logoi and Monads are linear figures of one dimension. The consciousness of the Cosmic Logos therefore works at a deeper level or in a higher dimension than the consciousness of the Solar Logoi and Monads, though the word "dimension" in this context should be taken in a deeper sense than the one we generally associate with it.

(4) It has been pointed out in a previous chapter that the point or centre from which a manifested system is projected mentally has a unique position. It commands the whole

system both in the sense that the consciousness functioning through it is aware of everything on every plane in it, and also that the system can be energized and controlled from it. We shall consider this point more fully in a subsequent chapter, but it should be noted here how this diagram with a common centre integrates symbolically into one unified and harmonized whole the different aspects of the manifested Cosmos, both in the aspect of consciousness as well as the vehicles through which that consciousness functions.

(5) As all the Solar Logoi and Monads are undergoing a process of continuous unfoldment in the realm of manifestation, the continuous expansion of all the circles, like the waves which are produced in still water by dropping a pebble, represents this universal unfoldment. It is this unfoldment of consciousness on the spiritual planes which is reflected in the process of evolution on the lower planes. Although these circles are expanding continuously they can never possibly touch each other or interfere with each other, thus illustrating how, in spite of the infinite number of solar systems and the vehicles of individual Monads in the Cosmos there is no interference or chaos. It is a cosmos in the true sense.

(6) The diagram given above is a figure in two dimensions. But it can be easily transformed into a three dimensional figure, an infinite number of expanding concentric spheres replacing the concentric circles and the surface of each *ideal* sphere replacing the *ideal* circle. In this case the Cosmic Logos will be represented by the solid sphere of infinite radius having the same common centre as the two-dimensional spheres. Here again we see that the solid sphere representing the Cosmic Logos is of three dimensions while the superficial spheres representing the Logoi and Monads are of two dimensions, i.e., the consciousness of the Cosmic Logos is functioning in a higher dimension than that of a Solar Logos or Monad.

CHAPTER XXV

THE POINT—III

(MAHĀBINDU)

WE have discussed already in the previous two chapters some mathematical properties of a point and their implications. We saw that a point by virtue of its having zero dimension can serve as a common passage or bridge between worlds of any number of dimensions. It is, therefore, inevitably a vehicle or instrument through which consciousness can function simultaneously in a number of mental worlds which have been projected from it and through it. These worlds of different dimensions in the realm of the mind are separate from one another and independent of one another owing to their functioning in different numbers of dimensions, but they are all open to the consciousness which has projected them and functions through them. We also saw that although the worlds of the different Solar Logoi and Monads function separately and independently they are all rooted in the Common Centre which is the Centre of Consciousness of the Cosmic Logos, so that while we are all living and functioning in separate worlds of our own, we literally live and move and have our being in Him.

We shall now proceed to deal with the properties of a radiating centre of energy enclosed within a sphere. The properties of such a radiating centre are very remarkable and have been referred to already in the chapter *Integrated*

Sound. They light up the whole field of the mechanism of manifestation and almost place some of our doctrines with regard to these things on a scientific basis.

The figure given below illustrates the behavior of light waves radiating from the centre of a spherical mirror as has been explained in detail in Chapter XXII.

If we consider the above phenomenon carefully we shall see that this repeated reflection of light waves with the tremendous speed of light really means that the radiation which was initiated from the centre fills the whole globe permanently. We know that light can travel for billions of years through empty space if there is nothing to stop or dissipate it.

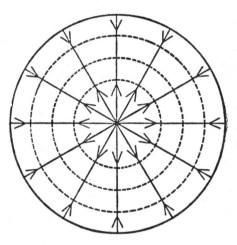

The inside of the sphere therefore becomes a globe full of the particular radiation and remains full as long as some external agency does not put a stop to the whole process. There are only two ways in which this can be done. Either the spherical wall of the sphere is made to disappear and the radiation allowed to pass out into space and disappear, or the radiation is stopped at the centre by the agency which started it.

Now, let us suppose that the radiation which is initiated at the centre is that of white light. In this case the whole globe will become full of white light and will remain full of white light unless and until the process is interrupted from outside. Every part, nay every point within the three dimensional globe will contain white light or will be permeated with white light. For this reason any colour of the spectrum can appear at any point within this globe at any time. In fact, the sphere of white light may be considered as a perfectly integrated form of seven spheres of coloured lights corresponding to the seven colours of the spectrum. We can imagine seven spheres of violet, indigo, blue, green, yellow, orange, and red colour integrated perfectly in one sphere of white light.

We have taken white light to illustrate the formation of a globe of radiant energy which automatically tends to become permanent and remains in existence as long as the impulse which produces it is not withdrawn. But it will be seen that any kind of vibration or impulse which is of the nature of radiation will produce similar conditions under the ideal conditions we have assumed. *Nāda* or the super-integrated vibration which lies at the basis of the universe will produce a globe of *Nāda* in which all possible kinds of vibrations are potentially present at every point within the globe.

According to the Occult doctrine the basis of a manifested system is a super-integrated vibration or *Nāda*, as it is called in Hindu philosophy. In fact, the word ' Logos ' means ' The Word ', or that primal Divine sound which brings the worlds into existence. The name used in Hindu philosophy for this primal Divine Sound lying at the basis of a mani-fested system is *Shabda-Brahma*, which means the Reality, considered as Sound, which produces and maintains a mani-fested system in existence. The above concept of a radia-ting centre forming a globe of the particular radiation shows how the impulse given by the Divine Will from the centre will lead to the automatic formation of a globe of *Nāda*, if we may say so. And since *Nāda* is integrated Sound—using the word Sound in its Occult sense—the globe thus formed will contain potentially all types of vibrations which may be needed in the manifested system. As *Nāda* is considered the

ultimate basis of a manifested system in all its complexity and
variety, and is capable of producing all kinds of forms,
we have here a very illuminating picture of the raw material
out of which a manifested system is made. Just as an egg
contains all the material out of which the body of a chick
is gradually made, so this globe of integrated vibration produced by the Logos of the system can, by its differentiation,
provide all types of vibrations and forms needed in the creation
and maintenance of the manifested system.

This phenomenon also provides us with a clue to the
shape of a manifested system. According to the Occult doctrine every solar system is an enclosed mental organism
pervaded by the consciousness of its Solar Logos and energized
by His life in its multifarious forms. It is called a *Brahmānda*
or the Egg of the Creator. An egg is of course ellipsoidal
in form, and not exactly spherical. But both forms have
a focus from which an impulse can be imparted to the
whole space enclosed within the walls of the organism.
Whether the phrase *Brahmānda* is used loosely for a manifested system having the form of a sphere or there are two
focii instead of one through which the life and consciousness
of the Logos function need not be considered here. The
important point to note here is that it is an enclosed organism
with a point from which forces, etc. can be poured into it
from above.

It may also be pointed out in this connection that the
Sanskrit word *bindu* means both a point and a drop, and so
the word used to indicate the centre of a manifested system
includes within itself the idea of a point as well as that of a
drop. It denotes not only the centre or focus round which
a manifested system is formed but also the manifested system
which is thus formed and is like a drop. A drop is a portion
of a liquid with an enclosing surface and approximately
spherical in form. It has also got a focus from which forces
radiate and keep the liquid in the spherical form. So the

word *bindu* used for the centre of consciousness belonging to a microcosm, or the word *Mahābindu* used for the Centre of a consciousness belonging to a macrocosm is more appropriate than the English word point which carries the idea of a centre but not of the manifested world which functions round that centre.

The fact that centres of consciousness or *bindus* of all *Jīvātmās* or Monads are concentric with the Centre of Divine consciousness or *Mahābindu* is of great significance in the realm of practical Occultism. It has been pointed out already that the point having zero dimension can serve as a bridge for consciousness between planes of different dimensions. It is through this common centre of the vehicles of a *Jīvātmā* working on different planes of the solar system that the yogi is able to pass from one plane to another. In *Samādhi* when consciousness rises from the lower to the higher planes there is no movement in space but only a sinking of consciousness into its own deeper levels. This sinking takes place through the common centre of all the vehicles. In *The Science of Yoga* this sinking of consciousness into deeper levels during the different stages of *Samādhi* is shown as taking place along a vertical line AO because it is not possible to show diagrammatically the sinking into a point. But this does not represent the process correctly because it will really mean that consciousness moves in space when it recedes into its deeper levels. Actually, it remains centred in the common centre of its vehicles and its rising from one plane to another merely means that while remaining centred in its *bindu*, it begins to function at a different level. It is only through a point-bridge that this can be done.

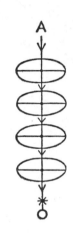

It will perhaps enable the student to gain a glimpse into this mystery of the sinking consciousness into deeper levels

through a point if he imagines himself looking down along the line AO from above. If he looks at the line AO from any side it appears a line but if he looks at it from above it is reduced to a point A and sinking along the line AO appears like sinking into the point A.

It is easy to understand how the spiritual vehicles of a *Jīvātmā* can have a common centre because they themselves are atomic. The Ātmic, Buddhic and Causal vehicles are atomic which really means that they are merely points or centres through which consciousness finds expression. But what about the lowest three vehicles, the lower mental, astral and physical which have an ellipsoidal form? Where is this common centre in the case of these three vehicles? In order to understand this mystery we have to remember that the vehicle through which the mind functions is different from the mind itself. The vehicle in the case of the lowest three planes is ellipsoidal but the mind itself being non-material and of the nature of consciousness, functions through a point and it is this point which is the real vehicle of consciousness. The outer material vehicle merely serves to receive and transmit external vibrations to the mind working through a point. This distinction between a vehicle and the mind is of great importance and should always be kept in view. Many students confuse the mental body with the mind itself. The first is called *manomaya kosha* while the latter is referred to as *manas*. It is this *manas* which functions through a point. It is this point which serves as the bridge for consciousness referred to above. This common centre of all the lower vehicles of a Monad or *Jīvātmā* is therefore called *mano-bindu* in Sanskrit which means ' the mental point '.

We may refer briefly here to the mystery of the secondary *Sushumnā* which is sometimes mentioned in occult literature. Very few people understand what this means. They understand by the word *Sushumnā* the hair-like passage in the spinal column in which *Kundalinī* rises from the *mulādhāra chakra* to the *Sahasrāra* at the top of the head. This passage activates various centres or *chakras* in the body and leads to the experiencing of higher states of consciousness. What is the function of the secondary *Sushumnā* and where is it situated? The secondary *Sushumnā* is a mysterious passage which connects the physical brain with 'the heart'. The word heart is used very frequently in mystic literature for the common centre of all the vehicles and is thus the seat of the mind. The secondary *Sushumnā* is thus the passage along which the vibrations in the brain centres reach the common centre of all vehicles through which the mind or *manas* functions. It is the mind which really perceives and the brain is merely its outpost on the physical plane. So the series of physical

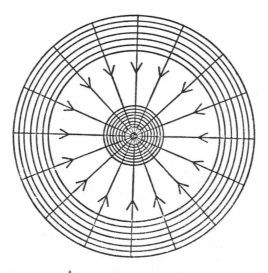

FIG. 17. The Macrocosm and the Microcosm

processes which lead ultimately to sensation do not end in the physical brain. They are continued along the secondary *Sushumnā* and terminate ultimately in the point through which the mind of the individual functions. What has been said above with regard to the physical body also holds true in the case of the other two subtler vehicles of the personality.

This common centre serves not only as a bridge for consciousness between different planes, but also as a vehicle for the transmission of different kinds of forces from one plane to another. Through this common centre the personality remains not only in touch with the individuality or the Monad but also receives the different kinds of forces which flow into the lower bodies either naturally or as a result of the response from above to aspiration or invocation of these forces. These forces may *appear* to descend into the lower vehicles through different centres or organs but they come actually through the common centre. And because the common centre of the *Jīvātmā* is concentric with the *Mahābindu* or the common centre of *Paramātmā* we may consider these forces as coming either from our own Higher Self or from the Logos. The bridge is the same and the *modus operandi* is the same as will be seen from Figure 17. In this figure:

> The outer ring represents the vehicles of the Solar Logos or the planes of the solar system.
>
> The inner ring represents the vehicles of the Monad or *Jīvātmā*.
>
> O is the Common Centre of the Over-Soul and the individual soul.

We might briefly discuss one more aspect of this common centre before bringing this interesting subject to a close. This is the relation between the individual mind of a *Jīvātmā* and the Universal Mind of the Logos.

It has been pointed out elsewhere that the world image produced in the mind of an individual is mostly the result of the interaction of the Universal Mind and his individual mind as shown below. The Universal Mind has many levels and so has the individual mind. At each level the interaction produces a certain image in the mind of the individual and this image is taken by him as his world. This phenomenon may be illustrated by a simple experiment. Suppose a glass globe which is silvered inside is suspended in a room. All the objects present in the room will produce a spherical image on the surface of the globe. If we imagine a point of consciousness at the centre of the globe which can see the image on the surface of the globe but not the room

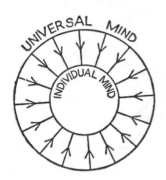

which produces that image we will see how to that entity the image on the sphere will appear as his world. He would not know that it was merely an image, and an image produced by an external agency acting on the surface of the globe. Similarly, we live in a world created by the Ideation in the Divine Mind. Our mind gets an ever changing impression from this unfolding world in the Divine Mind and this we consider to be our world because we identify ourselves with it.

The chief difference between the two images is that while objects in the room produce a changeless image on the surface of a stationary globe, the image in the mind of every individual is constantly changing. Even this phenomenon can be duplicated in the experiment by moving the globe from one place to another in the room, and thus changing the conditions of time and space. The changeless image will be immediately transformed into a changing image. The same effect can be produced by placing the globe in a surrounding of constantly moving objects such as a street.

In the above experiment the reflector is a material object with a spherical surface. The mind is not a material object and has no surface. The reflection of the Universal Mind in the individual mind is not therefore strictly speaking a process of reflection but of reproduction in a partial and distorted form according to the condition of the individual mind. The mental image appears really from within the mental centre. The mind itself being a modification of pure consciousness can function only from a point and therefore the mental image is really contained in a point or the *manobindu.*

How an image of a particular external environment can exist in a point will be seen from the figure on the right representing a number of concentric silvered glass globes hanging in a room. The objects in the room will produce an image on the outermost globe. If this globe is removed, the same image will 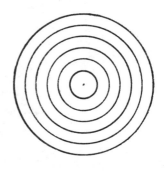 be produced on the next smaller globe, though it will be somewhat smaller. As we remove the globes successively the same image will be produced though it becomes smaller. Is there a theoretical limit to the size of the globe? Yes. The point representing the common centre of the globes is the limit from the mathematical point of view, and it follows logically and mathematically that the same image can exist in that point though now it is of infinitesimal dimensions. Now the size of the actual image formed does not matter as far as the mind is concerned as will be explained when we deal with the problem of Space. The image of the surrounding objects formed on the retina is extremely small, and yet when the mind perceives the surrounding objects through it, it is enlarged very greatly. Not only is it enlarged but it is invested with meaning. The image on the retina is a dead thing. The image perceived in the mind is a thing which is alive and full of meaning because it is a mental image illuminated by consciousness behind which is the whole Reality which underlies the universe.

The above considerations will show how the common centre of our vehicles through which alone mind and consciousness can function, serves as a sort of point mirror, i.e. a mirror which reflects the Divine Mind and Consciousness but is of the dimension of a point. Through this point we can become aware of our environment at whatever level our consciousness may be functioning. At the lower levels this point requires the paraphernalia of an enclosing vehicle to contact the external world, just as the lower mind requires the five sense-organs to contact the physical world. But on the higher spiritual planes of Ātmā, Buddhi and Higher Manas this paraphernalia is not necessary. The point itself is sufficient as a vehicle of consciousness. This is what is meant when we say that the Ātmic, Buddhic and Causal vehicles are atomic.

We see thus that this Point Mirror is multi-dimensional, that it can reflect consciousness at different levels or in different dimensions, or we may say that it is a multiple Point Mirror. The point is really one but it can function in different dimensions through different vehicles.

CHAPTER XXVI

DIMENSIONS OF SPACE

THERE are many truths related to the functioning of consciousness through vehicles which the student of Divine Wisdom finds it difficult to understand. He takes their existence for granted but is unable to comprehend them in the slightest degree. Let us take a few examples of such truths which are incomprehensible to us on account of the limitations under which our consciousness functions on the physical plane.

The consciousness of the Solar Logos can find expression through the minds of all the *Jīvātmās* in His solar system though they are scattered far and wide in the vast space in which a solar system functions. The Solar Logos is not only always aware of everything that is taking place in His solar system and in the minds of the *Jīvātmās*, but can bring about any change in any part of His realm. In a similar manner but at a much higher level the consciousness of the Cosmic Logos is in the most intimate touch with the consciousness of all the Solar Logoi and through the Solar Logoi with that of all the monads evolving in the different solar systems. Even an advanced yogi can create many artificial mental bodies for himself functioning at different places at the same time. Through these artificially created bodies he can function in different environments in the same manner as through his natural set of vehicles. All these facts we take for granted but have not the slightest notion of the *modus operandi* or how such extraordinary things are possible.

Then there is another set of phenomena which are difficult to understand on the basis of the laws with which we are familiar. According to the Occult Doctrine the whole universe in its manifested state is ultimately a mental phenomenon taking place in the consciousness of the Cosmic Logos, this consciousness being centred in and functioning through a Point which is called the *Mahābindu*. The Solar Logoi whose physical bodies are represented by solar systems and are scattered throughout the Cosmos are part of the consciousness of the Cosmic Logos and their consciousness is also centred in the *Mahābindu*. Similarly, the consciousness of Monads evolving in each solar system is centred in the consciousness of their respective Solar Logoi. We thus have the intriguing phenomenon of an innumerable number of minds at different levels or at the same level functioning from a common centre and all based on the Universal Mind. And the wonderful thing about the whole phenomenon is that these different minds function in their respective worlds without interfering with one another.

It is difficult for an ordinary man to imagine how different worlds of a mental nature can co-exist and function from a common centre of consciousness. The theory of dimensions throws some light on this problem and although it cannot enable us to visualize the *modus operandi* yet it shows us how this kind of thing is possible. A general theory of dimensions of space has been worked out by mathematicians and the idea of higher dimensions is familiar not only to occultists but also to scientists. But the mathematical theory of dimensions is a pure abstraction and more or less of academic interest. And because it does not relate the higher dimensions with any subtler worlds hidden within the physical, it has no significance to the scientist beyond the three dimensional world with which he is familiar and in which alone he believes.

It is necessary for us to understand how the same consciousness can manifest through vehicles or *upādhis* separated from one another in time and space. To imagine consciousness as some sort of fluid medium which spreads and fills our minds is philosophically untenable though this is the manner in which the average man tries to visualize the all-pervasiveness of Divine Consciousness. It is only on the basis of the hypothesis that consciousness on the subtler planes functions through a higher number of dimensions than the three with which we are familiar on the physical plane that it is possible to explain the doctrines which are generally held in the fields of religion and philosophy regarding the nature of Divine and spiritual consciousness.

The subject of higher dimensions is of great interest to the student of Occultism because unlike the orthodox scientist and the so-called intellectual of modern times the occultist believes that there are subtler worlds of matter and mind hidden beneath the physical world which the average man can perceive through his sense-organs. The consciousness functioning in these increasingly subtler worlds is considered to become less and less limited until we reach the bedrock of Divine Consciousness which is completely free from limitations and illusions as far as our solar system is concerned. These worlds interpenetrating the physical world are considered not only to be progressively subtler as regards their material and mental basis, but the consciousness which finds expression through the respective vehicles is considered to function in a greater number of dimensions as we penetrate from the periphery towards the centre. We do not know exactly the number of dimensions corresponding to each plane but that the number increases as we go deeper is taken for granted.

The occultist does not believe in leaving the ideas about our inner constitution and the manner in which consciousness functions through our subtler vehicles in a nebulous condition like the average orthodox religious man. The latter believes that there is some part of him he refers to as his 'soul' which survives the death of the physical body and he is content to leave the destiny of this dubious and nebulous entity in the hands of his guru, prophet or God; for while he is living his physical life he is too busy with its pursuits to bother about his soul. Time enough to attend to his soul during the 'eternal' life which he is going to enter on leaving this physical world. The occultist, on the other hand, believes in acquiring all the knowledge which he can get about our inner constitution here and now, not only because he thinks that it is possible to gain such knowledge to some extent, but also because our future depends upon acquiring such knowledge and utilizing it for our spiritual unfoldment.

As dimensions of space limit our consciousness and veil, as it were, the Reality which is hidden within us, it is of the utmost importance that we have some knowledge about their nature. Our approach to the problem should be practical and not academic. We shall therefore not deal with the question mathematically but in a comparatively simple manner. We shall also adopt the method of going from the known to the unknown because the study and understanding of the lowest three dimensions which the mind can grasp is the best method, or perhaps the only method of getting some idea regarding the nature of higher dimensions. But we should not expect to gain in this manner a clear conception regarding the nature of phenomena taking place in higher dimensions. In fact, in spite of our best effort we shall not be able to visualize clearly the world even of the fourth dimension, the world next to the one in which we are living. But it is a fascinating study and it shows us how the different planes of the solar system differ fundamentally from one another and how our consciousness is imprisoned on a plane until it is transferred to another plane, either in the natural course of transitions like death or by artificial methods of yoga.   And perhaps the most useful result of such a study is that it gives us a sense of perspective and wonder regarding the nature of this infinite universe.   We cease to suffer from the tendency to over-simplify the problems with which we are dealing and learn to approach them with the necessary humility and caution needed when a man with the imperfect instrument of the intellect begins to probe into this vast, wonderful and complicated universe in which God is enshrined.

The theory of higher dimensions has been developed so far only on the basis of mathematical analysis.   It is, as pointed out above, of pure academic interest and beyond the comprehension of any man who is not familiar with higher mathematics.   A few writers like Mr. Hinton have tried to develop the theory of the fourth dimension in a manner which will enable the layman to have some idea about higher dimensions, but as in these treatments no effort is made to relate the mathematical facts with the realities of life they lack that quality of vital interest which is aroused when some fact touches our life at some point.

We shall adopt a simpler method of treatment in dealing with the theory of higher dimensions.   In this we may not be able to go very deep into the subject but what we shall study will be understandable and have some significance with regard to the nature of consciousness and its functioning and unfoldment in human life. As has been pointed out before, the aspirant does not study these things for their own sake.   He has a definite object in view and he knows that his time and energy are limited.   So he confines himself to the study only of those subjects which throw light on the vital problems in which he is interested and which have some bearing on his life and its goal.

Let us begin with a few facts which everyone can understand.

(1) A point is a mathematical entity with zero dimension, that is, it has neither length, breadth nor thickness. Of course when we use the word point we mean an *ideal* point and not a very small dot made by means of a pen or pencil. The smallest *actual* dot that anyone can make will always have length and breadth and also some thickness as can be proved by placing it under a powerful microscope. It is impossible to make an ideal point in actual life. It is thus only an ideal point which has zero dimension. This fact, that a point has zero dimension, is of tremendous importance because the whole universe in its manifested state is centred in a point and comes out of a point as we saw when we discussed the nature of a point and its role in the mechanism of manifestation.

(2) The second fact we should note is that a line is made by the *movement* of a point. We can imagine a line as being traced by the movement of a point or as consisting of an infinite number of points placed end to end. We have to note two important facts with regard to a line. First, that it has only length and no breadth or thickness. It is therefore a mathematical entity of one dimension, i.e., length or direction with no breadth or thickness. The second important point we should note is that a mathematical line like the point is an ideal thing. We can never actually draw a line with no breadth and thickness.

(3) As the line is made by the movement of a point so a surface is made by the movement of a line not in its linear direction but different from it. A surface has length and breadth but no thickness. It has only two dimensions, length and breadth. Here again we have to note that a surface is an ideal thing. We cannot in actual experience have a surface without thickness. The thinnest film of matter must have at least the thickness of one atom and so we cannot have an actual surface without thickness associated with it.

(4) And lastly, we have to note that a solid of three dimensions is made by the movement of a surface not on its own plane but in any other plane. A solid has length, breadth and thickness. Since the human mind can function only in three dimensions on the physical plane, that is the limit beyond which we cannot go so long as our consciousness is confined to the physical plane. We can imagine a solid but we cannot imagine any figure or object with more than three dimensions.

Having considered the essential nature of a point, line, surface, and solid, let us now pass on to some interesting aspects of dimensions of space. It is possible to go much further into this question from the mathematical point of view, and some of the conclusions which we reach in this manner are extremely interesting, but we shall not go further into the mathematical aspects of the question however interesting they might be. In the first place, it is difficult to understand these things without some knowledge of mathematics, especially solid geometry, and we are likely to get confused rather than enlightened if we attempt this task without proper preparation. Secondly, it is not necessary to adopt the mathematical approach in order to gain a general idea with regard to the nature of dimensions of space, for the conclusions at which we arrive as a result of mathematical analysis, though interesting from the academic point of view, do not help us in gaining a more vivid conception of mind and consciousness functioning through the subtler vehicles. It is only when we transcend a plane that we can get rid of the limitations which are inherent in the functioning of mind and consciousness on that plane. So let us be content with a few general ideas regarding these higher dimensions which may throw some light on the well-known doctrines of Occultism.

The first general idea which we may note is that going into a higher dimension involves really adding a new kind of depth to our perception or understanding of any object or principle. This fact will be seen if we consider even the lowest three dimensions in relation to one another.

Suppose we take an ordinary object like a book. What we can perceive and know about the book will depend upon the number of dimensions in which our consciousness is functioning. If our consciousness is linear, i.e. confined to a line we can see only an edge of the book. Like a microbe we can crawl from side to side along one edge and can see neither the other edges nor the surface of the book, to say nothing of the solid aspect of the book. But suppose our consciousness instead of being linear becomes superficial, i.e., begins to function in two dimensions. Immediately a new world will emerge into the horizon of our perception and we shall discover a new depth in our knowledge of the book. Instead of our consciousness being confined to a line, an edge of the book for example, a whole surface will become available for our inspection and enquiry, though not simultaneously. We shall be able to crawl about freely on a particular surface, though we shall not be able to leave that surface and see another surface even though it is adjacent to it. An edge of the book will appear like a chasm where our world comes to an end, and we will not be able to see anything further. Now, the important point to note in this change in perception is that it introduces a new depth to our perception and understanding and thus enables us to see much more in the same object. Entirely new aspects of the object which were completely hidden from our view and which we could not even imagine emerge into our consciousness. They were there all the time but hidden from our view.

It is possible to go one step further on the physical plane in our knowledge of an object like a book. If our consciousness is raised to three dimensions from two dimensions we immediately begin to see much more in the book than what we saw as a two dimensional entity. Instead of our consciousness being confined to a surface it can now go into the third dimension and perceive the solidity of the book. We can now see different surfaces of the book. It is now a solid thing instead of being merely a superficial object. Here again we shall see that a new kind of depth in our perception and understanding of the object has emerged into our mental horizon. We see much more now in the same book simply because we see it in a higher dimension.

This example is enough to make us realize how the addition of new dimensions to our consciousness enables us to see much more in the same object. All the aspects of the object are already there, but they remain hidden from our view, as it were, according to the number of dimensions in which our consciousness is confined. When a new dimension is added to our consciousness as a result of our rising into a higher plane or to put it in other words, as a result of our going into a greater depth of our consciousness, these new aspects come into view and the same object appears far richer and more beautiful, without having undergone any change.

But our depth of vision and richness in perception is not confined to any particular object of the plane. All the objects on a particular plane share in being thus raised to a higher level of richness, beauty and significance. As our consciousness sinks into greater depths of Reality in its progress from the periphery to the centre, this whole universe round us becomes endowed with greater depth, richness, beauty and harmony owing to the removal, step by step, of our limitations. The universe in all its beauty, grandeur, divinity, is already there always. It is we who change and see more and more in it owing to the removal of our limitations.

And yet we do not go anywhere, move in any way, or even change with regard to our constitution. All that happens is that our consciousness sinks into the greater and greater depths of our own centre of being. That centre as we have seen is concentric with the Great Centre in which the whole universe in all its depth, richness, beauty is contained. So sinking into our centre really means sinking into that Great Centre in which the universe in all its fullness is contained.

If we could get the slightest realization of this truth of truths our whole attitude towards life and its problems would undergo a fundamental and dynamic change and the desire to pierce through these veils which hide the truths of the inner life from our gaze will be born within us. It is this strong urge which drives the *Jnāni* to know the Truth which is hidden within his heart. It is this intense desire which draws the devotee towards his Beloved. It is this irresistible will which urges the yogi to dive deeper and deeper into the unfathomable depths of his being to find that Reality which is hidden there. And it is this urge which we have to develop as a result of our training and self-discipline, for without this urge our life does not move towards its appointed goal.

CHAPTER XXVII

TIME AND SPACE—I

ACCORDING to the Occult doctrine the Ultimate Reality which underlies the universe exists in two states, the Manifest and the Unmanifest. The existence of this Reality in two states raises the question of the relation existing between these two states. This relation has been discussed already in detail in previous chapters and it is not necessary to go into the question here. All that we have to keep in mind is that the manifested universe is derived from and is essentially of the same nature as the unmanifest Reality which is hidden within it. The difference between the two lies in the fact that the former represents the differentiated and dynamic state of Reality while the latter represents the integrated and potential state of the same Reality.

The emergence of the manifested universe from the Unmanifest involves a definite mechanism of manifestation. The word mechanism may suggest the idea of a tangible or material instrument but it is not in this sense that the word is used here. It only means that in the manifestation of the universe from the Unmanifest a certain number of agencies are involved. These are related to one another and in their totality may be referred to as the mechanism of manifestation. The place of this mechanism or agencies of manifestation in the process of manifestation can be seen from the following table.

		THE ABSOLUTE		
THE EVER UNMANIFEST	{	THE POSITIVE—NEGATIVE PRINCIPLE		
		THE UNMANIFEST COSMIC LOGOS		

Mahākāla	Mahākāsha	Mahāmāya	Mahābindu	etc.

THE MANIFESTED DIVINITY	{	THE FIRST LOGOS	The Ādi Plane	
		THE SECOND LOGOS	The Anupādaka Plane	
		THE THIRD LOGOS	The Higher Ātmic Plane	
		THE MONADS		

Time	Space	Illusion	The Point	etc.

THE SPIRITUAL WORLDS	{	THE TRIPLE INDIVIDUALITY OR JĪVĀTMĀ	{	The Lower Ātmic Plane
				The Buddhic Plane
				The Higher Mental Plane
THE TEMPORAL WORLDS	{	THE TRIPLE PERSONALITY OR JĪVA	{	The Lower Mental Plane
				The Astral Plane
				The Physical Plane

It will be seen from the above table that these agencies of manifestation exist and come into operation in their highest form at the boundary between the Ever-Unmanifest and the Manifested Divinity. They exist and come into operation in their lower form again at the boundary between the Manifested Divinity and the spiritual worlds created by the Triple Logos. It is because they are a part of a total mechanism which brings about the world process that they begin to function together at the two boundaries.

Another point which we should remember is that manifestation is a repetitive and progressive process and the same process is repeated at different levels as has been shown in the chapter entitled " Reflections of Reflections ". In this repetition or reflection at lower levels the essential character of the process is retained, but owing to differences in the nature and density of the media the mode of expression is altered in many respects. It is for this reason that we ought to make an effort to understand the general principles and not get involved too much in the details. If our ideas regarding the general principles underlying any subject are clear we can not only understand the whole subject better but càn also apply our knowledge for the solution of any specific problem in a more effective manner.

We have already dealt with three agencies which are involved in manifestation, namely, *Māyā*, *Nāda* and the *Point*, and shall now take up for detailed consideration another agency involved in the working of a manifested world— *Time and Space.* As has been pointed out above, all the agencies involved in manifestation are related to one another and are really different aspects of the same integral process, but time and space are related to each other in a more intimate manner than the other agencies and we shall therefore consider them together.

Time and space are two enigmas of philosophy and have intrigued philosophers since times immemorial. A tremendous amount of speculative thought, some spurious and the other of a more serious and subtle nature, is available on the subject. A new and more practical interest has been aroused on the subject by the Theory of Relativity put forward by Einstein. Since this theory has led to far-reaching consequences in the development of Science, the conception of time and space given by Einstein in his theory is taken as the last word by the layman as well as the scientific world.

Here I may be pardoned for a little digression from my subject to say a few words about a tendency in human nature which has begun to find expression in an increasing degree in modern times, and which tends to warp our judgment and vitiate our sense of values. The tendency I am referring to is the extraordinary importance attached by the modern man to anything which is spectacular. The theory of Einstein was a brilliant achievement in the realm of philosophy and Science, but it remained of academic interest for a long time and only a few scientists took an active interest in it. But the moment the first atom bomb was exploded and it became known that the theory had been further corroborated by the discovery of atomic energy everyone began to swear by this theory and to consider its conclusions with regard to everything as final. The validity of the philosophy of scientific materialism was thought to be established beyond any doubt and the pursuit of purely physical aims in life was considered to be quite justified. If the enthusiasm of people in general for this philosophy of scientific materialism is not as great as it might have been it is because the discovery of atomic energy has lifted the lid of the proverbial Pandora's box and created problems of an extremely serious nature. People have realized to some extent that they have raised a Franken-stein's monster which will destroy them if it is not properly controlled. And they are also realizing slowly that for this purpose the materialistic philosophy is not sufficient. For, this control involves the mind and morals of man which the materialistic philosophy does not care to take into account.

Of course, those who are aspirants and believe in the pursuit of spiritual ideals have their own form of this general tendency to attach great importance to what is spectacular or sensational. The importance attached to so-called miracles or anything which is supernatural is an expression of this tendency. The highest expression of spiritual life will generally be passed by unnoticed while any miracle genuine or spurious immediately catches their attention and throws them into an ecstasy.

Now, the reason why I have referred to this tendency in human nature in this context is to point out that many people who are superficially acquainted with the subject or who are materialistic in outlook think that the question of the nature of time and space has been settled once for all by the Theory of Relativity.   But has not Einstein proved his conclusions by mathematical deduction? they say.   It is generally supposed, especially in scientific circles that if mathematical deduction is employed in proving anything the matter is finally settled and nothing more can be said about it.   They forget that most of such deductions are based upon many unproved assumptions, any one of which may be wrong or partially correct and vitiate the final conclusion.   They lose sight of the fact that a mathematical conclusion can be correct only if it takes all factors involved in the question into account and if some factors are left out the conclusion may be wrong or only partially correct.

These facts must be kept in mind when we consider the nature of time and space and the method Einstein adopted in dealing with the problem.   Einstein based his theory only on facts of the physical world and if other subtler worlds besides the physical also exist—and they do exist according to Occultism—then his theory can have no validity with respect to those worlds.   It is true that his theory is a brilliant achievement in the realm of mathematics, but since it is based only on physical facts, at best it can be valid only for purely physical phenomena.   It cannot be considered to throw light on the nature of time and space in general but only as they appear to the human mind working under the limitations of the physical brain.   The very fact that the conception of the time-space continuum as given in the theory is unintelligible to the human mind points to its limitations and the fact that it is merely trying to interpret imperfectly the shadows of some realities cast on the screen in a shadow play of the mind.

Anyone who studies the nature of time and space carefully will be convinced that the mind of man is also a very important factor in this problem and so in understanding

time and space we must take this factor also into account.
And since the mind of man is not only what finds expression through the physical brain, but has many degrees of
subtlety and modes of expression, the whole nature of man
is really involved in the problem of time and space. And
so only those who have dived within their consciousness and
unravelled its deeper mysteries and reached the source in
which time and space have their origin, are really competent
to say what the real nature of these basic realities of the universe is. Who is more competent to pronounce a correct opinion
about the nature of an orange, he who has merely scratched
the rind or he who has peeled the orange and eaten it?

It will be seen therefore that the Occult view of the
nature of time and space can be the only reliable one. We
may not be able to understand it except in a very hazy or
fragmentary manner on account of our limitations. We may
not be able to put the ideas in the framework of mathematical
formulae. But this does not really matter. We cannot escape
from the fact that a concept of time and space based on a
total view of the universe including its subtlest aspects can be
the only reliable concept however faulty and incomplete it
may appear to us down here on the physical plane. The
views of scientists may be apparently conclusive because based
on mathematics, but as pointed out above they can at best
have a very limited validity and scope. The views of Adepts
of Occultism may appear hazy and unconvincing but because
they are based on direct experience of the subtler planes and
take all factors into account they alone can be considered
generally valid and reliable by those who consider the physical
world merely as the outermost shell of the real universe that
exists hidden within it. So, while keeping an open mind on
the subject let us not give undue importance to what Einstein
or any other scientist has said on this question. Let us consider the Occult view of time and space however imperfect
and sketchy it may appear for the time being.

With this rather long but necessary introduction let us now come to the subject proper and consider some of its essential aspects. It is not possible for us to deal with the subject thoroughly and completely on account of the limitations of the lower mind. All that can be done is to present certain selected ideas which are suggestive and can stimulate thought in right directions. In these matters we must look for illumination within and dig out of our own mind gradually a coherent and meaningful conception of the reality which we want to understand. The ideas received from without can merely serve as signposts indicating the direction in which we have to explore our own mind.

I shall set the ball rolling by making the rather startling statement that according to the Occult doctrine both time and space are illusions. We shall discuss the nature of the illusion involved later and confine ourselves here to certain general aspects of the subject to clear the ground for deeper thought.

The doctrine that time and space are illusions created in the mind is not a mere interesting philosophical concept which has been evolved by intellectual analysis for the amusement of philosophers. It is a fact which is verified by every advanced occultist in his progress towards Self-realization. This concept is implicit in all spiritual doctrines such as those connected with the Unity of life, Liberation, Eternity, Omniscience, etc. There is a tendency among religious people to consider doctrines connected with subjects like time and space as of a purely philosophical nature and to regard only the doctrines connected with the Oneness of life, consciousness of our Divine nature, etc., of a spiritual nature. The fact is that all these doctrines hang together and are inter-related. We may go further and say that it is only through the doctrine of the illusion of time and space that we can to a certain extent throw some light on such doctrines as those of Eternal life, Liberation, etc., for this means going from the known to the unknown. Of course, such an intellectual analysis does not provide a proof of the truth of those doctrines which are based only on direct individual experience of those who have been able to dive into their consciousness and realized some of these verities of spiritual life. But it does provide a means of making intelligible, to some extent, doctrines which are essentially beyond the realm of the reasoning faculty. More than this is not possible for those who want either to explain or to understand these fundamental doctrines through the instrumentality of the intellect.

The doctrines of the illusory nature of time and space, matter, etc., are hard facts based on the experience of great Occultists—as hard as any facts can be. In fact they are harder than the facts of Science because they go to the very roots of scientific facts and make us see these facts from a higher and more real point of view. For example, they show us that what we had taken as objective tangible objects surrounding us are mere ideas in our minds, what we had taken as matter is merely motion in different permutations and combinations. Surely, if a person is dreaming and taking the objects perceived in his dream as facts, the realization that these facts are mere dreams when he wakes up, supersedes those facts and is therefore more valid than the facts noticed in his dream. This is exactly the relation between the facts of our waking life on the physical plane and the same facts as they are seen in the light of the Real. As long as we are dreaming, the facts of dream life appear as real. When we wake up they appear to be merely our own subjective thoughts. Similarly, when an individual is under the illusions of the lower planes, his life here appears real and made up of hard facts. But when he transcends these illusions and becomes aware of Reality, or in Reality, all these hard facts are seen to be not what they seemed but subjective or mental in character. This is not saying that they have no foundation in fact. They have. But they are not what they appear to be while we are subject to illusion. This is best illustrated by the well-known simile of the rope and the snake used in Hindu philosophy. We see a snake in a rope under the illusion created by darkness, and see the rope as rope · when a light is brought in and the illusion disappears.

The illusions created by time and space are due to the limitations imposed on consciousness by vehicles through which consciousness or mind works. On the physical plane where the density of matter and consequent limitations are maximum, these things, namely, time, space, distance, size, etc., seem to have an overpowering control on our consciousness. But as consciousness recedes inwards and begins to function through subtler vehicles the limitations seem to get feebler and almost fall away on the spiritual planes. Thus, on the mental plane where the mental body can travel with the speed of thought distance appears to have no meaning; because we can pass through objects and see them from all sides at once space loses its binding power. On still higher planes where the Adept is conscious of the past, present and future simultaneously, time in its ordinary sense naturally ceases to have any meaning. The stages in the gradual loosening of limitations as we penetrate inwards towards the centre of our Being are merely steps towards the realization of that state of consciousness in which time and space cease to exist as we know them down here. It is an Eternal Now.

I have used the expression 'time and space as we know them' purposely. We should always remember that time and space do not disappear suddenly and completely at any stage. They are subtilized more and more as we ascend into the higher realms of consciousness. Though time and space *as we understand them* are products of illusion they are not completely without foundation. They are derived from certain realities existing in the Eternal, and are shadows cast by these realities in the worlds of the unreal. Down here we take the shadows for the realities. Up there we *see* the realities and know the shadows as shadows. Because both time and space are shadows of realities it is not possible even to deny their existence. Such things of a fundamental character which play such an important rôle in the realm of the unreal do not disappear completely when consciousness emerges into the realm of the Real, but undergo a subtle transformation. They are seen in their real nature in the light of the Real. This is so because the unreal worlds are shadows of a Real world.

CHAPTER XXVIII

TIME AND SPACE—II

In the preliminary survey of facts concerning the nature of time and space which was made in the last chapter it was pointed out that time and space, as we know them, are illusions according to the Occult doctrine. This does not mean that they do not exist at all. It means that they are not what they seem to be. They are the products of our mind, depending upon the formation of mental images in our mind and their rapid succession as different kinds of forces play upon the mind. Is this a mere hypothesis which we have to accept on faith or are there any facts in our experience which, though not proving its truth, still show that such a thing is possible? Let us examine some of these facts within the realm of our own experience.

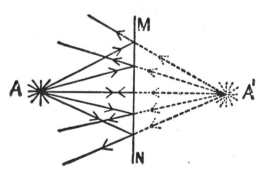

One of these simple facts with which we may begin the consideration of this subject is the phenomenon of the formation of a virtual image in a mirror. All of us know, of course, that the image of an object which we see in a mirror is not a real image but an unreal image which is technically called a virtual image. Those who have knowledge even of elementary science know how a virtual image is produced in a mirror. The process is so simple that it can be understood by everybody merely on seeing the following diagram:

A is an object and A' is its virtual image formed in the mirror MN facing the object A. It is called a virtual image because it is formed by rays not coming from A' but *appearing* to come from A' as shown in the above diagram. Although the object appears to be at the point A' behind the mirror, this is a pure illusion because there is no object behind the mirror and no rays can pass through the mirror. The illusion is produced by the fact that the rays from the real object A are reflected from the surface of the mirror in such a way that they *seem* to come from the point A' behind the mirror. The important point to be noted in this simple phenomenon is that an object can be seen at a place where it is not, and where there exists nothing at all corresponding to it.

In a similar manner the familiar world of forms, colours, sounds etc., which appears to exist outside us and in which we seem to live our life, does not exist there at all and appears outside us by a mysterious process of mental projection which is called *vikṣepa* and which may be represented

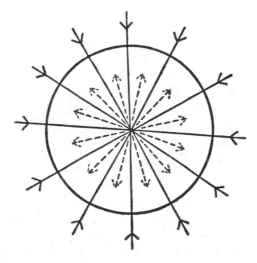

diagrammatically to some extent in the above figure.

The Universal Mind is really mirrored in the individual mind at the common centre of the two but the image is thrown outward as a virtual image. So we see outside us

a world which really exists within us. This is not speculation or a hypothetical assumption but a scientific fact.
According to Science the physical world in which we
live is nothing but a mass of atoms, molecules and
vibrations playing between them. When the vibrations
emanating from these atoms and molecules or the atoms
and the molecules themselves strike the sense-organs which
are also aggregates of atoms and molecules, sensations are
produced. The colours and forms, odors etc. we perceive
do not exist in the atoms and molecules constituting the
external objects. They spring up in our mind as a result
of the stimulus applied to our sense-organs. They exist in
our mind and as the mind throws outward the mental
image by the process of *vikṣepa* referred to above we see them
outside us and think they exist in the object. This is the
fundamental illusion of sense perception from which all of us
suffer and to which the *Bhagavad-Gita* refers again and again.
We are not aware of the illusion although it is a patent fact
and a conclusion to which our scientific knowledge leads
inevitably.

As this question has been dealt with thoroughly elsewhere
it is not necessary to go into it in further detail here. All
that is necessary to keep in mind is that the world which we
perceive outside us does not exist there as we see it. It exists
in our own mind.

The second important idea which is of special significance
in understanding the nature of space is that this mental image
which is projected outside by *vikṣepa* can be present in a point
—the centre from which the mind functions. Here again we
shall take the help of a diagram and consider a few illustrations which though hypothetical show us how a mental world
can exist in and appear to a point of consciousness which is
not encumbered with an ordinary vehicle. The use of such
hypothetical illustrations is quite permissible and is frequently
resorted to in scientific work and it is particularly justified in

this case because we know as a result of Occult investigations
that the spiritual vehicles of man are atomic in nature and
are free from many limitations of the vehicles functioning on
the lower planes.

Suppose a point of consciousness is viewing a line CC'
from the point 0, the line subtending an angle of 45° at the
point 0. Also suppose that the attention is concentrated on
the line and nothing else is in sight or in the mind. What
will happen if a bigger line BB' is substituted for CC' so that
it also subtends the same angle at 0 as CC' as shown below?
No change will be noticed provided no other object is in
sight for comparison. The same thing will happen if a smaller
line EE' is substituted
for CC'. The line will
appear exactly the same.
This shows that the
length and distance of
an object of one dimen-
sion do not matter to a
point consciousness if
they change proportion-
ately and there is no in-
ternal change involved.

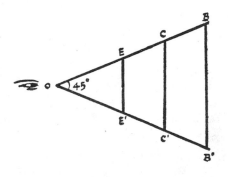

You may shift the line to a distance of one mile but if the
length and distance change proportionately so that the line
subtends the same angle at 0, and there are no internal
relative changes in the object such as in the intensity of light,
it will appear exactly the same.

Let us substitute a two dimensional object for a linear
object and vary its size and distance. Suppose a point
consciousness is seeing a circular disc which is perfectly black
with no other object in sight for comparison. The apparent
size of the disc will depend upon the solid angle it subtends
at 0. Whether the disc is at a distance of one yard or one
mile it will appear of the same size provided the distance

and size change proportionately and the disc subtends the same angle at 0.

We have chosen a black object for illustration because it is easier to imagine absence of internal change in a perfectly

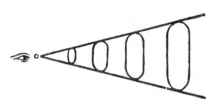

black object. We are considering an ideal case in which no internal change is noticeable. In objects like the moon etc. changes in the intensity of light or relative size of the objects on the surface will vitiate the argument.

Let us now go from the second to the third dimension. Suppose a point consciousness at the centre of a sphere is viewing a picture painted on the internal surface of the sphere. Whether the globe becomes larger and larger or smaller and smaller and all parts of the picture shrink or expand proportionately, the point consciousness will not notice the change in the size of the globe or the picture painted on its inner surface, for each object in the picture will continue to subtend the same angle at the centre 0.

The three points which should be kept in mind in all these cases we have dealt with are: (1) the distance and size should change proportionately; (2) there should be no external object in view for comparison or reference; (3) there should be no relative change between different parts or illumination of the object.

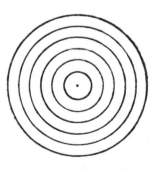

It will be seen that we have set no limit in all these cases to the extent of either expansion or contraction. The conclusion arrived at is a general one, not qualified by any limitations with regard to the size of the object or its distance from the centre of consciousness 0. Let us therefore suppose that we move any of these three objects on either side to the extreme limit and see what happens. What is the situation if it contracts or shrinks to the extreme limit? Obviously, the mental image remains the same as it was before, but it is now contained in a point. To the point consciousness it has not made the slightest difference whether it is contained in a point or at any distance from 0. If we go to the other extreme and the object shifts to an infinite distance from 0, again it will make no difference to the point consciousness. Here, therefore, we have a very intriguing phenomenon. *A mental image formed in a mind by mental projection can exist in a point and it is independent of the size of the objects as perceived by the mind.* It is also relative and therefore illusory. We do not know what the object itself is like in reality.

Now, size and distance are the usual yardsticks by which we measure objects in space and therefore space itself. If actual size and distance do not matter in mental perception and are relative in their nature, does it not follow logically that space is merely a mental impression produced in the mind or to put it in other words that space has no objective existence apart from the mind which perceives it? If the three dimensional world around us expands a thousand times or contracts a thousand times under certain conditions referred to above, it will not make any difference to the point consciousness which is perceiving it. The mental image of the world will remain the same because it is mental.

The reader should not misunderstand what is sought to be conveyed. We are dealing with a very subtle idea which is difficult to grasp unless we try to comprehend its deeper significance. The above conclusion does not imply that size and distance do not matter in the world in which we live. Only a lunatic could say that. What we should try to grasp is that these things are based ultimately on the mind and not on anything independent of the mind. And within the particular framework of the mind they are as valid as they would be if they were really based on an external world independent of the mind.

The discovery of a new world within the atom, consisting of electrons, protons etc., has not rendered the world of atoms and molecules invalid. It has merely altered the basis of the former world which was supposed to be composed of the ultimate particles called the atoms of the elements. In the same way the fact that the tangible world of physical forms etc., is essentially mental does not render the physical world and its laws, phenomena, etc., invalid. It merely enables us to see this world from a deeper point of view. In fact, even the mental world is based ultimately on consciousness from a still deeper point of view. This does not invalidate the mental world. Each world is valid and its laws hold good at its own level and we have to live within the framework of those laws and are governed by those laws as long as our consciousness is confined within it. It is only when we transcend a particular world that we can rise above its laws and limitations.

We have been referring all along to a point consciousness and discussing the question of space from the point of view of such a point consciousness. But we do not in our embodied life see things around us from a point consciousness which is just a hypothetical assumption. We see the world around us through a vehicle which has got a certain size and it is the size of the vehicle which brings in all the complications involving distance, size etc. of objects round us. For our vehicle gives us an internal standard of measurement of all objects around us, which are considered in relation to the vehicle. We can realize this fact by imagining that the world around us expands a hundred times leaving our body as it is. The whole picture of our environment in our mind will change completely and we shall not even be able to recognize it. A

new world like the one depicted in *Gulliver's Travels* will
replace the familiar world in which we are living. The
human beings round about us will appear as giants. Our
house will appear like a gigantic building. The table at
which we work will appear sky high. We will have to use
a ladder to see the top of the familiar objects round about
us. The same thing will happen if our vehicle becomes
smaller proportionately. An exactly similar world will be
present round about us. For it is the relative size of our
vehicle and the objects which surround it which really matters.
Who has not noticed when going to a place in which we lived
in our childhood and never visited during the intervening
years that everything seems to have shrunk in size? The house
in which we lived and which was remembered as a palatial
building in our imagination now appears very modest and
disappointing. The reason for this queer impression which
we generally get is of course that our body has grown in the
meanwhile and so all things which we saw and remembered
have shrunk in comparison with it. The change in the size of
the body is not great and so the shrinking though noticeable
is not marked.

So we see that the question of size, etc., and therefore
space is closely connected with the nature of our lower vehicles.
It is these which impose on our mind the ideas which are
associated with space. Although our consciousness works
through a point, the mental image in our mind is projected
outside through our vehicle and it is this which brings about
the complications in our perception. We perceive not through
our mental centre or *Bindu* as it is called in Sanskrit but
through our vehicle. The sense-organs are all distributed on
the surface of the body and the perception takes place through
these sense-organs. For example, the visual image of our
environment in our mind depends upon the retinal image
formed in our eye and any change in the latter will automatically be reflected in the former.

According to the Occult doctrine, unlike the lowest three
vehicles which are temporary and ellipsoidal, the vehicles on
the Ātmic, Buddhic and Higher Mental planes (which are
permanent and spiritual) are atomic; and the mind and
consciousness on those planes function through a point.   And
this accounts for the fact that the consciousness working
through these subtler spiritual vehicles is to a great extent
free from the illusions and limitations which are imposed by
time and space.   The capacity to become aware of anything
at any distance and to a certain extent see the past and future
at will, and many other such powers point to the fact that
time and space have not that degree of hold on these spiritual
planes as they have down here on the lowest planes, being
maximum on the physical.   Their hold has become loosened,
even if it has not completely disappeared and it is possible
to see at least partially that they are mere illusions or
impressions produced in our mind and have no objective
reality in themselves.

Two faculties referred to in the *Yoga-Sūtras* of Patanjali
which are called *Pratibhā* and *Vikaraṇa bhāva* are particularly
significant in this context.   They mean respectively non-
instrumental perception and non-instrumental action.   This
means that when consciousness perceives or acts through a
centre or a point vehicle—if I may use such a phrase—it is
free from many illusions and limitations which are present
when it is enclosed in a vehicle of the lower planes, and one
of these illusions is that of ordinary space.   Not only the
perception is free and unrestricted but the expression of will
is also to a great extent free and unhampered.   The transla-
tion of will into action is retarded or prevented by the complicated and cumbersome mechanisms of the vehicles on the
lower planes.   When it acts from a centre without having
to move through such a complicated mechanism it acts far
more freely and unimpeded.   That is why the spiritual will
of the Ātmā acting on the spiritual planes is comparatively

free while it can be thwarted and delayed in fulfilment on the lower planes.

It will be seen from the above that the natural and most powerful and effective instrument for the functioning of pure consciousness is a point and the complicated vehicles on the lower planes are gradually evolved and used only in the earlier stages of evolution when the spiritual vehicles functioning through a point are not ready. As soon as the spiritual vehicles have begun to function, the lower vehicles become dispensable though they may still be used for keeping contact with, and doing work on the lower planes. This is a general phenomenon observed in many spheres of evolution. Consciousness evolves a complicated mechanism on the lower planes and through this mechanism unfolds and perfects the functions of the higher vehicles, and when the higher functions have been perfected the lower mechanism which helped in the perfection is either discarded or used as an accessory. The sense-organs play such a role in relation to the lower mind, and the lower vehicles of the personality on the lowest three planes play a similar role in relation to the spiritual vehicles of the Individuality. And it is very probable that the spiritual vehicles on the Ātmic, Buddhic and Higher Mental planes in their turn play a similar role in relation to the Divine vehicles of the Monad on the Ātmic, Anupādaka and Ādi planes.

The illustrations and arguments which have been used above should give us some idea about the illusion which is produced in our perception of space. This is a very difficult subject to deal with and repeated and deep thought is needed to understand the real significance of the facts involved. But if we give such thought to it most probably a glimmer of the truth we are trying to grasp will gradually be seen and encourage us to pursue this subject further. Of course, such purely intellectual discussions cannot make us realize this illusion. All that they can do is to make us realize that there is an illusion involved in our perception of spatial phenomena and the statements of mystics and occultists in regard to this matter are essentially true. To realize the illusion actually requires freeing consciousness from the limitations of the lower vehicles which, as we have seen above, impose this illusion.

We have seen above that space as an objective reality apart from the mind does not exist. It is a product of the mind like all other things which form our familiar mental world. As we project this mental world outwards and see it as something outside us, the concept of space comes in necessarily to *contain* the things which appear to be outside but are really inside us contained in an image within our mental centre or *Bindu*. That is why the different spaces which appear in the mind on the different mental planes are called *chidākāsha*. The Sankrit word *chidākāsha* is compounded of two words *chit* and *ākāsha* and means *mental space*. Its nature is different on the different planes on account of the different number of dimensions in which consciousness functions on these planes, but on all planes it has the common characteristic of being essentially mental. The differences are due to the different degrees of fineness of matter, the different number of dimensions of consciousness and the different degrees of subtlety of the mind.

This mental space or *chidākāsha* is really the product of Divine Ideation. When the Logos of a solar system ideates and the solar system is projected from His Consciousness as a manifested system based on His Divine Mind *chidākāsha* appears as a part of this projected mental world to contain it. For though this world is mental in essence it is meant to function in the framework of time and space and to create the illusion of a real world in the minds of the Monads who are evolving in it. It is this Divine Thought of space at the back of this manifested world which creates the illusory conception of space in the individual minds of the Monads on different planes.

In contradistinction to *chidākāsha* or mental space is *Mahākāsha* the Ultimate Space or the Real Space, the container of Reality or the container of Chaos, Theos and Kosmos in their essence as H. P. Blavatsky puts it in *The Secret Doctrine*. All the mental spaces or varieties of *chidākāsha* may be considered to be derived from *Mahākāsha* and to reflect the *Mahākāsha* or Real Space in the same way as the different levels of the mind are derived from the differentiation of pure Consciousness or the colours of the spectrum are derived from the differentiation of white light.

We see, therefore, that space as we conceive it and understand it is an illusion but this does not mean that it is utterly without any foundation. There is a Real Space, *Mahākāsha* which lies at the basis of our mental spaces existing on the different planes and which really imparts the sense of reality to them. Everything in the world of the unreal is a reflection or shadow of a reality in the world of the Real. The illusion lies in our thinking and seeing the shadow as the substance, as the reality which casts the shadow.

CHAPTER XXIX

TIME AND SPACE—III

HAVING obtained some idea about the nature of space or *ākāsha* in the last chapter let us dwell for a while on its correlate time or *kāla* and the illusion which is involved in its perception. Here again a few illustrations taken from our common experiences will help us in grasping the ideas on the subject.

Suppose a person starts walking from one town to another on a road which connects the two. He will pass through the surrounding country and all the objects lying on the two sides of the road will be perceived by him one after another. If instead of walking he takes a motor car the same objects which he perceived before will be perceived by him in the same order but they will pass him with greater speed depending upon the speed of the vehicle. Now, imagine that the same person takes an aeroplane and goes high up in the air so that both the towns as well as the road connecting them are visible simultaneously from the air. What is the result of adopting this different mode of seeing all those objects? Obviously, he will now be able to see all the objects on the road simultaneously while he saw them in succession—rapid or slow—before. All those objects in the landscape are within his perception at the same time though their sizes and relative distances may appear different.

The essential points we have to note in these phenomena are:

(1) As long as we are confined to the ground and moving roughly in two dimensions the objects along the road are seen in succession but as soon as we go up into the air and our mind begins to work in three dimensions we see them simultaneously. I have used the word 'roughly' because when we move along the road we are not strictly in two dimensions. The third dimension also enters into our mental perception and it is this fact which enables us to see the objects near the road on the two sides. But relative to the height attained in an aeroplane we may say that we are moving on the two dimensional surface and it is this fact which makes the difference in the result of our perception. The above phenomenon shows that what is seen through a succession of mental impressions can be seen simultaneously by rising into a higher dimension.

(2) The second point we may note with regard to these phenomena is that the production of a series of mental images in our mind by the objects round us is due to movement, but this movement is relative, depending upon the relation between the vehicle and the environment. This relativity of movement is brought home to us to some extent when we are travelling in a train. As long as our attention is confined mostly to objects within the carriage it appears to us as if the carriage is stationary and the objects outside are moving past the window. If, however, we put our head out of the window we realize that it is the carriage which is moving amidst stationary objects.

(3) The third point we may note is that as we go up higher and higher more and more area comes within our view and we can see objects in this area simultaneously, and we may therefore say roughly that succession is eliminated from this area. The implication of these phenomena will be seen to be that whatever is within our consciousness simultaneously is outside the sphere of action of time. Going to the extreme limit we may say that if an individual is conscious

simultaneously of everything in the universe or to put it in other words is omniscient, he is above time. The existence of time is due to our limited range of perception. It is only when we cannot see the whole that we have to see the different parts one after another and it is this seeing of different parts of a whole in succession which produces the sense of time.

(4) If we consider a fast aeroplane or rocket travelling rapidly over continents at a high altitude we shall see that the area which is simultaneously within its view is very large and succession of perception ceases in that area. But succession on a grander scale is still there and continents are passed one after another where a pedestrian passes one field after another and a train passes towns one after another. It is only when the whole area is in view simultaneously that time ceases for that particular area. The Logos of a solar system is above time as far as His solar system is concerned because of His omniscience, but cosmic time still exists for Him and it is only the Cosmic Logos who is above cosmic time also. We see thus the relativity of time and Eternity. What appears as eternal at a lower level may be governed by a subtler kind of time and only the Absolute is absolutely above time.

(5) What has been said above shows also that some kind of relation exists between time phenomena and space phenomena. The two seem to change *pari passu* and a change in one brings about a change in the other also.

In order to go further into the nature of time and its relation with space let us take another illustration based on a scientific device with which we are all familiar, namely, the projection of a picture on a screen in cinematography. We all know how such a picture is projected. A roll of film containing a series of negative photographs passes in front of an aperture through which light is projected on a white screen. Each of the negative photographs in the film strip produces an image on the screen and the rapid succession of such images on the screen gives an impression of moving figures in the picture.

There are two points which we should note in this kind of projection. The first is that each photograph is projected separately. When a photograph comes in front of the aperture a beam of light is shot momentarily through it, thus projecting that photograph on the screen. The film moves on, another picture comes into place and the process is repeated. The second point is that the apparently continuous picture on the screen is really discontinuous and consists of a number of lighted images separated by periods of darkness. But since the human eye is not able to detect a change if the period is less than one-sixteenth of a second, the effect produced on the eye is that of a continuous picture with no periods of darkness.

This artificial phenomenon is of great importance to us in understanding the nature of time. Let us first note a few of its important features before we discuss their significance.

The first point to be noted is that an external agency can, by imposing a series of continuous artificial images on our mind, produce the effect of real life. This effect is particularly realistic in the case of three-dimensional cinematography which has been perfected recently. One almost gets the impression that one is living in the very midst of the scenes which are being shown on the screen. This shows clearly that it is not necessary to be in actual contact with so-called real and tangible objects to get the false impression of living among them. We can get the same impression without the actual presence of those objects in our environment. The reason for this significant phenomenon lies in the fact that in both cases what we really perceive in such experiences are our own mental images and not any objects outside us. And therefore how those images are produced in our mind does not matter. If somehow an exactly similar image is produced naturally or artificially the effect on the mind will be exactly the same and we shall have the impression or feeling of having exactly the same experience.

A similar phenomenon is observed in the case of hypnotic suggestion. The operator imposes his own mental images on the mind of the subject and the subject thinks and feels as if they are his own. If the operator says, 'Your legs are paralyzed', the subject thinks and feels that his legs are paralyzed and so cannot move them. So, the phenomena referred to above show how we live in our own mental images and the world we see outside us is produced by the projection outside of those images by the mind by a process which is called *vikṣepa* in Sanskrit and which has been explained already. The origin of those images or the manner in which they have been formed does not make any difference in our perception.

It will be seen therefore that there is nothing inherently improbable in the Occult doctrine that our individual mental worlds are mostly the result of the impact of the Universal or Divine Mind on our individual mind. If the world process has its origin in Divine Ideation it is natural to suppose that each individual will receive his own impression of the process according to his position in time and space and those who occupy practically the same position will receive similar impressions. This accounts for the common experiences of different individuals, coloured and modified, of course, by the condition and development of their own individual minds.

The second point we may note with regard to cinematographic projection is that a number of discontinuous mental images in the mind can give an impression of continuous experiences. It is all a question of the mind's inability to discern the breaks. Just as the mind seeing through the eyes cannot perceive spaces between objects which are too small and thus sees a continuous surface, so it cannot perceive gaps between events which are too small and gets the impression of a continuous event. That is why discontinuous matter appears continuous in the realm of space and discontinuous events appear continuous in the realm of time.

This inability to discern the discontinuity is related to the sense-organs and mind working on that plane and the latter are in turn again related to the density of the matter of that plane. On the subtler planes everything shrinks *in proportion* according to the subtlety of the plane and that is why the relation between these fundamental verities of manifestation—time, space, sense-organs, mind, etc., remains the same amongst themselves while it differs enormously in respect of the same verity on different planes. On the different planes, the density of matter differs, the subtlety of mind differs, measures of time and space differ, but the same kind of relation is maintained among these and so the phenomena of each plane are perceived harmoniously within the plane.

The projection of a cinematographic picture provides a very apt illustration of the well-known doctrine according to which the manifested universe is a discontinuous phenomenon and periods of manifestation and *pralaya* follow each other with inconceivable rapidity, thus producing in the mind an impression of continuity of manifestation and experiences which we go through on the different planes. The word *pralaya* is used in this context in a different sense from the usual one in which it stands for the long period of rest which follows every long period of manifestation. Here it stands for the infinitesimal period of time during which the manifested state disappears repeatedly during the long period of manifestation itself and this corresponds to the imperceptible period of darkness in the cinematographic projection of a picture. It is this swift alternation of *sṛṣṭi* and *pralaya* which is symbolized by the *damru* of Maheśa in Hindu symbolism.

It will be seen from what has been said above that the essential nature of time is the succession of mental images in our mind. If there is no succession of mental images there would be no time. It is this succession of mental images which produces the impression of change and the mind is led to assume that there must be ' duration ' in which the change takes place or that time is something independent of the succession of images. Let us consider a few experiences to see whether there is something independent of the succession of mental images which can be measured without reference to this succession.

We begin with experiences of the physical plane. Here we assume that time is an independent reality which can be measured correctly in terms of a definite unit of time called a second. This unit is derived from the period of time the earth takes to revolve round its axis and we divide it into so many hours, minutes and seconds. We assume that the earth revolves with a fixed speed and so the unit is constant. As far as the physical plane is concerned this idea that time is something independent of the changes which are taking place around us and can be measured independently of these changes, works satisfactorily because we measure it objectively and ignore the subjective phenomena connected with time which shows its relative nature. But as soon as we go out of the waking physical consciousness we immediately run into trouble.

Take the dream state for example. It has been shown by experiments and it is also within the experience of every individual that events which would normally take hours or days as measured in terms of physical time can take place in the subjective dream state in a few seconds or minutes. If we apply pressure on the throat of a person who is sleeping for a few seconds he may dream that he has committed murder, been caught and sentenced to be hanged and as soon as the noose is tightened round his neck in his dream he may wake up frightened and bathed in perspiration. And he may find on waking that the pressure on his throat which induced this lengthy dream did not last for more than one or two minutes.

Again, it is well known that before the soul passes out of the physical body at death, a review of the whole life normally takes place in a few minutes. The experiences of yogis on the subtler planes definitely corroborate this idea that the measures of time on the subtler planes are different from those on the physical plane and it is possible to condense a far greater number of experiences on the subtler planes in a given time as measured by physical standards. As consciousness recedes inwards toward the centre of Reality its range of perception as regards past and future seems to increase rapidly, and at a sufficiently deep level the past, present and future seem to lie before the Adept like an open book.

The conclusions which have been arrived at by Science about time as a result of the development of the Theory of Relativity are intriguing to a degree. For example, it has been calculated that for a person who is travelling in a spacecraft with the speed of light time will stand still or cease to exist. If he takes 100 years to reach another star according to our physical standards it will *appear to him* that he has taken no time. And not only time will cease to exist but the aging process which is a product of time will be halted for the time being, which encourages the modern scientist to hope that the difficulties of aging of the physical body and boredom may not stand in the way of inter-stellar travelling in the far distant future when spacecrafts have been perfected and can travel with speeds approaching that of light.

We should remember, however, that the conclusions of Science with respect to such matters are vitiated by the fact of their being based on the assumption that the physical world is the only world which exists and the mathematical deductions based on partial data of the physical world being forcibly applied to the time and space phenomena in general. But still, they are of great importance because they show the relative nature of time and the possibility of its annihilation under certain hypothetical conditions. This is merely another way of saying that Time has no existence apart from mind and is therefore an illusion.

Having considered a few facts of common experience let us now discuss very briefly the significance of these facts for the student of the Divine Wisdom. I may point out here that we are not dealing with a cut-and-dried theory of Time and Space but merely trying to understand, as far as this is possible, the phenomena connected with these two fundamental agencies lying at the basis of the manifested universe. We should never lose sight of the fact that we cannot really *know* anything in manifestation until we have transcended it. We shall deal with the inner significance of these facts concerning the nature of time, point by point, to enable us to make a mental note of them and remember them.

(1) We have seen just now that the sense of passage of time or 'duration' is connected intimately with the succession of mental images in our mind and that the succession of these mental images may be discontinuous like the images projected on a cinema screen without our being aware of the discontinuity. This succession of mental images can be at the individual level of the microcosm or at the Divine level of the macrocosmic Deity presiding over a particular manifested system. And just as our space sense is based upon and derived from the mental space created by the Logos, so our succession of mental images is based upon and is governed by the succession of mental images in the Divine Ideation at the solar or Cosmic level. And as for each plane there is a particular grade of mental space determined by its dimensions (three in the case of the physical) so for each plane there is a particular measure of time determined by the speed of the succession of mental images. This speed of succession, which is characteristic of each plane, is the basis of the differences which are noticed with regard to the rapidity or slowness

with which experiences can be passed through on the different planes.

(2) The relation of time-measures for the different planes shows that the experiences gone through by an individual depend upon the number of mental images and that the speed at which the images pass through the mind is immaterial. Just as empty spaces between particles are not seen and the things appear continuous at the surface at a particular level of visual perception so intervals between successive mental images are not perceived and events are seen as continuous. For the physical plane this limit is roughly one-sixteenth of a second.

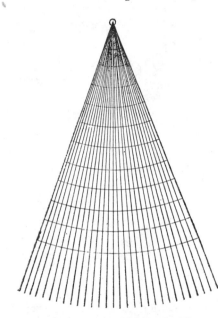

The Projection of Eternity in Time

Some idea of the manner in which a greater number of mental images can be condensed as we go into the deeper levels of consciousness can perhaps be obtained from the above figure which represents the spreading out of a number of lines as they leave the point of intersection and diverge more and more as the distance from the centre 0 increases.

The number of points of intersection on each arc in the diagram is the same but they become more and more condensed as the distance of the arc from the centre 0 decreases. When the arc merges with the centre 0 in the limiting case, all the points merge with the centre. This may help us to understand how time shrinks progressively as we approach the centre of our consciousness, and succession becomes faster from the physical point of view until it becomes simultaneity in the Eternal Now.

It will also be seen from the above figure that as the wheel of Time revolves, the events taking place on the different planes remain in step, as is required by the Occult doctrine that the lower is a reflection or shadow of the higher. Although the events are not the same on the different planes there is a mysterious correspondence between them, for it is the same Reality which is expressing itself at the different levels of manifestation. If the phenomena of the different planes are shadows cast on the different planes as the film roll of Divine Ideation turns upon its axis, then there should be some kind of correspondence between such phenomena.

(3) No discussion regarding the nature of time can be complete without a reference to the periodicity which characterizes all its phenomena and which is symbolized by the crescent moon in the symbology of *Maheśa*. We find cycles everywhere in the phenomena of Nature, smaller cycles within larger cycles, the cycle of day and night, the cycle of the seasons and the greatest cycle of creation and dissolution of the manifested systems. All these cycles are due to motion or revolution of some kind. We know the nature of revolution involved in the case of some cycles while in the case of others it is hidden, but that there is revolution or rhythm of some kind at the back of all of them seems to be certain. Everywhere in the universe we find revolutions according to Science, atoms, satellites, planets, solar systems, galaxies and probably the universe itself. And it is these revolutions on the physical or superphysical planes which are responsible for the cycles or the phenomena of periodicity. On account of these revolutions taking place everywhere, the universe in its material aspect appears like a gigantic clock containing billions of wheels of different sizes revolving in different ways and in different spheres and localities. We can see only a few of the wheels

of this clock, the rest being hidden from our view. Where is the mainspring of this clock of the universe? In the *Shiva-Shakti Tattva* or the Primary Differentiation of the Ultimate Reality into the Positive and Negative Principles as we have seen already in a previous chapter.

(4) In this periodicity which we find associated with time we have the clue to the curvature of Time-Space discussed in Einstein's Theory of Relativity. That Time-Space Continuum is curved is one of the mathematical deductions arrived at by Einstein. But no one can visualize or understand what this curvature of Time and Space means and it has been left as an unintelligible conclusion like so many others arrived at by scientists. Is not this periodicity which is an inherent feature of time phenomena the correct interpretation of the curvature of Time?

As regards the curvature of Space, it is probably in the Occult doctrine that we have the clue to this enigma of modern Science. According to the Occult doctrine each manifested system is an enclosed self-sufficient organism which resembles an egg in appearance. That is why it is called *Brahmānda* or the ' Egg of the Creator '. The life of the manifested system develops within this enclosed organism, energized by the Logos of the system acting from the Centre.

So, we see how a wider and deeper view of life and its phenomena which is given by Occultism provides a very intelligible explanation of many phenomena and theories of modern Science which even Science is unable to interpret intelligibly. But the orthodox scientist under the influence of intellectual pride and materialistic outlook refuses even to consider these Occult doctrines and prefers to remain in darkness and ignorance of these deeper aspects of life.

(5) We saw in the case of space that though space in the ordinary sense, as perceived in the realm of the manifest, is a product of the mind—Divine or individual—there is something in the realm of the Real which corresponds to these

manifestations of mental space. It is from this counterpart in the realm of the Unmanifest that all these different kinds of mental spaces or *chidākāsha* may be considered to be derived by differentiation as coloured lights of the spectrum are derived from the dispersion of white light by a prism. This Ultimate Space or the root of mental spaces is called *Mahākāsha* in Sanskrit.

A similar relationship exists between the different measures of time which we find in manifestation on the different planes and *Mahākāla* or the great Ultimate Time from which they may be considered to be derived by a process of differentiation. This *Mahākāla* is called Eternal Duration in *The Secret Doctrine* and is that aspect of Reality which produces the shadows of mental time on the different planes of manifestation. The human mind cannot conceive it though it must exist and does exist according to the Occult doctrine. So the statement that time is an illusion must be considered to refer to the mental times in manifestation which are the products of mind and not to that Ultimate Time or *Mahākāla* from which they are derived and of which they are shadows. It is in this *Mahākāla* that lies the source and potentiality of that relentless succession which characterizes all manifestation in contradistinction to the changeless, immutable nature of the Unmanifest.

(6) The consideration of the facts which we have been discussing above has, I hope, thrown some light on the nature of time and space, specially the question of their ultimate relationship and illusory nature. Space is a matter of the formation of mental images in the Mind of the Logos or the individual. Time is a matter of the succession of these mental images, again either in the Mind of the Logos or the individual. So both time and space depend on the mind and its mental images. When the mind is without images or there is *chitta-vritti-nirodha* according to yogic terminology, there is neither space nor time—only the Reality. But in

the above statement we should keep in mind the relativity of time and space. What appears as mindless, timeless and spaceless at a lower level may from a deeper level of consciousness be time, space and mind of a subtler nature. There is nothing absolute in existence except the Absolute.

CHAPTER XXX

THE CONCEPT OF PLANES AND VEHICLES

ONE of the most important contributions which Occultism has made in our effort to study the nature of the universe is the knowledge that hidden within the visible tangible world which we can perceive through our physical sense-organs are other worlds of a subtler nature which can be cognized with the help of subtler faculties which exist in an undeveloped state within every human being. It is possible to unfold these inner faculties by following certain methods of self-discipline and to come in contact with these subtler worlds. The idea that there are such subtler worlds hidden within the physical world is not new. Practically all religions of the world proclaim the existence of such worlds and the heavens and hells into which souls of men are supposed to pass after death, are nothing but popular versions of these subtler worlds. Occultists and mystics have also borne testimony to the existence of these worlds and asserted unequivocally the possibility of coming in contact with them while man is still living. But the whole idea as found in religious or mystic literature is surrounded by an atmosphere of vagueness, uncertainty and doubt and rests on blind belief or faith. It is only knowledge which has been given to the modern world by Adepts of Occultism which has placed the doctrines concerning the existence of the subtler worlds on a sure foundation and given us a fairly clear idea about their nature though not much about their contents. This knowledge has been amplified to a certain extent and made a little more definite by the researches of some theosophical workers who were able to develop the necessary faculties for investigating the phenomena of these subtler worlds and verified personally some of this knowledge by direct experience.

The student of Occultism or the Ancient Wisdom should have the proper attitude of discrimination towards this body of knowledge concerning the subtler planes. This knowledge may be divided under two broad sub-heads. Under one of these sub-heads we may place all those facts and doctrines which are of a general nature and pertain to the principles which underlie the nature and relations of the subtler planes. Under the second head may be placed all the detailed knowledge concerning the phenomena of these subtler worlds which is gathered by observation and experimentation, generally with the help of psychic faculties.

Now, strange as it may sound, it is much easier to deal with knowledge of the former class than with that of the latter. Not only is it easier to deal with from the point of view of the intellect, we are on much surer ground with respect to the former than with respect to the latter. Principles and relations between facts existing in great variety and number are far easier to grasp, formulate and deal with than the facts themselves. Once we have derived or discovered a principle by correct and reliable methods we can depend upon it under all kinds of circumstances. But when we are dealing with a mass of detailed facts we are liable to trip any moment. The reason for this is obvious. All principles and relations exist in the realm of the Universal Mind as eternal verities and are not subject to change or modification. The phenomena, on the other hand, form a flowing stream every part of which is changing all the time. It is true that these phenomena take place according to natural laws which are changeless and therefore reliable but the particular facts of those phenomena are variable and difficult to determine with certainty.

Besides this there is another fact to consider. As every archetype can find expression in innumerable forms, so every law or principle can express itself in innumerable ways. Therefore, in dealing with these variable expressions one is always dealing with the unknown and the unpredictable. We may be feeling quite sure of our particular facts and conclusions based upon them but anything may turn up at any time and make it necessary to change or modify our conclusions. The history of Science shows this constant appearance of new facts which have made it necessary to modify or change completely the general conclusions with regard to them. So in studying the facts and principles pertaining to the invisible subtler worlds it is advisable to distinguish between them and to adopt somewhat different attitudes towards them. Our ideas about the former should be clear, definite and firm and should form as it were the steel frame of our mental edifice. On the other hand, we should adopt a flexible attitude towards the latter and be prepared to change our ideas when the need arises.

This attitude is necessary in relation to knowledge with regard to the facts and phenomena of the subtler worlds for several reasons. In the first place, this knowledge is very difficult to communicate and grasp through the instrumentality of the physical brain. The phenomena and facts of each plane are best perceived and understood through the vehicle of the plane; for, that vehicle is particularly designed and suited for that purpose. Considering the tricks which dimensions of space and measures of time play with our mind one can see how difficult it would be to grasp these phenomena through the physical brain which has been designed to work in a world of three dimensions. That is why those who can function on those subtler planes do not make a serious effort to communicate these detailed facts of those planes to the people who are still confined to the physical plane. These people can wait until they can rise into these subtler planes and observe these things for themselves. The difficulty becomes still greater in the case of the realities and states of consciousness of the spiritual planes which are more removed from our physical brain consciousness and therefore still more difficult to comprehend.

In the second place, those who have risen to these higher planes of being and come in contact with the realities of the spiritual planes in greater or lesser degree have realized the illusions and limitations of these lower planes and the comparative unimportance of this knowledge concerning the phenomenal side of life. The tremendous expansion of knowledge with regard to the facts of the physical world is due to the lack of discrimination and proper sense of values in those who are blindly pursuing this knowledge without ever thinking of its real value. In itself most of it is not of much value from the higher point of view. Its chief value lies in the development of the intellect which takes place as a result of its pursuit. In the light of knowledge of the higher planes it appears trivial and becomes unnecessary. But since humanity as a whole is in that particular phase of its evolution in which the emphasis is on the development of the intellect, the expansion of this detailed phenomenal knowledge is inevitable.

The above should serve as a warning to the aspirant for Wisdom. He should see this phenomenal development of knowledge on the physical plane in the correct perspective and should not become hypnotized by the prevailing crazes and fashions of intellectual pursuits. It is ironical to a degree when those who spend their lives in studying the lives of insects and plants and atoms in the minutest degree, never give even a passing thought to the nature of their own life which holds within its deeper recesses the greatest and most profound secrets of the universe. The aspirant for Wisdom will also see from what has been said above that the craving for knowledge regarding the phenomena of the lower invisible worlds is really due to lack of discrimination. It is certainly interesting and enables us to see the universe in a better perspective. But it is not less phenomenal than the knowledge of phenomena concerning the physical plane. It is not of permanent and vital value to the individual who has realized the illusory and impermanent nature of life on the lower planes and wants to know the realities of the spiritual world. In fact, if we are not alert we are liable to be distracted by its glamorous illusions and to go off the track in our search for Truth. This is true of direct knowledge which is obtained through the development of psychic faculties. It is true in a greater degree of second-hand knowledge which we acquire through books, etc.

A considerable amount of information is available in theosophical literature about life and states of consciousness on the subtler planes, especially those which are nearer to the physical. This information is derived from different sources, is of different values, and is reliable in different degrees. As students of Theosophy are generally familiar with this literature it is not necessary to say anything about these superficial aspects of knowledge concerning the subtler planes. We shall, therefore, confine ourselves to the consideration of a few of its deeper aspects which will enable us to acquire a deeper understanding of the nature of these subtler planes and the manner in which mind and consciousness function on these planes. The understanding of the general principles which we shall consider will enable us to see all facts concerning the subtler planes in a better perspective.

The first point we may consider is the general relation of consciousness, mind and the vehicle through which they function. As this question has been dealt with in greater detail elsewhere I shall merely give a gist of the relevant ideas here. The relation of consciousness, mind and vehicle may be formulated concisely in this manner.

(1) Consciousness, mind and matter are three aspects of the One Reality. When integrated consciousness reacts with matter through a vehicle, the result of this interaction is mind, which forms the basis of all experience.   With regard to this interaction we have to note the following facts.

(a) As there is only One Reality and there can be nothing outside that Reality the whole process of this interaction is within the Reality itself and between its different aspects.

(b) Consciousness is the highest aspect of Reality and matter the lowest and mind comes in between.

(c) Experience is related to the mind. It is the result of the interaction of consciousness and matter in the widest sense of the terms.

(d) The experience which results on interaction of consciousness and matter differs according to the nature of the vehicle or the particular combination of matter which serves as an instrument of consciousness on a particular plane.

(2) We have seen already that the mind works through a point, and not only the different points corresponding to different levels of the mind in the case of an individual are concentric, but the different points corresponding to different individuals are also concentric.   This common centre of all vehicles of all the Monads and Logoi is called *Mahābindu* or the Great Point in Sanskrit.

The objection may be raised that our experiences on the physical or the superphysical planes do not show that we are all functioning in our minds from the same Centre or our mental worlds have, a common centre.   How then can we say that our different minds are functioning from the same

Centre? A little thought will show us that when we are functioning at a particular level of the mind through a particular vehicle we are not at all conscious of the vehicle through which our mind is functioning. Take the physical plane. The mental world created by our sense-organs or the independent activity of the mind functions through our brain and the nervous system. This is a scientific fact. Are we conscious of the brain while we are functioning on the physical plane? Not at all. The fact that our mind and sense-organs function through the instrumentality of the physical brain has been discovered indirectly by other methods and not through direct awareness of this fact.

Take another well-known fact. We all know that the visible panorama in front of us produces a tiny image in the retina of the eye. The process of seeing this panorama and the formation of its mental image takes place as a result of the contact of the mind with the retinal image. The mind is projected through the retinal image, as it were, and this results in 'seeing' a visual world which is an exact reproduction of the retinal image, though much enlarged and inverted. Are we conscious of this process? Not at all. So, we must note this important fact in relation to the mental world or image which appears in our mind as a result of the interaction of consciousness and vehicle. There is no awareness of the vehicle itself in this perception of the mental world which takes place through the instrumentality of the vehicle. And because there is no awareness of the vehicle it does not mean that the perception does not take place through the vehicle.

In fact, the awareness of the vehicle is a sign that there is something wrong with the vehicle. If our body is in perfect health we are hardly conscious of it. We become conscious of the part which is in an unhealthy or abnormal state. Similarly, if our lower mind or rather the lower mental body is in a perfectly healthy and harmonized condition, without any strain, distortion or tension, consciousness can function through it freely and effortlessly without any awareness of the mind itself. The more the mind gets disharmonized and distorted the more it obtrudes on consciousness as all people who are in a highly disturbed state know to their cost. On the other hand, those who have been able to purify, tranquillize and harmonize their mind can live without awareness of their lower mind though consciousness is still functioning through it. It is only under such conditions that the peace, power and knowledge of the higher planes can filter down into the lower mind.

Our not being conscious of the fact that our mind and consciousness function through the common centre of all the vehicles does not, therefore, mean that this Occult doctrine concerning the mechanism of mental perception is not true. The fact is directly realized in *Samādhi* by performing *Saṃyama* on the ' heart ' as pointed out in *Sūtra* III-35 of the *Yoga-Sūtras*.

3. Another important point we should note with regard to the vehicles of consciousness functioning on the different planes is that the function of the vehicle does not depend upon the complexity and size of the vehicle. Living as we do in the world of the lower mind where perception takes place through the complex agency of the five sense-organs and forms play a predominant role, size and complexity are the yard sticks by which we judge the value and importance of a thing. The lower mind is naturally and easily impressed by size and complexity and because the present civilization is based on the development of the lower mind we find everywhere a tendency to make bigger and more complex things in every sphere of life. Giganticism is the modern craze. Bigger buildings, bigger cars, bigger aeroplanes, bigger space ships, more sophisticated machines, bigger bureaucracies, bigger plans, all these things are considered as signs of progress and a more advanced civilization. This tendency is

also strengthened by the swing towards collectivism which necessitates the use of bigger things, but basically it is the result of the predominance of the lower mind which obscures spiritual values and revels in the pursuit of material aims.

But the falsity of our attitude towards these things and the comparative unimportance of size and complexity is shown by the fact that the deeper the level of consciousness the simpler the mechanism it requires for its expression. Thus, while on the lowest three planes we need fairly complex ellipsoidal vehicles for the expression of mind and consciousness, the vehicles on the spiritual planes are atomic, i.e., consciousness functions through a point. The higher spiritual consciousness can dispense with the complex mechanism of sense-organs etc., and both its cognitive and conative functions can be carried out through atomic vehicles as the *Sūtras* on *Pratibhā* and *Vikaraṇa Bhāva* in the *Yoga-Sūtras* show clearly. We should remember that the sense-organs are the real instruments of the mind working through a vehicle like the physical body. The rest of the mechanism is of an accessory nature, merely serving to keep in working order the organs of sensation and action.

The simplification of the mechanism and functioning of the vehicles as we descend into the deeper levels of consciousness does not mean any loss in the intensity and richness of life and consciousness which functions through them. On the other hand this richness and intensity increases tremendously with every plunge taken into a deeper level of consciousness. This is to be expected because the Ultimate Reality from which the whole of the manifested universe is derived by progressive involution is present at the Centre, at the deepest level of consciousness. The universe in all its complexity and degrees of subtlety comes into being by a process of step by step projection of this Ultimate Reality into less spiritual states of being, and so at each step in this externalization or condensation process there must be a loss of dynamism, richness, vividness and all those attributes we associate with the Real as opposed to the unreal. The coarseness of matter and the complexity of the vehicle which increase progressively at each step of this repeated projection do not facilitate but impede the expression of Reality.

We have seen above that the complexity and the size of the vehicle decrease as we approach the Reality from which the universe in its different degrees of subtlety is derived. And with this decrease in size and complexity, the dynamism, power, knowledge etc., which are associated with Reality increase tremendously at each step of this uncovering of Reality. This shows clearly that a vehicle is an obstruction in the expression of Reality; for, the greater the complexity of the vehicle, as consciousness descends lower in manifestation, the more limited and obscured it becomes. This is to be expected if Consciousness is what it is known to be, free, infinite and integrated. For the expression of an infinite and completely free Principle any vehicle which is finite and bound by limitations of time and space must be a limitation and this limitation must be greater the more complex the mechanism. Manifestation is a limitation which the Unmanifest places upon Itself even though it is not the whole of the Unmanifest Reality which gets involved in this limitation.

The above doctrine of Occultism finds complete corroboration in the concepts of the Point and the Void and their relation to Reality. In manifestation a Point is the least complex and the smallest vehicle we can conceive. It has zero dimension and as has been shown elsewhere it can serve as a vehicle of integrated consciousness with a minimum of obscuration and limitation placed upon it. The powers, knowledge and dynamism of consciousness in manifestation are maximum when it is manifesting through a Point.

The Point is a door or bridge connecting the Unmanifest and the manifest. On this side are all the worlds in manifestation in their increasing degrees of complexity, all centred

in the Great Point.   On the other side is the world of the
Ultimate Reality.   What is the vehicle of this Ultimate
Reality? What can be the vehicle of this Ultimate Reality
or the Absolute except a Void? This is the Occult doctrine
with regard to the vehicle of the Ultimate Reality if we may
use such a word as ' vehicle ' in this context.   According to
this doctrine the ultimate form of Space which is called
Mahākāsha and which must be infinite and boundless is the
' container ' of the Ultimate Reality which alone is truly
Unmanifest.   Not even the infinitesimal limitation of a Point
is possible for this Reality.   With the appearance of the Point,
limitation, however subtle, begins, and the first step has been
taken towards manifestation and increasing limitation and
obscuration of the different planes in manifestation.   The
concepts of the Void, Point and vehicles of consciousness
functioning on the planes of manifestation will thus be seen
to form a complete and magnificent picture in which are
integrated not only all the vehicles in manifestation but also
the bridge which connects the manifest and the Unmanifest.

CHAPTER XXXI

FOHAT (*AGNI*), *PRĀNA* AND *KUNDALINI*

WHENEVER we are trying to understand a difficult or complicated subject it always helps if we go back to first principles and consider the problem in the light of these principles, then come down step by step gradually to more detailed facts which are involved in the consideration. This method is effective because it enables us to see the specific question in the correct perspective and against the background of the fundamental principles. Adopting this method let us go back to the first principles which are involved in the consideration of the Occult concept of Fohat particularly and the two other allied forms of energy called *Prāna* and *Kundalini* in Sanskrit.

According to the Occult doctrine the vast universe in its totality, including the visible and invisible worlds, is the periodical manifestation of an unmanifest Reality which creates the universe, expresses itself through it for a limited though very long period and then withdraws it into itself, this cycle being repeated over and over again eternally.

In order that the unmanifest Reality may manifest it must first create the raw material which can be worked up into appropriate vehicles for its expression and it is only when such vehicles have been evolved that It can manifest through them according to their development and sensitiveness. We thus see that three well-marked stages are involved in manifestation, (1) the creation of the raw material, (2) the evolution of the vehicles, and (3) the expression of Reality through these vehicles and the unfoldment of the infinite potentialities which lie hidden within It.

All these three functions are performed by the manifested Deity who is called a Logos in theosophical literature and *Īśvara* in Hindu philosophy. The three aspects of the Logos which are related to these three functions are called respectively the Third Logos (*Brahmā*, the Creator), the Second Logos (*Vishnu*, the Preserver) and the First Logos (*Mahesha*, the Regenerator). It should be remembered however that the three Logoi are three aspects corresponding to the three broad functions and not three individuals.

In carrying out His respective functions the triple Logos makes use of three specific kinds of energies through the instrumentality of which His activity is carried on, regulated and controlled. The three functions of the Logos and the three specific kinds of energies with the help of which these functions are performed are given below:

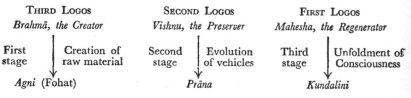

THIRD LOGOS	SECOND LOGOS	FIRST LOGOS
Brahmā, the Creator	*Vishnu, the Preserver*	*Mahesha, the Regenerator*
First stage — Creation of raw material	Second stage — Evolution of vehicles	Third stage — Unfoldment of Consciousness
Agni (Fohat)	*Prāna*	*Kundalini*

The facts represented above are well known and we need not consider them here. We shall consider only the nature of the three specific kinds of energies which are used by the three Logoi in carrying out Their respective functions. These three energies are called Fohat, *Prāna* and *Kundalini*. The name Fohat is taken from *The Secret Doctrine* because the nature of this creative force or agency is described in some detail under this name in her work, by H. P. Blavatsky. The word which comes nearest to Fohat in Sanskrit literature is *Agni* but this word has so many other connotations that it is better to use the word Fohat for the creative force of *Brahmā*.

If the student goes through the literature on Fohat in *The Secret Doctrine* without having a clear idea with regard to its essential nature he is likely to get confused. It is, therefore, necessary that he should first try to understand what this mysterious force is and should try to separate the essential ideas from the many details in which they are embedded. Many naive people think that what is given in *The Secret Doctrine* about any subject is the last word that can be said about it and we need not consider any other facts or views bearing on a particular topic being examined. They forget that H. P. Blavatsky was given the teachings embodied in *The Secret Doctrine* in a very general and incomplete manner and many of the concepts and doctrines were not and could not be properly understood at the time. Besides, she had to present some of these Occult doctrines of a profound nature in a rather hurried manner without first assimilating and relating them with one another. This accounts for the rather fragmentary manner in which the Occult doctrine has been presented in *The Secret Doctrine*. This work had to be elaborated, amplified and deepened. It was meant only to serve as a nucleus for further development in various directions by means of research and deep thought.

The Eternal Wisdom is a transcendent Reality which cannot be poured into a mould, preserved and then worshipped as a fetish. It must continually find expression in an ever-deepening, ever fresh and richer and richer expressions even in the realm of the intellect. The moment its expression becomes static and is treated as a creed, to be studied religiously and followed piously, it has really become dead, though it may still continue to inspire and help some people in a very limited manner. To treat the Occult doctrines discussed in *The Secret Doctrine* as a creed and to consider what has been said in it with regard to various matters as the last word on those subjects is therefore really a betrayal of the Eternal Wisdom which the book was meant to partially unveil. Let us understand this fact thoroughly and once for all if we want to preserve the freshness and dynamic nature of the Wisdom which was sought to be partially revealed and to be sown in the soil of materialistic thought so that it may provide humanity with a more meaningful and dynamic philosophy of life and purpose of spiritual endeavour.

Nowhere is this necessity for maintaining a dynamic outlook brought home more clearly than in the consideration of the subject which we are dealing with, namely, the nature of Fohat as an instrument of creating the raw materials for a manifested universe. When H. P. Blavatsky wrote *The Secret Doctrine* the sciences of physics and chemistry were in their infancy. What was known about atoms and molecules, the building material of the universe, and the forces acting in and between them, was very elementary and vague. So naturally when she had to interpret the significance of Fohat she was greatly handicapped by this paucity and indefiniteness of scientific knowledge and had to explain the nature of this force in very vague, general and sometimes misleading terms. To consider what she said about this force as the final word and not to take into account the results of the discoveries which have been made subsequently in the realm of Science with regard to the structure of atoms and molecules is really closing our eyes to patent facts of existence and doing the greatest harm to the cause which true Occultism represents.

Of the three specific types of forces which are related to the triple Logos, Science does not know anything and does not care to enquire into the nature of two of these forces, *Prāna* and *Kundalini*. But it has studied very thoroughly and in great detail the third force in its physical manifestation. This is nothing but the well-known form of force or energy which we call electricity and which is related in a mysterious manner to other physical forces such as magnetism, gravitation, etc. H. P. Blavatsky also used the phrase ' Cosmic

Electricity' for Fohat, which is very significant and shows that
she was trying to refer through the use of these names to that
universal principle or force which is the instrument for creating the raw material of the manifested universe—the atoms
and molecules of the different planes. That this is true at
least on the physical plane will be seen at once if we have
even an elementary idea regarding the structure of an atom
as discoursed by modern Science.

It may be mentioned in passing that the structures of
atoms and molecules are no longer in the realm of speculation
as in the time of H. P. Blavatsky. These things are now
known with definiteness, especially since the invention of
certain instruments in recent times, such as the electron
microscope. Very soon Science will have a complete picture
of the structure of atoms and molecules and its conclusions
in these matters cannot be ignored by those who are interested
in the study and interpretation of the Occult doctrines.

We need not go into the details of the structure of atoms
here but a brief reference to this subject in a general way is
necessary in order to show how modern Science has not
only to a great extent corroborated the Occult doctrine with
regard to Fohat but has also thrown a flood of light on it.

According to modern Science an atom consists of a
positively charged nucleus surrounded by a number of negatively charged electrons which whirl round the nucleus much
in the same way as planets go round the sun in elliptical
orbits. The electrons whirl round the positively charged
central nucleus in a number of shells, one inside the other,
the number of shells varying with the nature of the atom.
So the atom of an element as a whole is a multi-shelled structure with a central positively charged nucleus and a whirlpool
created by the whirling electrons round it.

As the electrons have negligible weight these shells may
be considered merely as a whirlpool caused by negatively
charged points moving in orbits round the nucleus. Science

does not know yet the nature of the mysterious electron. It may be a particle or a wave-motion or merely a probability function. In this mystery surrounding the nature of the electron lies the clue to the Occult doctrine regarding the production of matter from motion as will be explained later on.

Now, the points with which we are really concerned here in regard to the structure of the atom are that atoms of different elements are made by the addition of more and more negatively charged electrons to the surrounding shells and positively charged protons and neutrons to the nucleus in which the mass of the atom is concentrated; also, that it is the number and arrangement of the electrons in the surrounding shells which determines most of the properties of the different elements. Does this not show in a general way, if not definitely, that electricity is the instrument with the help of which the Creator prepares the raw material of the universe? Does it also not show that different atoms are whirlpools created by whirling motion in matter of a subtler nature and that different planes can be created by producing whirlpools within whirlpools?

This is in broad outline the Occult doctrine regarding the essential nature of Fohat and the genesis of the atoms of different planes which it produces by different permutations and combinations of particles and modes of motion of an electrical nature. Neither our knowledge in the realm of Science nor in that of Occultism is sufficiently detailed and reliable to enable us to make an exact comparison and formulate a satisfactory theory of Fohat. But it will be seen from the above that, on the whole, the facts of Science corroborate and are in harmony with the Occult doctrine. More definite and reliable knowledge about the structure of atoms and the nature of electricity will probably enrich further in the future our ideas about the nature of Fohat or ' Cosmic Electricity '.

Science has not investigated nor is it likely to investigate in the near future the other two specific forces which are related to the Second and First Logoi, namely *Prāna* and *Kundalini*, and all our knowledge with regard to them is derived from Occult investigations. Although these two mysterious forces are quite different from Fohat and should be dealt with separately it may be worthwhile recapitulating very briefly the main facts regarding their essential nature to show their relation to Fohat.

Prāna is the material instrument of the Second Logos or *Vishnu*. It enables the raw material created by the Third Logos to be worked up into ' living ' vehicles which have inherent in them the capacity for growth, etc., and for acting as instruments of mind in various degrees of development. An insentient vehicle like a machine cannot be used by the mind for the expression of thoughts, emotions, etc. It must be a living organism and these qualities which we associate with life are imparted to it by *Prāna*. As *Brahmā* the Creator evolves more and more complex atoms and molecules of different planes, so *Vishnu* the Preserver takes these atoms and molecules and organises them into living vehicles which can serve as vehicles of the mind and consciousness. Here also a process of evolution is involved and forms of a more and more complex nature are developed in the course of evolution which takes millions of years and requires a great deal of experimentation on the part of Nature.

The whole process of this kind of evolution on the physical plane has been studied in great detail by the science of biology. But biology studies merely the outermost forms made of physical atoms and molecules and physical and chemical forces acting between them. It recognizes the force of vitality which is present in these living forms. It knows that they evolve slowly and become more and more complex, which makes possible a fuller expression of mind and consciousness through them. But it does not know two things:

(1) that there is a definite vital force known as *Prāna* associated in an invisible form with the visible living forms;
(2) that these forms are evolving merely to serve as increasingly efficient instruments for the evolving life associated with
them. In other words Science does not know that the
main purpose of the evolution of forms is to provide more
efficient vehicles for the evolving mind and unfolding consciousness. This ignorance is quite natural because orthodox
scientists refuse to consider anything which is invisible and
cannot be handled by purely physical means. Occultism
supplies the missing knowledge and not only makes the
conception of the evolution of forms richer but also gives a
reason for the whole process without which it will be quite
meaningless.

The evolution of living forms prepared by the Second
Logos through the agency of *Prāna* is also not the last stage
in the preparation of forms for the expression of mind and
consciousness at different levels. It merely prepares the
ground for the descent of consciousness into the lower realms
of manifestation and the unfoldment of its hidden potential
powers and faculties through the occupation and use of these
living forms, especially at the human level. When the living
forms have reached a certain stage of evolution and rudi-
mentary powers of the mind can express through them, then
individualization takes place, leading to the formation of
the casual body by separation of an individual unit from
the group soul. So far evolution was collective; from
this point it becomes individual. A human soul is born,
as it were, or to put it more correctly, the Monad has descended into the lower planes to unfold his divine potentialities
there. Till then he was merely waiting as it were on the
higher planes for the preparation of adequate vehicles on the
lower planes. On individualization a definite connection is
established between the Monad and his casual body and
through the casual body with the still lower bodies. From

this point it is a human soul which evolves through human bodies and there is no limit to the unfoldment of consciousness which can take place through the vehicles prepared in this manner.

There is, however, one important point we should note in this connection. The physical body of man has not evolved from the physical bodies of animals, as assumed in the theory associated with the name of Darwin. It seems that the evolution of the animal bodies took place not to provide in the ultimate stage a physical vehicle for the Monad but only to prepare a mental vehicle in which individualization could take place. The evolution of animal bodies takes place to bring the ' group soul ' to a particular level of development and it is in this highest form of the ' group soul ' which is mental in nature that individualization takes place. And this individualized soul then incarnates in a human body derived from human parents.

The original human bodies were evolved by a long and peculiar process discussed in *The Secret Doctrine*. We need not enter into this question here. It is enough for us to remember that our physical bodies are not in continuation of the series of bodies evolved in the animal kingdom. There is a break in the evolutionary chain of bodies on the physical plane which has puzzled scientists. They have been trying hard to find the ' missing link ' but have not succeeded so far. Neither are they likely to succeed in the future for reasons given above. The dream of the materialist to have the proud privilege of being descended from the apes will therefore remain unfulfilled.

CHAPTER XXXII

REALITY, CONSCIOUSNESS, MIND AND MATTER—I

RELATION OF REALITY AND CONSCIOUSNESS

IF there is an Ultimate Reality underlying this universe and the manifested universe is a periodical phenomenon taking place in this Reality, then it is necessary for us to have some idea with regard to the various links which connect this Ultimate Reality with the three fundamental verities of the manifested universe, namely Consciousness, Mind and Matter. Of course we cannot know the nature of these relations which exist between the four in the true sense of the word 'know'. Only he whose consciousness has transcended the limitations and illusions of the intellect can have a faint glimpse into these ultimate mysteries of existence. But the purpose of philosophy and to some extent of Occultism is to interpret, as far as possible, these realities of existence to the human intellect, although there are great limitations and also some dangers inherent in such interpretations. If this kind of interpretation in terms of the intellect were not a necessity there is no reason why the great Teachers of the world and the sages and mystics who have appeared in the world from time to time should have spent so much of their time in trying to give us at least some idea with regard to these inner realities which transcend the intellect. They point out the impossibility of the human intellect comprehending these deeper mysteries and yet they try their utmost to make us understand these truths ' as far as we can' with the help of our intellect and intuition.

This shows that though the intellect is incapable of realizing the true nature of these transcendent realities of the inner life, still, it must have some knowledge with regard to them, even though this knowledge is merely intellectual. The necessity for such knowledge arises from the fact that man must have a philosophy of life to guide his conduct and to make the best of life in which he finds himself involved. Without such a philosophy of life he is just like a rudderless ship on an ocean carried about aimlessly hither and thither by the prevailing winds.

We have only to look around us in the modern world to realize the disastrous consequences of the vast majority of people in the world being without any kind of philosophy of life. They are bound to be at the mercy of human passions and natural instincts which must sway them in the absence of any principles to guide their life and any kind of ideals to point the right direction in which they should strive.

A philosophy which has as its fundamental object merely the control and exploitation of the forces of Nature to make the life of man as comfortable and pleasurable as possible is obviously inadequate and even dangerous. For, it places in the hand of a man who is still under the domination of his animal instincts and a slave of mere ideas, enormous powers of natural forces which he can use for spreading suffering and misery and even for destroying himself. No argument is needed to prove this fact. We have only to observe the chaotic conditions prevailing in the world at the present time to realize the inadequacy of the materialistic philosophy of life which is so fashionable these days.

So, we should not only have a philosophy of life. That philosophy should be based on Wisdom. But Wisdom cannot be gained by merely controlling and exploiting forces of

Nature and utilizing them for our material ends. It can come only from a deeper view of life, by going beyond its superficial aspects and finding those true and eternal principles upon which man's real life is based. And it is only those who have gone deep into the problems of life and discovered these true and eternal principles who can give us not only some knowledge regarding the true nature of life but also a philosophy which is true and adequate because it is based on Wisdom. Those who do not believe in Wisdom or the presence of a Divine Principle within the universe from which Wisdom is derived are obviously not in a position to give any reliable opinion on these deeper questions.

That is why all great Teachers of the world try to give us some knowledge regarding the realities of the inner life even though this knowledge is bound to be mostly on the plane of the intellect. This knowledge may not be real and adequate, but it gives us at least some idea regarding the true nature of life and the means which we have to adopt in order to gain real knowledge. I have pointed out this fact because there are some people with spiritual aspirations who have serious doubts in their mind as to the necessity of our acquiring this intellectual knowledge. They think that it is enough for the aspirant to know what he has to do in taking the next step and leave everything else. Some of them think that they can find these things themselves as they proceed, step by step, in this adventure of Self-discovery. This is nothing but an over-simplification of the problem which they have not really understood. Before an aspirant can tackle such a difficult and comprehensive problem he should know at least theoretically what it is and how it is tackled. Without such knowledge he has as much chance of success as a student who thinks he can discover the science of chemistry by his own efforts simply by going and working in a chemical laboratory.

In considering the relation of Reality, Consciousness, Mind and Matter we are dealing with a number of derivatives one derived from another as shown below.

Reality ——→ Consciousness ——→ Mind ——→ Matter. This chain contains three links and it is necessary to consider and clarify our ideas about all these links if we want to have not only some comprehension of these four basic realities of existence but also a general idea with regard to the philosophical concept of which they are integral and inseparable parts or aspects. Whenever we have to understand a composite thing it is always best to examine the parts separately as well as the whole together. It is only in this way that we can see the different parts in their correct perspective as well as invest the whole with a meaningful content.

As the basic realities with which we shall now deal in the above chain are beyond the realm of the intellect all that we can do is to try to gain a general idea of their nature with the help of analogies and similes. When the intellectual faculties are exerted to their utmost and earnest aspiration is present, the light of intuition can somehow illuminate the mind and accomplish to some extent what is beyond the power of the mere intellect. Analogies, symbols and similes are of great help in this work and are sometimes the only means available for understanding things under our present limitations. Their use depends, as has been pointed out before, on the principle that the phenomena of the lower planes are mysterious reflections of the realities existing on the higher planes.

Science has provided us with a vast fund of facts, laws and phenomena upon which we can draw for illustrating and symbolizing the hidden realities of the inner life, and it is now possible to deal with these problems more effectively than through parables and allegories which our great Teachers used in the past. The facts of science are not only more exact and reliable but far richer in detail and can thus illustrate these truths more effectively. One is sometimes startled on finding that a phenomenon in a scientific experiment is almost a perfect reflection of an inner principle or process and helps us to understand that principle or process more easily and effectively than a long and tedious philosophical explanation can do.

In considering the question of the relation between Reality, Consciousness, Mind and Matter we have to go back in thought to the nature of the Unmanifest for it is there that the roots of all these four lie. In considering the three aspects of the Ever-Unmanifest Reality, namely the Absolute, the Positive-Negative Principle and the Unmanifest Cosmic Logos we saw that they could be represented by a cross, one line of this cross symbolizing the primary differentiation into Consciousness and Power and the other line the secondary differentiation into Subject-Object relationship as follows:

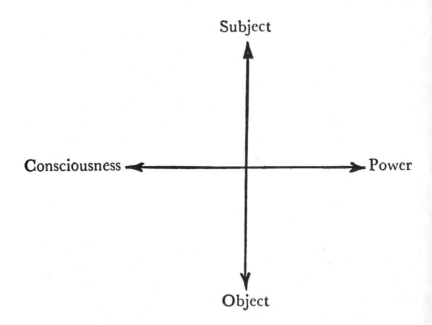

It is in this double polarity existing in the bosom of the Absolute represented by the point of intersection that the source of Consciousness, Mind and Matter and their relation is to be sought.

The nature of the Unmanifest has been dealt with in previous chapters and it is not necessary to repeat here what has been said already. All that is necessary is to state in a few sentences the essential nature of these three aspects of the Unmanifest to refresh our memory.

The Absolute is that Ultimate Reality which is referred to as *Parabrahman* in Hindu philosophy. It is that super-integrated state in which there is no differentiation of any kind, not even the extremely subtle primary and secondary differentiations which give rise to the Positive-Negative Principle and the Subject-Object relationship respectively. It is thus subtler than or above even the two highest *tattvas* or principles known as the *Śiva-Śakti Tattva* and the *Maheśvara-Maheśvarī Tattva*. In It all the principles, powers, qualities and opposites, etc. which find expression in manifestation exist in such a perfect equilibrium that nothing specific can be detected. It therefore appears like a void to the intellect, although it is a plenum containing potentially everything and actually nothing.

The result of the primary differentiation in this Ultimate Reality is a dual and polar Principle which is referred to as *Śiva-Śakti Tattva* in Hindu philosophy and the Father-Mother Principle in *The Secret Doctrine*. The emergence of this Principle from the Absolute marks the birth of Consciousness and Power in their purest and integrated forms. The name Śiva represents this pure integrated Consciousness or rather the root of Consciousness and Śakti represents pure integrated Power or rather the source from which all specific powers in the manifested universe are derived.

The result of the secondary differentiation in the Ultimate Reality is the emergence of another dual and polar Principle

which has been referred to as the *Maheśvara-Maheśvarī Tattva*
or the Logoic Principle. It is this Principle which is the
root of the Mind and source of Cosmic Ideation. It is also
this Principle which has been referred to as the Unmanifest
Cosmic Logos of which all the Solar Logoi who preside over
the innumerable solar systems in the˙ universe are partial
expressions. In fact, the name ' Maheśvara ' means the ' Great
Iśvara ' or the Cosmic Logos from whom all Solar Logoi
derive their power and plan.

The word ' reality ' is used generally in a rather loose
manner and frequently in a relative sense to indicate a more
real state in comparison with a less real state. But it will be
seen from what has been said above that the Absolute who
is referred to as the Ultimate Reality is the only true and
perfect reality and all other relative ·realities are merely its
derivatives or reflections at lower levels. Even the two
highest principles of existence derived from the primary and
secondary differentiations are relative realities as compared
with the Absolute.

It should be clear from what has been said about the nature
of the Ever-Unmanifest that the relation of Reality and Consciousness, the first link in the chain which we shall now consider, is rooted in the relation of the Absolute, the Ultimate
Reality, and *Śiva Tattva*, the pure, serene, integrated Consciousness in its highest state in which even the subtle disturbance of Cosmic Ideation is not present. All relations of
Reality and Consciousness (which are frequently considered
as synonymous) which manifest on the lower planes or which
we try to conceive with our limited intellect are really reflections of this primary transcendent relationship. This relation
is essentially a relation between a state which is absolutely
undifferentiated and another state which results when that
undifferentiated state is changed into another state in which
two polar and opposite states are present. These two polar
opposite states, though the products of a differentiation, are

yet completely integrated or undifferentiated in their respective spheres. The Consciousness at that level is pure, potential and integrated and the Power also, the other member of the primary duality, is pure, potential and integrated.

So we see that this relation of Reality and Consciousness is the relation of a superintegrated state with two polar, potential, integrated states. The integrated state still persists at the lower level but it is now a pair of opposite, polar states, each still integrated in its own sphere.

Can we find in the realm of physical phenomena artificially produced in a scientific experiment any analogous process which will throw light on this kind of change and thus help us to understand at least to some extent this relation between Reality and Consciousness? Let us take two very simple experiments which are of an analogous character and may serve to throw some light on this kind of internal change which brings about the contrast of a polar relationship and yet leaves the integrated nature of the two polar states unaffected.

The first experiment shows how, from a state of perfect uniformity, we can derive two states which are similar and yet have developed a potential between them. Let us take some water in a cistern as shown below. If we separate the water into two compartments and then lower one compartment as shown below

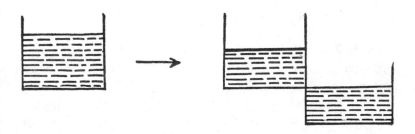

the amount of water and its nature remains the same as before but there is a difference of level in the water of the two compartments and so a certain amount of potential energy is available as a result of the rearrangement.

All that this simple experiment is meant to show is that by an internal rearrangement in any system it is possible to develop energy which can be drawn out gradually as we need it. It is true that this energy has to be put in before it can be taken out but the point we are concerned with here is that potential energy can be developed by internal rearrangement.

One of the most baffling enigmas of modern science is: Where does the energy which runs the machinery of the universe come from? According to science the whole universe is like a gigantic clock which is running down slowly and a time will come when all the energy will be spent and the universe will become dead. It is true that this awful fate will overtake us in the far distant future and we need not worry about it now but it will overtake us sooner or later. Now the question is: who wound up the clock of the universe, putting in the tremendous amount of energy which it requires for running for such unimaginable periods of time? Science has no answer to this pertinent question. To say that the energy is derived from fusion or fission of atoms means nothing, for it means only taking the question one step backwards. This question is so pertinent that many advanced scientific thinkers are now reluctantly considering the possibility of there being a Creator who put in this tremendous amount of energy in the process of creation. But this is considered so far only as an interesting speculation and not taken very seriously by orthodox Science which has a habit of ignoring inconvenient questions in its thoughtless pursuit of merely physical aims.

The Occult doctrine pertaining to this question is absolutely clear and unequivocal. The energy for running the machinery of any manifested system is derived ultimately from the *Śivā-Śakti Tattva* which is derived from the primary differentiation in the Absolute. That state which is present at the very heart of the universe, as has been pointed out, is a state of perfect equilibrium and tremendous stability and when the primary differentiation takes place and this perfect equilibrium is disturbed it tends like all systems in stable equilibrium to return to its original condition.   And so it is this tendency to regain the perfect equilibrium that is present in the Absolute which is the source of this tremendous amount of energy which is required for running the gigantic machinery of the universe. Just as there is no limit to the magnitude of equal and opposite quantities ($+$ & $-$) derived from zero so there is no limit to the energy derived from a Void State by polarization.

We have to remember that this differentiation takes place in the realm of Reality which is the root of Consciousness and Consciousness by its very nature is Self-sufficient and Self-determined and can alone bring about any change within Itself without the aid of an external agency.   Matter being insentient is incapable of this kind of change and so, while the material clock of the universe cannot wind itself it can be wound up by a Conscious Reality which underlies the universe.   This may sound rather anthropomorphic and over-simplified but the reader should try to grasp what is intended to be conveyed in this unsatisfactory manner. As this question has been dealt with in many other contexts it is not necessary to go into it any further.

The phenomenon of light provides us with an almost perfect analogy which illuminates wonderfully this extremely subtle conception and enables us to understand how a perfectly integrated or undifferentiated state can give rise to two similar undifferentiated states by means of an internal change or transposition.   In this way we get two states which are in contrast while previously there was perfect uniformity. The fact that this simile is provided by the phenomenon of light may not be a mere coincidence but a case of ' as above, so below'. Light is in some mysterious manner a representation or expression of consciousness on the physical plane

and its behaviour throws light on many phenomena of consciousness on the physical plane. This question is a very
interesting one but we cannot go into it here.

In order to understand how potential and contrast can
emerge from the absolute uniformity of a perfectly integrated
state without in the least affecting or changing the over-all
content and nature of the original state the reader is requested
to visualize a square which is uniformly illuminated by white
light of a certain intensity: We know that intensity of light
can be measured scientifically as so many quanta per square
millimetre or roughly in terms of candle power. For though
light is regarded as a wave phenomenon it can also be
considered to have a corpuscular character according to the
quantum theory. A uniformly illuminated surface can therefore be supposed to emit the same number of light
particles per square millimetre. In such a surface there
is nothing to distinguish one point from another, no contrast
of light and shade.

Now, if the light is supposed to be shifted from one
portion to another without changing its total amount, instead
of having a uniformly illuminated surface we shall have a
surface characterized by the contrast of light and shade. If
the light is shifted uniformly from the lower half to the upper
half of the illuminated square shown in the following diagram,

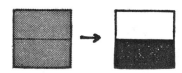

the upper portion will become more lighted than the lower
portion without any change in the total amount of light on
the surface. And the more it is shifted from the lower to the
upper portion the greater will be the contrast of light and
shade. If the light is evenly distributed in the two portions,

both the upper and lower portions will be uniformly illuminated though there will be contrast depending upon the relative intensity of light on them.

Only the initial and final stages of illumination are shown in the diagram as it is not easy to show the gradual increase and decrease of light in the two portions. The thing can be illustrated best by projecting light on a white screen.

We have assumed in the above experiment that the light is shifted uniformly from the lower half to the upper half of the surface and therefore only two surfaces of two degrees of uniform illumination are produced. But it is not necessary to have uniformity of distribution of the light. They can be distributed in an irregular pattern of light and shade. In fact it is possible to produce any pattern in black and white by mere redistribution and rearrangement of the light on the surface without affecting its total amount. I have used the words ' black and white ' purposely. We are not at the stage in which differentiation of white light into colours has any part. We are at a stage in which only white integrated light is present, though in greater and lesser quantity at different parts of the surface, thus producing the contrast of light and shade. It is merely the redistribution of white integrated light into more white light and less white light which is able to produce contrast and patterns of light and shade of any desired kind.

A recent discovery in the field of science has imparted added significance to this light phenomenon and made it almost a mirror of the Unmanifest state of Reality. This discovery is that of the silicon cell which converts sunlight into electricity. Scientists have been for a long time trying to devise a mechanism which will enable us to harness the energy coming from the sun and falling upon the earth. It is all wasted at present and if it could be utilized efficiently the power problem of the world would be solved for ever.

They have found that when light rays fall on a wafer of an element called silicon they dislodge electrons from the atoms of silicon which can then be drawn off in the form of an electric current. By suitably arranging a number of silicon cells a continuous current of electricity can thus be obtained.

The added significance of this interesting scientific discovery lies in the fact that it combines in one process light phenomena which can produce patterns of light and shade, and energy phenomena which give us power to do any kind of work. The same process in one aspect is a visual phenomenon enabling us to produce any kind of patterns of light and shade and in another aspect is an energy phenomenon giving us potential energy which can be utilized for doing any kind of work. Those who have studied the nature of the Ever-Unmanifest will see at once how this light phenomenon illustrates the combination of primary and secondary differentiations which give rise to Cosmic Power and Cosmic Ideation respectively in a double process represented by the mystery of the Cross.

CHAPTER XXXIII

REALITY, CONSCIOUSNESS, MIND AND MATTER—II

RELATION OF CONSCIOUSNESS AND MIND

WE shall now take up the second link in the chain of Reality ——→ Consciousness ——→ Mind ——→ Matter and try to understand its essential nature. We should not forget that we are here dealing in these discussions with the origins of the universe, the ultimates of existence, the subtlest mysteries of life, and should not therefore hope to find cut-and-dried solutions or precise ideas as is possible in the case of physical phenomena. But if we think deeply and constantly over these things, meditate upon them, pray that our intuition may be awakened, it is possible to gain a glimmer of these truths which are involved in our study. Even this would be impossible but for the fact that all these realities are hidden within our heart and are the very bedrock of our own consciousness.

We saw in the last chapter that the relation between Reality and Consciousness, the first link in our chain, is rooted in the primary differentiation in the Absolute which leads to the emergence of the primary polar duality of Consciousness and Power from the Void which the perfectly integrated and harmonized state of the Absolute appears to the intellect. We also saw that both the derivatives of the primary differentiation—Consciousness and Power or Śiva and Śakti—are integrated and harmonized in their own realms and precede the next further descent of the Absolute in the secondary differentiation. This secondary differentiation results, as we have seen, in the appearance of the subject-object or *Sat-Cit* relationship and forms the basis of Cosmic Ideation.

Let us now consider the nature of this subject-object relationship and try to gain a glimpse into the origin of the mind and its relation with consciousness. Western psychology studies mind as it finds expression through the physical brain and although there are now a large number of psychologists who are prepared to concede that the mind can exist and function apart from the physical brain, still, the tendency to regard with suspicion anything which is not based on the physical and cannot be verified by physical experiments is so strong that mind cannot be said to have acquired as yet an independent status of its own apart from the physical instrument through which it finds expression on the physical plane. We are still not very far, in the West, from the position taken by materialistic philosophy and enunciated by Lombroso in his famous dictum ' The brain produces thought as the liver secretes bile'.

Under these circumstances it is obvious that the relation existing between mind and consciousness cannot be usefully considered against the background of modern psychology. We have to fall back upon Yogic psychology which is based upon a study of the mind, not only apart from its instrument, the physical brain, but also upon an intensive penetration into its deeper recesses in order to discover what is its essential, ultimate nature. This intensive study of the mind has been undertaken and carried to its ultimate limit by a large number of investigators following the methods of Yoga. The subtlest phenomena of the mind have been thoroughly studied, the laws which govern its functioning have been discovered and formulated to some extent, the technique of this self-discovery has been perfected and verified again and again by innumerable unknown and unrecognized investigators

during the course of thousands of years. Of course, used as
we are to seeing people who have developed any little faculty
or power rushing out into the limelight to attract public
attention, we cannot understand how people who have worked
in these fields and have acquired such transcendent knowledge
and unusual powers can keep themselves deliberately unknown
and unrecognized by the world at large.

As a result of these researches we have at our disposal,
though not necessarily accessible to the public, a thoroughly
reliable and tested technique by the help of which every
individual, properly qualified, can undertake this voyage of
self-discovery in the realm of his own mind and consciousness
and verify for himself by direct experience not only the facts
and truths concerning mind but also with regard to the
universe in which he lives. In this way the doctrines of
Occultism which were to him matters of faith become a reality
based on direct experience. This technique as we all know
is the technique of Yoga.

It is therefore easy to understand that if we are to gain
any meaningful idea with regard to the relation existing
between consciousness and mind we can do so only on the
basis of Yogic psychology. For, Yogic psychology and technique is based upon the total nature of the mind, not on
the study of any aspect connected with a particular degree
of subtlety or expression. Unless we understand the totality
of a thing, all the phases of its derivation and development
fully, we do not understand it fully. How do we know that
we have understood the whole or totality of a thing? When
by investigating to the utmost limit we find that we have
transcended it and are beyond its operation and influence
altogether, not partially but wholly. Complete and real
knowledge of anything in manifestation is possible only when
we understand or know it so fully and in such a manner that
we go beyond it altogether and can perceive it, as it were,
objectively, separate from ourselves.

Now, as pointed out above, many people have tried and succeeded in penetrating so deeply into the inner recesses of their minds by the methods of Yoga that they have been able to free themselves completely from its action and influence, or in other words have transcended the mind. And what is their experience when they succeed in doing so? They find themselves in a state (which is not a state of mind) in which they become aware of that from which the mind is derived. They find that all the phenomena and experiences in the realm of the mind are merely modifications or differentiated forms of that basic thing, the substratum of the mental worlds, that all mental phenomena and mental experiences take place in that basic medium. It is this basic medium of mental phenomena and experiences which is called consciousness and it is the relation of this basic medium with the mind, its derivative, that we have now to consider.

Unfortunately, the word 'consciousness' is used very loosely in modern psychology and even in our ordinary parlance for indicating the principle of awareness in a general way. We use the words 'consciousness' and 'mind' almost synonymously. This is inevitable because both are so closely intertwined in their expression that we cannot distinguish between them. There can be no mind without consciousness because mind arises out of consciousness. It is only when mind is traced to its source by suppressing all its modifications that pure consciousness emerges and can be experienced. It is only then that we can know actually the difference between mind and consciousness. It is better to reserve the word 'consciousness' for the basic reality from which the mind of all degrees of subtlety is derived and the word 'mind' for the expression of that reality in its differentiated forms. Yoga recognizes this fundamental distinction and therefore uses two distinct words for the two—*citi* for consciousness and *citta* for mind.

The nature of the relationship between consciousness and mind has already been hinted at in the last chapter. It is rooted in the secondary differentiation in the Ultimate Reality which results in the establishment of the Subject-Object relationship in the perfectly pure and integrated consciousness which is referred to as Śiva. In the Self appears Not-Self and the integrated state called *Sat* becomes the triple state referred to as *Sat-Cit-Ānanda*. In the Unmanifest, however, this Subject-Object relationship based upon the separation of the One into the three is potential and not active. The Cosmic Mind which is referred to as the Unmanifest Cosmic Logos is so subtle that we can not conceive It. Yet It must be a tremendous Reality because It is the seat of Cosmic Ideation and the source of all the universes which follow one another in the eternal alternation of *Sṛṣti* and *Pralaya*. Each manifest Cosmic Logos when He appears after a *Mahāpralaya* brings the plan for His Universe from the Cosmic Mind of the Unmanifest Cosmic Logos. Each Solar Logos as He appears brings the plan for His solar system from the Mind of the Manifest Cosmic Logos. And the *Adhikāri Puruṣas* like *Manus*, etc. bring the respective plans for their more limited work from the Mind of their own Solar Logos. This is the concept of the Divine Plan in its totality which the Occult doctrine places before us. This is the concept of the Deity who rules over the universe containing countless solar systems. Where can we find such a grand and factual concept of the universe and its underlying Reality except in Occultism?

It will be seen from what has been said above that the ultimate root of the mind as we know it down here is in the Unmanifest Cosmic Logos, the seat of Cosmic Ideation, though the qualitative difference which must exist between the two owing to the difference of levels is so great that it would be absurd for us to visualize Cosmic Ideation or Divine Ideation of a Solar Logos merely as a subtle form of our own mental activity on the lower planes.

Judging by the intangible, impermanent and illusive nature of our own thoughts at the human level we are inclined to wonder how Cosmic Ideation can be the basis of this manifested universe in which we find laws working with mathematical exactitude, in which billions of solar systems are functioning in the framework of time and space and in which everything seems to suggest the very opposite of a mental origin. We forget when we entertain such doubts that we are dealing in Cosmic Ideation or Divine Ideation with an activity in Reality or of Reality. It is not ordinary thought which is the basis of the manifested universe. It is the Divine Thought of the Cosmic Logos at the cosmic level and the Divine Thought of the Solar Logos at the solar level.

Every activity in the realm of the Divine has the nature of Reality and Divine Ideation being a divine activity is therefore invested with that quality of factual existence which we associate with the word ' real '. In fact, it is tremendously more real than what we, with our limitations and illusions, can conceive as real on the lower planes. Our conception of Reality is an intellectual conception which comes nowhere near the realism of the real Reality. It is only such a Divine Thought or Divine Ideation which can serve as the basis of a cosmos or solar system in which everything is regulated by immutable laws, in which there is ordered progress according to a Divine Plan. We should be very careful in these things not to project our ideas based on our extremely limited and illusory experiences into the realms of Divinity and measure the Unlimited and the Real by our limited standards of the unreal. We should study these Occult doctrines which have been given to us by those who have experienced these truths with reverence, like one who treads ground which is holy, like one who is groping in the dark for some precious thing.

In considering the second link of our chain, i.e. the relation between consciousness and mind our real problem is to get some idea of that subtle process by which consciousness is transformed into mind or the integrated state of consciousness gives rise to the differentiated states of the mind. We have seen on previous occasions that in trying to get some comprehension of these incomprehensible truths similes and illustrations from the field of science are of great help to us; for, the realities of the higher worlds are reflected in the phenomena of the lower worlds and sometimes a simple illustration from life or a simple scientific experiment showing a natural phenomenon can give a clearer and more satisfying understanding of the problem than lengthy discussions of a philosophical nature.   Simple things are not necessarily less effective than complicated things in illustrating the realities of the inner worlds.   As has been pointed out elsewhere the realities of manifestation become simpler though also more profound as we approach the Centre from which the manifested universe is projected, owing of course to progressive integration. So a simple phenomenon or law in the lower world may reflect a reality of the higher worlds more effectively than a far more complicated phenomenon with many subsidiary aspects. That is why the great Teachers of the world always chose simple parables or similes to illustrate the truths of the higher and invisible realms.   These parables, similes and allegories could not only be understood by everybody but were generally very effective in illustrating the point which had to be emphasized.

In trying to understand how consciousness does not lose its essential character when it is transformed into the innumerable differentiated states of the mind let us take first the illustration of any basic substance which can be transformed into innumerable forms.   Let us take for example a sphere made of gold.   Not only the substance in this case is the most precious and beautiful from the ordinary point of view but the form is the most perfect which can be attained on the physical plane. Now, we can convert the sphere of gold into innumerable articles of different shapes and sizes, some ugly, others beautiful, some useful, others dangerous. In this conversion the integrity, the beauty and the perfection of the sphere is lost and what was perfect before now becomes a miscellaneous collection of articles all imperfect and different from one another.

But when the gold sphere is converted into articles of different forms and uses in this manner, is the nature of the basic substance altered? Not at all. They are still made of gold and are nothing else but gold though the forms assumed by the substance keep our attention diverted from the real basic substance to the unreal illusory forms.

This is, in a way, what happens when consciousness is transformed into modification of the mind. Instead of being aware of the basic substance from which the modifications of the mind are derived and in which the mental images are formed we become aware of the modifications and lose awareness of the medium, the consciousness itself. The basic substance, consciousness, is still there, always. It is the very medium or substratum in which the mental modifications and images exist and function and its presence is indicated by that vague sense of ' awareness ' which is present in all mental phenomena but we are not really conscious of consciousness. As the modifications become more and more subtle and the mind becomes more and more tranquil and pure, the vague awareness referred to above gradually becomes more vivid, pronounced and definite. And when the modifications subside or are eliminated completely this vague awareness is transformed into awareness of the integrated consciousness itself which we may call Reality in a relative sense. We are not now in the realm of the mind with its forms and modifications. We are now in the realm of consciousness itself.

It is, however, not necessary to eliminate all the forms in order to become aware of the substance. We can be aware of both simultaneously. In other words, the world of phenomena can co-exist in consciousness with the awareness of Reality, with change of focus from one to the other as desired or necessary. But we must have first known what the substance is by eliminating the forms before we can perceive it side by side with the forms. That is to say, we should be able to perceive the Real by transcending the unreal before we can see the Real in the unreal. Self-realization must be attained before the unreal can be truly seen as an expression of the Real.

We shall now consider another ordinary phenomenon which though less simple brings out more effectively the different aspects of this transformation of consciousness into mind. Suppose we have a glass cistern full of clear limpid water in which a powerful lighted electric bulb is suspended as shown below.

There is also a small turbine driven by an electric motor hidden in the bottom. This can churn the water at different speeds and the bulb can be seen through the transparent wall of the cistern.

The lighted bulb will be clearly visible and the surrounding water invisible as long as the water in the cistern is perfectly tranquil. As soon as the motor is started and the water begins to churn the electric bulb is not seen clearly but with a slight distortion. The water also begins to be visible. As the speed of the motor increases and the churning becomes more rapid the bulb becomes more and more distorted in appearance. After a certain stage patterns begin to appear and disappear in the water and make it more difficult to see the bulb. Ultimately, when the churning becomes violent the bulb becomes quite invisible, all the light radiating from it being assimilated by the rapidly changing patterns in the water appearing and disappearing rapidly. If the motor is gradually slowed down and the agitation in the water gradually subsides the whole process is reversed. When the water becomes absolutely tranquil the bulb is again seen clearly and the water becomes invisible as before.

In the above phenomenon we should note the following significant facts:

1. In the first place the patterns which are seen are really light phenomena, i.e. they are produced by the light of the bulb and are themselves of the nature of light. The water helps in producing the light patterns but it cannot by itself produce the patterns which are light phenomena essentially. For if the light is cut off, the visible patterns disappear even though the water may be churning and taking various shapes.

2. The second point to note is that in their material aspect the patterns are nothing but forms produced in water, the basic substance. There is nothing really in existence substantially in the phenomenon except water and motion. The innumerable patterns of various designs are produced just by imparting different kinds of motion to the water.

3. The third point to note is that three things—light, water and motion—are necessary to produce the phenomenon. If the light disappears the patterns disappear even though the water may be churning. If the water disappears, the

patterns disappear even though the light may be shining. If the water is perfectly tranquil even then the patterns disappear. The light shines as if the water did not exist.

Now, anyone who has studied the problem of the nature of the mind from the Yogic point of view, how it obscures our perception of Reality and how its purification and tranquillization is the essential technique involved in Self-realization, will see in this simple phenomenon almost a picture of the above process. For example, we can see reflected in the above phenomenon the following facts:

(1) Consciousness is assimilated with the modifications of the mind and, as it were, disappears in the mind as pointed out in *sūtra* I-4 of the *Yoga-sūtras*. (2) Consciousness emerges and again shines in its true and essential nature when there is *nirodha* or inhibition of the mental modifications; (3) Both consciousness and matter or *Puruṣa* and *Prakṛti* are necessary for manifestation and the production of mental phenomena, gross or subtle. (4) Both *Puruṣa* and *Prakṛti* revert to their integrated and harmonized condition from the differentiated condition when there is complete inhibition of mental modifications. The *Puruṣa* attains *Kaivalya* and *Prakṛti* attains its *Sāmyavasthā*.

A closer analysis of the phenomenon shows a still deeper similarity. What is matter, the material basis of this phenomenon, according to science? According to modern physics matter is nothing but bottled-up radiation or light as the quotation from Sir James Jeans' book given in another context points out. So the material basis of the phenomenon—water—which appears so different from the light illuminating it is really light in a condensed form. In one aspect light is the illuminator, and in another aspect it is the illuminated, one corresponding to the subjective and the other to the objective aspect of the mental phenomenon. And of course, the third element of the triplicity of illuminator, illumination and illuminated is also light.

Here again we see almost a perfect picture of the Occult doctrine that consciousness and matter are not essentially two different realities but two aspects of one and the same Reality. In one aspect the Reality becomes the perceiver or the subject and in another aspect—a lower or a degraded state—it becomes the perceived or the object. The two are essentially the same though at different levels of manifestation.

This relation between subject and object is thus relative and variable. This fact becomes clear in *Samādhi* when consciousness recedes progressively from the periphery of the mind, through different levels of the mind towards the centre of consciousness from where the mind arises or originates. It is found that what was subjective before becomes in its turn objective at a deeper level of the mind, as the moving partition separating the subjective and objective recedes continually toward the centre.

We see from what has been shown above that the difference between consciousness and mind is essentially a difference of the integrated and differentiated states and is rooted in the secondary differentiation of the Unmanifest state of Reality. Reality, Consciousness and Mind appear similar and intertwined with one another to the intellect working through the physical brain and it appears impossible to distinguish between them except through direct experiences obtained at the deeper levels of consciousness in *Samādhi*. But the problem is very important both from the philosophical and psychological points of view and it is necessary to make a definite effort to understand it intellectually and clarify our ideas on the subject.

CHAPTER XXXIV

REALITY, CONSCIOUSNESS, MIND AND MATTER—III

RELATION OF MIND AND MATTER
THE MENTAL BASIS OF MATTER (1)

In the chain we are considering, namely, Reality ⟶ Consciousness ⟶ Mind ⟶ Matter, the last link between mind and matter, though nearest to our ordinary experiences, is the most difficult to understand. The student is so much used to regard matter as something tangible and material that his mind finds it extremely difficult to consider it as an aspect of the mind itself. Yet the relentless logic of scientific facts recently discovered, the doctrines of Occultism and the facts of our common experience seem to point to the conclusion that we are living in a purely mental world and the so-called matter is merely an aspect of the mind. Let us first consider a few important facts from the realms of scientific knowledge and our common experience to prepare the ground for understanding this relationship between mind and matter.

(1) The first well-known fact that we may recall is that matter as known to Science is mostly empty space. It consists of infinitesimally small particles separated by tremendous distances and moving in many cases with unimaginable speeds. It has been roughly calculated that the proportion of space actually occupied by these particles to the empty space in which they move is so small that if all the empty

space in the physical body of a human being were to be eliminated the condensed matter would be reduced to a mere speck so small that we would require a magnifying glass to be able to see it. But this is not the limit at which Science has arrived in exploring the nature of matter. According to the conclusions of modern physicists even the infinitesimal particles of which matter is composed are nothing but radiation as the following quotation from the well-known book *The Mysterious Universe* by Sir James Jeans will show:

> 'To sum up the main results of this and the preceding chapter, the tendency of modern physics is to resolve the whole material universe into waves, and nothing but waves. These waves are of two kinds: bottled-up waves, which we call matter, and unbottled waves, which we call radiation or light. The process of annihilation of matter is merely that of unbottling imprisoned wave-energy and setting it free to travel through space.'

I think we should commit the above sentences from Jeans' book to memory and ponder over them, to let the ideas sink into our mind and enable us to realize their tremendous significance.

Now, what are waves? Waves according to Science are nothing but simple harmonic motion in a medium. We can have waves in the sea in which case the medium is liquid water. We can have sound waves in air in which case the medium is a gas. But the most extraordinary waves are those of light. These can exist in and travel through space without a medium. Formerly, physicists thought that an extremely tenuous medium called luminiferous ether filled all space and the electro-magnetic light waves travelled through this medium. But the most rigorous scientific experiments failed to indicate the presence of such a medium and the idea of an ether filling all space has been practically abandoned and light is now supposed to exist and travel without a medium of any kind. Einstein, after considering this question very thoroughly, formulated his Theory of Relativity without the ether.

We are thus face to face with another strange and rather startling fact discovered by Science, that light waves can exist and travel without a medium of any kind. They do not require any kind of tangible medium for their expression, not even such a tenuous thing as the hypothetical ether of Science. When light is travelling from one star to another for millions of years it is travelling in empty space. What is the significance of this phenomenon? According to Science and our own experience there is nothing else in existence except mind, energy and matter and if light can travel and exist without matter it means that it must travel and exist in the medium in which the mind works. Or, to put it in other words, light is a motion not of any material medium like the ether but of a mental medium. We have no idea what this mental medium is like but if there is nothing else in our experience which can serve as a medium except matter and mind and the very basis of matter does not exist it is natural to presume that light waves, or radiation as these are generally called, are somehow dependent upon the mind or are a function of the mind. All forms of matter are derived from radiation and·radiation itself is derived from mind in some way. Wave motion without some kind of medium, if we think about it, is an impossibility and the only other medium besides the material which we know of is the mental.

Let us look at the question from another point of view. We find in our experience that waves are harmonic motion in some kind of medium. But, as we have seen, light waves can exist without a medium, which really means that wave motion can exist without any kind of material substratum. If we look deeply into this problem we shall realize that from its very nature wave motion cannot exist without any medium and when it seems so to exist it is really a mental phenomenon with which we are dealing. The modern scientist in his eagerness to keep mind and consciousness out of the picture says that under these conditions wave motion takes place in empty space. But any one who looks at the question with an unprejudiced mind will see that if we knock out the medium from wave motion only motion is left and mere motion being physically impossible can be nothing but a purely mental phenomenon which can be expressed by a mathematical formula. The mathematical formulae expressing the phenomenon of light were previously considered to express motion in a hypothetical medium i.e. ether. But if there is no ether then we are left only with these mathematical formulae which are mere mental concepts. This means that light waves or radiation are waves in a mental medium. The disappearance of ether transfers the phenomenon from the material to mental level.

Let us pause for a while on the tremendous significance of this conclusion. It does not mean merely that the phenomenon of the material universe being either ' bottled up or free radiation ' are related to one another and can be expressed in mathematical terms. For, the relations of things which are tangible can also be expressed in mathematical terms as is done so frequently in all scientific work. The conclusion really implies not that all the phenomena of the universe can be expressed in mathematical terms but that they *are* mere mathematical expressions or a set of mathematical formulae. There is a great deal of difference between the two statements. The first implies the presence of ' things ' between which relations are established. The second means that there are no things but only ' relations ' in the form of mathematical formulae to consider in manifestation. The universe is thus deprived completely of a material basis (using the word ' material ' in its usual sense) and is reduced merely to a vast and complicated system of mathematical formulae of infinite variety *if we do not take mind into account.*

Let us now go a little further into the matter and consider what a mathematical formula is. What is its essential nature? The expression of a mere thought representing a principle, a relation, a mental image, a mode of motion, an archetype, etc. So if the whole manifested universe appears from the purely physical point of view as a vast system of mathematical formulae and these mathematical formulae can be nothing but representations of concepts and mental images, does it not follow that we are here dealing only with a mental world containing all these concepts and ideas.

We are thus led logically, step by step, to the conclusion that behind the apparently physical world and underlying it is a mental world containing all these principles, archetypes, modes of motion, images, etc. all mathematically related and co-ordinated into a harmonious whole. It is not that there is a physical world and underlying it is the mental world but there is only the mental world and this apparently physical world is merely an appearance in the mental world.

It should be noted that this statement is not based on the philosophical doctrine which considers the world an ' ideal ' world as a matter of speculation. It is based on the conclusion at which Science has arrived as the result of rigorous experimental work, which shows that there is no such thing as matter in the ordinary sense but only wave motion in the form of radiation and there is no material substratum like the ether in which motion can take place. Since waves cannot exist without a medium of some kind they must exist in the mind which is the only other reality of which we are aware.

We see from the above that the facts discovered by Science point to the probability of the physical universe being a purely mental phenomenon without any material basis whatsoever. This is the Occult doctrine with regard to the

essential nature of the universe which is regarded as an
expression of Divine Ideation. Of course, the mind itself
according to this doctrine is a modification of consciousness
or a phenomenon in the basic medium of consciousness as
we have seen already in the previous chapter. So the basis
of this universe is really consciousness or ultimately, Reality,
and the occult maxim ' Verily this manifested universe is
nothing but Brahman ' is not merely a philosophical doctrine
but a truth to which the latest researches in the field of Science
point unmistakably. Having familiarized ourselves with the
scientific conclusions and Occult doctrines regarding the
essentially mental nature of the universe we can now proceed
to the next step and consider how we can account for the
existence of an apparently tangible and material universe
existing outside us.

The appearance of a spiritual universe in Reality depends
as we have seen already upon the establishment of the subject-
object relationship in integrated Consciousness whereby Mind
comes into existence and Divine Ideation is made possible.
But on the lowest planes we have to account for the perception of an apparently material world outside us. We not
only see this world outside us but it seems to be composed
of particles like atoms and molecules and vibrations playing
between them.

In accounting for this phenomenon we have to take into
consideration two important doctrines. The first of these
doctrines may be simply formulated by saying that the mental
world of an individual is mostly the result of the interaction
of the Divine Mind and the individual mind. The second is
the well known doctrine of *Bhūtas* and *Indriyas* in Hindu
philosophy which is a part of the Yogic psychology.

Let us consider briefly the first doctrine and see what it
means. If we examine the contents of our mind and its
activities carefully we shall find that the mental world is
produced in our mind in the following ways:

(*a*) Without any contact with the external world as a result of the subjective activity of our own mind as in dreams, reveries, hallucinations, or when we are engaged in some concentrated mental effort.

(*b*) By the imposition of the mental images present in another mind on our mind as in thought-transference or as in hypnotic suggestion when the hypnotist is able to make his subject see, hear, or feel any thing he wills.

(*c*) As a result of the stimulation coming from the external world and affecting our mind through the sense-organs. This stimulation is provided according to Science by atoms and molecules and vibrations emanating from them and striking the sense-organs. The important thing to note about this kind of stimulation is that the world image which it produces in the mind has not the slightest resemblance to the external world. The external world contains only atoms and molecules and their combinations. The sense-organs through which the stimulation is received also contain nothing but atoms and molecules. But when the external world acts upon the sense organs it produces in the mind impressions of colour, form, smell, taste, etc., which obviously are not present as such in the aggregate of the atoms and molecules. The world which appears in the individual mind as a result of this external stimulation therefore comes really from within, though the source of stimulation is apparently external.

Still, we have to remember that there is a mathematical relationship between the nature of the stimuli provided by the external world and the corresponding sensuous images which appear in the mind as a result. Thus, for example, light vibrations of a particular wave-length always produce a definite colour sensation. Molecules of a particular structure produce a particular sensation of smell when striking the mucous membrane of the nose or a particular sensation of taste when coming in contact with the palate. The external stimuli do not produce sensations in a haphazard manner but according to definite laws which have a mathematical basis. The internal mental world of form, colours, etc. though quite different from the external physical world of atoms and molecules, is yet naturally and mathematically related to it.

This fact is of great importance because it shows that the mental world in which we live, like the physical world of Science is also governed by immutable, mathematical laws of Nature. The tendency of modern Science to keep the world of the mind outside the realm of natural laws, which is responsible for much of the confusion of thought and maladies of modern civilization, will thus be seen to be born of prejudice and narrow-mindedness and not any rational approach to the problems of life as a whole. Any fool can see that if two things are related to each other naturally and mathematically and the working of one is governed by natural laws which are precise and immutable then the working of the other also must necessarily be governed by such laws, otherwise no mathematical relation between the two would be possible. You cannot have a universe, half of which is cosmos and the other half chaos. But the modern scientist who prides himself on his rationalistic approach to life cannot see this simple fact and continues to treat the phenomena of mind and consciousness as if they had no scientific basis and took place in a haphazard manner.

Coming back to the question we are discussing, namely the contents of our changing world image, we find it to be a stream of two currents mingling most of the time and flowing singly at some times. One current is derived from the individual activity of our own mind and the other from the stimulus received from an external source. For example, when we are dreaming or imagining something or engaged in some intense mental activity, utterly oblivious of the external world, we are dealing with the individual activity of our own mind. When our mind is perceiving the external world through the sense-organs and the activity originating in our own mind is suspended for the time being, we are dealing with the activity of our mind which is stimulated by an external source. Generally, both these streams of thought are present together in a mingled state and it is difficult to separate them.

If we analyse the second stream of thought we shall find that it is derived from two kinds of sources and may be considered to consist of two currents. One set of stimuli is derived from the mental activity of other individuals and the other set from the mental activity of the Logos of our solar system. For example, when we are hearing a lecture or reading a book our mind is being stimulated by the thoughts of another person. When we are seeing a sunset or perceiving the world around us our mind is being affected by the activity of the Divine Mind, for the whole solar system is an expression of the Mind of the Solar Logos and as His Mind unfolds at different levels the Monads associated with Him receive in their minds impressions from the Divine Mind according to their location in time, space, plane of existence and the development of the corresponding vehicles.

It should be clear from what has been said above that there are only three kinds of mental activities in the universe (1) Cosmic Ideation which accounts for the appearance and unfoldment of the whole cosmos, (2) Divine Ideation which accounts for the appearance and unfoldment of solar systems, and (3) Individual ideation which accounts for the mental activity of the innumerable Monads who are evolving in the Cosmos and are at different stages of mental development. These three kinds of mental activities correspond to the three basic realities in the manifested universe—the Cosmic Logos, the Solar Logoi and the Monads—and may be considered to be derived from and to provide a means of expression to the Spirit at these three levels. The mental activity at each level may be considered to be a reflection of the spiritual unfoldment of the corresponding spiritual entity. It is true that there are tremendous differences in these mental activities referred to as Cosmic Ideation, Divine Ideation and Monadic or individual ideation but these differences are due to the differences of levels and degrees of unfoldment. Essentially the process is the same, because the Cosmic Logos, the Solar Logoi and the Monads are essentially the same, and mind at whatever level it works is essentially the same.

The mental phenomena classified under the above three heads account for the total Cosmic Process and the world images produced in the mind of any individual involved in this process. Leaving out of account for the present other aspects of this interesting subject let us consider briefly one aspect with which we are immediately concerned, namely, the interaction of the Divine Mind of the Logos and the individual mind of a Monad associated with Him in a solar system. Let us consider the nature of the stimulus provided by the Divine Mind for the individual mind through the mechanism of the different planes which the Logos has created for the evolution of the Monads in His solar system.

As has been pointed out already a great part of the current of mental images which are passing in the mind of an individual is the result of the impact of the Divine Mind on the individual mind. The Divine Mind functioning on each plane acts on the individual mind on that plane and produces a series of corresponding images naturally and automatically according to the nature of these images and the mechanism through which interaction takes place. We are using the word ' mind ' in its widest sense and not merely in the sense of the intellect or the lower concrete mind with which we are all familiar. As our consciousness recedes inwards towards its centre the nature of these images must necessarily change, for we are contacting the Divine Mind with a different mechanism of our own mind which we have been able to evolve on the particular plane.

Yogic *Samādhi* is nothing but a process or technique of contacting increasingly deeper levels of the Divine Mind with the help of increasingly subtler mechanisms of our own mind which we refer to as our vehicles. As pointed out in a chapter dealing with the nature of the Point, the common centre or *bindu* of every individual is like a multi-planar mirror which is capable of reflecting within itself the Divine Mind on each plane and as we dive into this centre of consciousness we come into contact with the different aspects of the Divine Mind.

It is easy to understand this interaction of the Divine Mind and individual mind in a general way but we have to take into consideration the important fact that there is a *modus operandi* involved in this interaction and unless we have some idea of this mechanism our ideas will remain vague and uncertain and the doctrine is not likely to find ready acceptance among those who adopt a rational approach to these problems. It is not enough to say merely that the world image produced in the mind of an individual is to a great extent the result of the impact of the Divine Mind on the individual mind. We should have at least some idea as to how this takes place. For example, on the physical plane the Divine Mind acts on the individual mind through the instrumentality of the sense-organs. How does this action of mind upon mind take place through the instrumentality of an apparently material mechanism?

The discoveries made in the realm of Science have provided us with some interesting facts and phenomena which throw some light on these interesting questions and enable us to get a glimpse into the nature of the mechanism which enables mind to act upon mind. We shall consider this matter briefly and generally in the subsequent chapter. We should not expect to understand fully this mystery of mental perception in this manner. These profound mysteries of existence cannot be understood in the real sense in this manner. They can be really understood only by going deep within the realms of consciousness and transcending the mechanism which lies at the basis of the world process as pointed out in aphorisms III-53 and IV-33 of the *Yoga-sūtras*. It is enough for us, while we are confined within the illusion-bound intellect, if we can manage to bring some definiteness and clarity into our generally vague and confused ideas concerning the Occult doctrines bearing on the subject.

CHAPTER XXXV

REALITY, CONSCIOUSNESS, MIND AND MATTER—IV

RELATION OF MIND AND MATTER
THE MENTAL MECHANISM UNDERLYING MATTER (II)

In considering how the Divine Mind affects the individual mind we should be clear in our mind generally as to what we are aiming at. In the first place, we are confining ourselves here to the interaction at the lowest level, namely, to the perception of an external world through the instrumentality of the sense-organs. This interaction takes place at different levels through the agency of vehicles which we have evolved on the successive planes, but as it is difficult to comprehend even partially what kind of world images appear in the mind at the higher levels as a result of this interaction, let us confine ourselves to the lowest plane with the phenomena of which we are familiar.

The mechanism of sense-perception as understood by Science is well known. The atoms and molecules send out vibrations of various kinds. These vibrations strike the sense-organs and produce in them responses which depend upon the natures of the sense-organ and the vibration. In the case of the sense of smell and taste it is the actual contact of the atoms and molecules with the sense-organ which produces the response, and the nature of the response depends upon the constitution of the molecule. These impressions produced in the sense-organs are converted into nervous impulses which are carried to the corresponding centres in the physical brain. Then something happens in the brain which converts these nervous impulses into sensations. Science knows nothing about the mechanism of this transformation and cannot say how purely physical nervous impulses are transformed in the brain into mental sensuous images. Occultism which has investigated the total constitution of man knows that this transformation is brought about through the agency of *prāṇa*. This is a special kind of matter which serves as a vehicle of vital force and may be considered as a kind of compound of matter and mind which enables mind to affect matter and matter to affect mind.

It will be seen, therefore, that there is a very complicated mechanism involved in the process of sense-perception and our knowledge of this mechanism is incomplete. Let us not enter here into the detailed consideration of this complicated mechanism which is more likely to confuse the mind than to lead to an understanding of the problem. The best method of dealing with such problems is to confine ourselves, at least in the beginning, to the general principles and broad facts and not involve ourselves in the meshes of details.

This is particularly necessary for the student of Divine Wisdom who studies these things concerning the mechanism of manifestation not for their own sake but as a stepping stone to real knowledge. He knows that nothing can be known definitely and fully as long as it is studied in isolation and is not seen as a part of the Whole, from which all things are derived and in which they really exist. He takes this partial knowledge with regard to everything lightly and tentatively, merely as a means of knowing that ultimate Truth which lies at the basis of the manifested universe and by knowing which everything can be known truly and fully. The pursuit of intellectual knowledge for its own sake and the zest for this kind of scrappy knowledge which is so much in fashion these days should have no place in his life. This is an ideal which can be accepted and fostered only among people who are not even aware of the realities of life and are content to live and die within the limitations and attractions of this illusory world without even giving any thought to the great mysteries of life which face us on every side.

In the second place, our object in studying the mechanism of sense-perception here is not to obtain a detailed and precise knowledge about its various constituents but to have a general and intelligible conception regarding the *modus operandi* of the interaction of the Divine Mind and the individual mind. The concept of this *modus operandi* should not be based upon the idea of atoms and molecules as physical entities because even according to Science atoms and molecules do not really exist as we imagine them. They are merely 'bottled-up radiation' or modes of motion. We have seen in the previous chapter that such a physical motion without a physical medium is impossible and so the mechanism and *modus operandi* of sense-perception must be basically a mental phenomenon. This will be in conformity with the highest Occult doctrines according to which the whole of this manifested universe is ultimately a mental phenomenon based upon consciousness.

But to say that the perception of an apparently external world consisting of atoms and molecules is a purely mental phenomenon and no matter is involved in the process does not necessarily mean that no mechanism is involved. In fact, scientific study of this phenomenon has proved beyond doubt that not only a mechanism is involved but this mechanism works in accordance with precise mathematical laws. So even though this mechanism is essentially mental it must be based upon definite laws which have a mathematical basis. What has happend as a result of recent scientific discoveries is not that the idea of a definite mechanism underlying sense-perception has been exploded but that a purely mental mechanism has replaced a purely physical mechanism or a physical-cum-mental mechanism. For, the existence of mind apart from matter is still not fully accepted by orthodox Science and there are still many die-hards who insist on believing that mind as we know it is merely a by-product of physical, chemical and biological processes.

If there is only a mental world in which all these apparently physical phenomena take place and the material world in the ordinary sense does not exist at all, this inter-mediate mechanism through which sense-perception takes place should also be of a mental nature. The Divine Mind must act on the individual mind through a mental mechanism and it is the nature of this mental mechanism that we shall now consider in a general way.

Let us begin our study with the brief consideration of a natural principle which operates in the realm of so-called physical phenomena and which may be referred to as the object-image principle. According to this principle it is possi-ble to convert one kind of physical phenomena into another kind of phenomena and back again into the original kind of phenomena through the instrumentality of an intermediate mechanism which works automatically. Let us take a num-ber of concrete examples to illustrate this principle. The sound waves produced in talking can be converted by the mechanism attached to a telephone into electrical impulses. These electrical impulses are carried along a wire and when they reach the receiving end are again converted into sound waves which are exactly similar to the original sound waves. Take another example. Music is broadcast from a trans-mitting station. An apparatus converts the sound waves into electro-magnetic waves which fill all space. Any radio which is tuned to those waves, catches them, converts them back into sound waves and we hear the music exactly as it was broadcast from the transmitting station.

This principle is utilized in many ways in scientific inventions of various kinds and can provide a clue to the mechanism of interaction between the Divine Mind and the individual minds. It shows how the ideas which are present in the Divine Mind may be reproduced in the individual minds but through the instrumentality of an intermediate mechanism. Divine Ideation may be considered to be like the broadcasting of music or pictures from a powerful transmitting station. The appearance of the mental images in the individual minds is like the reproduction of the music or pictures in the radio or TV sets.

There is, however, one point of difference which should be noted. The world image in the individual mind is not an exact reproduction of the Divine Thought, only a partial and frequently distorted reproduction on the spiritual planes and not even that on the lowest planes. This is obviously due to the limitations and imperfections of the individual mind. Even in the case of a radio we see that the quality of the instrument makes a great deal of difference. Each radio is sensitive only to certain bands of wave-lengths and can catch the electro-magnetic waves within those limits. Reproduction also depends upon the quality of the material used and the efficiency with which the parts are fitted together.

The limitations of the human mind are similar. In the first place, there are the limitations arising out of the differences of planes which work in different numbers of dimensions of space and measures of time. These impose certain limitations on consciousness functioning on each plane, the limitations increasing as the density of the plane increases. These limitations are inherent in the functioning of consciousness on that plane and restrict all minds working on that plane. Thus the lower mind working through the lower mental body can deal only with images of concrete objects and cannot really comprehend the abstract concepts and archetypes existing in the Divine Mind. Only the higher mind working through the causal body can do so.

The world image of unfolding Divine Thought in the mind of an individual also depends upon the position of the individual in time and space. It is not unlike the image produced in a silvered glass globe which is moved through a busy street. Its nature at any moment will depend upon the location of the globe and the time of the day and will be changing continually.

In the second place, there are the limitations of the individual mind arising out of the lack of development and sensitiveness. As the mind unfolds and its vehicles evolve on the different planes it is aole to catch more and more vibrations from the Divine Mind and obtain a fuller and truer comprehension of what is present in the Divine Mind on each plane.

The purpose of Yoga is to increase the range and sensitiveness of the individual mind and its vehicles so that the Divine Mind can be contacted on the different planes more and more effectively. As the consciousness of the individual recedes towards its centre and begins to function through the increasingly subtler vehicles it comes into touch with the different levels of the Divine Mind. The technique of *Sabīja samādhi* consists essentially in contacting a particular aspect or area of the Divine Mind which corresponds to a particular ' object ' of meditation of which the reality has to be realized by the Yogi. In the technique of *Nirbīja Samādhi* the realm of mind is transcended altogether and the Yogi contacts not the Divine Mind but the integrated Divine Consciousness which lies at the basis of the Divine Mind and illuminates the Divine Mind. He emerges into the realm of Reality itself.

A general idea of the principle involved in the interaction of the Divine Mind and individual mind can be obtained from the object-image principle referred to above. But this does not throw any light on the nature of the complicated mental mechanism through the instrumentality of which the ideas in the Divine Mind are transmitted to the individual mind. The reverse process by which ideas in the individual mind are perceived by the Divine Mind, of course, does not require any mechanism because of the capacity of the Divine Mind to exercise non-instrumental perception referred to in aphorisms III-37 and III-49 of the *Yoga-sūtras*. This complicated intermediate mechanism is needed, even in the case of an individual, only in the early stages of evolution and although the Self-realized person still uses it for the sake of convenience it is not obligatory for him. In the case of the Logos, of course, perception and action both are non-instrumental on account of His Omniscience and Omnipotence.

It is not easy to give yet a clear-cut and definite idea with regard to the nature of this intermediate mechanism simply because it involves so many occult doctrines of the subtlest nature and the links which connect them. No effort has so far been made to clear up this complicated question and obtain a satisfactory idea of the many factors which are involved in it. We are very prone to take things for granted in the sphere of religion and philosophy. We study the Occult doctrines of the greatest significance, we memorize them, we expound them, we extol them but we do nothing to understand them really. Where there are discrepancies we do nothing to explain them, where there are obscurities we do nothing to clear them up. Where we find disconnected parts of a wonderful concept we do nothing to put them together in an integrated whole. When there are certain ideas missing in an incomplete concept we do not take the trouble to find them and make the concept complete and meaningful.

That is how some of these ideas and doctrines which are of the greatest significance and importance to man have remained enveloped in an atmosphere of mystery and pious devotion and do not exercise any dynamic influence on our life and thought. They have been handed down from one generation to another, century after century, as heirlooms and remained practically unknown to the West. It was left to Western scholars to bring them to the notice of the world at large, mostly in the form of translations, and make us realize to some extent their value. But though these scholars put in a tremendous amount of labour and did monumental work in opening up this field of thought to the West, they lacked intuitive insight and could not appreciate and bring out the inner significance of these ideas. They treated them, as scholars are prone to do, as mere problems of scholastic research, with great care, precision and enthusiasm as regards the outer form but with utter indifference as regards the profound and significant truths which they enshrined.

The subject we are studying is one of these obscure areas of thought which require careful research in order to open it up and make it sufficiently intelligible for integration with the Occult doctrine. It is an indispensable constituent for evolving a coherent and intelligible conception regarding the spiritual nature of the universe which is in accordance with the Occult doctrine and the experience of those who have been able to penetrate into these innermost mysteries of existence. It is only such a rational and reasonable conception which can stand against the materialistic and irrational conception of orthodox Science which people accept without question because they are hypnotized by the spectacular achievements of Science. There is a general misconception present in the mind of the people that there is a vast array of scientific facts behind the theories of Science regarding the origin and nature of the universe. But the fact is that it is these very facts which have undermined the foundations of materialistic philosophy and provided an increasing corroboration of the doctrines of the Occult philosophy.

In considering this question of the mental mechanism which lies behind mental perception all that can be done in the present brief survey is to point out the salient features of the fundamental Occult doctrines which are involved and which can provide on careful examination the material for a systematic, coherent and reasonable theory of mental perception.

At the very root of this theory of mental perception we find the most fundamental doctrine of the Occult philosophy that the universe is based upon and derived from an Ultimate Reality which is essentially of the nature of pure Consciousness and the universe is a purely mental phenomenon using the words 'mental' and 'phenomenon' in their widest and deepest sense. As mind is considered to be a mere modification or derivative of Consciousness in this philosophy there is no contradiction between the two ideas in the above statement.

The second doctrine which is implicit in the Occult theory of mental perception, though not clearly stated, is that the mind not only works through the subject-object relationship but in its involution downwards divides itself into two streams as it were, one stream serving as the basis of the subjective function and the other of the objective function. We have already seen elsewhere how the very birth of the mind is due to the appearance of the subject-object relation in integrated Consciousness. This is stated in terms of Hindu philosophy by saying that owing to the functioning of the *Cit* aspect of Brahman a mental world appears from the integrated *Sat* aspect and as a result of this, the relation of Self and not-Self is established between the two. This is the root or the basis of the Mind Principle and all mental phenomena and mental operations from the highest to the lowest are derived from it. Cosmic Ideation, Divine Ideation and individual ideation are all expressions of the Mind Principle, both in its subjective and objective aspects, at different levels.

Now, this differentiation into subject-object relationship gives us an idea only of the general principle underlying the working of the mind at all levels. It does not give us any

indication regarding the *modus operandi* or the instrumental
aspect of the process. For this we have to understand the
doctrine of *bhūtas* and *indriyas* which is an integral part of
Hindu philosophy and the basis of Yogic psychology. Although frequent references to this doctrine are found in
different contexts in the literature of Occultism and Hindu
philosophy and there are also several aphorisms bearing on
the doctrine in the *Yoga-sūtras* of Patañjali it has never been
explained satisfactorily, at least not in terms of modern
thought, and has remained till now as one of those mysteries
whose truth is taken for granted and never sought to be
understood. So, we have still to piece together the different
ideas which lie scattered in the literature bearing on the
subject and put them together in the form of a coherent and
intelligible concept.

It may be pointed out that though the bifurcation of the
Mind Principle into two streams which serve as the basis of
the subjective and objective aspects takes place at a much
lower level it is really a reflection of a differentiation in con-
sciousness which takes place at a much higher level. In
Hindu philosophy the existence of this differentiation at
the highest level is indicated by ascribing two aspects to
Reality and using two separate phrases for the two aspects:
Brahma-Caitanya and *Śabda-Brahma*. *Brahma-Caitanya* is the
Reality as Consciousness in its subjective aspect while *Śabda-
Brahma* is the Reality in its vibrational aspect, the root of
the objective phenomenal universe.

Then again, in the symbolical representation of Maheśa,
the highest level of the manifest Reality, He is represented
both as *Pañca-vaktram* and *Tri-netram*. *Pañca-vaktram* means
' five-faced ' and *Tri-netram* means ' three-eyed '. This
obviously symbolizes the fact that the objective universe
which is cognized through our five sense-organs is nothing
but an expression of the same Reality which functions as the
cognizer and ' sees ' this objective universe through the three

eyes. Two of these normal eyes in the symbology of *Maheśa* represent instrumental perception while the third represents non-instrumental perception which is called *Pratibhā* in Yogic terminology. He is therefore not only the ' seer ' but also the ' seen '. The very stuff of which this universe is composed is an expression of His Consciousness and it is easy to see how this is possible only if the stuff is mental in nature. In one of His *mental* aspects He is the cognizer and in the other aspect, what is cognized.

It is these two subjective and objective aspects of Reality which in their instrumental aspects are referred to as the *indriyas* and *bhūtas* respectively in Hindu philosophy. The *bhūtas* may be considered generally as the instruments of the objective aspect and *indriyas* as those of the subjective aspect. It is much easier to understand their essential nature if we look upon them in this general manner and not identify them with their instruments on the lowest plane—physical. We should note, however, that the *bhūtas* and *indriyas* are not the functions themselves but the instruments of the objective and subjective functions. It is through them that the two opposite functions of the One Reality are exercised.

According to the doctrine of the *bhūtas* and *indriyas* it is at the junction of *bhūtas* and *indriyas* that mind in its objective aspect meets the mind in its subjective aspect and perception of the objective universe takes place. The perception of the physical universe through the five physical sense-organs is the result of the meeting of the subjective and objective aspects of mind at the lowest level. Some aggregates of atoms and molecules with certain specific properties stimulate particular sensations and serve as vehicles of the *bhūtas*. Other aggregates of atoms, molecules and cells which have been organized into sense-organs with special functions serve as vehicles of the *indriyas*. The basic material in the case of both is the same, namely, the atoms and molecules and vibrations playing between them, but the functions are different.

The doctrine of the *bhūtas* and *indriyas* is intimately related to other important doctrines which form an integral part of Yogic psychology. All these doctrines have to be considered together in some detail if we are to have a coherent and meaningful concept of the mechanism of mental perception. This can be done only in a systematic and detailed study of Yogic psychology.

GLOSSARY OF SANSKRIT WORDS

Adharma, unrighteous conduct

Ādi, the first and the highest

Adhikāri puruṣas, Liberated beings holding particular Office in the Divine Plan

Ādi-Śakti, Divine Power in its highest state

Ādi-Śiva, Divine Consciousness in its highest state

Agni, fire

Agni-tattva, fire as a cosmic principle

Ākāśa,
Ākāsha, } space as the subtlest of the five Elements

Akṛta, not made; beyond creative process

Ānanda, Bliss, one of the three aspects of consciousness

Aśvattha, the inverted Tree Life as a symbol of differentiation and integration

Atipraśna, a question concerning the ultimate mysteries of existence

Ātmā, The Spirit, individual or universal

Avidyā, lack of awareness of Reality

Aviveka, lack of discrimination

Bhakti-mārga, the path of devotion to God

Bhūta-Jaya, mastery of the five Elements

Bhūta-Shuddhi, the purification of the five elements in the body

Bhūtas, the five elements as stimulators of senses

Bīja-akṣaras, letters embodying operative powers of cosmic elements or Powers

Bindu, the point; the centre of consciousness

Brahmā, the creator; a member of the Trinity

Brahma Chaitanya, Reality as consciousness

Brahma Vṛtti, Cosmic or Divine Ideation

Brahman, the Reality underlying the universe

Brahman—Saguna and Nirguna, The Reality with and without attributes

Brahmānda, The Egg of Brahma, the Creator; an enclosed manifested system

Buddhi, faculty of direct perception; intuitive faculty

Chakra, a psychic centre in the body

Chidākāsha, mental space

Chit, one of the three aspects of consciousness

Chitta, mind

Chiti, Consciousness

Cidākāśa
Cit,
Citta, } see above
Citi,

Citta-Vritti, modifications of the mind

Damaru, a symbol

Deva, a member of a hierarchy on the subtle planes

Devata, symbolic representation of divine function in Hinduism

Devī, symbolic representation of divine Power in Hinduism

Dharma, righteousness; properties

Dharmi, substratum on which properties of all kinds inhere; Prakriti

Drstā, the seer; pure consciousness

Drśyam, the seen; the objective side of manifestation

Dvandvās, pairs of opposites

Gunas, fundamental qualities based on motion

Gupta Vidyā, secret Knowledge of Occultism

Guru, teacher

Hatha Yoga, a system of yoga

Ham, Yam, Vam, Lam, Ram, letters embodying the potency of the five elements

Indriya-Jaya, mastery of the senses

Indriyas, senses

Īśvara,
Ishvara, } God, Logos, presiding Deity of a manifested solar system

Jala, water; one of the five elements

Jatharāgni, gastric fire

Jīva, individual soul, personality

Jīvanmukta, liberated being

Jīvanmukti, liberation from bondage of the lower worlds

Jīvātmā, spiritual soul

Jñānāgni, fire of wisdom

Jñānendriyas, the five sense-organs

Jñani, a wise man; a man who has obtained knowledge of Reality

Kaivalya, liberation

Kāla, time

Kalpa, a period of manifestation

Kṛta, made; within the cycle of creation and dissolution

Kṣaṇa, a moment; the smallest unit of time

Kuṇḍalinī, serpent fire

Laya, absorption in a higher state

Līlā, divine drama; play of the Infinite

Mahābindu, The Great Point

Mahākāla, the ultimate and subtlest time

Mahākalpa, period of manifestation of a universe

Mahākāśa, the ultimate and subtlest space

Mahāmāya, The Great Illusion

Mahāpralaya, a period of dissolution or reabsorption of a universe

Mahātma, a great soul

Maheśa,
Mahesha, } The Great Lord; the Logos

Maheśwara, The Unmanifest Cosmic Logos

Maheśwara-Maheśwarī Tattva, The Logic Principle

Maheśwarī, the Power of the Cosmic Logos

Manas, mind as a principle

Mano-b'ndu, the point serving as a vehicle of the mind

Manomaya-Kosha, the subtle body serving as an instrument of the lower mind

Mantra, a combination of words with specific potency

Manu, a liberated being holding a particular office in the inner Government of the World

Māyā, Illusion

Mumukshattva, intense desire for Liberation

Nāda, integrated ' Sound ' which is source of all kinds of vibrations

Nataraja, The Dancing Siva as a symbol of cosmic rhythm

Niralamba, needing no support; not derived from any thing else

Nirbīja Samādhi, samādhi without specific 'object'

Nirodha, inhibition; suppression

Niruddha, inhibited; without modifications

Nirvāṇa, liberation; absorption into the Supreme Spirit

Nirvikāra, without any distortion or defect

Nirviśeṣa, without particular attributes; undifferentiated

Niṣkalā, inactive; potential

Pañca-Bhūtas, the five elements which are the stimulating agents
of five sense organs

Pañca-Mahābhūtas, the five Cosmic Elements

Pañca-Tattvas, the five 'Elements' as cosmic principles underlying manifestation

Parabrahman, The Absolute, the Ultimate Reality

Paramātmā, The Universal Spirit

Pariṇāma Vāda, the Hindu doctrine that manifestation means
modification of consciousness

Prakriti, nature, the harmonized and integrated condition of properties; correlate of Purusha

Pralaya, a state of reabsorption into a higher state; dissolution
of a manifested system

Prāṇa, vital force which flows in the subtler counter part of the
physical

Pratibhā, infinitive cognition; non-instrumental perception

Prātibhā Jñāna, knowledge derived from *Pratibhā*

Pṛthvī, One of the five Elements referred to as 'Earth'

Purāṇas, a class of Hindu scriptures

Pūrṇa, whole, perfect

Pūrṇatā, wholeness; perfection

Puruṣa,
Purusha, } Monad; eternal spiritual soul in man

Rajas, one of the three *Guṇas* related to activity

Rudra, one of the Hindu Trinity

Sādhana, Self-culture for spiritual unfoldment

Sakala, active, kinetic

Śakti, Divine Power

Śakti Tattva, Divine Power as a principle

Sādhaka, one who practises self-culture

Sabīja Samādhi, Samādhi with specific ' object '

Samkalpa, resolution to achieve some definite object

Samskāras, impressions left by action or thought

Samyama, the triple process of meditation

Scmyāvasthā, harmoured condition; integrated state

Sānkhya, one of the six systems of Hindu philosophy

Sarva-sākshi, All-seeing; the Eternal Witness

Sat, one of the three aspects of consciousness

Sat-Cit-Ānanda, the three aspects of consciousness

Sattva, One of the three *Guṇas* related to harmony

Shabda Brahman, Reality as ' Sound ' the basis of objective universe

Shānti, Peace

Shiva, Pure undifferentiated Divine consciousness, correlate of *Shakti*

Sṛṣṭi, Creation, manifestation

Sūtras, aphorisms

Sushumnā, the passage in the spinal column in which ' Kuṅdalinī ' moves

Svarūpa, real, essential form

Tanmātras, sensations

Tat, That

Tattvas, principles

Tejas, One of the five *Bhūtas* related to light

Trishṇā, thirst for life; desire for embodied existence

Upādhis, Vehicles; sheaths in which consciousness is enclosed

Vāyu, One of the five Elements or Bhutas called ' air '

Vedānta, The latter part of the Vedas dealing with problems of Liberation

Vikaraṇa bhāva, non-instrumental action

Vikṣepa, destraction of the mind; throwing of image present in the mind outwards

Viṣṇu,
Vishṇu, } one of the Hindu Trinity

Viśveśvara, The Lord of the Universe, the manifest Cosmic Logos

INDEX

A

ABSOLUTE: 1, 2, 4, 7, 9-14, 19, 63, 67, 71, 113, 118, 134, 137-9, 168, 188, 207, 225, 229, 234, 249, 304, 331, 354, 365, 376; aspect of, 72; concept of, 14, 15, 22, 145, 159, 173, 233; core of the universe, 37; ideal centre, 115; in mathematics, 233; manifest and unmanifest state, 22; Ultimate Reality, 20, 140; superintegrated state of, 77, 139; Ultimate Unmanifest, 80; universe rooted in, 18; void or plenum, 162; void state of, 32, 68, 118, 225; zero dimensions, 117

Adept(s): 100, 131, 335, 338, 359; of Occultism, xvi, xxv, 175-6, 280, 335-6

Adharma, 275

Adhikāri purushas, 273

Ādi; Anupādaka, Higher *Ātmic* Worlds, 72;—plane, 55, 61-2, 65, 92-3, 170-1, 193, 331, 349;—*Sakti*, 44;—*Siva*, 44

Agni: 210, 243-4, 377;—*Tattva*, 243-4

Ākāśa (Ākāsha), 187, 203, 210, 244, 350, 352

Ānanda: 124, 198, 199, 266; aspect of *Siva*, 44; bliss, 48-9, 86, 90; relation between *Sat* and *Cit*, 87-8

Ancient Wisdom: doctrines of, 102; student of, 367

Architect of Universe, xxxi

"As above, so below", 192, 197, 202, 207

Astral plane, 193-4, 331

Astronomers, 264

Astronomy, 253-4

Aśvattha, tree of life, 197, 208-9

Ātmā: 3, 9, 62, 94, 107, 211, 319, 348; —*buddhi-manas*, 119, 130, 195

Ātmic consciousness, 100

Ātmic plane, 54, 62, 72, 92, 170-1, 193, 196, 331

Atom(s), 259, 262, 346

Atomic bomb, 333

Atomic energy, 333

Avidyā, 244, 268

Aviveka, 252

B

BEING and Non-Being, 138

Besant, Dr. Annie, 195

Bhagavat-Gita: 342; quoted, 88

Bhakti mārga, 14

Bhūta jaya, 185

Bhūtas, 185, 227

Bhūta-shuddhi mantra, quoted, 96

Bīja-akṣaras, 245

Bindu, 287 et. seq., 312-3, 347, 350

Blavatsky, H. P., quoted, 290, 378-81

Bliss, 198

Boundless space—ideal point, 10

"Bottled-up radiation", 255-6, 259

Brahmā: 44, 80, 87-92, 168, 277; one hundred years of, 170; Third Logos, the Creator, 88, 90-2, 378, 383; *Vṛtti*, 156

Brahmaivedam Viśvam, 183

Brahman: 78, 117, 151, 154, 183, 270-2; *Chaitanya*, 153; egg of 286; electricity related to, 9, 91; Reality, 151; *Saguṇa* and *Nirguṇa*, 12-4; universe rests in, 82; "—, all is" 161, 185-6, 247, 270, 272

Brahmānda, egg of the Creator, 34, 286, 312, 363

Buddha, x, xxxv

Buddhi, 2, 3, 211, 275, 319; light of, 253

Buddhic faculty, 257; plane, 62, 72, 170-1, 193, 331, 348; vehicle, 314, 319

Buddhistic teachings, 13